*Joint and Family Interviews
in the Treatment of Marital Problems*

Joint and Family Interviews

IN THE TREATMENT
OF MARITAL PROBLEMS

By Elsbeth Herzstein Couch

Family Service Association of America
44 East 23rd Street, New York, N. Y. 10010

This project has been financed in part
by Public Health Service Grant MH–14735
from the National Institute of Mental Health.

Library of Congress Catalog Number: 77–90057

Copyright © 1969

by

FAMILY SERVICE ASSOCIATION OF AMERICA

Printed in the United States of America

 3

Foreword

This report reflects the results of an atypical approach to knowledge-building. The project on which it is based began not with formal data collection but with a call to counselors in family agencies throughout the country to formulate, record, and share on a national basis what they had learned about treating troubled marriages. This tapping of practice wisdom at its source was first suggested and later partially funded by the National Institute of Mental Health. The response from practitioners was so overwhelming that it nearly inundated the national project staff.

Of necessity, this unexpectedly large and varied inflow had to be processed and integrated before more than a trickle could be released for return to participants and the field generally. Now, finally, the sluice gates can be opened and the flow directed back to its point of origin. Publication of this volume signals the beginning of this new phase. A second volume will follow. Both reports seek especially to water the neglected dry spots and to support and encourage new green growth—growth in understanding, in research effort, and in practice skill.

The allocation of this entire initial volume to multiple-client approaches to treating troubled marriages reflects the well-deserved position of these modalities on the growing edge of practice, their critical challenge to theory-building, and the obvious enthusiasm of participants over their newly discovered potentials. Themes in this area not only stimulated especially rich individual comment but also were chosen as the prime favorite by participating local study groups. On every hand a major shift was evident—a movement from preoccupation with a closed one-to-one treatment relationship with a single client, focused on intrapsychic dynamics, to a readiness to experiment with involvement of an ever widening circle of treatment participants in a therapeutic process focused largely on here-

and-now interaction. This shift is of vital, almost revolutionary, importance to the treatment of couples with marital problems.

Also evident was a pervasive difficulty the social work profession was experiencing in revising the theoretical base of practice to accommodate the implications of these new approaches. An obvious conceptual challenge was therefore inherent in the theme itself: developing a system-level restatement of the intervention process when joint and family interviews are used in marital conflict situations. Moreover, this formulation would need to take into account not only the patterned relationships between the partners but also the total family system and its many-sided involvement in the wider social structure.

The author of the present volume, therefore, was faced with a triple task: to reflect adequately a complex network of views of project participants, to examine these views in the light of the rapidly expanding literature, and to effect a creative engagement with this newly emerging conceptual challenge. The volume differs from most previous casework literature in three respects: It is focused specifically and at length on the values of, and criteria for the use of, joint and family interviews in the treatment of marital problems. It makes systematic use of practice wisdom collected in written form from a large number of participants. And, finally, it ventures a system-level interpretation of the dynamics of these modes of treatment intervention in family interaction.

The decision to release this specialized volume in advance of the more comprehensive one covering project results as a whole is based entirely on practical considerations. In essence, these considerations are simply that this volume was ready first; it can stand alone; it is too timely to be delayed; and it should be permitted as soon as possible to make whatever contribution it can to this rapidly evolving area of practice. The second report, to follow as soon as feasible, will trace the treatment of couples with marital problems through all phases from intake to termination and will undertake to delineate as a total process the dynamics of marital conflict and its resolution or modification through casework treatment. Both volumes endeavor to utilize to the maximum the exceptional perspective on internal family processes available to family agencies by reason of their direct responsibility for the helping process.

The decision of the Family Service Association of America to give high priority research attention to the whole area of marital problems and their treatment reflects the results of wide consultation with its member agencies. It took into account the pervasiveness of marital problems and the seriousness of consequences among family agency applicants, the paucity of relevant research, and the urgent need for improved understanding of marital conflict and better ways of resolving or moderating it through casework.

Because of the wide gaps in knowledge in this area, the approach has been, by intent, an exploratory one. In essence, the process has involved tapping, piecing together, consolidating, and, when possible, conceptualizing the practice wisdom of those actually involved in counseling troubled couples and their families. As already mentioned, the initial step was to elicit comment from experienced practitioners. Topics highlighted in the request included the goals of treatment, prognostic clues, diagnostic processes, treatment modalities, typical outcomes, patterns of marital balance, and the sources and processes of marital conflict. In response to these queries, some nine thousand pages of unstructured comment were submitted. Both reports present a systematic analysis and integration of these comments as seen in the light of relevant theory, prior research, and recorded practice experience. The goal throughout has been to map this area of treatment for future research exploration, to identify its central dimensions and processes, to separate areas of consensus from those of controversy, to reveal gaps in knowledge and awareness, and to highlight the resulting implications for needed research directions, innovative experimentation, practice modifications, and theoretical effort.

The attempt to collect and consolidate practice wisdom on behalf of research planning and related theoretical and practice goals has necessarily been a pioneer venture. Caseworkers have indeed been involved in research on many occasions, but primarily as interviewers, as judges of written records, as reporters of their own cases, and as subjects in academic experiments. Their potential contribution to identifying hypotheses, relevant variables, and hidden predictors has seldom been tapped except on a minimal and informal basis. Researchers have understandably not been attracted to the study of practice wisdom since it cannot be structured to meet usual research norms for rigor, objectivity, accurate measurement, and experimental design without destroying its essence. In spite of this deterrent, however, this project was deliberately designed at the outset to seek out the ideas and observations of those directly involved in helping distraught marital partners untangle their conflicts and difficulties. Though unorthodox from a research point of view, this choice stemmed from the conviction that these counselors have opportunities rarely available to outsiders to penetrate the hidden dynamics of families in turmoil and to observe significant repetitive patterns in the ways they regain equilibrium in response to help. These clues, in turn, can provide important guidelines that will help keep more formal research endeavors on target and productive in relation to the central concerns of practice.

The approach selected has required a massive investment by member agencies of the Family Service Association of America and their staffs, by project staff, and by the Association as a whole. When both reports are considered, the number of local agencies contributing comes to more than a hundred and the number of participating practitioners and supervisors to more than four hundred. Summarizing and integrating the returns, placing them in the context of the literature, and reporting them in a two-volume sequence has required many man-years of time from numerous authors. The resulting manuscripts have been reviewed and criticized in whole or in part by more than fifty persons, including members of the Association's Research Committee and consultants. The costs of the project have also been widely shared. Each local agency financed its own contribution. The National Institute of Mental Health provided major grants for a five-year period. The Association has also contributed substantially to costs at the national level, including the financing of a particularly heavy investment of time by the principal investigator.

Even the best co-operative effort, however, can add only a small increment in the long, slow process of knowledge-building. It is essential that this type of mutual effort and exchange continue long after both volumes become available. The next step is the selective pursuit by caseworkers and executives in many diverse settings of some of the numerous leads here offered, as their interests dictate. Some of the criteria proposed and some of the approaches described should be subjected soon to formal research testing. Other formulations should be clarified and refined at the theoretical level; still others would benefit most from study by increasingly sensitive and aware observation and reporting by practitioners. Regardless of method, however, consistent grappling with both clinical and conceptual issues must continue if a truly comprehensive and valid system-level view of both family life and the treatment of marital problems is to be achieved.

In due time the yield from such many-sided efforts will need to be brought together once more in a co-ordinated interagency effort involving again a national-local partnership of researchers and practitioners. By that time improved theoretical perspective and observational tools should be available so that a relook at essentially the same phenomena can provide new insights. Only by continuing this necessary circular exchange involving repeated study and feedback can the enormous gap between minimal knowledge and massive need eventually be bridged. In this period of rapid flux, it is earnestly to be hoped that the present report will add thrust and momentum to the co-operative effort urgently needed to improve the knowledge base for practice.

Dorothy Fahs Beck, Ph.D.
Principal Investigator,
Research Project on the Treatment
of Marital Problems,
and
Director of Research,
Family Service Association of America

Acknowledgments

This monograph is based on the labors of many people. I am most deeply indebted to all the practitioners who answered the questions posed by project staff and took part in the related study groups. Over three hundred caseworkers submitted written statements on one or both of the two questionnaire items directly concerned with the use of multiple-client approaches in relation to marital problems. Numerous additional practitioners replied to other questions also drawn on in this report. A full listing of all the respondents and participating agencies will appear in the forthcoming report on the project as a whole. The names of those who participated in the nine study group reports utilized in this specialized monograph are listed in the chapter bibliographies. Though participants never met with each other as a total group or with the author, their candor and their willingness to share their experiences have made this book truly a joint venture.

Invaluable help and guidance as this report evolved were given by the members of the FSAA Research Committee, who consistently encouraged efforts at further conceptualization. The full list of committee members during the period of the project appears on pages xii–xiii of this report. Special acknowledgment and thanks are due those members of the committee who gave time to extended conferences with the author over and above their committee participation. These included, in alphabetical order, Professor Dorothy Aikin of the University of Chicago School of Social Service Administration; Mrs. Frances L. Beatman, Executive Director of the Jewish Family Service of New York; Miss Gertrude Einstein, Casework Director of the Jewish Family Service of Philadelphia; and Dr. Reuben Hill, Professor of Sociology at the University of Minnesota.

Further stimulus and enrichment were gained from consultations with other outstanding thinkers, leaders, and practitioners in the field. Listed in chronological order of their assistance, these included a group of supervisory staff at the Jewish Family Service of Philadelphia (including, in addition to Miss Gertrude Einstein, Miss Rose Potasky, Mrs. Edith L. Shapin, and Mrs. Mollie Spector); Dr. Hilda Goodwin, then Assistant Professor at the University of Pennsylvania; Mrs. Doris Wolfenstein of the Jewish Family Service Bureau of Cincinnati, Ohio; Mrs. Gertrude T. Leyendecker, Senior Associate of the Department of Family Services of the Community Service Society of New York; Mrs. Margaret C. Lovell, then Casework Director at the Family Service Organization of Worcester, Massachusetts; Mrs. Elsa Leichter, Director of Group Therapy at the Jewish Family Service of New York; Mrs. Frances H. Scherz, Casework Director of the Jewish Family and Community Service of Chicago; and Mrs. Ruth E. Ronall, then on the staff of both the present project and the Family Treatment and Study Unit of the Department of Psychiatry of the New York Medical College. Briefer discussions were held with other practitioners and professional leaders too numerous to mention.

Thanks are also due the secretarial and editorial staff members who labored so carefully to produce the finished manuscript, and particularly to Mrs. Patricia Ann Lynch for her careful copy editing.

No statement of gratitude can quite express my indebtedness to Dr. Dorothy Fahs Beck, the principal investigator and content editor for all the project reports, who was unfailing in her patient guidance and always helped to bring the woods back into focus when glimpses of particularly interesting trees threatened to lure me into bypaths.

Finally, thanks are due the National Institute of Mental Health, without whose financial support, Public Health Service Grant MH–14735, this exploration would not have been possible.

Research Committee
Family Service Association of America
Composite List of Membership, 1961–69

* Chairman, 1967–69:

David Fanshel, D.S.W., Professor and Director of Child Welfare Research Program, Columbia University School of Social Work, New York, N.Y.

Chairman, 1957–67:

Stanley P. Davies, Ph.D., Deputy Director of Planning (Mental Retardation), New York State Department of Mental Hygiene, Albany, New York

* *Dorothy Aikin, Ph.D.*, Professor, School of Social Service Administration, University of Chicago, Chicago, Illinois

* *Mrs. Frances Levinson Beatman*, Executive Director, Jewish Family Service, New York, N.Y.

John J. Blasko, M.D. (deceased), formerly Director, Psychiatry, Neurology, and Psychology Service, Department of Medicine and Surgery, Veterans Administration, Washington, D.C.

Bernice Boehm, Ph.D., Professor, Graduate School of Social Work, Rutgers University, New Brunswick, New Jersey; previously Director of the Research Center, Child Welfare League of America, New York, N.Y.

Dawson Bradshaw, Executive Secretary, Family Service of St. Paul, St. Paul, Minnesota

Harry Brill, M.D., Director, Pilgrim State Hospital, West Brentwood, New York

Genevieve Carter, Ph.D., Chief, Intramural Research Division, Office of Research Demonstrations and Training, Social and Rehabilitation Service, U.S. Department of Health, Education, and Welfare, Washington, D.C.; previously Associate Executive Director, Los Angeles Welfare Planning Council, Los Angeles, California

Ralph Colvin, Ph.D., Executive Director, Johnny Cake Community, Family, and Child Study Center, Mansfield, Arkansas; previously Director of the Research Center, Child Welfare League of America, New York, N.Y.

Leonard S. Cottrell, Jr., Ph.D., Professor, Department of Sociology, University of North Carolina, Chapel Hill, North Carolina; previously Secretary, Russell Sage Foundation, New York, N.Y.

* *David Crystal, D.S.W.*, Executive Director, Jewish Family Service Agency, San Francisco, California

* *Ruth S. Downing*, Director of Professional Services, Family Service of Memphis, Memphis, Tennessee

* *Joseph W. Eaton, Ph.D.*, Professor of Social Research and Social Work, Graduate School of Social Work, University of Pittsburgh, Pittsburgh, Pennsylvania

---

* Member of Research Committee, 1968–69. Former members of the Research Committee are identified by affiliations current at the time of their membership.

* *Gertrude Einstein,* Director of Casework, Jewish Family Service of Philadelphia, Philadelphia, Pennsylvania

Mrs. Garret J. Garretson, II, FSAA Board Member 1956–64, Green Farms, Connecticut

Naomi Goodard, Seattle Area Office, Washington State Department of Social Welfare, Seattle, Washington; previously Assistant Director, Family Counseling Service, Seattle, Washington

Jeanette Hanford, Director, Family Service Bureau, United Charities of Chicago, Chicago, Illinois

Elizabeth Herzog, Chief, Child Life Studies Branch, U.S. Department of Health, Education, and Welfare, Washington, D.C.

* *Reuben Hill, Ph.D.,* Professor of Sociology; previously Director of the Family Study Center, University of Minnesota, Minneapolis, Minnesota

* *Howard Hush,* Executive Director, Family Service of Metropolitan Detroit, Detroit, Michigan

* *Mrs. Ruth Janowicz,* Executive Director, Family Service of Central Connecticut, New Britain, Connecticut

* *Leonard S. Kogan, Ph.D.,* Professor of Psychology and Director of Center for Social Research, City University of New York, New York, N.Y.

* *Jean M. Leach,* Casework Director, Family Service of the Cincinnati Area, Cincinnati, Ohio; Lecturer and Supervisor of Research, Smith College School for Social Work, Northampton, Massachusetts

Mrs. Norma D. Levine, formerly Assistant Director, Jewish Family and Community Service, Chicago, Illinois

* *Henry J. Meyer, Ph.D.,* Professor, School of Social Work and Department of Sociology, University of Michigan, Ann Arbor, Michigan

* *Mignon Sauber,* Director, Research Department, Community Council of Greater New York, New York, N.Y.

* *Paul Schreiber, J.D.,* Professor and Director of the Hunter College School of Social Work, New York, N.Y.

* *Mrs. Maria E. Shelmire,* Executive Director, Family Service of Delaware County, Media, Pennsylvania

* *Ann W. Shyne, Ph.D.,* Director of the Research Center, Child Welfare League of America, New York, N.Y.

Mrs. Michael Straight, FSAA Board Member 1958–61, Alexandria, Virginia

Dorothy V. Thomas, formerly Director of Casework, Family and Child Services of Washington, Washington, D.C.

* *Cornelius Utz,* Director of Casework, Family Service Association of Cleveland, Cleveland, Ohio

Wayne Vasey, Professor, School of Social Work, University of Michigan, Ann Arbor, Michigan; previously Dean, Graduate School of Social Work, Rutgers University, New Brunswick, New Jersey

Mrs. Viola W. Weiss, Director, Community Services, Jewish Children's Home Service, New Orleans, Louisiana; previously Director of Casework, Family Service Society, New Orleans, Louisiana

Joseph L. Zarefsky, Executive Secretary, Community Council, Houston, Texas

Contents

1

2

Contents

3

4

5

Contents

Contents

1

An Introductory Orientation
to the Study

Within the past two decades caseworkers have been making increasing use of multiple-client approaches to the treatment of marital problems. This trend toward direct therapeutic involvement of both the marital partners, and at times even of other family members, has been generally characteristic of the treatment of various forms of family difficulty. It reflects a cautious hope on the part of practitioners that the worker may offer increased help with marital and family problems if he can work with the problem participants together.

Before the efficacy of these approaches to the treatment of marital difficulties can be tested with any accuracy, certain questions need to be clarified: Do caseworkers see joint or family interviews as making any distinctive contributions to marital treatment as compared with those of the exclusively individual approach? What are the special assets of these modalities? If multiple-client sessions are used primarily, or in varying combinations with other approaches, including individual sessions, is it possible at this stage to identify any of the conditions on which the decision for or against their use for treatment of marital problems should be based? And what of such variants of these approaches as the use of several therapists at once or group sessions in which several couples or even several families are seen together? The questions are a sampling of the major concerns to which this monograph is addressed.

Perhaps such technical questions seem remote from the burning issues of social planning and action that have come to be recognized as necessary if the lot of families and of society as a whole is to be improved. Yet they are not. Even deep conviction and committed professional and civic activity on the practitioner's part do not remove his responsibility, as a clinician, for undertaking the task of helping individuals and families with today's pain. He cannot ask them to wait to experience the results of action now pending or not even undertaken, if they need his help *now* to make the best of the inner and outer resources currently available to them. Indeed, even if all the necessary social changes were miraculously accomplished at one fell stroke, conflicted marital partners would still be likely to find themselves so entrapped by their habitual patterns in relation to each other that they would still need skilled caseworkers to help them become free enough to make use of their better environment and opportunities. Conversely, the disruptive effects of marital conflict range so wide that help to unhappy couples is likely to have positive repercussions not only within the family but far beyond its boundaries.

PURPOSE OF THE MONOGRAPH

The present monograph undertakes to throw light on these questions not through a formal research analysis of reports of actual cases, but rather through an intensive content analysis of the ideas and observations of family caseworkers and others experienced in the use of the newer modalities. The themes that will be examined relate principally to the values of joint and family interviews and their variants and to the conditions relevant to their use in treating marital problems. Because of this specialized focus, the monograph necessarily reports only a portion of the findings of the larger study of marital treatment in general that was first undertaken in 1962 by the Family Service Association of America with the help of grants from the National Institute of Mental Health. The results of this more comprehensive study, like those reported in the present monograph, were based in the main on the responses of experienced family caseworkers to a series of unstructured questions, plus the results of a number of study group efforts in participating family service agencies. The results of this larger study are being reported in a separate publication (17).

In keeping with the purposes of that wider study, this monograph aims to tap the "practice wisdom" of caseworkers in FSAA member agencies in the conviction that caseworkers know more about marital treatment than they have ever put in writing. As an essential preliminary to more formal research testing of these ideas, it undertakes to examine and organize their views and concurrently to explore possible ways of conceptualizing the realities of this type of practice (16, p. 2). By providing an improved base for research planning, it is hoped that such effort will eventually contribute to closing the gap between needed research and what can actually be accomplished. Insofar as this goal can be realized, the end result should at the same time foster more effective service to clients.

BACKGROUND

As already noted, the focus of this monograph on multiple-client interviews mirrors the shift that has taken place in the field of casework over the past two decades. In previous years, caseworkers had unhesitatingly used individual interviews to treat partners in marital turmoil. While this approach undoubtedly resulted in enhanced individual growth and family harmony in many instances, there must also have been numerous occasions when a possible conflict of interest inherent in this dual goal became evident. Certainly, over the past twenty years the basic assumptions underlying the exclusively individual approach have come increasingly into question, partly owing to soul-searching as a result of failures and dropouts in therapy, and also because of the frequent observation that some marriages disintegrate even though one or both partners may be improving as individuals in the course of treatment, while other families seem to respond to individual help by rotating symptoms among their members.

Further pressure for a reconsideration of basic treatment assumptions came from the growing community demand for service, from the frequent requests of married couples themselves to be seen together or as a family group, and from the impact of theories about the family as a system whose hidden rules exert tremendous influence in determining what kinds of behavior will be initiated, maintained, favored, or punished within the family circle. Thus interest in family-centered casework and, in some quarters, increased familiarity with group treatment approaches have grown apace, accompanied by a revived concern with integrating social science con-

3

cepts into social work thinking. All these trends combined to create new opportunities for family casework to move from self-criticism to experimentation—cautiously, but with hope. Even a cursory glance at the literature and a quick survey of the respondents' replies show the varied approaches and striking creativity with which the challenge of this opportunity has been met.

Three main interview approaches may be identified among the various casework orientations toward treatment of the family in general and of marital partners in particular. One is the family group interview approach used by such casework practitioners as Satir (30, 31) and Bardill and Ryan (14), and by such psychologists as Bell (18, 20). This orientation has deeply influenced some of the project respondents, although none seems to have adopted it in its "pure" form. Its advocates are convinced that, with few exceptions,[1] the family member showing overt difficulties will be helped most effectively if the modality used to treat him includes the other family members who are affected by his problems and also play a vital part in his life. In this view, all the family members should be seen simultaneously by the same worker, since usually in such situations the family system itself will need to be modified to some extent if it is to incorporate healthier patterns of mutual behavior and feeling. On the whole, these authors would concur with Bell's view that any member excluded from the sessions will be driven toward sabotage against therapeutic change or into alienation from the remaining family members who are working together to repattern old ties in new ways (20, p. 5).

At the opposite end of the spectrum are those who oppose all multiple-client approaches and believe that interaction can be handled by working with one individual at a time. Three individual respondents and one study group (6) stanchly represented this point of view and therefore offered no criteria for any shift away from individual sessions. Even though the focus of this monograph is on joint and family interviews and therefore excludes full consideration of individual treatment as an exclusive modality, the existence of this approach must be clearly acknowledged and understood here since it was widely held in this unqualified form until quite recently. In contrast, today's advocates of individual treatment

---

[1] Bell excludes children too young to express themselves well verbally (19). Satir usually sees the marital pair first at least twice because they are the family leaders and mates as well as parents (30).

seem to have moved from a general use of the approach to its discriminate application on the basis of specific diagnostic clues. Thus Blanck, for instance, suggests exclusive use of individual treatment when either partner did not have his early symbiotic needs adequately met (21, p. 71). According to this view, personal growth must precede marital improvement if there were significant deficits in early nurturance. Such growth, according to Blanck, requires an undiluted intrapsychic confrontation, which he sees as best accomplished in individual sessions focused on enhancing the individual's ability to cope with his environment, or at least on minimizing its negative impact on him.

Between the advocates of the family interview or the individual session as exclusive modalities lie most of the literature and practice in current social work and in specialized marriage counseling, where combinations of joint and individual interviewing have long been in use, at times even including group methods (28). Philosophically, this flexible approach, which also characterized most of the responses, links with the theoretical framework of the transactional school, which stresses the mutual interdependence of the individual, the family system, and other wider social systems, their constant state of mutual transaction and influence (26, p. 4), and the multiple determinants of most phenomena within any of these systems. The pioneering labors of the Jewish Family Service of New York (11, 12, 15, 32); the Jewish Family Service of Philadelphia (23); the Midwest Seminar on Family Diagnosis and Treatment, led by Dr. Otto Pollak (13, 29); and the Committee on Family Diagnosis and Treatment of the FSAA Midwestern Regional Committee, under the chairmanship of Mrs. Frances Scherz (22), all belong in this context.

Scope and Approach

The present monograph seeks first to identify and classify the views of respondents in the larger study insofar as these relate to the values of joint and family interviews for diagnosis and treatment of marital problems or to the conditions favorable and unfavorable to their use. Although values and criteria must obviously be weighed in relation to each other in actual practice, they will be considered separately here. In reflecting the respondents' views, the report aims first to explore their full range and content and to include every nuance of opinion irrespective of the amount of stated support for any given position. Second, it attempts to place the respondents' views within the larger context provided by an overview of the totality of their comments, by consultation with leaders in the field, and by perusal of relevant literature from social work and allied disciplines. It will undertake to explore the implications of the composite replies and to infer from them the orientation they may reflect. Areas of substantial agreement or disagreement, striking insights, gaps, and sparsely covered areas needing further inquiry will be noted. At intervals, an attempt will be made to restate the respondents' largely psychodynamic comments in terms of a system-level conceptualization of treatment. Finally, some implications for practice, theory-building, research, and training will be suggested as emerging from the composite picture.

Although the comments analyzed in this report focus mainly on joint and family interviewing, the monograph will also include consideration of the use of several therapists and of couples' and multi-family groups, because of the close conceptual links among all these multiple-client approaches. On the other hand, the separate treatment of two marital partners through individual participation in group sessions with unrelated individuals will not be discussed. Questions on this issue were raised in the original queries, but responses in this area were too sparse to warrant intensive analysis, especially since the values identified by respondents in this context often overlapped with those of the joint or family interview techniques that they discussed more fully.

The monograph similarly excludes full consideration of the role of individual interviews in the treatment of marital problems, a topic examined more fully in the over-all project report (17). However, their contribution to marital diagnosis in the context of multiple-client sessions is discussed. In addition, the section on contra-indications to the use of multiple-client approaches also throws indirect light on the use of individual interviews. Their value and importance, when appropriately used, are implicitly acknowledged throughout by virtue of the preference of most respondents for a combination of approaches in marital treatment. In fact, the respondents most articulate about the values of multiple-client sessions and about indications for or against their use were also the ones to spell out most clearly and most frequently the need for individual interviews in clearly specified circumstances. Since issues relating to the use of specific casework processes in joint and family interviews were not probed in the source questions on multiple-client modalities, this aspect will not be discussed in this monograph. However, it is considered in the general report of project findings (25).

Sources

Since the full-scale research project tapped a wide range of sources, a varied group of basic materials was available for this specialized monograph. First among these are the carefully analyzed replies of caseworkers to two direct questions on the values and criteria associated with the use of multiple-client interviews in the diagnosis and treatment of marital problems.[2] Both these queries were part of the approximately sixty open-ended questions used in the larger project. The question focused on diagnosis was answered by 146 individual respondents or co-operating respondent groups that pooled their ideas, while 59 replied to the question on treatment.[3] In line with the total project's methods and aims, these questions were framed to capture the widest possible range of views and to permit the workers to reveal their own conceptual thinking, expressed in their own words. For this reason, the questions were unstructured to allow the respondents' own ideas to determine, as far as possible, the choice of issues and content to be offered on each given topic. Consequently, these replies do not provide an adequate basis for determining the full extent of agreement or disagreement on any given viewpoint.

Further sources include comments from scattered related questions not analyzed intensively in relation to the theme of this mono-

---

[2] Question 9, first installment of the questionnaire: "Do you use any special procedures to assist you in diagnosis? If so, what are these and when do you use them? (For example: Joint interviews, total family interviews, group intake, home visits by workers or homemakers, etc.; psychiatric evaluation or consultation; psychological or medical evaluation, consultation, or testing; client questionnaires; or other types of diagnostic aids.) In what ways do you find them useful?" Also question 16 of the third installment: "How do joint interviews, family group interviews, or group treatment, or combinations of these, contribute to change? When in the treatment process are these approaches indicated? When are they contraindicated? When both joint and individual interviews are being used, at what points in the treatment are joint interviews introduced? Why?"

[3] Although study group participants are identified in the bibliography, the names of project respondents are not listed in this monograph, but their comments are quoted or acknowledged as responses. Respondents' names are identified in the over-all project report (17).

graph,[4] responses to follow-up letters to practitioners interested in couples' groups, and answers to supplementary inquiries sent out in 1965 to clarify the experience level of respondents in family interviewing. Use was also made of nine study group reports submitted in connection with the larger study. Five of these were directly concerned with multiple-client interviewing (1, 4, 6, 7, 9) and another four focused on issues relevant to some of the criteria for use of these methods (2, 3, 5, 8). Other unpublished agency studies utilized included relevant reports developed through the National Experiment in Staff Development, itself an outgrowth of the over-all marital research project of which this monograph is a part (33). Selected articles and books from the extensive literature of social work and allied fields were also used to deepen discussion of the responses, to bring it up to date, and to add perspective. Finally, consultations were arranged with a small number of outstanding practitioners and teachers thoroughly experienced in the study and practice of multiple-client interviewing.[5]

Nature of the Respondent Sample

Since respondents in this study were essentially self-selected on the basis of interest in and experience with the treatment of marital problems, the responses available for analysis cannot be said to represent the typical viewpoint of family agency thought and practice even at the time of the study. Both the agencies and the caseworkers who participated did so voluntarily, and not all member agencies of FSAA chose to take part. In fact, several of the agencies pioneering in family therapy and a number of the smaller agencies representing the more traditional approaches did not participate in the question-answering phase of the project. The viewpoints of both are therefore underrepresented. Agencies that did volunteer were asked to nominate as participants principally workers with extended experience in the treatment of marital problems. Those nominated were, in turn, encouraged to choose from among the large number of questions posed those to which they wished to respond, and to do so either on a group or individual basis. Presuma-

[4] The questions most frequently tapped in this group probed the workers' possible efforts at new approaches to diagnosis and treatment and their methods for interrupting repetitive conflict.
[5] For a partial list, see pp. x–xiii.

bly those choosing to answer the specific questions on joint and family interviews analyzed here did so out of special interest in these approaches. The practitioner sample is therefore far from random. Instead, the selection process deliberately favored the more experienced and interested practitioner in the hope of maximizing the yield of practice wisdom. Nevertheless, it must be remembered that the views expressed represent the perceptions of caseworkers only, and not of clients or impartial observers. For this reason, the findings must be viewed as simply reflecting how at a given point in time practitioners saw their own experience in working with partners in marital difficulty.

Analysis of the actual prior experience of these respondents, as shown in Appendix Table 1, in fact confirms that almost all who answered the questions used in the present analysis were well experienced in the use of joint interviews. In contrast, less than one-quarter of those answering the question on treatment had used family interviews extensively either for diagnosis or treatment of marital problems, although over two-thirds had made occasional use of the modality. As for those commenting on diagnosis, nearly one-half had only occasional experience in family interviewing, and over one-third had none at all. Thus, the respondents' interest in family sessions by far outstripped their actual experience at the time of their writing. It is possible that questions focused on parent-child problems might have elicited a different approach to family interviewing. Undoubtedly the project's concern with marital problems influenced workers to lean toward joint rather than family interviews as the preferred interviewing modality. In fact, many of the respondents who wrote on family interviews mentioned that they had gained their experience with this approach from the treatment of parent-child difficulties and did not use it for the treatment of marital conflict unless the children were directly involved.

It must further be borne in mind that the comments reported here reflect an experience level below that which undoubtedly now prevails in the family service field. Replies to the basic questions were received in 1963 and early 1964. All the study group reports were in by early 1965. Since then, many respondents have reported an increase in their use of family interviews in the context of marital diagnosis, and some have also stepped up their use of family interviewing in marital treatment. Many more are likely by the time of publication to have found their practice and views changing in this rapidly evolving field. By 1966, 94 percent of all FSAA member agencies were using family interviews for some purposes (24), although the statistics do not specify how extensively or in relation to what problems.

Method of Data Analysis

Although all the materials used were studied carefully, only the responses to the two main source questions (see footnote 2, page 7) were subjected to a systematic content analysis. Each separate point offered in each response to either question was identified and copied onto a separate sheet. The points were then sifted and classified. Care was taken to avoid superimposing an organizational scheme and to let the classificatory groupings be suggested, instead, by a systematic perusal of the materials themselves. The full range of worker views was thus accommodated regardless of the amount of expressed support for any given position. All the values that respondents attributed to the use of joint and family interviews in the treatment of marital problems are listed and summarized for quick review in Appendix Table 2, together with the number of workers suggesting each asset. Appendix Table 3 similarly summarizes the respondents' views regarding possible criteria for the use of joint interviews and states how many workers expressed support for any given view or disagreed with it. The number of criteria comments applicable to family interviewing was too small to warrant tabular presentation.

In the text itself, minimal emphasis is placed on the actual number of respondents supporting a given position. This policy seemed appropriate since the source questions were open-ended and the phrasing of the responses therefore did not allow an accurate evaluation of the full extent of support or disagreement regarding any given view. Such assessment could only have been obtained if all respondents had been asked to respond pro or con to identical checklists.

Taken together, the points gleaned from the responses with respect to each of these topics amount to a list of values and criteria longer than any similar list known to the author either from the literature or from the reading of any individual response. This suggests that careful analysis of pooled practice experience really does make possible an exceptionally broad and inclusive perspective that can contribute to improved understanding, research, and service for couples in conflict. One cannot overstress the central role of the responses in this monograph. It was through their juxtaposition with each other that the author could gain an overview that none of the respondents themselves, writing in isolation from each other, could enjoy. This allowed recognition of an over-all configuration of ideas and experiences and made certain gaps and areas needing clarification strikingly evident. These could not have emerged with the same clarity from perusal of the separate responses. At the same time, this perspective suggested ways in which insights from recent literature might be used to fill in some of these gaps, clarify some of the questions, and open up further avenues of exploration. In this sense, the monograph illustrates how much practitioners and theoreticians need each other. It is thus hoped that it will offer some demonstration, however small, of the potential rewards of close exchange between them. The pressures of practice leave caseworkers little time for theory-building, which is yet needed to focus and sharpen their understanding and skills. The theory-builders, on the other hand, need contact with the green shoots of practice to remain alive to the real needs, problems, and limitations of the field.

ORGANIZATION OF MONOGRAPH AND DEFINITION OF TERMS

The rest of this monograph is devoted to reporting the findings resulting from analysis of the responses and to viewing their conceptual, research, and practical implications in the light of the literature.

For the sake of clarity, values and criteria and considerations of timing are treated separately even though in practice they must always be weighed in relation to each other. Thus the first two chapters following this introduction deal with the values of joint and family interviewing for the diagnosis and treatment of marital difficulties. The next two deal with the conditions favorable or unfavorable to the use of joint and family interviews respectively. These four chapters lean heavily on the project responses, although separate sections in Chapters 3 and 5 respectively attempt to restate from a system-level perspective the values and criteria associated with joint and family interviewing. Chapter 6 departs from this

heavy reliance on responses to discuss the uses of multiple therapists, couples' groups, and multifamily groups with a view to their
conceptual link with the joint and family interview modalities. The
last chapter summarizes the total sequence, with special emphasis on
broad themes, restating the contribution of joint and family interviews at the system level, and suggesting some implications for practice, theory-building, research, education, and in-service training.

Throughout all chapters the term joint interviews refers exclusively to sessions with a married couple and one caseworker. It is
thus quite distinct in meaning from the family interview, which is
considered here to include at least one family member in addition
to the marital pair. Since the total monograph excludes group
treatment of unrelated individuals, the term multiple-client session
is used in its narrower meaning in the context of this volume, to em-
brace any of the modalities in which more than one client from the
same family participate simultaneously with one or more workers in
the same interview. Any of these approaches, or all, and individual
sessions as well, may be used in the course of family treatment, which
in this report denotes an over-all treatment orientation and not an
interviewing modality.

GENERAL ORIENTATION

Several points of view are implicit in the author's approach to the
materials of this study. These should be made explicit as far as possible so that this orientation and bias may be clear from the start.

For example, although family treatment as an over-all orientation
has been taken for granted throughout, as it also was by most
respondents, it has been assumed here that treatment focused
specifically on the relationship between the partners may be
regarded as a legitimate and at times crucially necessary phase of
family treatment and that, as such, it can be made the focus of
special study. Even though the patterning of the marital relationship often represents only one of several one-generational or intergenerational subsystems within the family, the role of this relationship is seen as central to the total because the partners are the
family founders and have primary leadership responsibilities.
Marital treatment, from this point of view, affords a means of
dealing directly with a pivotal segment or subsystem of the family,

one that is so critical to the whole that it influences significantly and may even substantially determine the life and future of the whole family group and its success in coping with the larger environment. Although some of the respondents and study groups seemed uneasy about singling out marital treatment for special concentrated attention, the implicit tone of the majority of responses suggested concurrence with the views of those writers who, although deeply committed to a family treatment orientation, yet acknowledge marital treatment as a legitimate adaptation of it, "specialized for the specific features of a marital problem" (10, p. 163), and who do not necessarily identify family treatment with the exclusive use of family interviews (13, 22, 23, 27).

In the present attempt to analyze the treatment of the marital subsystem from a total family orientation, two strands of thought will be found interwoven throughout: one of these is represented by the mainly individual orientation of most of the respondents, the other by the system-level orientation of some of the literature and a few of the respondents. It has been assumed here that there is value in probing the comments for their system-level implications, in presenting these implications, and in attempting to push them further, without loss of the worker's traditionally deep respect and concern for the individual, but with gain of a new perspective on the marital unit and on the total family configuration.

The system-level view favored by the author is, it should be emphasized, a dynamic rather than a static one. There is no intent to suggest that preservation of the system or of a stable equilibrium within it should take priority over the welfare of its members. On the contrary, it is the author's strong conviction that, if the family is to last as a unit, making room for the changing and often conflicting requirements and resources of its members as well as for normal changes over time, it must be open to initiatives for change emanating from its individual members and subsystems, as well as from the outside. If it is not geared to growth, it is likely either to stultify the partners' and members' lives or to be burst asunder by the pressures of their struggles against its overly tight strictures and boundaries.

The author's concern with maintaining a system-level perspective goes beyond the use of this approach to the family to encompass a system-level view of the treatment process itself. As the worker temporarily enters the marital and family system for therapeutic purposes, he and the partners or family members are seen as forming a new and transient system together. It is this system that provides the testing and training ground within which the partners and other participants learn to build on existing strengths and resources inside and outside the family system and, if necessary, to evolve system changes adapted to their specific needs and capacities. The success of this treatment system is demonstrated by its eventual dispensability and also by the capacity of its client participants to request and enter into treatment again in the future if they recognize a need for it, for remedial or preventive reasons or both.

Finally, it should be stressed that separate scrutiny of the various elements of treatment is not intended as an endorsement of a manipulative or atomizing view of treatment. Theoretical clarity may make some analytic dissection necessary, but this is merely a temporary expedient for clarifying the nature and basis of knowledge and for devising ways of testing its validity. In the author's view, treatment is and must be, above all, an encounter, a total experience involving worker and clients as whole human beings and the worker-couple or worker-family system as a total entity. This means that the possibilities of insight and encounter, of liberation and healing, are many, but that they must remain largely unknown, a part of the mystery of life. Agency clients are likely to benefit most, as the profession labors to enlarge the areas of transmittable knowledge, if it at the same time preserves a sense of wonder at the mystery.

BIBLIOGRAPHY

Study Group Reports

1. AKRON, OHIO, FAMILY AND CHILDREN'S SERVICE SOCIETY OF SUMMIT COUNTY, *Joint Interviews as a Method of Treatment with Marital Partners Where There Is Hostile Interaction.*
   Study group participants: Mrs. Martha Van Valen (Leader), John C. Freeman, Christian C. Heim, Ronald Kerkhoff, Mrs. Annette McGunnigal, Margaret Minich, Mary C. Monsour, Rosemary Nagy, Mrs. Emily J. Roth, Mrs. Edith Weigl.
2. BALTIMORE, MD., FAMILY AND CHILDREN'S SOCIETY; JEWISH FAMILY AND CHILDREN'S SERVICE; also TOWSON, MD., CHILDREN'S AID AND FAMILY SERVICE SOCIETY: *Practices and Methods of Different Agencies in Handling Marital Relationship Problems.*

14

Family and Children's Society study group participants: Ellen Power, Mrs. Mary Rauh, Albert Tarka.
Jewish Family and Children's Service study group participants: Mrs. Pauline Graff, Mrs. Elsie Seff, Mrs. Anita Weiss.
Children's Aid and Family Service Society study group participant: Mrs. Dorothy Melby.

3. CINCINNATI, OHIO, FAMILY SERVICE OF THE CINCINNATI AREA: *The Relationship of Emancipation to Marital Conflict.*
Study group participants: Mrs. Pauline Cohen (Leader and Recorder), Mrs. Margaret B. Ballard, Mildred Bateman, Sarah Benedict, Mrs. Gretchen Bode, Mrs. Madge Cone, Mary Elizabeth Dodson, Ruth L. Lampley, Mrs. Sarah Lusby, Lois Margot Marples, Mrs. Marilou McCreadie, Janet Rae McKee, Mrs. Jean Powers, Mrs. June B. Ruger, Mildred Ryan, Mrs. Frances Wise, Mrs. Roberta Wooten.

4. CINCINNATI, OHIO, JEWISH FAMILY SERVICE BUREAU, *Family Diagnosis and Treatment as Related to Marital Counseling.*
Study group participants: Morton R. Startz (Leader), Anne Billinkoff, Miriam H. Dettelbach, Mrs. Paula Edelstein, Mrs. Ruth Goldberg, Rose L. Greenstein, Margarete Hirsch, Helen Lampe, Jacqueline Lancaster, Michael Meyer, Mrs. Miriam O. Smith, Mrs. Bernice Temin, Mrs. Miriam Tsevat, Mrs. Doris Wolfenstein.

5. DETROIT, MICH., JEWISH FAMILY AND CHILDREN'S SERVICE: *Treatment of Couples Where the Man Is Passive and the Woman Dominant.*
Study group participants: Rose Kaplan (Leader), Mrs. Rose H. Buchhalter, Mrs. Ida Kost, Mrs. Mildred Littman, Mrs. Hilda Lucas, Mrs. Lillian Weisberg.

6. FLINT, MICH., FAMILY SERVICE AGENCY OF GENESEE COUNTY, *Marital Research Study of Interaction.*
Study group participants: Lorraine Lull (Leader), Mrs. Catherine B. Farner, Mrs. Ruth E. Spurlock, Mrs. Fonda M. Williams; Warren Kennison, M.D., Psychiatric Consultant.

7. GLEN ELLYN, ILL., FAMILY SERVICE ASSOCIATION OF DUPAGE COUNTY, *Criteria for Use of Joint Interviews in the Treatment of Marital Couples.*
Study group participants: Margaret Bates (Leader and Recorder), Frances Barry, Mrs. Marjory Casey, Sema Levinson, Mrs. Anne Ross, Juanita Thorn, Margery Whitcomb, Don Yohe; Mrs. Frances Scherz, Jewish Family and Community Service, Chicago, Consultant.

8. PHILADELPHIA, PA., FAMILY SERVICE OF PHILADELPHIA: *Casework Intervention in Marital Conflict Where the Man Is Passive and the Woman Is Dominant.*
Study group participants: Mrs. Mildred Rosenstein (Leader), Mrs. Hilda Cassert, Mrs. Matilda Mick, Mrs. Bernice Mopsik, Jacob Rubin, Evelyn Stiles, Mrs. Lois Taber, Anna Wiggins.

9. ST. LOUIS, MO., JEWISH FAMILY AND CHILDREN'S SERVICE, *Some Criteria Used by Family Caseworkers in Their Decision To Use Joint Interviewing as the Primary Method of Treatment.*
Study group participants: Michael A. Solomon (Leader), Mrs. Winifred Gross, Margaret Milloy, Mrs. Clara Rosenthal, Mrs. Charlotte Schwarzenberger.

Outside study group participants in second phase of study: 54 staff members from Family and Children's Service of Greater St. Louis; 16 staff members from Family and Children's Bureau of Columbus, Ohio; 8 staff members from Family Service Association of Cleveland; and 20 staff members from Family Service Bureau, United Charities of Chicago.

General References

10. ACKERMAN, NATHAN W., "The Family Approach to Marital Disorders," in Bernard L. Greene (ed.), *The Psychotherapies of Marital Disharmony*, Free Press, New York, 1965, pp. 153–67.

11. ———, BEATMAN, FRANCES L., and SHERMAN, SANFORD N. (eds.), *Expanding Theory and Practice in Family Therapy*, Family Service Association of America, New York, 1967.

12. ———, BEATMAN, FRANCES L., and SHERMAN, SANFORD N. (eds.), *Exploring the Base for Family Therapy*, Family Service Association of America, New York, 1961.

13. AIKIN, DOROTHY, "A Project on Family Diagnosis and Treatment," *Social Work Practice, 1963*, Selected Papers of the National Conference on Social Welfare, Columbia University Press, New York, 1963, pp. 3–18.

14. BARDILL, DONALD R., and RYAN, FRANCIS J., *Family Group Casework: A Casework Approach to Family Therapy*, Catholic University of America Press, Washington, D.C., 1964.

15. BEATMAN, FRANCES L., "The Training and Preparation of Workers for Family-Group Treatment," *Social Casework*, Vol. XLV, No. 4 (April 1964), pp. 202–208.

16. BECK, DOROTHY FAHS, "Practice Wisdom as Data," paper presented at the National Conference on Social Welfare, Los Angeles, 1964 (mimeographed).

17. ——— (ed.), *The Treatment of Marital Problems*, Family Service Association of America, New York (in preparation).

18. BELL, JOHN ELDERKIN, *Family Group Therapy*, Public Health Monograph No. 64, U.S. Government Printing Office, Washington, D.C., 1961.

19. ———, "Recent Advances in Family Group Therapy," *Journal of Child Psychology and Psychiatry*. Vol III, No. 1, (January/March 1962), pp. 1–15.

20. ———, "A Theoretical Position for Family Group Therapy," *Family Process*, Vol. II, No. 1 (March 1963), pp. 1–14.

21. BLANCK, RUBIN, "The Case for Individual Treatment," *Social Casework*, Vol. XLVI, No. 2 (February 1965), pp. 70–74.

22. COMMITTEE ON FAMILY DIAGNOSIS AND TREATMENT OF THE MIDWESTERN REGIONAL COMMITTEE OF THE FAMILY SERVICE ASSOCIATION OF AMERICA, *Casebook on Family Diagnosis and Treatment*, Family Service Association of America, New York, 1965.

23. EINSTEIN, GERTRUDE, *Report on Family Group Treatment Project at Jewish Family Service*, Jewish Family Service of Philadelphia, 1964 (mimeographed).

24. FAMILY SERVICE ASSOCIATION OF AMERICA, *Agency Program and Service Statistics: 1966 (Summary of 1966 Yearly Report Questionnaires, Part III)*, Family Service Association of America, New York, 1967, pp. 1–2.

25. FROSCHER, HAZEL B., "Intervening in the Conflict," in Dorothy Fahs Beck (ed.), *The Treatment of Marital Problems,* Family Service Association of America, New York (in preparation).

26. GAP, COMMITTEE ON THE FAMILY, *Integration and Conflict in Family Behavior*, Report No. 27, written by Florence R. Kluckhohn and John P. Spiegel, Group for the Advancement of Psychiatry, New York, 1954 (reissued June 1968).

27. HALEY, JAY, *Strategies of Psychotherapy,* Grune & Stratton, New York, 1963.

28. MUDD, EMILY H., and GOODWIN, HILDA M., "Counseling Couples in Conflicted Marriages," in Bernard L. Greene (ed.), *The Psychotherapies of Marital Disharmony,* Free Press, New York, 1965, pp. 27–37.

29. POLLAK, OTTO, and BRIELAND, DONALD, "The Midwest Seminar on Family Diagnosis and Treatment," *Social Casework,* Vol. XLII, No. 7 (July 1961), pp. 319–324.

30. SATIR, VIRGINIA M., *Conjoint Family Therapy: A Guide to Theory and Technique,* Science and Behavior Books, Palo Alto, Calif., 1964.

31. ———, "Conjoint Marital Therapy," in Bernard L. Greene (ed.), *The Psychotherapies of Marital Disharmony,* Free Press, New York, 1965, pp. 121–133.

32. SHERMAN, SANFORD N., "Joint Interviews in Casework Practice," *Social Work,* Vol. IV, No. 2 (April 1959), pp. 20–28.

33. SMITH, NEILSON F. (ed.), "Family Phenomena, Problems, and Treatment: Some Family Agency Studies" (A Terminal Progress Report on the Project, "Casework on Marital Problems: A National Experiment in Staff Development"), Family Service Association of America, New York, 1968 (mimeographed).

2

Special Values
of Joint and Family Interviews
for Diagnosis

Can joint and family interviews reveal any diagnostic information regarding a couple's marital problems and their interaction with each other that cannot be learned at least as well in individual sessions? If so, what are the special diagnostic values of such interviews? This chapter will attempt to answer these questions in the light of more than three hundred comments from respondents on this theme and in the perspective of related literature. Chapter 3 will undertake a corresponding analysis of the values of multiple-client interviews for treatment.

While this separation of diagnosis from treatment is bound to be artificial to some degree, it is introduced here to facilitate an orderly presentation. It is not intended to suggest that in actual practice diagnosis can be chronologically or dynamically isolated from treatment. In fact, almost every step in diagnosis has either therapeutic or antitherapeutic impact, or at least sets the tone for the treatment that is to follow. In recognition of the inseparability of the two, some agencies are no longer referring to a "diagnostic phase," but rather to "exploratory treatment."

An organized view of the comments analyzed in this chapter is presented in tabular form in Appendix Table 2, which itemizes, in relation first to diagnosis and then to treatment, each value seen by respondents as stemming from joint or family interviews and cites the number of respondents commenting on each. While the large volume of response in this area mirrors the growing interest and enthusiasm of practitioners regarding the use of joint and family interviews, the bulk of practice experience involved joint rather than family interviewing. Not only did the comments on joint interviewing outnumber those on family interviewing about two to one, but those who did discuss family interviewing had in most instances used this modality only occasionally or not at all at the time they wrote, whereas those who discussed joint interviews almost always wrote from intensive experience with the approach. The comments therefore reflect a degree of interest in family interviewing that far outstripped respondents' actual experience with it at the time they wrote.

In general, irrespective of experience, respondents almost universally saw the diagnostic values of multiple-client interviewing as stemming from the opportunity provided for simultaneous observation and evaluation of both partners or the entire family. This opportunity was reported to lead to (a) faster and better diagnosis in general, (b) improved understanding of the individual family members and their patterns of interaction, (c) a clearer picture of the reality situation, (d) a better history of the couple and the family as a unit, and (e) a more direct view of their reaction to both the initial conditions of treatment and changes occurring during treatment. The present chapter will discuss each of these advantages in some detail and will also include consideration of the diagnostic contribution of individual interviews when these are used in combination with multiple-client sessions.

Increased Speed and Accuracy of Diagnosis

Respondents valued joint and family interviews both for their general diagnostic usefulness and also for their tendency to accelerate diagnosis as compared with exploration through the use of individual interviews alone. Several workers hailed this acceleration, which some attributed to the usefulness of multiple-client interviews in highlighting the central conflict and the role of each partner in it, a view shared by Mitchell (25, p. 285). Not only difficulties but also assets, such as the couple's or family's potential for mutual gratification of needs, were seen as emerging more quickly as a result of joint or family interviewing.

The majority of respondents addressing themselves to this question wrote about joint rather than family interviews and spoke generally of their usefulness in the diagnosis of dynamics. The special diagnostic virtues of four-way interviews were also noted. One group stressed that they "contribute to the workers' understanding of the spouses where two caseworkers have similar methods of work" and mutual respect. Their experience suggests that two workers, by sharing their observations and reactions, can spot and correct each other's distortions and thus clarify and enrich each other's diagnostic impressions.

As for the general diagnostic value of family interviews, respondents discussed these in much the same terms as joint interviews, although one stated specifically that she would use them only "if the children are included in the difficulty." Several testified to the usefulness of home visits with the whole family, but some disapproval was voiced regarding their use in the early stages of treatment, when establishment of the casework relationship was thought to have priority over the amplification of diagnostic data.

IMPROVED UNDERSTANDING
OF FAMILY MEMBERS AND THEIR INTERACTION

By far the greatest volume of comment dwelt on the value of multiple-client interviews for the observation and evaluation of both the individuals within the family and the interaction itself. Included under interactional patterns and their components were various ways of relating, functioning, viewing the marital problem, managing role allocation and role assumption, communicating, clashing, using mutual defenses, sharing positives, and holding certain sociocultural stances and values.

Ways of Relating, Interacting, and Adapting

The difficulties experienced by caseworkers as they reach out from the more familiar ground of individual psychodynamics to the dynamics of interaction were reflected in this material. Respondents tended either to use words describing individual reactions, such as relating, adapting, and revealing feelings, or else they remained quite general in their statements about interaction, communication, and the like. They seemed to be groping for ways to pinpoint what they saw going on between partners and within family constellations, but found that they lacked the words and concepts to describe their diagnostic discoveries. As they strove to express a sense of reciprocity, of mutual or manifold reverberations, certain phrases recurred. Various workers spoke of learning, through joint or family interviewing, about verbal and nonverbal interaction, constructive and destructive patterns of behavior, and the marital or familial balance.

Most of the time, the comments on the way in which family interviews reveal interaction were almost the same as those on joint interviews, but there was a sense of increased subtlety of understanding and of progressive complexity of observation as they ranged from viewing the single client to seeing the couple together and, finally, to including in the session all members of the family living under one roof. Several brought out how their diagnostic view of an individual spouse seen alone tended to differ from their impressions after seeing the marital partners together. Often the joint interview will "throw into relief the psychological changes within each when in the presence of the other." At other times, the change may lie less in the partners' reactions than in the caseworker's response. A shift of impressions and evaluations was seen as likely to result from such a joint interview following individual contact. Such a shift was described as even more likely when separate workers usually see the two partners but bring them together for periodic four-way interviews to observe the interaction.

While most workers prized the increased understanding of the marital relationship revealed by joint interviews, some saw it as further illuminated by family sessions. They regarded such interviews as offering added insights into the couple as parents, while enabling the worker at the same time to catch a subtler understanding of the marriage itself in this wider net of relationships. The few who stressed this point saw the family interview as "further refining our understanding of something which we jointly perceived in part but needed to perceive more fully, if it was to be modified." Such interviews, as another put it, "can be helpful in identifying elusive, interfering attitudes of partners." "One set of relationships may be seen to be affected by other family relationships. . . . The mother relates differently to the son, for example, when the father is not present. Why?" Use of a combination of interviewing modalities offers the caseworker a chance, as Mitchell has pointed out (24, p. 121), to observe the family members engaged in contacts almost as various as those natural within the family itself, thus offering rich opportunities for diagnostic comparison and contrast.

Increased subtlety of diagnostic understanding may also spring from the "deeper and keener understanding of the individuals themselves and of their problems" that may be gained in such sessions. Thus no single aspect of the caseworker's field of concern is allowed to dominate the diagnostic picture. The majority seemed to be reaching for an approach to diagnosis that would encompass the nature and needs both of the individuals and of the systems of which they are a part, even though they did not state their views precisely in this manner.

How accurate is the worker's impression of family interaction likely to be? Will the family members not feel uncomfortable in the office and constrained by his presence? Over half of the respondents commenting on the value of family interviews for observing the family's interaction cited the particular usefulness of the home setting for such interviews. Although many of these did not define the special contribution of the home visit, a good number stressed that it could give an especially vital impression of a family's ways. Families were thought to be less guarded (especially if such visits are planned at dinner time), even though the members may be on their "best behavior." Often the home itself reflects a couple's feelings about themselves, their marriage, and their family. Besides, a home visit might well include important family members who might not come to the office and whose interaction with the other members could round out the diagnostic picture. Watching the "enactment of . . . family relationships on home territory" and seeing "how a father handles his little boy at the dinner table may be more revealing of how he relates to his wife than anything he has said in the office." To this group of values Speck would add the rather delightful one of seeing the family together with its pets as yet another diagnostic bonus of home visits (37).

Emphatic disapproval of home visits for diagnostic purposes was voiced by two respondents fairly inexperienced in this approach. They feared that the caseworker's presence in the home might invite distorted or inhibited behavior, or that the home atmosphere would encourage acting out. Such comments suggest that some practitioners, as well as clients, may feel more relaxed and more in control of the situation when on their own home ground, at least until they perceive the values of venturing forth.[1]

Clearly the diagnostic value of a specific modality cannot be seen in a void. It is closely tied not only to the family's situation but also to the worker's attitudes. Furthermore, it must be used in such a manner that diagnosis is not enhanced at the expense of treatment. If a worker can observe acting out in the home and also handle it therapeutically, as Friedman shows in his article on home visiting (15, p. 140), he is likely to find both his diagnostic understanding and his helpfulness enhanced.

Interacting, relating, and the rest are highly general terms. A great many respondents tried to define more specifically what the added plus was that they could see and weigh as they observed interaction in multiple-client interviews. Their comments ranged from the couple's and family's attitude toward the marital difficulty, their patterns of role allocation and functioning, communication, conflict, and mutual defenses, to the family's strengths and sociocultural patterns and values. These categories, even though overlapping, help organize respondents' offerings.

Attitudes
toward the Marital Difficulty

The married couple's view of their conjugal difficulties is an aspect of both their mutual functioning and their individual pain. No wonder, then, that some respondents felt they could best learn each partner's view of the marital difficulty in an initial individual interview while others believed it important to use a joint interview even at intake. By this means the latter group felt able to gain a sense of the couple's ability to face the reality of the marital problem, of their awareness of individual involvement, and of the severity of the conflict. They saw value not only for their own diagnostic understanding, but also for the couple, in having each state his view of the problem in front of his partner. However, no respondent saw interviews with the total family as the appropriate choice for an intake interview in situations in which the problem was understood at

---

1 Bell (10, pp. 6–7) states unequivocally that he will not engage in any meetings with a family outside the office: ". . . for even though I might learn from such occasions, I would be sacrificing the advantages and speed of treatment that follow a more . . . structured role for myself. . . ."

the time of first contact to be one of marital tension. At the same time some did favor the use of family interviews during the early diagnostic period to understand the marital problem in all of its ramifications, although they apparently did not see themselves as starting the contact by exploring the full extent of the difficulty in the presence of the children. This approach coincides with that of most of the writers in the social work field (7, p. 78; 31, p. 213). Even so strong an advocate of family group interviewing as Satir usually sees the couple first for at least two sessions, because they are family leaders and mates as well as parents (30, p. 137). However, the therapeutic implications of the initial exploratory contact must not be overlooked. Thus one of the study groups cautioned (2, p. 6) that "it is important to set up a family interview early in the exploratory phase. Then when a family interview is suggested during treatment it . . . [will] seem more natural and acceptable to the family." What happens early in the contact is thus recognized as setting the tone for treatment. Everything that happens in any interview has impact— for better, for worse, or for keeping the status quo—even when the worker is temporarily focusing on diagnosis.

While there were relatively few comments on the values of joint interviews for revealing a couple's total stance toward the marital difficulty, this was more than balanced by the volume of responses that covered the areas of mutual feeling and functioning, both conscious and unconscious, that together make for harmony or cacophony in wedded and family life. The topics covered by these more specific responses included role, communication, conflict, defenses, strengths, and sociocultural attitudes. An overview of their content will reveal the respondents' convictions about the unique contribution of multiple-client interviews to improved understanding of the gamut of mutual gratification and friction among couples and families. It should also begin to reveal something of the respondents' underlying view of treatment, since the diagnostic values stressed must surely give a clue to the problems regarded as either most in need of change or most receptive to improvement.

Patterns of Leadership,
Control, and Role Allocation

Of the comments regarding the patterns of leadership, control, and role allocation as revealed in multiple-client interviews, only a few referred to family interviews. Such sessions—in the office or in the home—were valued by the respondents for revealing the respective roles of various family members and were thought to point up role failure especially clearly. As for joint interviews, they were thought to show "who assumes the burden of responsibility," at least within the interview situation, and "whether there is a mutual sharing or one of the partners prefers to remain relatively uninvolved." They could also reveal "the role that each is fulfilling in marriage" and whether "this is a source of dissatisfaction to one or both." Moreover, they were regarded as useful for observing a couple's response to the fee scale "(who withholds, who pays, and who is ignorant of the actual family income)."

The remaining comments in this category referred to strength and leadership, on the one hand, and to methods of domination and manipulation, on the other. An especially lively illustration was offered by a worker who had been unable to understand what was happening in one marriage until she held a joint interview. She then found that the wife, who in individual interviews had complained of her husband's failure to tell her what he thought, cut him short each time he tried to speak. The diagnostic picture began to clear.

Clues to benign, self-defeating, or destructive forms of dominance were seen to emerge in the course of joint interviews. Workers praised them for revealing who shows leadership, who is the stronger of the two, who is dominant or controlling, who uses manipulation, and who is passive, submissive, or dependent. Workers did not indicate whether they used the joint interview to see whether there were specific situations that evoked such behavior while quite different or even opposite behavior might be shown by the same partner in other circumstances or vis-à-vis other persons.

Posing the problem in this fashion suggests that even though respondents did not address themselves to this directly there might be considerable value in the use of family interviews for illuminating the chronicity or flexibility of such stereotyped patterns. To see the partners in the broader context of the family might show, for instance, whether the dominant spouse needs to control all family members or can relate in a quite different manner, for example, to one of the children. This would give a clue to the worker as to whether he is dealing with a pervasive attitude or with attitudes and behavior tied to a specific relationship. Joint interviews, then, used in combination with individual and family sessions, offer a unique

25

opportunity for avoiding hasty generalizations. This is a point of the utmost importance, especially since almost all the respondents used a variety of approaches.

The richness of materials offered by the use of diverse modalities may eventually make it possible to spell out more clearly the various components of the role concept and to explore whether certain of these components may tend to occur in typical clusters. Such an increase in specificity—already pioneered in other contexts in the work of Spiegel (38) and Perlman (27)—should do much to gear a global term such as *role* to the requirements of daily practice.[2]

Patterns of Communication

The tendency for respondents to write in general terms that characterized the material on role was also prevalent in the comments on communication, which were mainly focused on joint interviewing and did not state whether the understanding of communication patterns gained in total family interviews differed in degree or kind from that gained from the joint interview. Various respondents noted the value of observing the nature or pattern of communication between the marital partners and the opportunity to observe or confirm the lack of communication, to identify areas in which communication has broken down, or to see the comparative impact of individual and joint interviews on the partners' ability to communicate with each other. Above all, caseworkers remarked on the joint interview as an aid to understanding both verbal and nonverbal communication. Some highly pertinent and specific questions were posed: "Is each free to present the situation as he sees it? Does the other partner really listen, or look out of the window in impatience? Do the complaints come from only one side? Is there easiness or uneasiness about being revealed in front of the other?"

These are questions that relate not only to feelings—an area long familiar to caseworkers—but that also point in the direction of the newer understanding of communications developed in recent years, in part through the work at Palo Alto, California. Easiness or uneasiness about revealing oneself in front of one's partner, complaints emanating from one quarter exclusively—such conditions raise diagnostic issues akin to the questions considered by such writers as

---

[2] For some discussion of such existing refinements as Spiegel's concepts of role modification *see* (38).

Bateson, Jackson, Weakland, Haley, and Satir: What are the rules within this family or between this marital pair regarding "who is to talk about what" (17, p. 133)? Do they handle their "differentness" from each other "in terms of *war* and *who is right*" or "on the basis of *exploration* and *what fits*" (30, p. 90)? Viewing communication with these questions in mind will give diagnostic clues, in Satir's view, as to whether the clients are tending toward "stalemating, retardation and pathology" or to "growth, individuality and creativity" (30, p. 90). Even more detailed questions useful for the diagnostic evaluation of communication between spouses or among all the family can be formulated from the writings of this group. They are summarized in the report of the Jewish Family Service of Philadelphia (13, pp. 8–9) about their own Family Group Treatment Project: "Messages have to be carefully evaluated by the counselor: Are they what they seem to be, or is some hidden meaning involved? Is there a contradictory double message, denying what is said on one level . . ." by what is conveyed on another more hidden one? Clearly, the whole body of communications experience and theory built around the concept of the double bind (6) can be brought into the service of casework by skillful use of joint and family interviews. Thus both respondents' comments and the literature regarding communication reinforce the previous impression that the diagnostic value of these sessions increases in direct proportion to the specificity of the concepts with which the practitioner is operating. Paradoxically, such increased specificity also leads to a better sense of the characteristics of the over-all pattern of communication. One might say, by analogy, that the clear delineation and distinctive coloring of each individual mosaic piece add to, rather than detract from, the wholeness of the finished and blended picture.

While communication problems may result in misunderstanding and conflict, it is also true that a breakdown of communication between the partners may be due to anger or conflict felt so intensely that they interfere with the appropriate expression and reception of other feelings between the partners or among the family members. Such obstacles will be considered next.

Extent and Nature of Conflict

How much conflict is there between the partners? How intense is it? Which family members are most caught up in it? To what degree are they involved in the strife? What are the loci of their disagreements or their divergencies of need? Several respondents saw answers to such questions as being facilitated by joint or family interviews.

Patterns and degree of mutual hostility and destructiveness and specific areas involved in the marital conflict. Joint interviews were seen as useful for revealing both overt and covert patterns of mutual hostility and destructiveness and for casting light on the actual areas of conflict. They were described variously as showing the "sado-masochistic byplay" of the partners and as revealing "the weapons these people punish each other with and why . . . they work." The extent and modes of indirect expression of aggression were seen as delineated, along with the points of pain, sensitivity, and friction. They were found to afford an understanding not only of the difficulty in the marriage, but also of the sources of the conflicts within the individuals. Thus, once again joint interviewing was recognized not only as a diagnostic aid in understanding the partners in relation to each other but also as a means of deepening the worker's understanding of each as an individual. "When the focus is on interaction," Mitchell once put it (25, p. 284), "neither the individual nor the group is submerged, but the group medium is utilized in the interests of the participating individuals."

Extent and type of relationship of the children to the marital conflict. The extent and manner of the children's involvement in the marital conflict has always had to be a part of the worker's diagnostic assessment in the treatment of marital problems. Material from individual interviews will offer a basis for inferring the children's part in the problem. Joint interviews, as one respondent pointed out, can allow the worker "to observe the reactions of each partner as he talks about the children." Therefore, they help evaluate "the extent to which the relationship of each parent to a particular child or children enters into the marital conflict." However, confirmation—or refutation—of such impressions is only possible by direct observation. Therefore total family interviews were welcomed to test whether the relationship of one partner to one of the children threatens the spouse and whether either is using the children against the other.

Two unique contributions of total family interviews to an understanding of marital conflict were identified. On the one hand, respondents saw them as revealing (especially during home visits) who the key clients are and what the impact of the marital problems is on the children, especially in situations of "extreme, pervasive conflict." On the other hand, they recognized, to quote the study group report of the Jewish Family Service Bureau of Cincinnati (2, p. 1.), "that children are not only the recipients of marital difficulties but also contribute to them." Several pointed out that family sessions may show the way in which children "participate in the family dysfunctioning" or, more specifically, how "the child plays one parent against the other." One group mentioned especially families in which "a child's behavior or emotional, intellectual, or medical problems are a significant factor in the marital conflict," but indicated that their own inclination was to use joint interviews in such situations. Another group, confronted with the same reality problems, might have favored family interviews.

Still other comments related to using a child against the partner, playing one parent against the other, or, in other words, making use of family members as allies. The value of family interviews for highlighting "family alliances [and] shifts in these alliances" was made explicit by the Jewish Family Service of Philadelphia report (13, p. 8) and by a respondent group commenting on another question altogether. "Because marital problems often are reflected in the upset behavior of children," they wrote, "we are increasingly interested in seeing the total family as soon as possible. The enables us to assess family interaction and alignments."

The question of alliances raises more than the issue of anger, which may unite some against others. The pioneers of multiple-impact therapy, for example, suggest that anger and hostile alliances are not usually concealed as desperately as the bonds of tenderness and of collusion "which may, in fact, represent the most resistive ele ments in the total family picture" (21). Since collusion, unlike tenderness, is not a constructive force in family life, it is to be hoped that joint or family sessions might help the worker to distinguish those bonds and coalitions that are rooted in mutual affection and can be used to build marital and family strength from those anchored in mutual need based on fear, misperception, and the like, to guard the pathological adaptations of individual family members or the dysfunctional patterns of the marital or family group as a whole.

Such concepts as collusion (36) or pseudomutuality (43, p. 108) suggest the necessity for some caution about identifying the key members. The member most intensely involved in the marital conflict may not be the one who "bears the brunt of the stress" (31, p. 213), the one who is being scapegoated (41). Scapegoating, as the Cincinnati Jewish Family Service Bureau study group pointed out (2, p. 4), may be revealed in family interviews to be "a reflection and displacement of problems between the marital partners. . . . The developing sexuality of the . . . [adolescent, for instance,] may arouse latent conflict in the parents . . . [and] . . . cause scapegoating of the adolescent as a way of avoiding an examination of . . . their own attitudes around sexuality." The overt sufferings of one or several members may thus conceal the problems and conflicts of the ostensibly more effective partner. Similarly, as Sonne *et al.* have pointed out (36), the "good" or "healthy" child may be heavily implicated in the conditions making for marital and family upheaval and its continuance. Interviews with the total family can make a most valuable contribution to diagnosis by revealing and documenting the nature of these complex networks.

An aspect of conflict not mentioned by the respondents in connection with diagnosis, but raised in the context of treatment, was the value of both joint and family interviews for an improved understanding of the family's maturational stage and of the extent to which marital strains may be associated with it.[3] Some authors speak of the "dissimilar requirements for change and possibilities for action" characteristic of different age groups (9, p. 5) and of "the incompatibility of the diverse developmental strivings of family members at critical points of growth" (40, p. 149). Such disparities may be clearly observable in family interviews. Their recognition may prove an especially valuable diagnostic contribution in situations in which divergencies due to growth must be distinguished from "tensions created by disparities between individual striving and group pressures" (25, p. 285), which may be due to other causes and may therefore require different remedies.

Operation and Effectiveness of Mutual Defenses

Failure or inadequacy in communication, family harmony, distribution of responsibilities, and the like may be due to a variety of factors ranging from unalterable realities such as organic retardation

[3] *See* pp. 44–45 for a discussion of Spiegel's view of maturational changes and role problems (38).

to such intangibles as the operation of individual defenses or shared defensive maneuvers. Respondents had a great deal to say about the value of joint and family sessions for *handling* various defenses, but they offered fewer references to their usefulness in diagnosing what the partners or family members were defending themselves against, how they managed to do this, and why. Some commented in a general way that joint interviews offered a valuable opportunity to observe types of defenses or methods of coping with anxiety, their appropriateness, and their degree, but only one cited the value of total family interviews for such purposes. These workers seemed to be thinking mainly in terms of individual defense mechanisms, but did not explain whether they saw these as springing into action because of intrapsychic pressure or as the result of strains in interpersonal relationships.

The defense mechanisms singled out for specific comment by most respondents were those of projection, distortion, and denial. It was not clear from the comments whether these three ways of avoiding responsibility for a problem were usually seen as arising from conscious or unconscious motives, but all three were described as emerging more clearly in joint than in individual interviews. Presumably the patent incompatibility of the partners' accounts or attitudes is harder to evade in joint interviews and defenses are more likely to emerge because of the presence of real or felt attack.

One respondent spelled out the added usefulness of family interviews in the diagnosis of defenses. She recalled that children are often "effective in putting their finger on important things that parents are too defensive to reveal."

Extent and Nature
of Existing Strengths

While the diagnosis of problems and difficulties has been the center of attention so far, references to adaptation and to assumption of responsibility and leadership have already suggested the importance of recognizing also the precise areas of health and effective functioning in the couple's and family's life.

Ability to function jointly and realistically. Most references to the couple's capacity for joint and reality-oriented functioning were general. Half of those commenting in this area valued joint interviews because they enhanced their understanding of the individual

partners' capacities. They found these interviews useful for apprais-
ing a couple's capacity for reality functioning, as did the few respondents who cited family interviews for revealing family functioning
and dysfunctioning. Joint interviews, one of the respondents elabor-
ated, could show "who is the stronger of the two" and "how a couple
handle stress." The remaining half of the comments stressed mutuality. They suggested that joint interviews helped the worker to observe how the couple functions as a unit and how they mutually
evaluate or handle problems.

Other positives in the marital or familial relationship. When a
client comes to the office alone, positives in the marital or familial
situation are hard to spot. Often in such situations hints of success,
satisfaction, or strengths within the marriage and family have in the
past been lost or overlooked. Workers therefore lauded joint and
family interviews for adding a new dimension to their understanding.

Three different groups of respondents each highlighted the special
contributions of the home visit—one set speaking of such visits to
the partners alone, the other two recommending home visits to the
total family. One reported that "husbands often fare much better in
a home visit," especially "the husband who feels that his wife
brought him to the agency for counseling. In his own home, he be-
gins to indicate strengths and capacities which were not evident in
the office interview." By way of illustration, this practitioner stated
without explanation that one father seemed to take the home visit as
an indication that no "threat of loss of face" was involved in discussion of his troubles—another indication of the intricate interweav-
ing of diagnostic and therapeutic elements. Any given mode of interviewing may be seen as tending to provoke, by its very structure,
certain types of diagnostic information that might otherwise remain
hidden.

Office visits by the couple or the family were described as revealing
both their potential for mutual gratification and their actual
strengths. Those who wrote about joint interviews stressed their
value for revealing what the couple have in common, how they fit
each other, and what they have achieved in terms of mutual closeness, sensitivity, intimacy, warmth, and "togetherness on ideas
[about] having and rearing a child." Similarly, family interviews
were thought sometimes to reveal "natural little courtesies or affec-
tionate gestures which indicate that family life is not as totally bad

as described" or to give a glimpse of strengths in the marriage that had not become evident in individual or joint sessions.

The importance of these points is confirmed by some of the literature (23, p. 63; 31, p. 213; 34) and by the views of the study group from the Cincinnati Jewish Family Service Bureau (2, p. 3). They cannot be overstressed. Diagnosis must always seek to identify the best point of leverage, whether to effect improvement, to revert to a more comfortable previous state of affairs, or at least to arrest the further deterioration of the marriage and family. No more effective leverage is likely to be found than one based on already existing powers within the family itself.

Sociocultural Patterns and Values

So far no mention has been made of sociocultural patterns and values. Respondents and writers alike have been quoted as if the only problems relevant to the marital difficulty resided in and were expressed through facts, attitudes, and interactions within the family alone. To some extent this omission reflects a pattern obvious throughout the responses. Yet even without Spiegel and Bell's brilliant formulations of the intertwining among the systems of the culture at large, the family, and the individual (39, p. 140), such an approach would have to be dismissed as narrow and unrealistic. Some of the respondents did show considerable interest in understanding the family in a wider context, but did so mainly within the focus of treatment. Another commented briefly on the usefulness of the joint interview for revealing the cultural and social attitudes of the partners and spoke of home visits to the whole family as illuminating their values as a group and their place in the culture. No doubt the revived national concern in the past few years with problems of the poor would have been reflected in more concentration on these factors if the responses had been written more recently.

An understanding of the couple's and family's cultural patterns and values may not always contribute to an understanding of the genesis or development of the marital difficulty. It is, however, always essential for the worker, since he cannot develop a meaningful treatment plan with the family unless he understands clearly whether and in what ways their culture and value system differ from his own. Without this knowledge, the worker will have difficulty in understanding the partners and in accepting them, **if** their values happen to differ from his own (28, p. 219). With **it,** he may well be able to bridge the gap (3).

IMPROVED KNOWLEDGE OF THE REALITY SITUATION

The life situation of a couple or family seen in individual interviews is accessible to the caseworker only through inference from their various accounts and from such direct familiarity with their environment as his own life or collateral contacts may have afforded him. Clearly, a new world for seeking and validating diagnostic impressions is opened up when both partners or the whole family are seen together in the office—and even more when they are seen at home. No wonder, then, that only the topic of family interaction and mutual relating attracted more comment than the value of multiple-client interviews for understanding the reality situation. This topic was also the only one, except for the relatively few comments on sociocultural attitudes and on the role of children in the conflict, on which comments about family interviewing far outnumbered those about the joint interview.

Two main points stood out with respect to joint interviews. Half of the respondents speaking on this issue saw such interviews as a valuable means of observing the facts or the reality situation as such. The remaining half praised this approach as a means of clarifying the situation after conflicting statements by the partners had obscured it. In this fashion, the joint interview could serve the double diagnostic purposes of illuminating the situation and the partners' defenses simultaneously.

Except for a few comments referring to office interviews with the family group, all the responses on diagnosing the reality situation through family interviews differed sharply from those on joint sessions in that all of them referred to home visits. For this reason they were focused more on the realities of the clients' environment, although the emotional angle was not ignored by any means. Several workers expressed regret that they lacked time to make home visits or to make them as often as they thought appropriate. A few saw only certain kinds of families at home: the "chronically disorganized family," when the influence of the environment on the conflict needed clarification, or, more generally, families who claimed conditions in the home to be part of their particular problem.

On the whole, however, the workers' comments did not specify whether they were using the family home visit only for specific situations, for just one session, or for repeated meetings. Instead, they concentrated on spelling out the diagnostic values of such visits, with their opportunities to sense the meaning of "home" to each member and to see and feel its environment and climate. They also saw home visits as casting light on the family's socioeconomic status, their living standards, the severity of external pressures on them, and, in certain cases, the special handicaps or mental retardation of a family member. The housekeeping capacity of the wife was another factor noted, especially in situations in which the husband complained of inadequacy in this respect.

The liveliness of some of the illustrations offered bore out how greatly such visits also contribute to the caseworker's sense of the clients as real people in real families. One wife, a respondent wrote, had complained of her husband's "saddling her not only with the children but with animals as well" and then going out all the time. This meant little to the worker until she visited and literally tripped over a dog (female), a cat (female), and their respective offspring. Another used an illustration to buttress her view that "even the physical layout of the house" can give clues to the home climate. She told of a family whose "whole house was planned around the recreation room which had been set up as a ballet studio for the wife. She had not mentioned her interest in dancing, but this was an absorbing concern . . . and aggravated the husband who wanted a wife, not a dancer."

These comments support the value of home visits as discussed by such authors as Friedman (15, p. 137), who feels that "families do not as readily ignore or hide their real ways of living and relating to each other when they are seen in their own homes." Faucett (14, p. 442) moves beyond the issue of milieu to point out the value of home visits for a clearer view of the impact of changes in the family life cycle on the members—changes that range from reactions to developmental change in children to reverberations from moving, taking in an aged parent, or even doing better financially.

Home visits, like any other interview modality, are not automatically useful. One respondent warned that the worker "must be conscious of the clients' feelings" and weigh the possible effects of such a visit on the casework relationship in situations in which "environmental factors must be observed to assess a reality situation." Diagnosis, to repeat a familiar theme, will be useless if it involves actions or reactions that are antitherapeutic. Conversely, a respondent group suggested that a request for home visiting may be the client's way of showing that he does not feel understood or that more time should be spent on "the practical aspects of where and how he lives." The psychic reality of his need is as much a diagnostic clue as the physical reality to be observed.

Just as the couple or family need opportunities for clarifying their understanding of their own situation, so the worker needs to keep alert simultaneously to his own reactions to the clients' emotional and interactional situation, to their reality situation, and to the wider world in which they are all functioning. Only if the worker is open to all these systems and ready to turn his attention to whichever one requires it will he be able to help the couple and family break out of the imprisonment of their interlocking problems to reach more open, resourceful, and constructive levels of functioning and more mutual growth and satisfaction—provided such liberation is possible within the limits of their personal, familial, and environmental situation. This is the diagnostic balance toward which the totality of comments so far seems to point.

Perhaps it may not be out of place to suggest here that multiple-client interviews and home visits also offer an opportunity to diagnose weaknesses in the environment. They may highlight, for example, a lack of needed resources. A heightened awareness of the need for community action may thus be yet another value that may accrue from the use of multiple-client interviews, especially in the case of multiproblem families in deprived neighborhoods, who may lack the verbal facility or the knowledge to point out what they need, or who may have failed to recognize either their own strength for obtaining it or the limitations preventing them from doing so.

FULLER REVELATION OF THE FAMILY HISTORY

Most agencies use individual interviews to gather historical background on the individual spouse or family member, but several respondents specifically mentioned the value of multiple-client interviews for obtaining a history of the family. Half of the admittedly sparse comments on this topic came from workers who found joint interviews generally helpful for clarifying the partners' shared past—some because a partner may be able to "recall events his mate cannot," others because joint interviews might illuminate the histories of the individual partners. The latter group acknowledged "some practical difficulties for the worker in obtaining a clear chronological picture," but found the attempt doubly fruitful diagnostically (and therapeutically) because "each partner can hear the other and interact as this material is reviewed." The remaining comments suggested that family interviews were well suited for obtaining "accurate background more readily" and for helping the worker to understand the family's past through perusal during home visits of the " 'historical record' as reflected in the surroundings." [4]

Although most respondents preferred to see clients individually to discuss their historical background, one type of situation was mentioned as specifically requiring joint interviews, even for history-taking. This involved the couple with whom any individual interviewing would, in the respondent group's opinion, have implied a "false promise" for the wife, leading her to hope for more closeness in her relationship with the caseworker than she could expect from her husband. Otherwise, the general inclination of respondents to use various modalities for various ends held good, with joint or family interviews emerging as an added tool for history-taking rather than as a substitute for the individual approach. To quote Weiss (42, p. 113): "Knowledge about the family's operations can give the worker insight into the central family themes, but only the significant history of each family member can furnish clues as to the adaptive functions these themes serve for each individual. A family theme that permits successful adaptation for the parents may be maladaptive for the children." Her summation makes a case for combining different types of interview in order to explore personal and family history. This approach goes beyond the reasons given by respondents and links them with the need for clues about the nature and development of disparate strivings and maturational tensions within the family (see p. 30).

Similarly, a concern with the possible development of the marital conflict, as outlined by Beck (8), suggests a highly useful role for

[4] For mention of the importance of the family's understanding of its own past, *see* this volume, Chap. 3, p. 75.

joint and family interviews in tapping shared memories and reactions of the partners in relation to their courtship, to the evolution or explosion of conflict, and to the factors precipitating their request for help.

MORE DIRECT KNOWLEDGE
OF REACTIONS TO THE TREATMENT SITUATION

Of the comments so far reviewed, all but those concerning the hastening and general enrichment of diagnosis have centered on the clients and their situation. Now the focus shifts. The last two categories identifying diagnostic values relate to the way in which joint and family interviews illuminate the couple's or family's reactions to the treatment situation. These reactions are stimulated first by the initial conditions for treatment, which also persist throughout the contact, and then by changes in the marital relationship—the successes, failures, or omissions—that become evident in the course of treatment or even after termination. These are the categories of diagnostic concern that will guide the worker and the clients as they struggle to integrate the process of treatment with the changing needs and realities—both emotional and practical—in the family's total situation.

Reactions to Agency and Worker

Most of the workers who discussed the couple's or family's reactions to the agency or the worker spoke of these in connection with the development of a plan for treatment. A few also mentioned the value of joint and family interviews for gaining a diagnostic impression of the couple's or family's reaction to the worker and the agency. Half of those commenting on this topic spoke of family interviews and focused entirely on their usefulness in seeing how clients relate to the worker and "what role [they are] attempting to cast the worker into." This was also the tenor of almost all the comments on this specific value of joint interviews. A simultaneous reaction to agency policy was, however, involved in the comment citing the usefulness of noting "differences in response (as between the partners) to the fee scale." Further contributions of joint and family interviews for an understanding of the family's reactions to treatment are suggested by the theories of Bell (9, 10), Haley (17), and Satir (30), among others, who have urged a view of the family as a system. Some of the possible implications of their analysis for diagnosis will be discussed later (see pp. 46–47).

Readiness for Involvement
in Treatment

While the individual client's readiness to involve himself in treatment can be weighed in individual interviews, joint and family interviews were seen as shedding light on the extent to which the worker may expect mutuality of motivation and involvement from the couple or family. Almost all the comments on this topic centered on joint interviews, but there was mention of family sessions as useful for revealing "whether both partners wanted help or one of them was there under pressure from the other." In addition to conscious or hidden individual reactions, that which is revealed may include the nature and mechanisms of the family system itself. This was recognized by the Jewish Family Service of Philadelphia when they stated that part of the diagnostic evaluation made possible through family interviews "was a direct testing of the family's readiness and ability to face their problem and to tolerate intervention in a destructively set pattern" (13, p. 7).

If such a pattern exists in the family, it must yield satisfactions of some kind or it would hardly have persisted. In some families it may even have evolved from the couple's distorted perceptions about the conditions necessary for their very survival as a marital and family unit (16) and may therefore be especially difficult to challenge. How can the worker get an indication of the family's readiness for involvement in treatment under such circumstances? The study group report of the Jewish Family Service Bureau of Cincinnati (2) envisaged a diagnostic as well as a therapeutic role for family interviews in this connection. "If the family is to give up their current destructive mode of satisfying needs," they wrote (p. 6), "then they must be offered an alternate and more satisfying method. We must determine the clients' motivation for such new adaptation, their tolerance to examine current patterns and their personal capacity to assume new ways of satisfying each other. In many situations we may need to settle for a restoration of a less than totally satisfying relationship."

39

Assessment of motivation is thus an ongoing process requiring that clients also be given a sense that help and a measure of satisfaction are possible for them. "It is important," as this same study group report pointed out (p. 2), "to determine the immediate core problem on which the family is ready and able to work," and to understand "the family's perception of themselves." At the same time, without a diagnostic awareness of what the agency and the worker can offer the couple, a diagnostic assessment of the family's readiness to use help would be incomplete. Thus, joint and family interviews, like individual sessions, demand a high capacity for growing self-awareness on the part of the worker, who needs to maintain a constant alertness to the impact of his personality, skills, strengths, and shortcomings on the couple of family. Joint and family interviews also contribute a new dimension to his view of himself vis-à-vis the family as a group, their predicament, and the possibilities for hope. Thus they deepen and enrich his diagnostic understanding.

More Adequate Periodic Evaluation of Changes during Treatment

Whether one approach is used exclusively or a variety of interviewing modalities is brought into play, the joint or family interview was acknowledged by many as especially useful for the evaluation of change or impasse in the marital relationship, for a view of the impact of such change on the children, for an assessment of the direction of treatment for both partners in split cases, and for a delineation of areas needing further individual work. The joint interview was also cited as useful for the evaluation of a couple's progress after termination. One respondent reported scheduling such a check-up for two months after the end of the contact.

Even in situations in which the partners are usually being seen individually, respondents saw joint interviews as appropriate for evaluating progress or regression on the part of the marital pair, for seeing what changes had occurred in their situation, and for evaluating jointly what the service meant to them. Some planned joint interviews at regular intervals for such assessment throughout the period of treatment, while others scheduled joint check-ups whenever timely. Similarly, one of the respondents thought occasional family interviews valuable even in the course of treatment mainly by joint interviews, in order to assess what was happening to the children and to their relationship with the parents.

A NOTE ON THE CONTRIBUTION OF INDIVIDUAL INTERVIEWS TO DIAGNOSIS

This monograph, as mentioned earlier, is based on responses to questions focused on multiple-client interviewing. At no point were the respondents asked to spell out the distinct values of individual interviews as compared with multiple-client approaches either for diagnosis or for treatment. Their full thinking on these important questions is therefore not available. However, a number either stated or implied views on that modality's values for diagnosis.

Some saw individual interviews as useful for diagnosis in combination with other methods, when there was a need for a better understanding of the basis of repetitive behavior on the part of one spouse. Others singled out their value for history-taking. While thoroughly familiar with the joint interview, these respondents expressed a preference for seeing clients individually in order to discuss their personal background or to "clear up a specific point related to a client's past." The importance of using such interviews in order to link an understanding of central family themes with clues to the adaptive functions they serve for each individual (42, p. 113) has already been discussed (see p. 37). It is reflected in the reported practice of holding at least one interview with each partner and one with both before any diagnosis is attempted. Thus the couple can "reveal alone what they cannot reveal in the presence of each other, and they can enact together what they cannot tell about individually."

This practice raises the issue of using individual interviews for an airing of feelings or information that one partner may not have previously acknowledged to the other. Such interviews were seen by some workers as necessary under special circumstances (see p. 151). A few advocated individual interviews at intake as a regular practice prior to later joint sessions, so that each partner might separately give his view of the marital problem. The overwhelming majority, however, stated a preference for joint interviews at intake. Needless to say, great caution must be exercised by the worker lest individual sessions become antitherapeutic traps interpreted by the other spouse as an alliance against him. There are some theoreticians and therapists—in particular Bell (9, 10)—who see all requests for separate interviews as resistance and will not see any family member alone at any time. However, the workers represented in this study took no global stand of this kind.

To summarize, then, workers who identified certain special diagnostic values of individual interviews when these are used in combination with multiple-client interviews did not speak as partisans for any approach. Like the vast majority of all respondents, they seemed to prize the complementary contributions to diagnosis gained when all available modalities are used with discrimination and with full awareness of their special assets and risks. They saw individual, joint, and family interviews, used in this fashion, as each supplementing and deepening insights derived from the others. Their approach would, therefore, seem to be in general agreement with that of the Jewish Family Service of New York (7), the Jewish Family Service of Philadelphia (13), the Midwest Seminar led by Dr. Otto Pollak (4), and the Committee on Family Diagnosis and Treatment of the Midwestern Regional Committee chaired by Mrs. Frances Scherz (11), to mention only four of the several pioneering groups in the field.

IMPLICATIONS FOR FURTHER EXPLORATION

A review of all the findings reported so far suggests certain gaps in the responses as compared with the literature and some possible implications for further study and exploration. Particularly evident are a need for greater specificity of diagnostic concepts, for more diagnostic attention to certain neglected areas and to the dovetailing of agency resources and family strengths, and for further exploration of the usefulness of family interviews for the diagnosis of marital problems.

Need for Greater Specificity of Diagnostic Concepts

Caseworkers' comments on the values of multiple-client interviews for diagnosis of marital conflict and its participants made use of a wide range of concepts, but terms were for the most part used globally and vaguely without clear identification of their meaning or components. A great deal of work evidently remains to be done by the field, (a) to absorb and integrate into practice the advances reflected in the literature and (b) to refine these global concepts to the point at which they may become enriching and refining for both diagnosis and treatment. The author's plea at this point is for movement toward greater specificity and clarity of concepts. To urge this does not imply any downgrading of feelings, but merely their assignment to a more definable place in the diagnostic picture. While granting the great importance for casework of intuitive insight, partly inexplicable hunches, and so on, alertness to specifics should sharpen and deepen diagnostic impressions, both with respect to the particulars and the total configuration of patterns within the marriage and family, and should make such impressions more relevant therapeutically.

Some concepts needing attention. Illustrations of concepts needing further attention include communication, role functioning, involvement, and mutual defenses. A little amplification in each case may help to make clear what greater specificity could mean for the sharpening of diagnosis through the type of observation possible in multiple-client interviews.

In the area of communication, several subconcepts are already available (6, 17, 30) to allow the identification of various methods and levels of communication and a range of possible communication paradoxes. An attempt to apply these concepts more consistently in general casework practice and to develop them further would make it possible to sharpen the worker's diagnostic awareness with regard to the web of mutual involvements in a particular pathological family system and the habits, fears, and gratifications that sustain it. Without such mapping of the pathological family system of communication in a specific situation, the worker may focus on intrapsychic difficulties of a member, with the result that problems rotate among the rest of the family group. On the other hand, if he limits his view to the family system of communication exclusively, he may fail to perceive an intrapsychic problem, to the

concepts
allowed
redients

came through clearly in the responses. Caseworkers cited willingness to come in and to work together on the problem as clues to the
clients' stance. There was little hint, however, of what such involvement might mean to the partners themselves. Follow-up interviews with couples might help reveal further components of involvement. What did the partners themselves see as the factors
that did or did not induce them to try, and then to continue, to
tackle their marital problems with the help of a caseworker?

Greater specificity also seems indicated in relation to the term
mutual defenses, as used to refer to defenses at the family rather
than at the individual level. Respondents did refer to a number of
defensive maneuvers in terms of individual psychopathology, using
such terms as projection, distortion, and the like. However, references to defenses that require description at the group or system
level, such as scapegoating, collusion, displacement onto children,
rotation of problems, and so on, abound in the literature and are
reflected in some of the study group material, but only occasionally
in the questionnaire comments. Similarly, little reference was made
to healthy family defenses that might appropriately be used to
ward off attack or to protect and nurture the realistically vulnerable
family member or the family as a whole. Further identification of
system-level defenses, both positive and negative, could contribute
to improved awareness of both the strengths and weaknesses of
couples and families as they may be revealed in multiple-client
interviews.

An illustration from role theory. A plea for smaller, less global
concepts that might bring the large thoughts of social scientists into
useful conjunction with the highly specific requirements of the
casework interview was issued long ago by Sanford Sherman (33).
Just how such "smaller concepts" might be forged and what this
might mean for the practitioners can be illustrated by a glance at
Spiegel's development of the concepts of role complementarity and
of role modification and their subcomponents (38) within the wider
context of role theory. His formulations are mentioned here not
to recommend role analysis as the method of choice for caseworkers,
but merely to illustrate how a theoretical concept, in the form of
practically applicable subconcepts, may enrich the worker's observations and hence increase his diagnostic and therapeutic effectiveness.

"Role complementarity," as Spiegel (38) develops the concept, serves the essential function of preserving economy of psychological effort. Agreement on complementary roles cuts down on the need for making decisions about most actions because every player knows his part so well. It would follow from this view that a multiple-client interview that revealed friction and doubt about roles would point to a situation of severe strain since the members may be dissipating in role strife the energies needed for problem-solving. Identification of the areas of role conflict, their effect on the family's coping capacity, and the possible spiraling of problems resulting from inadequate attention to external problems may all become possible, at least in some degree, through the use of multiple-client interviews, provided the worker has been alerted to think in these terms.

As a further refinement of role analysis, Spiegel also identifies five factors making for failure in role complementarity [5] and eleven re-equilibration processes [6] that may come into play either to restore the status quo by manipulation or to move through mutual insight to a new equilibrium. Every one of these sixteen factors could become evident at some time in a joint or family interview and could illuminate the family's direction toward further conflict or away from it, provided the nature and significance of these factors were understood by the worker. They even suggest issues for the sake of which a skilled worker may at times want to provoke diagnostic information, whether by creating a suitable situation or by verbal inquiry.

Without going into further details on Spiegel's theories or describing Perlman's application of role theory to the individual casework approach (27), it would seem possible that caseworkers not only might benefit from theoretical refinements of interactional concepts in allied fields—selectively used and adapted—but also may be able to develop such refinements themselves through careful evaluation of the content of multiple-client interviews. The result, paradoxically, of such heightened attention to detail is not

---

[5] These are (a) ignorance of or lack of familiarity with the required role, (b) discrepancy in goals that determine role function, (c) disagreement about a member's claim to a role, (d) lack of means for executing an accepted role, and (e) confusion or conflict about cultural values and concomitant roles.

[6] These consist of (a) five manipulative processes—coercion, coaxing, persuasion, evaluation (e.g., praise or blame), and denial, masking, or postponement, (b) five processes of role modification—joking, referral to a third party, exploring, compromising, and consolidating, and (c) one transitional re-equilibration process—role reversal, which stands between the manipulative and the modifying processes (38, pp. 373–380).

likely to be a flood of minute irrelevancies. Set within an expanded framework, such details are likely, instead, to contribute to a more integrated understanding of people in their "operational situations" (22, pp. 546–548) and to sharpen the practitioner's view of the problem-to-be-worked—the one that is not only the most burdensome for the family and its members but also the most likely to respond to therapeutic intervention (4, 26).

Need for a language of interaction. The development of greater conceptual specificity is linked with the need for a vocabulary that can describe interactional phenomena and their ingredients more clearly than present language apparently can. Current language appears to be more adapted to dyadic and linear causal thinking than to the complexities of multiple determination and to the description of complex systems involving reverberations, feedback, and multifaceted equilibria.[7]

To suggest one possible area for the expansion of the language of interaction in relation to casework, one might try to develop terms to describe a family's reaction to a worker. Several authors have urged the importance of approaching the couple or family as a unit (9, 10, 17, 30), although many also stress the simultaneous necessity of thinking of them as individuals (4, 7, 31). Is it conceivable that a couple or family also reacts as a unit to a worker or, for that matter, to any given person or situation? Bell (9) speaks of the tendency of humans to react "dyadically" even in group situations, and uses this tendency diagnostically and therapeutically. Haley (17) seems to suggest that there is a systemic aspect to a couple's or family's reaction in any encounter. He sees this response in part as an attempt to suck the outsider into the system—or to eject him from its sphere—in accordance with the survival needs of the system rather than of its constituents.

If this view holds true, it may become possible, given enough diagnostic alertness, to identify the nature and direction of this thrust, develop terminology to describe it, and plan treatment accordingly. Whether or not such a diagnostic orientation would necessarily be opposed to the more conventional one remains to be seen. Further study of these concepts in practice may well show that the

[7] However, some fascinating efforts have already been made at developing concepts that might describe the complexities of family interaction in terms that are equally relevant to individual personalities and to the characteristics of whole families, whether "normal" or otherwise (18, pp. 4–19).

two approaches supplement each other. Enhanced awareness of the family as a system and increased alertness to the participants and their reactions within it may reveal pathways in both for greater mutual flexibility and growth at both the family and the individual levels. Neither the individual nor the family nor any other psychological or social system is really closed, although severe pathology or totalitarianism may strive to make it so.

Need for More Diagnostic Attention to Certain Neglected Areas

Sociocultural and economic factors. Lack of language, however, can hardly be the reason for the comparative dearth of comments on sociocultural and economic data as revealed through joint or family interviews. The tendency to omit these factors held generally true of all responses. It is possible, as already mentioned, that attention to their diagnostic importance may already have increased sharply in recent years in the wake of federal programs to fight destitution and demoralization among the poor. Certainly a keen awareness of the diagnostic relevance of sociocultural and economic data is likely to reward caseworkers with a broader understanding of strengths and resources. Since the influence, for instance, of the extended family in both the development and amelioration of marital conflict differs widely among the various cultural subgroups in society, it needs to be thoroughly understood in terms of the group's usual customs and the family's particular dynamics and idiosyncracies. Greater sensitivity to this aspect of diagnosis should help the resourceful worker to identify relatives or other persons who might reinforce the healing process. At the very least, it may enable him to prevent sabotage from quarters beyond the nuclear family.

Similarly, the worker needs to understand how the family's immediate environment and the larger forces of the society may help to bolster or undermine their struggles. Although multiple-client sessions can provide essential data about the couple's or family's views of their place in the larger world, other sources of information regarding the wider social network may be needed if multiple-client approaches are to be used with maximum effect, especially when deprived or traditionally disadvantaged minorities require worker clarity about a family's reality situation and about the availability and relevance of existing services for them. It is striking, in this context, to note the absence of comment on multiple-client interviews as a source of diagnostic data on the ethnic, religious, or national status of the family members, particularly in a society deeply moved by these issues. To the extent to which facts or feelings about these issues set up barriers among the clients or between them and their caseworker, these must be understood before help can be given or used. This calls for a good deal of searching study and sensitive exploration—a process in which multiple-client interviews can play a real part.

Residues from past experience within the family or in other intimate groups. The increasing use of multiple-client sessions is also likely to yield data or hints regarding residues, in the present, from the partners' experience as members of their original family systems or of some other intimate social group. The helpful or hampering effects of such residues on the partners' current attitudes, behavior, and expectations may thus become clear and illuminate their respective roles as shapers and maintainers of their own family system. Greater diagnostic alertness to these residues may help workers to achieve better understanding and handling of some resistive family maneuvers. It may even reveal and partly explain the structural weaknesses built into the evolving family system because one or the other partner was prevented by his reactions to past family experience from making sure that certain of his basic needs could be met and contributions received within the marital system. Adequate attention to these factors should yield data essential for treatment that may be needed to remedy or counterbalance such structural weaknesses, e.g., by allowing a "strong" partner (who may have been "the good child") to make more room for competence on the part of the "passive" partner (who may have been a scapegoated child), so that each may be able both to give and to take more fully within the marriage.

Maturational stresses. The various stages in the family life cycle give rise to much inevitable change (19). Multiple-client interviews are especially suited for prompt diagnosis of the attendant tensions and discrepancies among family members and within the total group (9, 14). They could thus help the worker to differentiate acute from chronic problems and to weigh the family's capacity to handle them. Family interviews offer a unique opportunity to observe and evaluate maturational frictions and their effects. Such observations may even be valuable for preventive purposes since they are likely to include not only overt but also latent points of friction that may be responsive to early therapeutic intervention, but which, if left alone, may later explode into conflict.

Stages of conflict. Although respondents did not on the whole relate their diagnostic comments to the phases of the marital conflict, attention to this factor might also prove helpful in differentiating chronic from acute difficulties in the marriage. Thus failure in communication may be due to habitual and deeply rooted individual or family patterns, or it may reflect an early phase of marital strife, such as a period of latent conflict when differences may be deliberately concealed, or it may be a time of spreading conflict when expression and understanding of mutual feelings may already have been cut off (8).

Similarly, preoccupation with problems of the children, acting out, excessive mutual competitiveness, hostility, suspiciousness, or excessive one-sidedness in intrafamilial relationships may be due to entrenched factors, to the simmering, exploding, or spreading of marital conflict, or to a combination of these. A disorganized family may turn out to be not chronically chaotic but rather disintegrating in response to the paralysis or despair felt in the face of waning hope for the marriage and of abandonment of the family as a source of gratification.

Need for Sharpened Understanding of Marital and Family Strengths

Most of the comments on strength were general but reflected a great interest in diagnosing positive ties within the marital and familial relationships so that these might be put to therapeutic use. The increased use of multiple-client interviews offers great opportunities for further observation and study of the nature of supportive and nurturing balances within the family at any given time or at different developmental stages. Such study would supplement the growing body of understanding about pathological balances within the family and would help to pinpoint further the elements of complementarity and strength in families, even when pathology or severe problems may exist.

The field's growing interest in aid to families in crisis has already led to some inquiries of this kind and has sharpened awareness of the manner in which agencies may organize their services and resources to fit the family's needs and capacities more closely. More specific understanding of how to build strengths and prevent their erosion may also grow from the study of such settings as those described by Cumming and Cumming (12, p. 56) where "graded crises" are deliberately brought about, in dosages of small but increasing toughness, "under circumstances that maximize . . . [the patient's] chance of resolving them." The mastery of identifiable problems by means of identifiable strengths—the clients', the agency's, and the worker's—is a highly therapeutic experience. Inasmuch as multiple-client interviews may illuminate how these sets of strengths may dovetail, they will be contributing not only to diagnosis but also to a revision of the meaning of effective help, which in the past was all too often thought synonymous with long-term "once-and-for-all" contact.

Further Uses of Family Interviews
for Diagnosis of Marital Problems

As previously indicated, the volume of comment on diagnostic values of family interviews was relatively meager in comparison with that on joint interviews, probably because of the marital focus of the study and the fact that use of family interviews in family agencies was still in its early developmental stages at the time the comments were submitted. Yet when it came to fathoming the extent and manner of children's involvement in the marital conflict, the sociocultural attitudes and values of the family, the areas needing further work, and the impact of marital change on the children, the number of comments on the value of family interviews—although often still sparse—exceeded those on joint interviewing. This suggests that in relation to a marital focus, workers view family interviews, used diagnostically, as mainly useful for illuminating the ramifications of the marital conflict beyond the partners and for revealing the family's place in society at large. Some comments not reflected in the headings of Appendix Table 2 also suggest that workers saw particular usefulness in family interviews for clarifying subtle aspects of the marital relationship.

On the other hand, joint interviews were mentioned—to the almost total exclusion of family interviews—for a wide range of purposes directly related to the diagnosis of marital problems. These included detection of the partners' patterns of mutual hostility, mutual defenses, and communication; their allocation or assumption of roles and control; their mutual readiness for involvement in treatment; the changes or impasse in their relationship resulting from treatment; the success or failure of efforts to keep treatment coordinated; and their progress after termination.

It is possible that joint interviews were valued for all these purposes not because hostility, communication problems, and the rest did not often encompass the children too, but because the burden of their development and alleviation was seen as devolving on the marital partners as mates and parents responsible for the continuation or breakup of the family. On the other hand, it may be that the project's marital focus led respondents to overlook some of the potential contribution of family interviews to the diagnosis of marital problems. It might be profitable to compare the partners' behavior in joint and family interviews and to observe whether their hostilities, defensiveness, manipulativeness, or role failures are concealed or heightened in the presence of the children. Comparisons of interactions in the two settings are likely to reveal their attitudes and capacities regarding self-control. New light may also be cast on their mutual functioning as parents and as partners and on possible conflicts between both sets of roles. Similarly, family sessions may well play an illuminating part in the evaluation of changes resulting from treatment, of puzzling impasses, or of developments after termination.

The whole question of the impact on the children of the use of family interviews for the diagnosis of marital problems requires further exploration. The married pair are the founders and maintainers of the family. Exposure to both the full depth of their difficulties and the vagaries of their progress in treatment may have damaging effects on the children under some circumstances or on the parents' status as heads of the family, although it may be relieving in others. It would be helpful indeed to obtain further clarification of the circumstances under which family interviews may or may not be fruitful for diagnosis.

SUMMARY AND OVERVIEW

If volume of comment is any indication of degree of interest, then the respondents in the project were mainly preoccupied with the diagnostic contribution of joint interviews to the worker's understanding of interaction, to greater speed and accuracy of diagnosis, and to a clearer view of the couple's reality situation. These topics also received by far the greatest proportion of the comments on family interviewing. Indeed, the number of comments on the yield from family interviews in terms of improved understanding of the reality situation exceeded the number of similar comments regarding joint interviews. The same was true of the comparative volume of comments on family interviews as they contribute to an understanding of the children's involvement in the marital difficulty, to a clearer view of the family's sociocultural patterns and values, and to an identification of the areas in which further casework help might be needed. For all the other categories, joint interviews commanded the bulk of the respondents' attention. However, there were only four subcategories out of nineteen in Appendix Table 2, PART I, on which there was no comment at all concerning family interviews.[8]

Judging from the responses seen as a whole, one can conclude that workers see the major contribution of joint and family interviews to the diagnosis of marital problems to be fivefold: (a) They illuminate the way in which family members interact with pathological destructiveness, restrictiveness, and mutual pain. (b) They reveal the often hidden strengths and positive mutual bonds within the marriage and the family that may become essential therapeutic aids. (c) They offer greater clarity about the life situation of the couple or family (especially if home visits are also used). (d) They make possible greater speed and accuracy in diagnosis. (e) They provide improved opportunities for the worker to observe the impact— or lack of effect—of treatment on the couple and family members.

Glimpses of disagreements appeared only in the comments on the usefulness of joint or family interviews for history-taking or at intake. The bulk of the responses describing the values of these methods reflects an affirmative—even enthusiastic—point of view toward these approaches. It was only in their consideration of possible criteria for and against the use of these methods that respondents revealed some sharp disagreements. These will be discussed in Chapters 4 and 5 of this monograph.

---

[8] These four subcategories were attitudes toward the marital difficulty, evaluation of change or impasse in the marital relationship, success or failure (in split cases) in working in areas jointly delineated, and evaluation of progress after termination.

Although the questions on which the present chapter is based were concerned with the special diagnostic contribution of joint and family interviews, it was clear that the majority of the respondents did not see these approaches as supplanting individual interviews. Several respondents thought the joint interview to be a natural vehicle in the case of marital problems, but there were few who advocated its use, or that of family interviews, as the exclusive modality. Even those who did use joint interviews exclusively did so only for specific reasons with specific couples. They valued both the individual and the multiple-client sessions as mutually complementary. In most cases, the individual interview was seen as a great diagnostic aid when used in combination with joint or family sessions, since it could throw light on the individual background and behavior of the partners or family members. Some respondents also saw it as helpful in offering the individual an opportunity to share with the worker information or feelings that the client may not ever have acknowledged to the partner, but there was some disagreement about the wisdom and timing of such individual revelations.

In the opinion of respondents the range of diagnostic values stemming from multiple-client interviews seems large by comparison with any list of such values offered by leading authors in the field (21, 32, 42). However, the literature, in particular that on role and communication theory, is far more specific in its articulation of diagnostic concepts than were the comments of the respondents. Indeed, the lack of specificity on these topics and on the issues of diagnosing mutual defenses or the degree of a couple's involvement in treatment were points that seemed to warrant much further work and exploration, as did the conceptualization of the reactions of the couple or family as a group in relation to the worker. Other gaps that appeared to call for further diagnostic attention and study were the role of economic, ethnic, and sociocultural factors in marital and family problems and their treatment, the existence of residues from past experience within other family systems, and the differentiation between acute and chronic problems, especially as these may relate to different stages of the conflict spiral or be linked with the presence and attempted resolution of conflicts arising from maturational discrepancies within the family. Further enrichment of the diagnostic content of multiple-client interviews also seemed possible from study of the couple's or family's strengths seen in juxtaposition with the agency's resources—a question already familiar to students of crisis theory. Finally, it was recommended that the feasibility and wisdom of expanding the diagnostic use of family interviews be explored further. Through all these considerations of gaps ran an acute awareness of the lack of a proper language for clear description of interactional phenomena. This is a crucial problem that must be surmounted if substantial progress is to be made in related areas.

Even taking into account the existence of disagreements and gaps and the fact that most of the respondents commented in isolation from each other, it does seem possible to infer a fairly consistent approach to diagnosis from their combined comments on the values of joint and family interviews. First, there seems to be a decided trend toward emphasis on the "here and now" of diagnosis, although historical data are not being neglected. Second, there are signs among some of the responses that the line between diagnosis and treatment, even as reflected in agency structuring of intake and assignment, may be giving way to an early merging of both elements. Finally, the diagnostic microscope has been fitted with a wide-angle lens, with the result that the picture under scrutiny looks different. No longer does the individual loom largest, with marriage, family, workaday world, and the wider society seen as a background for him. Instead he is now viewed at one and the same time as a unit and as a functional part of various groups, each of which is in turn part of a larger cluster—the marital combination, the family group, the work group, and similar face-to-face associations. Beyond these, the wider society and the great universe itself form, as it were, concentric circles infinitely expanding outward, with no hard and impenetrable lines dividing the individual unit from the marital or the family constellation or from other family groupings and the encompassing wider circles.

If the present analysis represents a reliable reading of project responses, then the worker's diagnostic microscope is centered on the constellation of the family he is treating, with the light flowing over each individual, each subgroup of individuals within the family cluster, and on the family constellation itself. As yet he has directed limited attention to the remaining clusters and circles, unless movements from them are infiltrating one or more parts of the family cluster, with further repercussions. On the whole, workers no longer think that they can understand a marriage if they have direct access only to the inner circle of each partner's special world by means of exclusive separate interviews with each spouse. They are scanning both the marital and, at times, the family cluster in order to detect the areas of greatest agitation and of greatest steadiness and mutual support, either within one unit or subgroup or within the basic constellation.

By keeping the family cluster and its constituent units simultaneously in view, the diagnostician sees new light cast both on the individual units and on the patterning of the constellations. In other words, the individual, the marriage, and the family, viewed as systems, are each seen as open to and permeable by influences from each other, from surrounding clusters, and from the wider circles within which they are placed. Forces from any one or a combination of them need to be identified as helping or hurting the marriage, as opening or sealing off the couple's or family's access to their own inner and outer worlds.

Not one of these units or circles can be properly understood if viewed as self-sufficient, or almost so. Yet each can legitimately become a temporary focus of diagnostic study since a clearer understanding of each unit enriches the worker's knowledge of its interrelationships with the rest. In the respondents' view, the focus of diagnostic concern clearly influences the choice of methods. When the modification most sought relates to the marital relationship, it is the marital dyad that comes under particular scrutiny through joint interviews—but not without the realization that these revelations will be distorted or fragmentary without attention to the other constellations. Thus the respondents' almost total concurrence in the combined use of various interview modalities mirrors the necessity of intensive diagnostic concern with at least the family cluster and its constituents at all times, but acknowledges that varying operational foci may call for corresponding interview approaches. Whether some of the persons involved in relationships in the workaday world could or should be included in interviews, for either diagnostic or treatment purposes, is a question that was not touched on in the material.

One further image emerges from the mosaic of these responses. It is not expressed well in terms of the microscope analogy, since the viewer himself is now to be viewed. The project responses make quite clear that diagnosis must at the very least encompass not only the individual, marital, and familial spheres of the partners' lives, with a sense of their mutual openness or closedness; it must also include a worker who can see himself in relation to all of these and can adjust his feelings and vision to take in the clusters and concentric circles around and beyond the inner circle that has often dominated his view in the past. Not only has there been an expansion in the diagnostic landscape, as pictured in the composite drawn from the responses, but the worker's personality and awareness have had to expand simultaneously to take in not only the larger view but also the comings and goings among all its different components. Just as the individual, joint, and multiple-client interviews may offer diagnostic pointers that may make it possible to open channels hitherto closed between the individual and his inner needs, between the partners, and among all family members, so they are also seen to call for including in the overview the worker's own needs and prejudices vis-à-vis a couple or a family group. Unless he recognizes these, both his diagnostic and his therapeutic effectiveness will be impaired because he will be unable to help the family recognize or clear new paths if he shrinks from following them himself.

The foregoing is not intended to present all the respondents as adherents of the transactionalist point of view. It merely shows that the respondents' comments and illustrations regarding the diagnostic values of multiple-client interviews can most easily be described in language partly borrowed from transactional and general systems theory since the use of all interview methods in combination reflects a readiness to examine all relevant influences. This approach on the part of the respondents mirrors a dominant trend in the field of casework as a whole (4, 7, 11, 21, 23). Although the literature includes advocates of total or almost exclusive use of family interviewing (5, 9, 30), it should be noted that these come from settings in which problems of children or their mental illness are the dominant presenting concern rather than marital difficulties, although the latter may have an important part to play in the former.

The respondents' general willingness to use various types of interview and to examine the marital problem in relation to all the therapeutically relevant systems suggests the immense potential usefulness and relevance of recent literature regarding system-level patterns. The caseworker is likely to recognize intrafamilial patterns only if his conceptual resources allow it. Given such a conceptual orientation he will be able to use these interviews to formulate two kinds of diagnostic impressions. One relates to the operations of the marital or family system, its characteristics, norms, rules, role configurations, alliances, and defensive maneuvers. It also includes the overt and covert family themes and myths that represent a shared consensus about what the couple or family needs to preserve and protect, ward off, or encourage, in order to safeguard or enhance their chances of survival as a family or the reciprocities they need and enjoy from each other. The second is formulated as the worker assesses these system-level patterns in relation to the welfare and treatment needs of the family group and its constituent subgroups and individual members: Do the family patterns serve the individual growth and satisfaction of each member as well as of the family group as a whole, or are they geared mainly to constant re-equilibration of an unstable marital balance or to the protection of one member's stability? Do they combine to allow change and growth for the individuals within the system and for the system itself, or do they operate mainly to inhibit change and to maintain a rigid dysfunctional status quo? Have they become significantly altered in the course of mounting marital conflict, and are such changes beneficial, ameliorative, or increasingly destructive? In the latter case, are they reversible, and, if so, how? Do they allow the members to provide mutual supports for each other that counterbalance their individual shortcomings, or do they increase the vulnerability or destructiveness of some or all of the members?

Clearly, if system-level diagnosis can offer even tentative answers to such questions, it represents no idle intellectual exercise, but rather a source of major insights into family needs and resources in relation to treatment. It thus points the way for the worker to intervene in the precise manner needed to help the couple or family develop or use their resources more effectively and modify their system in ways suited to their specific needs and their capacities as individuals and as a group. One might say that diagnostic understanding of pathology in individual psychodynamics at first grew mainly from attempts to classify observable phenomena in such a way that patients falling into similar categories might be recognized and treated accordingly. Diagnostic classification of interaction types is still in the process of development, but joint and family interviews, by revealing the characteristics of particular marital or family systems, are seemingly offering therapeutic opportunities for buttressing the weaknesses and reinforcing the strengths of each system. Indeed, this close hewing of diagnostic insight to the system's strengths and deficiencies and the opportunities available through treatment may be one of the major diagnostic contributions of joint and family sessions at this time.

Diagnosis, as it has been discussed throughout this chapter, provides for mapping the course of treatment. The next chapter will be concerned with the special contribution of multiple-client interviews to actually navigating that course, either by means that make for change and improvement in the marital relationship or by modifying the processes of deterioration.

BIBLIOGRAPHY

Study Group Reports

1. AKRON, OHIO, FAMILY AND CHILDREN'S SERVICE SOCIETY OF SUMMIT COUNTY: *Joint Interviews as a Method of Treatment with Marital Partners Where There Is Hostile Interaction*
   Study group participants: Mrs. Martha Van Valen (Leader), John C. Freeman, Christian C. Heim, Ronald Kerkhoff, Mrs. Annette McGunnigal, Margaret Minich, Mary C. Monsour, Rosemary Nagy, Mrs. Emily J. Roth, Mrs. Edith Weigl.

2. CINCINNATI, OHIO, JEWISH FAMILY SERVICE BUREAU: *Family Diagnosis and Treatment as Related to Marital Counseling*
   Study group participants: Morton R. Startz (Leader), Anne Billinkoff, Miriam H. Dettelbach, Mrs. Paula Edelstein, Mrs. Ruth Goldberg, Rose L. Greenstein, Margarete Hirsch, Helen Lampe, Jacqueline Lancaster, Michael Meyer, Mrs. Miriam O. Smith, Mrs. Bernice Temin, Mrs. Miriam Tsevat, Mrs. Doris Wolfenstein.

General References

3. ACKERMAN, NATHAN W., "The Future of Family Psychotherapy," in Nathan W. Ackerman, Frances L. Beatman, and Sanford N. Sherman (eds.), *Expanding Theory and Practice in Family Therapy*, Family Service Association of America, New York, 1967, pp. 3–16.

4. AIKIN, DOROTHY, "A Project on Family Diagnosis and Treatment," in *Social Work Practice, 1963,* Selected Papers of the National Conference on Social Welfare, Columbia University Press, New York, 1963, pp. 3–18.

5. BARDILL, DONALD R., and RYAN, FRANCIS J., *Family Group Casework: A Casework Approach to Family Therapy*, Catholic University of America Press, Washington, D.C., 1964.

6. BATESON, GREGORY, *et al.*, " A Note on the Double Bind—1962," *Family Process*, Vol. II, No. 1 (March 1963), pp. 154–161.

7. BEATMAN, FRANCES L., SHERMAN, SANFORD N., and LEADER, ARTHUR L., "Current Issues in Family Treatment," *Social Casework*, Vol. XLVII, No. 2 (February 1966), pp. 75–81.

8. BECK, DOROTHY FAHS, "Marital Conflict: Its Course and Treatment as Seen by Caseworkers," *Social Casework,* Vol. XLVII, No. 4 (April 1966), pp. 211–221.

9. BELL, JOHN ELDERKIN, "Recent Advances in Family Group Therapy," *Journal of Child Psychology and Psychiatry,* Vol. III, No. 1 (January/ March 1962), pp. 1–15.

10. ———, "A Theoretical Position for Family Group Therapy," *Family Process,* Vol. II, No. 1 (March 1963), pp. 1–14.

11. Committee on Family Diagnosis and Treatment of the Midwestern Regional Committee of the Family Service Association of America, *Casebook on Family Diagnosis and Treatment,* Family Service Association of America, New York, 1965.

12. CUMMING, JOHN, and CUMMING, ELAINE, *Ego and Milieu: Theory and Practice of Environmental Therapy,* Atherton Press, New York, 1966.

13. EINSTEIN, GERTRUDE, *Report on Family Group Treatment Project at Jewish Family Service,* Jewish Family Service of Philadelphia, Philadelphia, 1964 (mimeographed).

14. FAUCETT, EMILY C., "A Re-evaluation of the Home Visit in Casework Practice," *Social Casework,* Vol. XLII, No. 9 (November 1961), pp. 439–445.

15. FRIEDMAN, ALFRED S., "Family Therapy as Conducted in the Home," *Family Process,* Vol. I, No. 1 (March 1962), pp. 132–140.

16. GEHRKE, SHIRLEY, and KIRSCHENBAUM, MARTIN, "Survival Patterns in Family Conjoint Therapy," *Family Process,* Vol. VI, No. 1 (March 1967), pp. 67–80.

17. HALEY, JAY, *Strategies of Psychotherapy,* Grune & Stratton, New York, 1963.

18. HESS, ROBERT D., and HANDEL, GERALD, *Family Worlds: A Psychosocial Approach to Family Life,* University of Chicago Press, Chicago, 1959.

19. HILL, REUBEN, and RODGERS, ROY H., "The Developmental Approach," in Harold T. Christensen (ed.), *Handbook of Marriage and the Family,* Rand McNally & Co., Chicago, 1964, pp. 171–211.

20. JOLESCH, MIRIAM, "Casework Treatment of Young Married Couples," *Social Casework,* Vol. XLIII, No. 5 (May 1962), pp. 245–251.

21. MACGREGOR, ROBERT, *et al., Multiple Impact Therapy with Families,* McGraw-Hill Book Co., New York, 1964.

22. MEIER, ELIZABETH G., "Interactions Between the Person and His Operational Situations: A Basis for Classification in Casework," *Social Casework,* Vol. XLVI, No. 9 (November 1965), pp. 542–549.

23. MITCHELL, CELIA B., "Integrative Therapy of the Family Unit," *Social Casework,* Vol. XLVI, No. 2 (February 1965), pp. 63–69.

24. ———, "Problems and Principles in Family Therapy" in Nathan W. Ackerman, Frances L. Beatman, and Sanford N. Sherman (eds.), *Expanding Theory and Practice in Family Therapy,* Family Service Association of America, New York, 1967, pp. 109–124.

25. ———, "The Use of Family Sessions in the Diagnosis and Treatment of Disturbances in Children," *Social Casework,* Vol. XLI, No. 6 (June 1960), pp. 283–290.

26. PERLMAN, HELEN HARRIS, "Family Diagnosis: Some Problems," in *Social Welfare Forum, 1958* Official Proceedings, 85th Annual Forum, National Conference on Social Welfare, Chicago, May 11–16, 1958, Columbia University P.ess, New York, 1958, pp. 122–134.

27. ———, "The Role Concept and Social Casework: Some Explorations. Part I. The 'Social' in Social Casework. Part II. What Is Social Diagnosis?" *Social Service Review*, Vol. XXXV, No. 4 (December 1961), pp. 370–381, and Vol. XXXVI, No. 1 (March 1962), pp. 17–31.

28. POLLAK, OTTO, "Entrance of the Caseworker into Family Interaction," *Social Casework*, Vol. XLV, No. 4 (April 1964), pp. 216–220.

29. ROBERTS, ROBERT W. "The Diagnostic Process," in Dorothy Fahs Beck (ed.), *The Treatment of Marital Problems*, Family Service Association of America, New York (in preparation).

30. SATIR, VIRGINIA M., *Conjoint Family Therapy: A Guide to Theory and Technique*, Science and Behavior Books, Palo Alto, Calif., 1964.

31. SCHERZ, FRANCES H., "Exploring the Use of Family Interviews in Diagnosis," *Social Casework*, Vol. XLV, No. 4 (April 1964), pp. 209–215.

32. ———, "Multiple-Client Interviewing: Treatment Implications," *Social Casework*, Vol. XLIII, No. 3 (March 1962), pp. 120–125.

33. SHERMAN, SANFORD N., "Discussion" (covering papers by Joseph J. Reidy, "An Approach to Family-Centered Treatment in a State Institution," and Harold A. Goolishian, "A Brief Psychotherapy Program for Disturbed Adolescents"), *American Journal of Orthopsychiatry*, Vol XXXII, No. 1 (January 1962), pp. 148–151.

34. ———, "Joint Interviews in Casework Practice," *Social Work*, Vol. IV, No. 2 (April 1959), pp. 20–28.

35. SKIDMORE, REX A., and GARRETT, HULDA VAN STEETER, "The Joint Interview in Marriage Counseling," *Marriage and Family Living*, Vol. XVII, No. 4 (November 1955), pp. 349–354.

36. SONNE, JOHN C., SPECK, ROSS V., and JUNGREIS, JEROME E., "The Absent-Member Maneuver as a Resistance in Family Therapy of Schizophrenia," *Family Process*, Vol. I, No. 1 (March 1962), pp. 44–62.

37. SPECK, ROSS V., "Family Therapy in the Home" in Nathan W. Ackerman, Frances L. Beatman, and Sanford N. Sherman (eds.), *Expanding Theory and Practice in Family Therapy*, Family Service Association of America, New York, 1967, pp. 39–46.

38. SPIEGEL, JOHN P., "The Resolution of Role Conflict within the Family," in Norman W. Bell and Ezra F. Vogel (eds.), *A Modern Introduction to the Family* (rev. ed.), Free Press, New York, 1968, pp. 391–411.

39. ———, and BELL, NORMAN W., "The Family of the Psychiatric Patient," in Silvano Arieti (ed.), *American Handbook of Psychiatry*, Vol. I, Basic Books, New York, 1959, pp. 114–149.

40. STRYKER, SHELDON, "The Interactional and Situational Approaches," in Harold T. Christensen (ed.), *Handbook of Marriage and the Family*, Rand McNally & Co., Chicago, 1964, pp. 125–170.

41. VOGEL, EZRA F., and BELL, NORMAN W., "The Emotionally Disturbed Child as the Family Scapegoat," in Norman W. Bell and Ezra F. Vogel (eds.), *A Modern Introduction to the Family* (rev. ed.), Free Press, New York, 1968, pp. 412–427.

42. WEISS, VIOLA W., "Multiple-Client Interviewing: An Aid in Diagnosis," *Social Casework,* Vol. XLIII, No. 3 (March 1962), pp. 111–114.

43. WYNNE, LYMAN C., "The Study of Intrafamilial Alignments and Splits in Exploratory Family Therapy," in Nathan W. Ackerman, Frances L. Beatman, and Sanford N. Sherman (eds.), *Exploring the Base for Family Therapy,* Family Service Association of America, New York, 1961, pp. 95–115.

3

Special Values

of Joint and Family Interviews

for Treatment

The diagnostician may have good reasons for seeing some or all family members together, at least at times, but is the treatment of marital problems also furthered by this approach? Do joint interviews offer something to couples in conflict that they cannot gain in individual sessions? Is there any value in using family interviews for treatment even when the focus is chiefly on the amelioration of marital problems? The present chapter will explore these and related questions in an effort to identify the unique values of these approaches for marital treatment.

This exploration will first encompass the contribution of joint and family interviews to the general facilitation of treatment and to the avoidance or attenuation of some problems often associated with the exclusive use of individual interviews. Each value identified is drawn from detailed content analysis of the responses summarized in Appendix Table 2, and each will be introduced by a presentation of relevant respondent views. In the ensuing discussion, these views will be examined in the perspective of the author's overview of the composite replies and in the context of the relevant literature. In the light of this juxtaposition, potential treatment values that received little attention will be suggested. Finally, an attempt will be made to restate in system terms the sources of potential therapeutic gain inherent in a multiple-client approach.

Throughout, the spotlight will shift freely between joint and family interviews. Any temporary concentration on a specific approach is not to be taken as endorsement of its exclusive use. Respondents repeatedly made clear that they used joint, family, and individual interviews, alone or in any combination, as the diagnostic picture, the treatment plan, the worker's skill, and the phase of treatment indicated. It is to be hoped that the possible components of a valid choice regarding treatment modalities will be clarified as the special values of each approach are progressively spelled out.

In contrast to later chapters, and in accord with the respondents' approach, the focus here is on the positive values of joint and family interviews. The special risks and problems associated with their application and the disagreements regarding their use will receive detailed consideration later, as specific conditions favorable or unfavorable for their use are analyzed. Meanwhile, the potential treatment gains flowing from the use of these modalities will be highlighted. They are defined broadly to encompass not only direct improvements but also the countering of deterioration, arrest of the spread of conflict, and evocation of the strengths needed to grow or adapt in the face of change and to sustain these modifications.

CONTRIBUTION TO THE
GENERAL FACILITATION OF TREATMENT

Respondents described a wide range of values that joint and family interviews may contribute directly to the treatment of marital problems. These were related to enhancing the speed, relevance, and efficacy of treatment; increasing opportunities for handling dysfunctional attitudes and interactional patterns; confronting the marital conflict; and enhancing awareness of self and others. Greater opportunity for promoting constructive mutuality and for experimenting with new behavior and joint problem-solving were also noted, as were special benefits for couples who had been found hard to reach in individual interviews.

Gains in Treatment Momentum
and in Mutual Clarification
of Agency Service

Great gains in treatment momentum and in mutual understanding of the applicability of agency service were seen as stemming from the discriminating use of joint and family interviews. These assets were attributed to one or more of several sources: the reduction in problems and delays related to confidentiality, the sharpened treatment focus thought to result from the increased opportunities for mutual validation and correction among all family members, and improved and more relevant diagnosis. Also mentioned as a source of increased momentum were the opportunities provided for jointly discussing and evolving the focus for and goals of treatment.

The impact of some or all of these factors on speed and efficacy of treatment was seen as manifold: The directness of the contact may enable the worker to tackle interactional patterns the existence of which might have remained unknown to him in individual interviews. The treatment gains achieved may also be more readily and thoroughly transferred into everyday life. Furthermore, some initial constructive communication and heightened mutual awareness may be sparked as the partners discuss use of the service or of referral, see each other's reactions, and begin to recognize mutual needs, wishes, feelings, and perceptions emerging around this focus.

Although respondents concentrated on the values of joint interviews for clarifying the means of change available through the agency, one of the study groups pointed out the importance of recognizing with the whole family "that a marital problem affects the total family" (3, p. 3). They saw great value in having all share in the initial treatment "contract" and thought that early use of family interviews made later involvement of other family members in treatment seem much more natural, should it become necessary (3, p. 3). It seems implicit in this view that fear, anxiety, or misconceptions regarding the meaning of the parents' contact can thus be aired, hope for constructive change conveyed, and treatment sabotage by family members lessened.

The literature suggests a further explanation of the momentum derived from the use of joint and family interviews. Identification of the family, rather than of any individual, as the patient "immediately confronts many resistances other than that of the one who has been identified as the patient," and thereby dilutes the burden of guilt. As a result, new responses are called forth—an acknowledgment of anxiety, perhaps, instead of an accustomed show of bravado. Thus, in skilled hands the family interview "provides a rapid method for disentangling interlocking psychopathology" (31, p. 62). Similarly, the joint session may hasten experimentation with noncombative behavior because the focus on the marriage performs a face-saving function. Each, instead of feeling that he is surrendering to the spouse's resented demands, can see himself as responding to the worker's suggestions on the basis of a shared concern for the marriage (21).

This approach clarifies the views of those writers (40, 23) who do not necessarily agree with the respondents and with such authors as Kempler (31) and Levine (34) that multiple-client interviews save treatment time. They see the main gain as one of momentum, of getting more quickly to the core difficulty and more effectively sustaining the necessary commitment to treatment.

Some authors have offered persuasive evidence that added treatment momentum plus speedier transfer of treatment gains into daily life may result from the use of family group treatment in the clients' home—especially in work with severely deprived (34, p. 21) and disturbed (20, p. 133) clients. Yet surely gains from individual treatment in the office must often have been quite effectively transposed into the clients' home life too, although the worker no doubt lacked dramatic evidence of this feat if he did not see the couple or family together. Probably the crucial point here is the effectiveness of either approach in providing at home the liberating and enabling climate of the office. A controlled examination of the interview and family conditions most conducive to successful transfer of such a climate would no doubt make a valuable contribution to casework practice in this respect.

Increased Opportunity
for Handling Mutually Restrictive
or Damaging Attitudes
and Interactional Patterns

More than one out of three comments on the treatment values of joint and family interviews concerned the handling of mutually restrictive or damaging attitudes and interactional patterns evolved within the family. Strong—even enthusiastic—conviction regarding the unique assets of the method was expressed in this respect. These benefits were not regarded as inevitable but as possible, given a valid diagnostic appraisal, a worker capable of therapeutic intervention in the marital and familial interaction, and a family capable of allowing such intervention.

Respondents saw joint interviews and, on the whole, family interviews as useful when the partners compete excessively, their conflict is affecting their life situation, and this conflict is repetitive and spreading.[1] They valued them, furthermore, for use in situations in which there are various signs of constant strain, such as role or sexual difficulties, or when perception of mutual interaction is unrealistic and trigger actions have remained unrecognized. Joint or family sessions were also described as helpful for partners with communication problems who find it difficult or impossible to hear or feel with each other, are constricted, are defensively silent, feel helpless in the face of the partner's apparent failure to understand, and are in need of support to express their feelings to each other. Included also were partners who have expressed hostile feelings enough in individual interviews to be able to engage constructively in some mutual communication. No unique contribution of the family interview was mentioned in any of these respects, though the comment was made that the presence of children may be an advantage in that they may tellingly delineate the marital interaction and their own reactions to it.

With reference to defenses and defensive maneuvers,[2] respondents described joint and family sessions as supremely useful when partners and family members use distortions, projections, denials, and discrepant statements and are unaware of the dynamic link between problems ostensibly outside and those within the marital relationship. For this last subcategory, the number of comments on values of family interviewing exceeded that on joint interviews almost two to one—the only instance of such a ratio in all the responses regarding treatment values of multiple-client modalities. Family sessions were seen as uniquely helpful in situations of this latter kind, including those in which the partners' main concern is focused on a specific "problem child" or on mutual disagreement about handling the child or getting help for him. They were also valued for situations in which children have become involved, consciously or unconsciously, in the marital conflict or have been

---

[1] For a fuller discussion of this issue in individual as well as multiple-client interviews, *see* Beck (11) and Froscher (21).

[2] The term *defenses* is used here to cover both attempts within the self to deal with intrapsychic threats and attempts of the self to deal with threats felt to be arising in interpersonal relationships. *Defensive maneuvers* are collusive attempts —conscious or otherwise—on the part of two or more participants in a social system to ward off actual or felt threats coming from other persons, from a social system consisting of two or more members, or from the environment in general.

used as allies or pawns by the parents. Similarly, they were thought productive when marital friction may have been precipitated by family conflict over coping with a maturational task [3] or when children are reacting to changes resulting from treatment of the parents. In contrast, joint interviews were regarded as especially valuable in situations in which the partners need to focus on their marital problems, as, for example, when they remain absorbed in difficulties relating to the children or in-laws in an apparent attempt to avoid facing a marital conflict.

The power of joint and family interviews for modifying this great variety of damaging and constricting family patterns was seen to stem in part from the possibilities offered by their very structure for focusing on shared anxiety and frustration; for mobilizing, containing, and utilizing these feelings for treatment; and for sustaining change by building, right in the interview, on the mutual easing of strains. In multiple-client sessions, the various damaging and constricting patterns within the marriage or family can become highly visible to all. The worker can then focus on and explore them and demonstrate their frequency and extent, especially to members inclined to deny them or to be blind to them in the absence of overt conflict and recriminations. The very structure of joint and family interviews was seen as exerting pressure toward the challenge of unrealistic defenses, including the displacement of marital problems onto others. Family interviews were seen as particularly valuable in this last respect, since a child's comment in the session or alleviation of his symptoms through such interviews may at last press the partners to face and tackle their marital difficulties.

Through joint and family sessions, mutual distortions and projections can be corrected and a more realistic basis for interaction thus created. Focus on the whole family was seen by some respondents and one of the study groups (3) to be especially effective when a child—e.g., an adolescent—may have been labeled "the problem," even though marital tension may have played a crucial role in the development of his symptoms. In family interviews the onus is removed from any one member, since all are shown to be involved

---

[3] One of the study groups (3, pp. 4–5) enlarged on the value of family interviews when oedipal attachments seem to be causing resentment and competition between the parents of adolescents and to be arousing old and long-dormant conflicts, as well as the fear of being left without the children or with a partner who offers less emotional solace than the offspring.

in maintenance of the family's difficulties. Thus all can be freed to contribute to the amelioration of these problems. Referring to a family that had presented a "perfect front" to the world, one worker described his success in puncturing their illusions by reflecting back to them the covert feelings evident in the session. This freed them to "attack . . . and defend each other," thus releasing anxiety and motivation for treatment as their mutual anger was exposed and the web that they had jointly spun to imprison themselves and each other was unraveled.

The structural focus of joint and family sessions on the marriage or family operates to sustain change because it implies the worker's conviction that both can survive and develop, even while tough individual and mutual problems are being tackled. It thus supports the evolution of a climate permitting new ways of communicating, behaving, interacting, and carrying roles. Such changes involve not only technique and etiquette but also deep feelings, since a profound sense of anger or of helplessness, for instance, may have to be tackled before a couple's communication can improve. Joint and family sessions, then, are likely to enhance hope, self-esteem, and mutual esteem and to strengthen the couple in their roles as partners and family heads.

Returning to a more individual or bilateral approach, many responses showed how mutual strains may be eased through multiple-client sessions, as, for example, through appropriate airing of feelings. Thus, joint interviews may offer an opportunity for discussion of sexual problems in a manner that stresses the partners' relationship, obtains their mutual support, and perhaps dilutes transference feelings toward the worker. Family interviews, on the other hand, may lead children to become more aware of the precariousness of the marital balance and thus reduce their provocation of parental conflict.

Simultaneous clarification of the reasons underlying mutual strains, misunderstandings, and trigger actions was seen as another potential outcome of joint and family sessions. A lively illustration showed the resolution of one such misunderstanding in a family in which the wife thought her husband sneered at her whenever she discussed money matters. Through joint interviews she learned that he grinned helplessly in the face of his own sense of inadequacy on the subject. That recognition led to the couple's eventual success in solving financial problems co-operatively.

Some few respondents believed that sadomasochistic couples with sufficient ego strength could sometimes be faced in joint interviews with the pleasure they get from their interactions and could then look into the basis for this, with the stress on the relationship. Even mutually destructive partners, it was thought, could occasionally be helped to see that they were relating self-destructively to each other and to the worker and to explore the reasons behind their behavior, with beneficial results.

Desensitizing of irritation points in the actual interview situation emerged as another possible effect of multiple-client interviewing. This seemed to be achieved, at least in part, both by dealing with trigger actions and by toning down excessive reactions to every negative stimulus. These in turn were accomplished by universalization of the particular problem and by encouragement of mutual recognition of residual influences from the partners' individual pasts that were no longer appropriate in the present.

It is hardly necessary to add to the respondents' acknowledgment of these various values of multiple-client interviews for the handling of interactional problems the warning that these assets are likely to be realized only if the worker does not continue an exclusively dyadic approach in these sessions but rather uses them to treat the interaction of the couple or family (see pp. 108–109). Treatment of this interaction may also involve inclusion of the parents or other relatives when these are emotionally involved with the current nuclear family. Interest in working directly with the three-generational or extended family unit, when indicated, is evident in some of the literature (9, 48, 61). Clearly, there may be real value in directly tackling in multiple-client sessions the possible displacements of feeling and misallocations of responsibility among the family members, provided that the worker does not structurally address himself to the members in such a way that his interpretations, although accurate, strengthen inappropriate role allocations or assumptions or other entrenched and dysfunctional patterns (see 37, p. 347).

The reach and effectiveness of these modalities, it should be pointed out, is likely to be greatly enhanced as recent theoretical developments (such as those in role theory) come to be increasingly studied and applied to them,[4] and as improved diagnostic under-

---

[4] *See* pp. 90–91 of the section on "Potential Treatment Values that Received Little Comment" for a discussion of some possible assets of role theory for multiple-client interviewing.

standing of the total marital or family system offers the worker an opportunity for exerting conscious therapeutic influence in areas of which he might previously not even have been aware. He may, for example, come to recognize an undercurrent of family desperation that may be keeping all from bringing to the surface and confronting their real, as distinct from their felt, survival needs as a couple or family (22). Being himself directly involved in their interactional system, he can confront them with the effect of these misperceptions on their actual functioning and survival chances and point out the urgency of their realistic survival needs, perhaps especially in relation to the children's growth.

Alertness to the system as a whole, one might speculate, may also direct therapeutic attention to the amount of energy being used up by the couple and others in their constant efforts to reestablish the family equilibrium, which is then repeatedly disrupted owing to the mutual pushes and pulls resulting from the members' ambivalent feelings about each other. The presence of all of the ambivalent members together in the interview enables the worker to help them directly with the resolution of whatever conflicted feelings can be resolved and with the acceptance of those that cannot.

Provision of an Environment
Suitable for Confronting Conflict

Both for those unable to express their feelings and needs and for those only too ready to express them impulsively, joint and family interviews were seen as valuable because they can provide an environment suitable for confrontation of the marital conflict and, at the same time, for offering controls where needed. All the comments on the value of such interviews for providing confrontation and control referred to the current interaction between the partners and among the family members. Included were situations in which one or both partners act out habitually,[5] one spouse seems to be "downtrodden," and couples find it hard to contain their anger or, conversely, to express pent-up feelings, especially of hostility. The assets attributed to joint and family interviews were

[5] Several respondents advised against joint interviews with such couples if their destructive acting out seems or proves to be beyond the worker's control (*see* p. 140).

quite similar in this context, except for partners needing help in expressing withheld feelings. With reference to these, joint interviews alone were mentioned—a reflection, perhaps, of some caution about exposing children to the unmasking of parental conflict that they may never have experienced openly. At the same time, the project responses as a whole included comments revealing the usefulness of the family interview for puncturing a "perfect family front," for instance, when indicated.

A combination of two factors was identified from the responses as accounting, at least in part, for the value of the joint or family interview in helping couple and worker to confront but at the same time to channel the marital conflict: on the one hand, the provision of an atmosphere of acceptance—at times even of protectiveness—to encourage the verbal expression of negative or conflicted feeling when indicated, and, on the other hand, the institution of controls when needed. One of the study groups (1), which had chosen multiple-client interviewing of hostile couples as its special topic, spelled out some of the more explicit controls. They saw the worker as actively interrupting the partners' hostile interchange if it had grown too destructive, perhaps by asking them to speak to him directly so that he could understand, or by insisting on keeping the focus on the present. Other respondents suggested that partners be asked to "try to present their complaints in ways not provocative of counterhostility." They made clear that the worker "might terminate the interview if it became a damaging experience," with a plan for separate interviews or later joint interviews, if indicated. The importance of explicit structuring to reassure clients that "they would not be overwhelmed by their own impulses" was thus generally acknowledged.[6] It was even seen as useful for some couples who do not openly fight and argue, since they may gradually discover that "nothing so terrible happens" when disagreements and irritations are discussed more openly.

Respondents saw several kinds of change as emerging when the joint or family interview is used to help the couple or family confront their conflict in a setting providing some safeguards against excessive expression of anger or impulsivity. Hostility may be

6 One respondent stressed that she did not use home visits with a couple at the initial diagnostic stage because she felt that the structure of the office interview as such made clear that the couple should discuss their conflicts, not act them out.

brought out into the open but contained,[7] acting out may be reduced or prevented, clients with poor impulse control may be taught to behave in ways less provocative of frustration, and the conflict may be interrupted, at least temporarily.

One respondent cited a dramatic example of conflict interrupted in a joint interview with a young couple. They had each been punishing the other with infidelity and had been getting nowhere in individual interviews. In the joint session each repeatedly accused the other of having given more pain than he had received. "Why do you stay married?" the social worker asked. The couple responded by halting their battle and starting to tackle the problems between them. Another comment suggested that the effects of confrontation might even be multiplied by the mixing of various interview modalities and by seeing different combinations of family members in various settings.

However, not every result mentioned depended on confrontation of the meaning or effect of the interaction. The presence of the worker as a protective factor was in itself seen as enabling the "downtrodden" partner to risk himself more, while the angry couple's outburst in the worker's presence was thought to lessen the "puncture value" of their anger at home and to strengthen the partner under attack (1, p. 11). At an educational level, partners who had previously been unable to acknowledge the presence of disagreement were seen as capable of learning in multiple-client interviews to accept the need for a more open exchange of feelings and opinions.

Moving from the respondents' comments to consider those issues in a broader light, one might point to one similarity between group therapy and multiple-client interviewing that is relevant here. Just as the milieu of group therapy can be seen as providing an atmosphere opposite to that within which the individual's pathology developed (10, pp. 111–114), so the joint or family interview can be thought of as offering the couple or family what is *currently* missing but needed in their life. Such interviews can provide controls for those who express or act out their feelings and needs impulsively; encouragement of expression for those who may have been too fearful or withholding to reveal their real attitudes, perhaps even to themselves; and reassurance for those whose constric-

[7] For discussion of bringing unacknowledged positive feelings into the open, *see* p. 77.

tion has been due to the strength and vehemence of feelings previously concealed that the worker will not allow them to become overwhelmed by their own impulses.

The worker's recognition that a particular element is missing but needed in the couple's current interaction rests in the last resort on his implicit or explicit stance toward the family's current state in the light of his own concepts of what social and therapeutic standards are appropriate. The nature and effect of this confrontation and the role of the worker's own value system in it need to be understood more fully if joint and family sessions are to yield their maximum value for treatment. Moreover, the use of confrontation and intervention must be geared to diagnostic awareness of the "optimum degree of anxiety" that the participating clients can tolerate in an interview, as Weisberg has pointed out (59, p. 2). The elasticity of every marital and familial system is also likely to have limits. Unless the worker is aware of both these sets of factors, he may find the individual and collective defensive maneuvers of his clients springing into operation to counter the threat of the confrontation he has provoked or identified or to elude the controls he has set. A good sense of timing and a recognition of the specific supports that may temporarily be needed are therefore essential if the potential values of control and confrontation are actually to be realized in multiple-client sessions.

Provision of Conditions
Favoring Heightened Awareness
of Self and Others

Heightened awareness was cited by many respondents as one of the common results of joint and family interviews. Three major constituents of awareness were seen as enhanced through such approaches: awareness of oneself and one's impact on others; awareness of the feelings, needs, expectations, and thoughts of others; and awareness of the current impact of residual influences from the past. Interviews involving more than one family member were thought to have special value when partners or family members lacked self-perception, had closed off understanding or feeling for each other, or had failed to make an adequate appraisal of certain aspects of their reality situation because of these limitations.

The enhancement of awareness of self, of others, and of mutual impact was thought to stem from three factors: (a) the juxtaposition of partners or family members with each other and with the worker in multiple-client sessions, (b) the opportunities afforded there for current reality-checking, and (c) the help provided in sorting out the now inappropriate reactions to past experience.

Seeing oneself in dynamic interaction with one's partner or other family members and with the worker in the joint or family interview is likely, in the view of many, to heighten self-perception and to add perspective—the more so when various interview modalities in various settings are combined. Given such opportunities to check mutual distortions and projections, the individuals and the family group were thought to see themselves more sharply and realistically —as if through an observer's eyes. In addition, the exchanges and events of the multiple-client interview were seen as likely to bring home to the partner what his behavior means for the spouse and in what unexpected ways he may be important to his mate. Thus he may be prompted to recognize some personal share in the interactional problems and—given the will and ability—may begin to assume some responsibility for amelioration and change. Attitudes or behavior previously thought offensive may come to be recognized as being due not to pure hostility but to frustrated affection or inarticulate and disappointed need for the perceiving partner's attention and caring. Realizing this, the partner may be freed to take more responsibility for his feelings and behavior as they affect others.

A heightened awareness gained in joint or family interviews, regarding mutual needs and expectations, was seen as making for various positive reverberations within the family, including greater empathy. If such new perceptions should lead partners or family members to try to meet each other's needs in some measure, and if their efforts should be at all successful, then the total family may be strengthened. A series of positive responses may thereby be evoked, as implied by a client's remark that "a little generosity repays me doubly."

Not only actions but also basic attitudes may be affected by changes in individual and mutual awareness. Clients may, in the view of some, become able to accept the fact that things "have not changed as much as they might like . . . . They may even shift the value they place on different things, finding them less important than they had imagined." A few commented on the deeper "recognition of the individuality of other family members" that springs from greater mutual awareness and saw the incipient readiness of a spouse to allow his mate to be different as creating for both partners "a feeling of great freedom and release . . . intensifying . . . their ability to feel pleasure about many things."

Finally, a clearer perception of self and others provides a sounder basis for constructive interaction. To the extent that joint and family interviews help the partners and family members to test out their assumptions about each other's motives, such interviews were seen as reducing the tendency to fantasize about the meaning of the other's behavior and as offering, instead, a more realistic view of the members' actual and potential capacities.

Of all the many comments on heightened awareness gained through joint interviews, only one made any reference to the mutual recognition of influences from the past as a possible development in such interviews. This respondent believed it possible, after some individual and joint sessions, for partners to "sort out their feelings" after examining their mutual expectations in the light of "their expectations of marriage as based on their own parental families." Presumably the result might be some mutual reduction in inappropriate demands. The absence of further comment on the remnants of past influences alive in the present is especially interesting in the light of the strong psychoanalytic influence on casework thinking and its stress on the therapeutic value of insight into past origins.

Although a clearer perspective was seen by several respondents as resulting from the increased awareness gained through multiple-client interviews, they did not spell out just how it might lead to change. One can speculate that the individual, as he becomes more cognizant of his own ways of feeling and acting in differing interview situations, may also become more tolerant and flexible about the variability of others. Thus the intensity of the partners' mutual feelings and interaction may be diluted and the family become receptive to more flexible, or even new, mutual approaches.

As the partners or family members become better able to clarify their mutual attitudes, they may simultaneously learn how far their individual perceptions are congruent. This increased perspective can help reverse the conflict and contribute to improved understanding, emotional ease, and more effective action, whether joint or individual.

75

Increased mutual awareness or self-awareness is not, however, an automatic guarantor of progress. Some capacity, will, and opportunity for a better marriage are necessary if growing awareness is to lead to greater mutual acceptance, change, or accommodation rather than to flight, strife, or even despair. The step from shared guilt to shared hope is unlikely to be taken without the presence and use of at least some minimal strengths in the marital relationship and some individual self-esteem. Furthermore, the partner who is seriously lacking in a sense of self-worth is unlikely to believe himself capable of meeting the spouse's newly perceived needs even if he should deeply wish to do so. He may also need to downgrade the partner to bolster his own ego. It is no coincidence, therefore, that many leading practitioners and thinkers in the field have stressed the value of multiple-client interviewing for enhancing self-esteem (45, p. 217; 49, pp. 164–165).

Possible gains in awareness are not limited to the clients in joint or family interviews. The worker's misperceptions or misinterpretations are also likely to be corrected, especially if he uses a combination of interviewing methods, since different environments bring "out different sides of the personality that could well be lost in individual treatment" (24, p. 137).

Increased Opportunity
for the Promotion
of Constructive Mutuality

In considering the promotion of constructive mutuality by means of joint or family interviews, the respondents seemed to be describing a process of mobilization about which they felt a good deal of assurance and conviction. They valued these methods for situations in which current cohesion or coping capacity were a part of the problem, but in which some community of goals and values was either latent or attainable. Although some comments referred only to joint and others only to family interviews, the values and influences toward change they identified seemed equally applicable to both. They included the "impartial and equally supportive atmosphere of the interview" and the contrast between physical proximity and emotional distance.

A focus on common values, responsibilities, and goals was pictured as a natural outgrowth of the special social structure involved in these multiple-client interviews. This structure was also thought to dramatize and activate the involvement of the partners or all family members, to foster joint acceptance of responsibility for problems and problem-solving, and to demonstrate and reinforce positives within the marriage and family.

Common values or goals may be discovered or rediscovered by the partners or family members themselves in these exchanges, and achievable goals mutually determined. At times, however, it may be the worker who recognizes a possibility for mutuality of which the couple themselves may not have been aware. This possibility was illustrated by two contrasting comments. One described excessively dependent couples who could "progress from clinging to the worker to grasping a mutual goal for the marriage and the family, which the worker can offer them." The other illustration referred to a basically pleasure-loving couple who had denied themselves much of the relaxation that the worker now began to encourage. This "relieved pressure, relaxed a too rigid conscience," gave the couple genuine pleasure, and enabled the mother to let the children "live their own lives more." In this way, unacknowledged or unrealized as well as identified areas of mutuality may be used by the skillful worker to build or reinforce a foundation for conjugal reciprocity.

By their structure, joint or family interviews also demonstrate a focus on the relationship and on areas of complementarity and "symbolize and implement the idea of joint responsibility." The very offer of a joint interview may serve to foster more even involvement of both partners, as one respondent found after her agency had come to insist on seeing couples jointly for the first interview. This may be especially true in the case of the "guilty" partner, since he is likely to use every means to elude contact if he believes that the worker already disapproves of him owing to contact with the applying spouse. Once in the interview it becomes hard, however, to "walk out or refuse to talk" when the other partner is there to speak his part. In addition, the "impartial and equally supportive atmosphere" provided by the worker may help to mobilize a couple to work together.

Clearly, no structure or procedure can be valid for all situations. Some instances were cited, but not further described, when most of the sessions are joint but it was found necessary to see one or both partners individually to keep both involved.

Apparently because of the project's focus on the treatment of marital problems, references to the fostering of joint responsibility for problems and problem-solving occurred mainly in discussions of joint interviews. However, both joint and family interviews were seen as offering not only the possibility of discovering and developing shared thinking around areas that all can deal with, but also the opportunity to combine efforts to work out a solution. In joint interviews the worker was seen as specifically focusing on mutual responsibility rather than on the "judgmental projections which the couple bring," and as helping the couple to arrive at joint decisions, most often on charged issues such as the handling of children or finances. Thus a specific point of conflict between the partners was thought resolvable or a joint attack on environmental problems feasible in joint interviews. Participation of all the family members was valued for alleviating a situation in which all could play a part, such as developing shared understanding and acceptance of the needs arising from chronic illness or handicap of a family member. Furthermore, it was regarded as useful "to increase the individual's range of choice for problem-solving," since family members in the interview can compare their different ways of handling common problems.

The live process of the joint or family interview was thought to offer many opportunities for pointing out and reinforcing strengths and assets in the marriage or family. Thus, in joint interviews couples may come to recognize their own realistic achievements or the strong mutual pulls and positives that "years of struggling may have obscured for them."

While the responses suggested many factors accounting for the value of joint and family interviews in promoting constructive mutuality, the effects of these factors on the couple or family were barely spelled out. Presumably they include some reassessment of situations that have become bogged down, some positive spiraling, and some increase of individuation within the context of strengthened family integrity, provided there is some minimal initial will and capacity for co-operation.

Going further beyond the respondents' own statements, one might suggest that a focus both on mutual responsibilities and on individual and complementary strengths may help the couple to redefine their situation, to see it not as the "trap" it may have seemed to become, but also as the result of choice and of some positive factors. When the marriage or family has become fragmented, leaving its members mutually alienated, suffering, and lonely, the structurally reinforced shift of emphasis from the individual client's problems to their joint capacities for working them out may call forth new or abandoned reactions. More active and responsible attitudes and behavior may then enable the clients to use their individual and complementary strengths to better advantage—and demonstrably so—even in the interview situation. In such a context it may become possible, to use Mitchell's analogy, for the "potential corrective influences within the family [to] begin to act on the focal sources of infection within the individual and the group" (39, p. 285).

Even a slight success in the move from fragmentation to mutuality may become evident to all in joint or family sessions. Each increase in hope, mutual regard, or self-esteem is likely to lead to further success or, failing that, to help the couple or family to begin to weather their disappointments together—an essential and cementing experience for family living and for maintaining hope and strength. In multiple-client sessions these experiences and their attendant fluctuations of feeling can be worked through together right in the interview, which may mean a speeding and deepening of treatment effects.

Another contribution of multiple-client sessions may be the strengthening of the sense of the family as an integral unit, with distinct characteristics of its own, even in the presence of conflict or of some fragmentation. Exceptionally deprived or inadequately functioning families have often been thought to hamper the individuation of their members. In part, this may be due not only to pathology, ignorance, and chaotic conditions, but also to the fear that individual growth might be at the expense of family solidarity in the face of a dangerous and hostile world. When such families experience a strengthened sense of family identity or integrity as a result of the partializing of problems and the focus on mutuality and strengths, they may also become freer to allow individuation, with enormous benefits for the marital partners, the children, and the society to which they might otherwise become a burden.

All these advantages of multiple-client sessions in strengthening mutuality also suggest a potential hazard when shifts in treatment modality are undertaken. For example, if joint or family interviews are used only for diagnosis and then abandoned, the partners may take this as a tacit admission by the worker that he can help each one of them but that they cannot help each other in treatment. Thus, unless the reasons for such shifts are made quite clear, these changes may undermine the mutuality necessary for progress. Overlapping groups, as Bell has pointed out, tend either to coalesce or to split (13, p. 22).

Promotion of Direct Experimentation with New Behavior and Problem-solving

A few respondents directly discussed the role of support from the worker and of identification with him in stimulating new behavior and problem-solving in joint or family interviews. They saw these influences as directly encouraging couples and families to try new ways of interacting. Immediate guidance in the pinpointing and partializing of problems and direct support of the marriage rather than of any one individual were seen as powerful stimulants to experimentation with new behavior.

In joint and family sessions there are many opportunities for the worker to be observed as he reacts to the partner or family members, relates to them, and has them relate to him in ways that differ from the family's usual pattern among themselves. Since the worker, moreover, does not give up in the face of the couple's problems and regressions, the participants begin to feel renewed hope for the marriage. They are emboldened to try some of the attitudes and behavior that have begun to seem possible for them as a result of their observation of and identification with the worker. Thus they may learn to stand against pathological behavior and yet try to understand it and not to reject the person exhibiting it. They may focus more on the meaning and effect of their mutual behavior with each other than on mutual condemnation and thus become freer to work out more effective and gratifying interaction.

The structural focus of the joint or family interview on the marriage or the family as a whole was also seen as tending to mobilize the positive forces in the family. Thus the multiple-client session can become "a laboratory for testing out changing patterns in a protective setting." The worker can encourage new behavior right in the multiple-client session as he comments on and reinforces new and constructive ways of interacting that may be emerging. The setting also permits the worker to give all the participants simultaneously some immediate guidance in facing and partializing problems and in reducing them to manageable proportions. Together with him they can begin to sort out whether the difficulty is due to external, interpersonal, or maturational stress and mobilize their joint resources to attack one aspect of their problems at a time.

Some authors particularly interested in viewing the family as a system are convinced that the first change must almost certainly be induced by the worker because the family will inevitably cling to the status quo. However, "the acceptance of one major change . . . may serve as the starting point for a chain reaction" (40, p. 18). One might argue that even minor changes may have this effect. It may be the hope born of some evidence of success or change— whether in attitudes or behavior—that lessens the grip of individual fear and mutual clinging to the status quo.

Once he has experienced the comparative advantages of the various multiple-client and individual treatment approaches, the worker himself is likely to respond with a greater flexibility of therapeutic approach and readiness to use different interactional systems for therapeutic advantage. Friedman's selective inclusion (20, p. 139) of crucial "outsiders" (such as the identified patient's prospective bride) in family interviews provides one example of such an effect.

Greater Effectiveness
with Certain Types of Couples
or Families

So far, the outstanding characteristics distinguishing joint and family interviews from the exclusively individual approach have been seen as stemming mainly from these sources: their structure, their direct revelation both of familiar friction and of unfamiliar yet successful handling of conflict, and their use of approaches opposite to those habitual with the couple or family prior to treatment. To these characteristics of multiple-client interviews one might further add the immediacy and observability of interaction in these sessions. Here each participant can see for himself what the worker and the partner or other family members are doing or talking about together. As a result, mutual distrust and fantasies regarding the other's relationship with the worker are reduced and motivation for treatment may be better sustained for those who need a constantly clear and present sense of either the need for or the usefulness of help.

It would seem to follow from these characteristics that multiple-client techniques might be of special value in relation to individuals, couples, or families who need such direct experiences if they are to find it possible to give up or ease their defenses and defensive maneuvers and to try less rigid or self-defeating ways of getting along together. Almost by definition these are likely to be families for whom the road to change often may not involve much insight into causes [8]—either because they would find such insight too intolerably painful, too irrelevant, or too unintelligible, or because they are doers better able to respond to direct experience than to "just talking." The occasional descriptions by respondents of successes with couples previously unreached by the individual approach seem to fit in well with the theoretical expectations just outlined, as well as with some of the literature on this subject (see pp. 83–84).

The types of couples or families who often respond better to the multiple-client than to the individual approach were described by respondents partly in terms of symptoms and partly in overlapping diagnostic terms. No neat classification of these comments is therefore feasible, but they are interesting enough to bear listing: couples in which one or both partners are excessively suspicious,[9] excessively hostile, suffering from character disorders, or referred by coercive authorities; couples whose complementary patterns have become accentuated into opposing extremes, including sadomasochistic couples; those where one partner is excessively passive or both struggle extensively for power; and, finally, partners who find a one-to-one relationship with the caseworker intolerable. Only one respondent cited joint interviews as being especially helpful with young couples. The study group especially focused on the relationship of marital conflict to incomplete emancipation from parents believed this modality to become truly effective with un-

---

[8] This is not to say that insights into past causes cannot be gained through multiple-client sessions. However, many clients with whom the individual approach was thought to have failed in the past seem to fall into the category of those with whom such an approach may be inappropriate, at least for a time.

[9] For discussion of the pros and cons of seeing suspicious partners together or separately, *see* pp. 127 and 152 ff.

emancipated couples only after individual interviews have enabled the partners to experience some personal growth and to modify some of their attitudes or behavior (2, p. 2).

The first four categories of couples just listed as responding best to the multiple-client approach were those mentioned most frequently by the respondents. In fact, one full study group report was devoted to the question of treating hostile couples through joint interviews used exclusively or in combination with other modalities. This report confirms, in relation to extremely angry couples, the special values and distinguishing dynamics of joint interviews cited throughout this chapter. It describes variations in the approach and in its values depending on the basis of the partners' anger and suggests that limitations may be placed on the use of the modality depending on the degree of the partners' destructiveness, the extent of their inability or reluctance to become involved in joint interviews, the degree of their pathology,[10] and the presence of unclarified countertransference elements (1, p. 4).

Generally speaking, treatment decisions appeared to be made by workers on the basis of specific dynamics rather than over-all typology. However, it seems appropriate to state that confrontation of the conflict through the institution of controls was seen by respondents as especially relevant for excessively abusive couples and those manifesting character disorders.

Many of the leading authorities in the field of joint and family treatment buttress the conviction that these approaches have something special to offer certain groups of families with whom other approaches have failed, even though several concur that development of a typology of families most suited to family treatment is as yet not feasible (23, p. 525; 38, p. 64). Families in which one or more members are suffering from character disorders (4, p. 4; 27; 31, p. 58; 45, pp. 217–218; 53, p. 122; 58) and multiproblem families from impoverished environments (31; 60, pp. 150–151) stand out in this respect. As for extremely hostile couples, the crucial role of the worker's attitude is stressed by such writers as Weisberg (59, p. 3) who see the potential values of joint interviews as becoming available to hostile partners if the worker can cease to be alarmed by the couple's fighting and see their very presence in the interview as evidence of the wish for a better relationship.

---

[10] For some differing views regarding the presence of severe pathology as a criterion for or against the use of multiple-client interviews, *see* p. 127.

In relation to the treatment of very young couples, the work of Jolesch (30) provides a further basis for the view of the Cincinnati study group (2) that maximum values from joint interviews accrue only after a period of previous individual contact with each partner. Only after such an opportunity for personal growth may some of these couples cease to experience their marriage—and therefore the joint interview focus on mutuality—as a threat to their sense of individual identity. Jolesch, in this context, cites yet another asset of joint interviews introduced after a period of individual treatment. In such sessions, the worker may be able to help the more mature partner use his increased tolerance and freedom, gained in individual sessions, for helping to sustain the less motivated partner until he in turn becomes truly involved in treatment (30, p. 251). On the other hand, some of the literature on family treatment in relation to adolescents (51) suggests, by implication, the possibility that emancipation may at times require that those needing to evolve a new type of relationship and to gain some emotional distance from each other should be seen together so that they may all learn this simultaneously. This suggests that some further careful experimentation may be fruitful in relation to bringing the parents of immature couples into the sessions under certain conditions or for certain ends.

CONTRIBUTION TO
ATTENUATION OF PROBLEMS ASSOCIATED WITH
EXCLUSIVE USE OF INDIVIDUAL TREATMENT

Long experience with individual interviewing has given caseworkers a rather refined understanding of the limitations as well as of the values of this basic approach. Joint and family sessions were seen by many respondents as helping to overcome some of these limitations. For partners being seen mainly in individual sessions, either by the same worker or by separate workers, and for partners undergoing differing types of treatment (such as group therapy for one spouse and individual treatment for the other), joint and family interviews were thought to avoid certain problems commonly encountered in exclusively individual treatment. Such problems fall into two categories: difficulties not uncommon in the treatment of life companions through separate individual interviews and complications arising from the one-to-one relationship with the caseworker.

Difficulties Inherent
in Individual Treatment

When couples are being treated mainly in individual interviews, whether by the same or by different workers, respondents described periodic or occasional joint or family interviews as highly useful if the development of discrepant directions, rates of progress, or goals for the partners is to be avoided or checked.[11] They did not, on the whole, attempt to explain specifically how such multiple-client interviews might bring about improved co-ordination of treatment. Instead, they seemed to imply that this followed from structural factors that made changes in mutual feelings, needs, and aspirations evident in the interview and therefore susceptible to therapeutic handling directed toward mutual development or accommodation.

Respondents were somewhat more explicit about the factors enhancing the productivity and flexibility of treatment, about those permitting the highlighting and reinforcement of treatment gains, and about those providing for mutual weighing and implementing of termination. When an impasse or deterioration in the marital relationship has developed in individual sessions, respondents saw joint or family interviews as stirring productive anxiety, bringing conflict into the open, or stimulating new interest.

A well-timed shift of interviewing methods was seen as useful for groping toward or accomplishing a shift in treatment focus into the area of greater current urgency or potential productivity—e.g., away from a child's problems to the underlying marital difficulty. It seemed implicit in these comments that the change in structure was regarded as swinging the spotlight onto the marital or familial relationship now captured, as it were, in the new interview structure. A change to joint or family interviews was also seen as often enabling the worker to reinforce, test, or highlight the fact that the partners were becoming able to hear each other and to explore their

11 The great majority of these responses centered on the value of the periodic or occasional joint interview. Values of the family interview in this context were generally phrased in terms similar to those regarding joint sessions, except for one comment about using family sessions to allow participation of a family member previously absent from treatment.

respective roles in the marital problem, or were beginning to move closer together. Sometimes a shift to multiple-client interviews may represent a deliberate change in treatment approach, e.g., from an individual intrapsychic focus to demonstration and education or even to direct guidance regarding the marital or familial interaction.

Joint and family interviews were also thought by respondents to be valuable near the time of termination, because they could dilute the one-to-one casework relationship and thus smooth the transition to dependence on each other and independence from the worker. Joint interviews were further described as helping the partners to face the satisfying elements in their relationship and to sum up and affirm the changes accomplished in treatment and those left unachieved.

Complications Arising from
the One-to-One Relationship
with the Worker

Many problems often associated with the ostensibly exclusive client-worker relationship in individual treatment were thought by respondents to be attenuated or even avoided by the use of multiple-client sessions. However, they did not specify how much multiple-client interviewing was necessary for those attenuating influences to become operative. The partners' co-presence with the worker in joint sessions that are focused mainly on their interaction were thought to minimize the illusion of an exclusive relationship with the worker and to reduce the fantasies of emotional gratification from and total empathy with him, since one spouse is constantly being reminded in the interview of the needs and capacities of the partner or other family members. Joint participation of the couple or family group was further seen as offering a brake on the possible "wish-fear conflict" of clients about dependence on the worker. Secondary gratifications that might tend to prolong treatment unduly also seemed minimized in multiple-client sessions in which the need to share the worker's attention with others is inescapable. In addition, such interviews were thought perhaps to dilute excessive guilt through recognition of shared responsibility for problems and their solution. When the outcomes were favorable, family members were seen as growing freer to work out their problems, and the more highly defended client as being reassured through the presence of others less anxious.

In multiple-client interviews, partners have less chance to succeed in misrepresenting the worker's views or in using him as a weapon or judge against the spouse. On the contrary, the worker was thought more likely to become a "family resource" person through family interviews. Working in relation to several participants at once, he is in all probability perceived more realistically and may himself be checked in the tendency to overidentify with one spouse or to see the clients' situation unrealistically. The sense of dilution that may result from sharing a case with another worker is also avoided.

More effective co-ordination of direction, pace, and goals in treatment and periodic evaluation of progress would seem to be valuable assets of joint or family interviews even when they are the main (although not necessarily the exclusive) method, rather than the auxiliary one. It would be helpful to learn from actual comparative case studies under controlled conditions whether the predominant use of these methods in the treatment of interactional problems may not save treatment hours by greatly diminishing the danger that discrepant therapeutic directions and goals will develop in the course of the partners' treatment. Such studies may also reveal special pitfalls of multiple-client treatment, such as the possibility suggested by Bell (13, p. 24) that the chances of the partners' successfully joining in manipulation of the worker may increase with the length of the joint contact.

In any case, it goes without saying that the multiple-client structure as such can never provide a guarantee against misperceptions in and misdirection of the treatment situation, and that shifts of method can be no substitute for diagnostic thinking and therapeutic resourcefulness. The worker's personality and skill, as well as the family's stance and situation, are still essential codeterminants of the effectiveness of treatment.

Potential Treatment Values That Received Little Comment

Perusal of the responses as a whole in the light of the literature, discussions with consultants, and theoretical speculation suggest a few additional treatment values that might have deserved further comment. The most obvious gaps relate to the positive uses of value differences and to socioeconomic and cultural concerns, which generally received little attention. However, the enhancement of self-esteem through joint and family sessions also received little comment. In addition, the values of such interviews in handling problems regarding separation and divorce were left mainly unexplored.

Widened Opportunity
for Therapeutic Use
of Value Discrepancies

No comments were offered on the positive uses, if any, of the possible differences between the worker's and the clients' hierarchy of values. True, these may also differ in individual sessions, but a situation in which the worker is outnumbered, suffers the onslaught of a different value system, and yet maintains his position and authority as a "helping" person implicitly suggests the possibility that his values may be more achievable or more likely to be rewarded than the family's. Differences between the worker's and the client's sense of values tend to be discussed as aspects of the counter-transference. In this context respondents stressed the need of workers to be alert to all the nuances of their attitudes toward the individuals or families concerned and warned that workers should not try to impose their own values on clients. However, inasmuch as the multiple-client interview is structured to allow handling of the marital or familial system as such, it necessarily involves tangling also with the rules and therefore the values—conscious or otherwise—that underlie the functioning of the system. Thus, couples who apply may often feel that they have failed to live up to their own or to society's values or that the latter may be remote, unattainable, or inevitably frustrating. This sense of alienation may perhaps be modified in multiple-client interviews in some instances, due to the impact of the worker's values.

The absence of condemnation in the worker's stance, even for those who lack necessary controls, combined with his therapeutic optimism, his stress on the effect of behavior and on the opportunity to learn more effective, more satisfying ways of interacting, all amount to a recognition that standards of behavior are necessary but need not be rigid and unattainable. In this fashion, it would seem, joint and family interviews have a special contribution to make to treatment, particularly of character-disordered family members. When, for instance, one or both partners have failed to develop adequate internal values and controls, multiple-client interviews, with an emphasis on what does and does not work in their relationship, may help the couple to evolve standards to which they *can* live up because these are more realistically geared to their own capacities and provide at least some fairly immediate satisfactions, as demonstrable in the joint session.

Greater Likelihood
of Acceptance by Families
from Specific Sociocultural Groups

No reference was made in the responses to the possibility that some national, ethnic, economic, or religious groups may typically find one-to-one contact an unfamiliar experience and may be more comfortable in a setting in which other family members may participate. Exploration of such cultural factors might increase and broaden the reach of casework treatment among groups, such as those in the lower socioeconomic strata, whom this approach has often failed to touch in the past. However, since the worker's background or value system may differ sharply from the family's, their nature and impact need to be better understood if the multiple encounter is to be put to full therapeutic use.

Greater Range of Opportunity
for Coping with
Environmental Problems, Realities, and Opportunities

Respondents did not discuss whether and to what extent joint or family interviews might become a model for solving problems in relation to people and situations outside the family. Some did stress the values of multiple-client sessions for distinguishing between intrafamilial and external problems and for helping the family to see environmental problems more clearly and to tackle them more effectively. However, further possibilities deserve attention. Haley, for instance, has pointed out (26, p. 137) that the couple's encounter with the worker tends to change their use

89

of third parties. Whether such a carry-over effect does indeed take place might be a subject for further study. If it does, direct discussion of the couple's use of third parties might also be found to affect their handling of confidences with outsiders, their use or avoidance of outside resources such as babysitters, and even their handling of money.

Multiple-client sessions may also be useful for revealing how environmental resources might be used to dovetail with therapeutic requirements. Thus, partners who function well together provided they can reverse conventional roles can perhaps be helped to become more independent of external criticism (12). An overly pugnacious spouse's energies might be constructively diverted into sports or political activities. A mother, left lonely in the "empty nest" with a somewhat cool spouse, might be steered toward volunteer work in a children's ward. Although all these new relationships of the family to its larger social setting could also result from individual treatment, the joint or family session may have special values both in highlighting in the presence of all the need for such measures and in enlisting the co-operation of all the family in their initiation and maintenance.

Enlarged Possibilities
for Enhancing Self-esteem
and Mutual Regard

Although the literature stresses the values of multiple-client sessions for building self-esteem and mutual regard, there was barely any discussion of this asset on the part of respondents. Some further study of why and how these modalities further such ends might well contribute to improve practice. It might also advance the development of clearer criteria for choice of approach, especially in relation to individuals and couples who are deficient in self-esteem.

Improved Climate for Resolution
of Role Conflict

At the time when respondents were drafting their comments, the application of role theory to casework was only beginning to be explored. Such concepts were therefore reflected in only a generalized sense in those few comments that mentioned role perception and functioning. The combined contributions of Spiegel and Kluckhohn, Perlman, and Tharp (25, 41, 42, 43, 57) now make it possible to see ways in which joint and family interviewing might become highly useful in the modification of role conflicts, even though none of these authors has given any particular emphasis to this approach. Spiegel's analysis of the various methods of re-establishing role equilibrium, for instance, may serve to increase the possibilities of the worker's intervention in the multiple-client interview by making him newly conscious of re-equilibrating techniques.[12] It may also alert him to the possibility that clients, who may have been accustomed to being approached manipulatively, may react to his attempts to explore, to create opportunities for compromise, and so on as if he were merely masking in a new way an effort to coerce, coax, blame, or pretend. Aware of the specific possibilities, the worker may be able to use joint or family interviews to help the clients shed their inappropriate reactions, recognize the limitations of manipulation, and perhaps switch to new approaches more respectful of one another's identity and worth.

A further point of special relevance for the multiple-client interview is implicit in Perlman's view that improved role functioning may lead to improved mental health, although the inverse effect has in the past held the attention of caseworkers (41, pp. 310–313; 42, pp. 379–380). Joint and family interviews, although not singled out by Perlman, would certainly seem uniquely suited to the clarification of role requirements, role allocations, and role performance within the family since the participants can simultaneously become aware of their own misperceptions of role requirements and may mutually experiment with revised role definitions. They can, with the worker's help, define the extent to which their role problems may have resulted from unclear definition by society, from conflicting role expectations of the two partners, or from incompatibility of their personal needs and capacities (or those of their system) with social role requirements.[13] Common recognition can confront common resistances and lead to common readjustments. These, in turn, may spur "positive spiraling" since improved

[12] For a summary of Spiegel's concept of re-equilibration processes, *see* footnote 6, p. 45.
[13] The causes of role failure cited in this paragraph are derived from Perlman's much more exhaustive account (43, pp. 25–30).

role functioning has social as well as personal rewards that further reinforce and consolidate the improvement.

The preventive value of such an approach, used as one of several perspectives in the joint or family interview, is clear if role discord between the partners in one area will produce, as Tharp claims, role discord in the same area between the children or between parents and children (57, pp. 533–535).[14]

Widened Resources
for Resolving Problems
Related to Separation and Divorce

Many respondents, in the context of criteria for the choice of interview modality, stressed the clients' wish for joint interviews or for continuation of the marriage as a criterion in favor of such sessions. In keeping with this position, some recommended switching to individual interviews if the couple were struggling with the question of separation (28). Nevertheless, there was occasional comment suggesting the usefulness of one or more joint interviews for couples involved in the separation process who need to plan for their children or to state their decision to separate "responsibly in each other's presence." There was no discussion of the feasibility or value of joint sessions for couples with totally divergent feelings about the future of their marriage or for partners who are both considering separation or divorce. Although the structure of joint interviews may war inherently with such a purpose, it might nevertheless be worth exploring whether they could be used in conjunction with individual interviews to extend the depth and range of the couple's consideration of feelings and problems related to their joint or individual future. Similarly, it may be worth testing, in cases in which the marriage is to be terminated, whether and to what extent this structure may be used to reinforce the need for common planning regarding the children and the legal and financial arrangements and for mutual modification of the strains involved. Still to be identified are the circumstances under which such a negation of the inherent "pull toward mutuality" in joint

---

[14] Tharp offers five classes of marital functions (57, p. 533): solidarity, sexuality, external relations, internal instrumentality, and division of responsibility. A deficit in parental solidarity, for example, may mean an excess of solidarity between one or both of the parents and one or more of the children.

interviews and its conversion into mutuality for the limited purpose of joint planning and mutual considerations of issues related to separation are likely to be feasible, desirable, or self-defeating.

ASSETS RESTATED
FROM A SYSTEM-LEVEL PERSPECTIVE

With minor exceptions, respondents tended to conceptualize the values of joint and family interviews principally in terms of the dynamics of the individual participants. This final section will undertake, with the help of insights from relevant literature,[15] to provide a second and somewhat different perspective by restating these values in system-level terms.

The key factor that distinguishes joint and family interviewing from individual sessions, and even from group treatment of unrelated individuals, is obviously the worker's direct intervention in an operating social system that exists as such outside the treatment situation and consists of clients who share each other's lives and are crucially important to each other. In contrast to individual sessions, the worker no longer aims exclusively at separately influencing one or more members of that system or at preparing them to modify the system as a result of individual changes within themselves. Instead, he himself enters the system, hoping not only to influence it directly, but also to teach its participants, through direct experience, how to modify it and how to maintain its resilience in the face of further threat. By directly and simultaneously exposing to his treatment initiatives all relevant system participants involved in a marital conflict, the worker sets in motion a circular feedback between his impact on the marriage and family networks and that of the participants on him and on his progressively evolving diag-

---

[15] A discussion of this kind could not have been attempted without the wide range of concepts and insights offered in the works listed in the bibliography. These concepts include some fertilized by the influence of sociology, anthropology, and communications analysis: the open system (16, 36), equilibrium (35), boundary (29), role (25, 41, 42, 43), congruence in communication (8, 49, 55), alliances and collusion (18, 62), family myths (22), and norms as applied to therapy (10). Some others derive from a wide spectrum of therapeutic thinking, ranging from those recommending exclusive use of family interviewing (7, 13, 15) to those advocating discriminating use of all methods (5, 6, 38, 39, 52, 54, 55). Without the aid of these concepts, the author would have lacked the tools for even attempting to view the responses in a manner groping toward integration of the systematic and individual approaches.

nostic assessment of the interaction. In successful cases, the end result is not only moderation of the conflict but also some modification of the underlying system that gave rise to it.

In the case of marital conflict, the partners are likely to be caught in a seemingly irreversible escalation of negative and stereotyped exchanges. If this process is not interrupted, it tends to undermine the marriage, to extend to involve the children and other family members and friends, and eventually to break up the marriage and family union altogether. However, the attempt to intervene in any established social system whose members have become habituated to functioning together according to long-established patterns tends to activate the processes directed toward reinstating the old dysfunctional equilibrium. This presents a treatment dilemma that joint and family interviews seem especially suited to solve. They place the practitioner in a position in which he can work directly and simultaneously with both partners in the conflict and with other family members when they are involved. Hence he is in an exceptionally strategic position to facilitate the interruption of this conflict cycle and at the same time to counter the pull toward reinstatement of the former habitual but dysfunctional exchange. The ultimate effectiveness of the treatment is determined largely by the extent to which the forces making for a modified and improved balance and a positive cycle of interchange succeed in triumphing over those favoring system retrogression, immobility, or breakup.

To push a system-level analysis beyond these global generalities, one must ask further just how the joint and family interview structure enables the worker to influence the marital interaction constructively. In what ways does it facilitate modifications so that the family system may more flexibly accommodate the paradoxical requirements of family well-being: necessary cohesion, anchorage, and mutual meeting of needs, on the one hand, and individuation, growth, and self-reliance for its members, on the other? In more specific terms, still stated from the system perspective, the advantages of these types of interview structure would seem to be the following: (a) They facilitate a direct therapeutic relationship with all system participants. (b) They simultaneously enhance the motivation of all system participants for change. (c) They facilitate group recognition of system characteristics and effects. (d) They provide for simultaneous exposure of all system participants to the worker's treatment initiatives directed toward system modification.

(e) They promote group consideration and action regarding the relation between the marital and family system and the larger environment. (f) They facilitate early attention to the obstacles in the path of needed change. (g) They provide multiple supports for facilitating and sustaining change. (h) They improve the long-term preventive potential of casework intervention.

Facilitation of a Direct Therapeutic
Relationship with All
System Participants

The first asset of a joint or family approach to marital problems is apparent immediately at the point of the worker's entry into the system. For caseworkers, the development of a therapeutic relationship with marital partners in conflict has always been a delicate and hazardous undertaking. Usually only one of the partners seeks help initially. More than likely he is overflowing with complaints about his spouse and may seek to involve the worker as his direct ally in the conflict. Often he has delayed seeking help until repetitive bitter exchanges have all but destroyed the marriage. To achieve a constructive solution in spite of these strong counter-pressures, the worker must relate not simply to the individual applicant, but also to his estranged partner and to the pattern of interaction between them.

In using the individual approach, the worker all too easily becomes identified with the problems and perspective of one spouse, with the result that he tends to reject or be rejected by the other. However, if early in the contact all those involved in the conflict can be seen together, the worker is less likely to slip into overidentification or unwitting collusion with one or to be perceived by the other as playing this role. Even if this should occur, the reactions of the partner who feels affronted are likely to pull the worker up short without delay. Thus the structure of the interview itself eases his task of keeping the focus on the marriage or family. It also enables him to develop early a direct therapeutic relationship with all those who must change if the conflict is to be resolved.

By entering the system without letting himself be absorbed by it, the worker exerts the double influence of the basically uninvolved outsider and the temporary participant. As an outsider, he is able to offer new attitudes and ways of behaving. As a participant, he can, through direct experience, gain some grasp of the couple's or family's predicament and be alerted to the complex mutual requirements that must be met if marital balance and family cohesion are to be achieved without infringement on individual growth.

Through this same dual role, the worker also introduces a measure of uncertainty into the stereotyped choreography of the family system. As the partners face together an unknown temporary participant in their relationship, they are forced, in a limited and protected way, to face and tackle together uncertainty, discomfort, and the threat of change. For couples who lack the capacity to handle uncertainty this may in itself be therapeutic and may serve to reveal to both partners some unexpected capacities for resilience and co-operative problem-coping. In any case, the inclusion of an unknown outsider as a temporary but necessary observer and even participant in discussion of the marital relationship of itself represents a transient modification of the marital system because most of the intimacies of marriage usually remain undisclosed, at least among families with middle-class standards, except as the process of conflict escalation leads the partners increasingly to reveal them in their search for allies. The very act of disclosing intimacies to a nonpartisan worker thus interrupts and to some extent modifies a customary pattern and may therefore be a first step toward change.

One might well ask why partners at the height of conflict would ever consider allowing the social worker even a temporary role in the crucial issues that divide them. Usually it is only the pressure of deep pain, prolonged frustration, intense fear, and the hope of relief, based perhaps on the expectation that the partner alone will be made to change, that will lead one or both to open their relationship to the worker and allow him to remain in contact long enough to help start and guide the process of change. If such consent is to be given, it must inevitably rest on their both viewing him and his behavior, attitudes, and potential recommendations as at least minimally acceptable, effective, and relevant to their difficulties and goals. This consent is likely to remain in effect only as long as the family decision-makers participating in the interview see him as related to the marriage and family as a whole and not exclusively to one spouse or individual alone. The structure of the joint or family interview is especially suited to achieving this result.

Here, then, is the beginning of a parallel, at the system level, to the concept of the casework relationship at the individual level. At the core of both lies a deep respect for the autonomy of the treatment target (within socially and ethically acceptable limits), whether it is the individual or the system, and a willingness on the worker's part to make available all his resources for the more effective, rewarding, and socially viable or even useful exercise of that autonomy.

It is important to articulate this system-level view of the casework relationship because the increased and direct focus on the marital and family relationships in multiple-client interviews may have obscured the fact that the worker can hope to affect the system directly only as long as this relationship holds. His permit for entering and staying temporarily within the system is likely to be canceled if he threatens its basic requirements by forming untherapeutic alliances with some participants or pushing his challenges against its malfunctioning aspects too far. It will also be revoked if he disappoints the partners' hopes by not challenging the system enough to offer hope for constructive change or if he assuages the couple's anxiety prematurely or falsely. He is likely to continue as an aid in starting and sustaining change only if he can steer clear of these extremes and can avoid succumbing to the unrealistic myths consciously or unconsciously shared by the family members, while at the same time sensing the realistic possibilities for positive change.

The partners' consent for treatment is never final. It is subject to many stresses, but in joint and family sessions these can be seen and handled in the presence of all. Thus the worker can gauge more promptly and realistically whether his reaction to the threat that precipitated the couple's request for help has been sufficient either to release the coping and healing forces available within the family or to enable the partners to become involved in treatment. Such interviews will also make it easier to detect and handle efforts on the part of some participants to reject the worker, nullify his influence, or involve him in destructive family alignments. Misunderstandings about the worker's role and suspicions about his focus and relationship with the partner or other members are less likely to occur in multiple-client than in individual treatment since the exchanges between worker and clients are directly accessible to all at once.

In addition, discouragement about progress in treatment and

fear of the worker's becoming too important to the individuals or to the maintenance of system gains are eased or made more accessible to handling, since the treatment relationship has been understood by all to be temporary. This transience implies that the worker is hopeful about the family and that their ability to do well without him is as much a prestigious and desirable goal for him professionally as for them personally and as a group. When irrational reactions on his part or theirs interfere with this mutual goal, they are likely to be more evident in the group, to evoke discernible reactions, and therefore to be handled directly.

Simultaneous Enhancement
of the Motivation
of All System Participants for Change

Several factors operating in joint and family sessions tend to enhance the motivation of all participants for beginning treatment and staying with it. Since they experience the worker's optimism together and see him as ready and able to involve himself in an unfamiliar system, their capacity for hope and for risking change is enhanced. They are faced as a group with the opportunity to confront the problems that led them into treatment, to examine their effects, and to pool their resources for tackling them. All this together may revive or awaken their sense of shared purpose and responsibility. A recognition that all are contributing to or affected by the marital difficulty and its ramifications may spur them to join together in an effort at amelioration. In so joining, they may find or rediscover mutual strengths and satisfactions that can be highlighted and reinforced in the presence of all, thus helping further positive spiraling.

As setbacks arise, the fact that all shared in the development of the treatment contract may increase the participants' motivation for adhering to it. A decision may seem the more binding by having been shared and public, and treatment goals more realistic, relevant, and worth striving for because the family members have helped to shape them. Because the mutual and shifting needs of all the participants are constantly being made known, there is also less danger that one participant will develop too far in a direction intolerable to some of the others. As a result, the couple may feel less tempted to withdraw from treatment prematurely.

On the other hand, when both partners have come to feel that the interests of cohesion and of individual welfare are irreconcilable, treatment cannot be aimed chiefly at system modification. In such situations it may instead need to be geared to helping the partners assess the wisdom of separation or divorce or to helping them to implement the dissolution of the marital system with as little avoidable damage to the individual partners and the children as possible. The many values of multiple-client interviews for such purposes and for helping in the formation of a new family system that will accommodate the new circumstances will not be included in the present summary, which focuses exclusively on values of multiple-client sessions for families in which the partners want to preserve the marriage.

Facilitation of Group Recognition
of System Characteristics
and Effects

Because of his knowledge of other family systems, the worker has a perspective that enables him to recognize underlying patterns that the family may take for granted or even fail to realize. As these latent patterns become manifest he can, as appropriate, point them out, question them, and help facilitate their modification. For example, mutual distortions and projections may become evident, or defensive maneuvers, overt and covert family norms and rules, incongruent communication patterns, or dysfunctional family myths and themes may emerge. Destructive alignments and splits, with such related intrafamilial patterns as scapegoating, may also be revealed, as well as restrictive, inappropriate, or unclear role patterns, unrealistic family goals, excessive cohesion or separation, or failures in reciprocity. Finally, individual behavior patterns and their effects on others within the system can be pointed out. Such discoveries may be thrown into relief even more when various interview modalities are being used and participants can be helped to notice how their attitudes and behavior may differ in various social contexts and what this may imply for their relationship with present and absent members and for their feelings about the marriage and family as a whole. With some couples a shared focus on insight into the possible sources of these dysfunctional patterns may be indicated, while others may need to concentrate

99

on joint evolution of the changes necessary if the ill effects of these patterns are to be avoided.

Careful attention to the stress or crisis that precipitated the request for help may reveal, for example, where and why the marital balance broke down. If such stress cannot be bypassed or eliminated, it may be possible for the couple or family to recognize with the worker the basic vulnerabilities existing within their system and the need either to accommodate to or to remedy them. It is at such points that the couple's or family's norms and rules, shaped by their fears about surviving as a unit, may become open to shared recognition and more realistic assessment.

Simultaneous Exposure
of All System Participants
to Worker's Treatment Initiatives

In contrast to the treatment approach in individual interviews, treatment initiatives in joint and family interviews can be directed simultaneously to all system participants and can focus more directly on the modification of the patterns by which their dysfunctional system is being maintained. As the family drama is acted out, the worker can, in word and deed, challenge the system and the patterns of relating shared by the family members, as well as the role of each individual participant in their maintenance. He can point out the unrealistic basis of many of these patterns and their constricting or destructive effects. In the presence of all he can challenge inappropriate family norms, press for their modification, and legitimate, by his stance, the establishment of modified norms.

By what gauge, one might ask, may the worker judge the appropriateness of family norms? Clearly, his personal sense of values may not be a legitimate yardstick; yet the very fact of his challenge implies criteria for judgment. Their source, it is assumed here, lies mainly in the norms of the therapeutic culture of which the worker is a part. Typically, these encompass the inevitability of conflict within the family and the desirability of expressing thoughts and feelings openly, but with a realistic awareness of and a sense of responsibility for the possible effects of that expression. It is essential, if the worker's challenge is to be constructive, that he struggle for thorough clarity about his own hierarchy of values,

100

the extent of its congruence with the family value system and with the norms of the therapeutic culture he represents, and the effects of any differences among the three on the therapeutic situation.

The worker's questioning of the dysfunctional system is in itself a demonstration of his conviction that the family can change and that new approaches need not destroy their cohesion. Since all participants can observe his spontaneous handling of a "variety of feelings, disagreements, and conflicts" that would be unavailable in individual interviews (33, p. 329), the success of his different stance can become evident right in the midst of their deadlocked and repetitious interaction, thus making clear that different ways are also feasible for them. Because the worker resists their pressure for compliance with overt and covert rules of the previously dysfunctional marital or family system, he presses the participants toward change in their relationship to each other, through their new relationship with him (26, p. 137). He shows how the push and pull of their customary incongruities, their collusive or disruptive alliances, their scapegoating or mutual blame may be successfully resisted without lasting loss of affection and esteem and without loss of identity. He evokes, at the same time, new reactions and initiatives among the family members by eliciting the "public behavior" of each (14, p. 10).

Since the family members' reactions to the worker's impact may differ considerably, his influence is likely to enter the system through more than one participant. Thus the marital or family system is opened up to changes from within as well as from the outside, and each participant may become an agent for further system modification. As a result, constructive change is made more likely, provided that these reactions are well utilized for breaching the dysfunctional system and that the multiple points of resistance, which also become directly evident, are adequately dealt with. For this to be possible, the worker needs to remain constantly alert to the realistic requirements of the essential as distinct from the dysfunctional marital and family balance and mindful of opportunities for enabling the partners and others to adapt their mutually changing ways in such a way that the marital and family balance will be kept viable and family cohesion will not be fostered at the expense of individual growth.

If the members can make use of the worker's fresh responses, the family will move toward greater system flexibility and a beginning

101

of positive escalation. If they reject or bypass his responses or initiatives, short of withdrawing from treatment, they force the worker to test for yet other ways of entry or to take a new diagnostic look at what the family may be trying to preserve or protect.

The new attitudes or ways of behaving experienced by the participants in multiple-client sessions may relate to problem-solving, handling of human difference, living through an unfamiliar group experience, expressing and controlling mutual feeling, or sharing recovery from error and failure. Feelings about authority and the couple's use of authority may be influenced by their joint encounter with an outsider who does not wield it for its own sake, but rather to release and encourage the family's constructive powers. As they undergo this shared experience, the couple or family can come to realize that mutual ties may be strengthened and individual growth enhanced if they pay less attention to who makes the rules and more to what the rules are designed to achieve.

Aided by their shared exposure to the worker's perspective as an outsider who has worked with other couples and families and seen the effects of their system, the couple or family members may together come to expand their view of the range of permissible and worthwhile behavior. They can also be helped, through the worker's introduction of the missing elements, to amend some of the excesses and lacks of their own family system. When, for instance, closeness has been carried to extremes within the marriage, the worker can try to arouse more concern about the children, neglected during the couple's intense mutual involvement. With partners who have grown apart and turned to the children for emotional satisfaction, the worker may need to strive for a strengthening of the marital axis so that the children may be freed from overly close involvement with a parent and helped to more healthy relationships within the family and among their peers. When the need for marital distance is great—at least in one partner—the other may be steered toward outside satisfactions that will not disturb the partner but may fill some of the emotional needs left unmet by the spouse.

When the family has evolved a system that inhibits the expression of feelings and thought, the worker may introduce the norm of freer expression. If self-expression and impulsive behavior have been allowed to run rampant, he may demonstrate within the multiple-client situation some or all of the full range of possible controls. When a false image of total harmony has been enforced, he will uphold the inevitability of conflict and the need to cope with it openly. When the partners or family members have each been hugging their isolated suffering, he will stress their inescapable mutuality. Thus joint and family interviews serve not only to bring submerged conflicts into the open but also to teach ways of controlling or even resolving them.

Change may also be initiated through reinforcement of constructive tendencies already latent or even active within the marital or family system, such as co-operativeness and a joint striving for maturation. The worker can foster communication among the participants, encourage them to tackle feelings and realities immediately at hand, and enlist their efforts as a group in examining their common problems and tasks. He can also help them evaluate the relevance of agency service and take appropriate action. He can, further, encourage them to face and meet reciprocal needs more fully and plan for new satisfactions together.

In joint and family interviews, the worker provides and promotes a safe milieu in which the partners or family members can try, test, and practice new ways. In this setting they can test out for themselves the satisfactions possible through more constructive mutuality or greater individual development and can experiment with new behavior in a setting in which they can get immediate help with any negative repercussions that develop. Thus, system adaptations can be geared to the amounts and kinds of change that are tolerable to the couple or family as a group, and a viable balance can be fostered between the need for personal growth and independence on the one hand and for a family offering anchorage, cohesion, and mutual satisfaction on the other.

When basic changes seem impossible or inadvisable, joint or family interviews can still become a living experience in increasing the elasticity of the marital or family system. When one partner, for instance, dominates excessively and the other submits excessively, with resultant loss of self-esteem and coping capacity, the partners may be helped to work out a less extreme balance right in the sessions, with the dominant partner allowing somewhat more room for his spouse and the spouse using the opportunity to share more in the expression of feelings and thoughts and in the making of decisions. Facilitation of such a shift may help to some extent to heal the intrapsychic split represented by the choice of so opposite a partner (19, p. 9).

Promotion of Group Consideration and Action Regarding Relationship of the System to the Larger Environment

Unlike individual sessions, joint and family interviews can directly clarify for worker and family alike in what ways the members may concur or be at loggerheads regarding their relationship to the world beyond the family and that world's role, if any, in precipitating, increasing, or alleviating their problems. The existence, absence, quality, and relevance of job resources and health, educational, religious, and recreational facilities; the impact of political, financial, and military forces; and the network of relatives, friends, and community groups all have a profound effect on the family and may be affected by it in varying degrees. The multiple-client session, by helping all participants to clarify the role of such forces, groups, and institutions in their family difficulties and to learn new ways of using outside help, can enable them to become active rather than passive or goal-directed rather than merely defensive or explosive in reaction to these wider networks and systems. By increasing their realistic awareness of their capacities and limitations as a family, on the one hand, and the opportunities and limitations of their environment, on the other, the worker in joint or family sessions can help the participants jointly to weigh and then to act on the necessities of the moment. This may involve the development of shared approaches for more effective handling of some environmental issue, modifying some aspect of the environment, or coming to terms with its immutability. It may involve the couple or family in deciding to shift from a damaging to a more hopeful environment or from one occupation to another. It may also lead the family to join with others in movements they see as essential for bringing about necessary local or wider social change. Such sessions can also serve as an arena for dealing with the differing repercussions of resulting environmental, marital, and family changes on the participants as individuals and on the couple or family as a group. Any or several of these uses of the joint or multiple sessions may be considered and undertaken in order that therapeutic change within the family system may be realistic in terms of the participants' total life setting and not merely a means of keeping the family from disturbing the social framework.

Facilitation of Early Attention
to Obstacles in the Path
of Needed Change

In addition, joint and family interviews offer a favorable arena for the unmasking of entrenched and often unconsciously shared "survival myths" (22) as equally unrealistic and more destructive in their effects than the dangers they were intended to ward off. Buttressed by the shared experience of newly emerging satisfactions and supports within the family, the interview participants may be helped to remove such roadblocks in the path of change.

Another obstacle to progress may be revealed in multiple-client sessions if contradictory pressures of deeply ambivalent individual and mutual feelings and behavior constantly engage the family's energies in efforts at re-equilibration. In such situations the worker can help the participants to resolve such ambivalences whenever possible and to tolerate those that are unavoidable, thus freeing their powers for realistically essential efforts that might lead to a more constructive modified system.

In situations in which multiple-client sessions reveal that the marital and family difficulties are precipitated by the severe personal problems of one of the marital partners, joint or family sessions may have made clear the spouse's current inability to contribute to or to benefit from them. Individual treatment may then need to be offered to ease these problems. Meanwhile, the other spouse and the children may be seen in separate or family subgroup interviews, in traditional forms of group treatment, or in combinations of some of these, to help them with the difficulties of the transition period. After adequate progress, joint or family sessions may again become useful, not to clear away the major obstacle to change, but to channel and tailor necessary system modifications.

Since the effects of therapeutic errors are more likely to become evident in joint or family than in individual interviews, the worker can more promptly allay the fears of participants if they have been pressed beyond their current tolerance for change or flexibility. He can also counteract the discouragement of those who feel that basic needs or problems are being bypassed. As a result, relapse into the old dysfunctional system or breakup of the family system itself may be forestalled.

When misunderstanding and conflict have been temporarily heightened by treatment, these can also be dealt with by all before these reactions become so entrenched as to hasten system retrogression or breakup. In addition, the worker can point out to the participants the effects of their evasive or resistive maneuvers and the shared satisfactions and system modifications that these endanger. Thus temporary chaos and dislocation due to change can be tackled. Better integration of treatment, greater flexibility of focus, and more effective reinforcement of treatment are also likely to result since the shared sessions directly reveal discrepant rates and directions of movement that can then be handled before they threaten the family's newly emerging patterns.

Provision of Multiple Supports
for Facilitating and Sustaining Change

Used skillfully, joint and family interviews seem to favor not only the initiation of therapeutic change but also the sustainment of such change until constructive modifications in the marital and family system may be consolidated. While differential challenges and learning help loosen the stranglehold of the dysfunctional system, differential supports are also greatly needed to help participants bear the pains and risks of anticipated or actual change. Cohesive forces within the family must be directly reinforced while at the same time room is made for individual growth. Participants' constant exposure to the worker's concern both for the whole family and for the individual members constitutes in itself a basic supportive element for change. It reassures them, implicitly, that he will intervene correctively if change should come to threaten either family cohesion or individual development unduly, thus lending power and hope to the participants' deep wish for both togetherness and separateness.

Since the partners and family members live together between sessions and know that their feelings and behavior during these periods may be brought up for discussion, therapeutic controls from the interviews may be carried into the clients' daily life and thus help to support them through the reverberations of change.

The partners and family members are also bolstered in their

ability to tolerate individual frustration and temporary group instability, since mutual supports within the system can be spotlighted and mobilized. Mutual goals can be kept in clear focus and emerging individual strengths and assets identified, highlighted, and reinforced, together with the family's natural maturational strivings and the rewards of newly evolving family patterns that are more satisfying and more realistically effective than the old. In this light, the dangers whose evasion had previously engaged much of their shared energy may seem less threatening and alternative ways of surviving become clearer. As a result, more realistic and less defensive mutual attitudes may emerge and more energy become available for coping with the outside world. A growing sense of personal liberation, wholeness, competence, and renascent mutual feeling is likely also to sustain change and perhaps even to release new creative powers for family living.

Joint and family interviews offer the participants an opportunity to test and practice their newly evolving ways under circumstances in which they are most likely to be successful and to be noted as such, interviews tailored to individual as well as group needs and resources. As a result, the new ways are less likely to be abandoned in favor of the old system, and their transfer into the clients' daily life is made more feasible. If this is achieved, system modification is more likely to be sustained because participants will have learned that they have not only a need but an ability to develop continued resilience in the face of growth and change.

Improvement of the
Long-Term Preventive Potential
of Casework Intervention

Inasmuch as joint and family interviews may facilitate both the arrest of deterioration and the improvement of the marriage and family as systems, they have vital preventive values for the development of the children and the future of the partners. It may well be that their preventive contribution will prove their most distinctive feature as compared with the contributions of the exclusively individual approach. The new ways of interacting and the new flexibility learned together in the interview add up to a therapeutic atmosphere that the partners and family members can together transfer into their daily situation. The simultaneous experience of the members with the worker, if at all successful, provides them with an approach to authority, pain, anxiety, and conflict that has many mutually corrective elements, especially if the shared responsibility for problem-solving in the office can be carried into daily living.

If modified norms have emerged, some profoundly re-educative and preventive factors may arise from family treatment. Under the impact of such changed norms, parents may in varying degrees become able to develop in their children a more adequate and varied social competence than they themselves brought into the marirage originally, a less rigid approach to new situations, and a greater capacity to manage anxiety, to keep defenses flexible, and to solve problems. To the extent that more environmental supports and resources become available to the family as a result of these changes, the family system will also undergo a further increase in resilience and effectiveness.

Some of these results can also be achieved by treatment limited to an exclusively individual approach. However, under favorable conditions the marital conflict and its ramifications within the family are directly interrupted and modified in joint and family interviews and the integrity of the marriage and of the family as systems directly reinforced. This makes for consolidation of the marital axis and for enhanced opportunities for growth and emancipation for the children. Both these effects contribute immensely to the viability of the family as it passes through its various maturational stages.

As yet these potential advantages of joint and family interviews can be stated only speculatively. Careful comparative analyses and follow-up studies are needed to show whether the gains made in such interviews are really maintained better over a longer period than are the gains from individual treatment, whether and under what conditions they may be achieved with less expenditure of time, and whether they truly confer added skills for functioning in other systems of social relationships.

Requirements of the Worker
in Relating to the System as a Whole

If the worker is to capitalize on the numerous advantages of working with families or couples at the system level, he cannot merely carry over the exclusively dyadic approach of the individual interview. He needs to be able to relate to the couple or family as a group and to foster communication between the clients rather than between himself and the clients as individuals only. Moreover, he has to be constantly alert to the therapeutic implications of his relationship to the marriage and family as systems even when he is for the moment engaged with just one participant in the joint or family session. Unless both his manifest communications and his implicit communications in the interview are congruent with his conscious objective of helping the marriage or family as a whole, his goal of helping all the participants is likely to be frustrated.

In brief, then, the worker's temporary therapeutic participation with the couple or family multiplies his opportunities for direct and constructive intervention in the dysfunctional system. Conversely, it also increases his chances of error and failure. His success in making the special values of the joint and the family interview available to the family will depend largely on his capacity for living through a highly charged group experience, for intervening appropriately and at the optimum time, for coping with the results of his intervention or his failure to intervene, and for perceiving and correcting the effects of therapeutic misjudgment in the system context.

He needs also to recognize the pivotal nature of his role as a buffer, mediator, and bridge between the couple or the family on the one hand and the wider environment with which they are in transaction on the other. Acquainted with the strengths, needs, excesses, and deficiencies characteristic of the particular marital or family system, he can help to enhance the members' self-esteem and competence as a group because he symbolizes at one and the same time both society's concern for their well-being and the legitimacy of family resistance against illegitimate social pressure as, for example, in some cases of marital role reversal. He may also need to teach them as a group to use social resources to compensate for some of the deficiencies in or moderate some of the excesses characteristic of their family system.

The special skills and qualities required of the worker who seeks to use joint and family interviews to approach the family as individuals and as a system will be discussed in more detail elsewhere (46, 47, and Chap. 7).

SUMMARY AND IMPLICATIONS

Reviewing the responses as a whole, it is clear that the respondents welcomed joint and family interviews for their distinctive contribution in enlarging the area of direct therapeutic impact. In the main, they used this approach in combination with individual interviews, but in some instances they reported using it exclusively. They saw these modalities as capable of effecting a prompter and more realistic grasp of the applicability of agency service for a specific couple or family and as enhancing and possibly accelerating treatment owing to the offer of experiences in the joint expression of feelings, the handling of mutually restrictive or damaging attitudes and interactional patterns, and the joint confrontation of the conflict in the interviews, together with safeguards for that expression and opportunity for enhanced mutual respect and self-esteem.

New ways of behaving and interacting were seen to emerge as the anxieties and dissatisfactions aroused or intensified by these experiences were turned into energy for change owing to the spur of renewed hope, a sense of shared responsibility, and the demonstrated feasibility of change. Recognition of that feasibility was seen as emerging for family members as they gained through multiple-client interviews a more realistic appraisal of themselves, of each other, and of their total situation. It was also linked to the worker's refusal to react as if he were a member of the family and to his success in thus showing and evoking different responses and initiatives.

Joint and family sessions were further seen as attenuating certain problems often encountered in exclusively individual treatment. These included lack of co-ordination of movement and goals in treatment, the clients' enjoyment of secondary gains from the one-to-one relationship, and the development of mutual distortions in perception and role functioning for clients and worker. Similarly, certain kinds of families that had often failed to gain from individual contact in the past were thought to be able to benefit from joint or family sessions.

With few exceptions, these respondents saw joint interviews as the multiple-client approach most valuable and appropriate for the treatment of marital difficulties. However, they saw family interviews as playing a vital role in such treatment in that they

110

could serve to make clear or demonstrate the impact of marital conflict on the children and could offer the family the relief of facing openly and together a situation long known but not shared openly. Family sessions were also valued for helping couples to face a marital conflict previously displaced onto children and for handling and easing family tensions resulting from such conflict. Apart from the accomplishment of these specific purposes, the values of family interviewing were described by respondents in terms that did not develop any basic distinction between their assets and those of the joint session. Like the latter, family interviews were seen as accomplishing their goals through offering opportunities to foster freer communication, to diminish mutual projections and provocations, and to clarify and improve role functioning. A chance to focus on behavior that may ease the situation for all, to build on strengths and on the capacity to tackle common tasks and responsibilities, was also seen as an important although not unique contribution of the family session.

The major proportion of total comment regarding the values of joint and family interviewing focused on their use to reveal and handle interactional problems, to provide better integration of the partners' progress, and to promote mutuality. Much less was said about the use of these modalities to control the conflict enough for fruitful confrontation or to develop new behavior and problem-solving in relation to the issues at stake. Perhaps this may be taken as an indication that the workers, at the time of their writing, were still concentrating primarily on those values that allow correction of some of the most acute lacks in individual treatment. They were only beginning to articulate those areas of greatest potential treatment value that are unique for these approaches. As experience with them continues to grow, these positive and unique therapeutic contributions, especially in relation to marital conflict, should become increasingly evident and identifiable.

The final sections of this chapter attempted to explore some potential values of the multiple-client approach and some related issues that had received little attention. A tentative attempt was also made to restate the workers' practice wisdom regarding the values of joint and family interviews in system terms, as far as the author's grasp of their views, relevant literature, and consultants' opinions would allow.

It seems clear from all the materials that caseworkers are struggling to integrate their concern with the individual with their interest in understanding and treating the marital and familial systems as a whole. By bringing not only the individual but also the couple, or even the family, into the treatment arena, they are distributing the burden of change more realistically than before. Yet the wider society that the caseworker as such cannot change may also help or hinder the family's development or improvement. Its impact cannot be overlooked without again misplacing the burden of change exclusively onto the participants in the interview situation. Three configurations, then, need to coexist in the worker's mind as he enters into the marital interaction: the intrapsychic system, the marital and familial systems, and the wider society. It is the tension between their often conflicting demands that operates to create, require, and maintain a flexibility and versatility of therapeutic orientation and intervention that offer great promise for the future.

BIBLIOGRAPHY

Study Group Reports

1. AKRON, OHIO, FAMILY AND CHILDREN'S SERVICE SOCIETY OF SUMMIT COUNTY: *Joint Interviews as a Method of Treatment with Marital Partners Where There Is Hostile Interaction*
Study group participants: Mrs. Martha Van Valen (Leader), John C. Freeman, Christian C. Heim, Ronald Kerkhoff, Mrs. Annette McGunnigal, Margaret Minich, Mary C. Monsour, Rosemary Nagy, Mrs. Emily J. Roth, Mrs. Edith Weigl.

2. CINCINNATI, OHIO, FAMILY SERVICE OF THE CINCINNATI AREA: *The Relationship of Emancipation to Marital Conflict*
Study group participants: Mrs. Pauline Cohen (Leader), Mrs. Margaret B. Ballard, Mildred Bateman, Sarah Benedict, Mrs. Gretchen Bode, Mrs. Madge Cone, Mary Elizabeth Dodson, Ruth L. Lampley, Mrs. Sarah Lusby, Lois Margot Marples, Mrs. Marilou McCreadie, Janet Rae McKee, Mrs. Jean Powers, Mrs. June B. Ruger, Mildred Ryan, Mrs. Frances Wise, Mrs. Roberta Wooten.

3. CINCINNATI, OHIO, JEWISH FAMILY SERVICE BUREAU: *Family Diagnosis and Treatment as Related to Marital Counseling*
Study group participants: Morton R. Startz (Leader), Anne Billinkoff, Miriam H. Dettelbach, Mrs. Paula Edelstein, Mrs. Ruth Goldberg, Rose L. Greenstein, Margarete Hirsch, Helen Lampe, Jacqueline Lancaster, Michael Meyer, Mrs. Miriam O. Smith, Mrs. Bernice Temin, Mrs. Miriam Tsevat, Mrs. Doris Wolfenstein.

General References

4. ACKERMAN, NATHAN W., "The Future of Family Psychotherapy," in Nathan W. Ackerman, Frances L. Beatman, and Sanford N. Sherman (eds.), *Expanding Theory and Practice in Family Therapy*, Family Service Association of America, New York, 1967, pp. 3–16.

5. ———, BEATMAN, FRANCES L., and SHERMAN, SANFORD N. (eds.), *Expanding Theory and Practice in Family Therapy*, Family Service Association of America, New York, 1967.

6. AIKIN, DOROTHY, "A Project on Family Diagnosis and Treatment," in *Social Work Practice, 1963*, Selected Papers of the National Conference on Social Welfare, Columbia University Press, New York, 1963, pp. 3–18.

7. BARDILL, DONALD R., and RYAN, FRANCIS J., *Family Group Casework: A Casework Approach to Family Therapy*, Catholic University of America Press, Washington, D.C., 1964.

8. BATESON, GREGORY, et al., "A Note on the Double Bind—1962," *Family Process*, Vol. II, No. 1 (March 1963), pp. 154–161.

9. BEATMAN, FRANCES L., "Intergenerational Aspects of Family Therapy" in Nathan W. Ackerman, Frances L. Beatman, and Sanford N. Sherman (eds.), *Expanding Theory and Practice in Family Therapy*, Family Service Association of America, New York, 1967, pp. 29–38.

10. BECK, DOROTHY FAHS, "The Dynamics of Group Psychotherapy as Seen by a Sociologist: Part I, the Basic Process, and Part II, Some Puzzling Questions on Leadership, Contextual Relations, and Outcome," *Sociometry*, Vol. XXI, Nos. 2 and 3 (June and September 1958), pp. 98–128 and 180–197.

11. ———, "Marital Conflict: Its Course and Treatment as Seen by Caseworkers," *Social Casework*, Vol. XLVII, No. 4 (April 1966), pp. 211–221.

12. ———, "Variations in Treatment in Relation to Type of Marital Interaction" in Dorothy Fahs Beck (ed.), *The Treatment of Marital Problems*, Family Service Association of America, New York (in preparation).

13. BELL, JOHN E., "Contrasting Approaches in Marital Counseling," *Family Process*, Vol. VI, No. 1 (March 1967), pp. 16–26.

14. ———, "Recent Advances in Family Group Therapy," *Journal of Child Psychology and Psychiatry*, Vol. III, No. 1 (January/March 1962), pp. 1–15.

15. ———, "A Theoretical Position for Family Group Therapy," *Family Process*, Vol. II, No. 1 (March 1963), pp. 1–14.

16. BERTALANFFY, LUDWIG VON, "General System Theory," in N. J. Demerath III and Richard A. Peterson (eds.), *System, Change, and Conflict*, Free Press, New York, 1967, pp. 115–129.

17. BOSZORMENYI-NAGY, IVAN, and FRAMO, JAMES L., eds., *Intensive Family Therapy: Theoretical and Practical Aspects*, Hoeber Medical Division, Harper & Row, New York, 1965.

18. ELLIS, BARBARA GRAY, "Unconscious Collusion in Marital Interaction," *Social Casework*, Vol. XLV, No. 2 (February 1964), pp. 79–85.

19. FAMILY DISCUSSION BUREAU, TAVISTOCK INSTITUTE OF HUMAN RELATIONS, *The Marital Relationship as a Focus for Casework,* Codicote Press, Welwyn, Hertfordshire, England, 1962.

20. FRIEDMAN, ALFRED S., "Family Therapy as Conducted in the Home," *Family Process,* Vol. I, No. 1 (March 1962), pp. 132–140.

21. FROSCHER, HAZEL B., "Intervening in the Conflict," in Dorothy Fahs Beck (ed.), *The Treatment of Marital Problems,* Family Service Association of America, New York (in preparation).

22. GEHRKE, SHIRLEY, and KIRSCHENBAUM, MARTIN, "Survival Patterns in Family Conjoint Therapy," *Family Process,* Vol. VI, No. 1 (March 1967), pp. 67–80.

23. GRALNICK, ALEXANDER, "Family Psychotherapy: General and Specific Considerations," *American Journal of Orthopsychiatry,* Vol. XXXII, No. 3 (April 1962), pp. 515–526.

24. GREENE, BERNARD L., BROADHURST, BETTY P., and LUSTIG, NOEL, "Treatment of Marital Disharmony: The Use of Individual, Concurrent and Conjoint Sessions as a 'Combined Approach,' " in Bernard L. Greene (ed.), *The Psychotherapies of Marital Disharmony,* Free Press, New York, 1965, pp. 135–151.

25. GAP COMMITTEE ON THE FAMILY, *Integration and Conflict in Family Behavior,* Report No. 27, written by Florence R. Kluckhohn and John P. Spiegel, Group for the Advancement of Psychiatry, New York, 1954 (reissued June 1968).

26. HALEY, JAY *Strategies of Psychotherapy,* Grune & Stratton, New York, 1963.

27. HALLOWITZ, DAVID, and CUTTER, ALBERT V., "The Family-Unit Approach in Therapy: Uses, Process, and Dynamics," *Casework Papers, 1961,* from the National Conference on Social Welfare, Family Service Association of America, New York, 1961, pp. 44–57.

28. HELGASON, ARTIE, "Counseling in Relation to Separation and Divorce," in Dorothy Fahs Beck (ed.), *The Treatment of Marital Problems,* Family Service Association of America, New York (in preparation).

29. HESS, ROBERT D., and HANDEL, GERALD, *Family Worlds: A Psychosocial Approach to Family Life,* University of Chicago Press, Chicago, 1959.

30. JOLESCH, MIRIAM, "Casework Treatment of Young Married Couples," *Social Casework,* Vol. XLIII, No. 5 (May 1962), pp. 245–251.

31. KEMPLER, WALTER, "Experiential Family Therapy," *International Journal of Group Psychotherapy,* Vol. XV, No. 1 (January 1965), pp. 57–71.

32. KING, CHARLES H., "Family Therapy with the Deprived Family," *Social Casework,* Vol. XLVIII, No. 4 (April 1967), pp. 203–208.

33. LEADER, ARTHUR L., "The Role of Intervention in Family-Group Treatment," *Social Casework,* Vol. XLV, No. 6 (June 1964), pp. 327–332.

34. LEVINE, RACHEL A., "Treatment in the Home," *Social Work,* Vol. IX, No. 1 (January 1964), pp. 19–28.

35. LIPPITT, RONALD, WATSON, JEANNE, and WESTLEY, BRUCE, *The Dynamics of Planned Change,* Harcourt, Brace and Co., New York, 1958.

36. MACGREGOR, ROBERT, *et al., Multiple Impact Therapy with Families,* McGraw-Hill Book Co., New York, 1964.

37. MINUCHIN, SALVADOR, "Family Structure, Family Language and the Puzzled Therapist," *American Journal of Orthopsychiatry*, Vol. XXXIV, No. 2 (March 1964), pp. 347–348.

38. MITCHELL, CELIA B., "Integrative Therapy of the Family Unit," *Social Casework*, Vol. XLVI, No. 2 (February 1965), pp. 63–69.

39. ———, "The Use of Family Sessions in the Diagnosis and Treatment of Disturbances in Children," *Social Casework*, Vol. XLI, No. 6 (June 1960), pp. 283–290.

40. MURRELL, STANLEY A., and STACHOWIAK, JAMES G., "The Family Group: Development, Structure, and Therapy," *Journal of Marriage and the Family*, Vol. XXVII, No. 1 (February 1965), pp. 13–18.

41. PERLMAN, HELEN HARRIS, "Identity Problems, Role and Casework Treatment," *Social Service Review*, Vol. XXXVII, No. 3 (September 1963), pp. 307–318.

42. ———, "The Role Concept and Social Casework: Some Explorations. I. The 'Social' in Social Casework," *Social Service Review*, Vol. XXXV, No. 4 (December 1961), pp. 370–381.

43. ———, "The Role Concept and Social Casework: Some Explorations. II. What is Social Diagnosis?" *Social Service Review*, Vol. XXXVI, No. 1 (March 1962), pp. 17–31.

44. POLLAK, OTTO, "Disturbed Families and Conjoint Family Counseling," *Child Welfare*, Vol. XLVI, No. 3 (March 1967), pp. 143–149.

45. ———, "Entrance of the Caseworker into Family Interaction," *Social Casework*, Vol. XLV, No. 4 (April 1964), pp. 216–220.

46. RONALL, RUTH E., "The Caseworker's Objective Characteristics and Background as Factors in the Treatment Process," in Dorothy Fahs Beck (ed.), *The Treatment of Marital Problems*, Family Service Association of America, New York (in preparation).

47. ———, "The Caseworker's Personality and Skill as Factors in the Treatment Process," in Dorothy Fahs Beck (ed.), *The Treatment of Marital Problems*, Family Service Association of America, New York (in preparation).

48. SAGER, CLIFFORD J., et al., "Selection and Engagement of Patients in Family Therapy," *American Journal of Orthopsychiatry*, Vol. XXXVIII, No. 4 (July 1968), pp. 715–723.

49. SATIR, VIRGINIA M., *Conjoint Family Therapy: A Guide to Theory and Technique*, Science and Behavior Books, Palo Alto, Calif., 1964.

50. ———, "Conjoint Marital Therapy," in Bernard L. Greene (ed.), *The Psychotherapies of Marital Disharmony*, Free Press, New York, 1965, pp. 121–133.

51. SCHERZ, FRANCES H., "The Crisis of Adolescence in Family Life," *Social Casework*, Vol. XLVIII, No. 4 (April 1967), pp. 209–215.

52. ———, "Exploring the Use of Family Interviews in Diagnosis," *Social Casework*, Vol. XLV, No. 4 (April 1964), pp. 209–215.

53. ———, Multiple-Client Interviewing: Treatment Implications," *Social Casework*, Vol. XLIII, No. 3 (March 1962), pp. 120–125.

54. SHERMAN, SANFORD N., "Joint Interviews in Casework Practice," *Social Work*, Vol. IV, No. 2 (April 1959), pp. 20–28.

55. ———, "The Sociopsychological Character of Family-Group Treatment," *Social Casework*, Vol. XLV, No. 4 (April 1964), pp. 195–201.

56. SMITH, NEILSON F. (ed.), "Family Phenomena, Problems, and Treatment: Some Family Agency Studies" (A Terminal Progress Report on the Project, "Casework on Marital Problems: A National Experiment in Staff Development"), Family Service Association of America, New York, 1968 (mimeographed).

57. THARP, ROLAND G., "Marriage Roles, Child Development and Family Treatment," *American Journal of Orthopsychiatry*, Vol. XXXV, No. 3 (April 1965), pp. 531–538.

58. WATSON, ANDREW S., "The Conjoint Psychotherapy of Marriage Partners," *American Journal of Orthopsychiatry*, Vol. XXXIII, No. 5 (October 1963), pp. 912–922.

59. WEISBERG, MIRIAM, "When Difficulties Relate to Marriage—Techniques in Joint Interviewing," paper given at Biennial Conference, Family Service Association of America, Detroit, Mich., November 11, 1965 (mimeographed).

60. WILTSE, KERMIT T., "The 'Hopeless' Family," *Social Welfare Forum, 1958,* Columbia University Press, New York, 1958, pp. 135–153.

61. WYNNE, LYMAN C., "Some Indications and Contraindications for Exploratory Family Therapy," in Ivan Boszormenyi-Nagy and James L. Framo (eds.), *Intensive Family Therapy: Theoretical and Practical Aspects,* Hoeber Medical Division, Harper & Row, New York, 1965, pp. 289–322.

62. ———, "The Study of Intrafamilial Alignments and Splits in Exploratory Family Therapy," Nathan W. Ackerman, Frances L. Beatman, and Sanford N. Sherman (eds.), *Exploring the Base for Family Therapy*, Papers from the M. Robert Gomberg Memorial Conference, Family Service Association of America, New York, 1961, pp. 95–115.

4

Conditions

Considered Favorable or Unfavorable

to the Use of Joint Interviews

What are the conditions under which the values of multiple-client interviewing are most likely to be realized? Are there any circumstances that would bar the use of such approaches? Is it possible to outline some of the special skills that would make the assets of each operative or would increase practitioners' ability to recognize situations that may call for a shift in modality? Are there any areas of wide agreement or disagreement with respect to workers' views on these issues?

The present chapter will attempt to examine some of these topics in relation to joint sessions, the type of interview discussed in about three-fourths of all the criteria comments volunteered by respondents. Chapter 5 will deal similarly with the conditions relevant to family interviewing, to which about one in five of the criteria responses was devoted. Careful analysis of both sets of responses showed that they could be grouped into five broad categories linking the choice of modality with conditions related to (a) the characteristics of the partners as individuals, (b) the interaction between the partners or family members, (c) the worker-client, worker-couple, or worker-family relationship, (d) worker skills and characteristics, and (e) reality factors and objective characteristics of interview participants. These categories will be discussed in turn, with the focus shifting from favorable to unfavorable conditions within each group.

There is a very real danger, in reporting on some practitioners' criteria for their choice of approach, that opinions that are really in flux and still subject to further experimentation and study may be prematurely codified into rules. This is not intended here. In fact, an original attempt to comb the responses for a possible list of basic requirements necessary for use of multiple-client interviews yielded nothing except the un-enlightening truism that no multiple-client session can be held unless all the necessary participants are available at the same time. What did prove possible was the formulation of various conditions that respondents, on the basis of their daily experience, tentatively considered to be favorable or unfavorable to the use of any particular type of interview.[1] It is in this sense and this sense only that the term *criterion* should be understood in this monograph. It is used to denote a principle providing a tentative basis for discriminating between favorable and unfavorable conditions for the use of a particular interview modality and does not represent the results of documented and tested research.

The flexibility of approach that characterized most of the workers' responses is also needed for interpretation of their criteria comments. Except for those committed to one exclusive mode of interviewing, there was general agreement that no single condition favorable or unfavorable to the use of multiple-client interviews should lead directly to use of a particular type of interview. The choice of modality must depend on a number of interdependent groups of variables, such as the characteristics of the personalities or interactional patterns of the couples or families seeking help, worker attitudes and skills, and considerations of diagnosis and timing. It may be possible at a later stage in the development of

---

[1] Many conditions can be phrased in either positive or negative form with little change of meaning. Usually the placement of a specific condition among those favorable or unfavorable to joint interviewing was determined by the spontaneous wording of most comments on that condition. For instance, willingness to come in together was listed as a circumstance favoring joint interviews, because most of those commenting had seen it in this light. Of course, comments on reluctance about coming in together as an unfavorable condition were included in the counts and discussion as agreeing with the positive criterion since they were merely phrasing it negatively. Exceptions to this organization are found in the presentation of comments on the absence of any wish to share goals (*see* pp. 149–150) and the lack of trust in the worker (p. 156). These are listed with the conditions unfavorable to joint sessions even though respondents mainly wrote on the presence of mutual goals and of trust as desirable. To place them with favorable conditions would have caused the Appendix tabulation (Table 3) to imply, absurdly, that those disagreeing believed partner mutuality and trust of the worker to be conditions unfavorable to joint interviewing.

these approaches to define certain clusters of conditions as basic
minimum requirements that must exist if a given type of interview
is to be used. At this stage, however, it would be premature to
attempt such groupings.

Conditions Related to
the Partners as Individuals

Dramatic illustration of recent changes in casework thinking and
practice is offered by the fact that only about a quarter of all the
responses offering criteria regarding joint interviews were focused
on conditions related to the marital partners as individuals. These
comments were either directly concerned with the partners' ego
functioning, broadly defined, or they were focused on the predominance of intrapersonal concerns as compared with interactional
difficulties (see Appendix Table 3, PART I and PART II, Item B2, respectively). By contrast, 65 percent were concentrated in the area of
marital and familial interaction. Even granting the special interest
in multiple-client approaches on the part of respondents choosing
to answer the two source questions, this is a striking demonstration
of direct concern with interaction, especially considering that individual contact was the norm for marital treatment in family agencies until fairly recently. Although the whole family was always
to be kept in mind even in the days of the exclusively individual
approach, it seems nevertheless reasonable to assume that joint
interviewing has greatly heightened the alertness of caseworkers to
interactional phenomena and that such phenomena have come to
be regarded as increasingly important in the diagnostic and treatment decisions of caseworkers.

The pendulum, however, has not been allowed to swing to an
extreme. In welcoming the new ways, respondents also tended to
uphold the profession's traditional concern with individual needs,
as evidenced by their references to intrapersonal dynamics and
personal needs. No doubt it was this capacity to hold fast to the
concern for the individual, while reaching out into the interpersonal realm at the same time, that steered most of these
respondents toward using a flexible approach, encompassing a variety of modalities, that was mentioned in Chapter 1 of this
monograph.

Individual Characteristics Considered Favorable

Some Self-awareness

Only one individual trait favorable to seeing partners together was identified in the analysis. A small group of responses offered by practitioners thoroughly experienced in all phases of joint interviewing noted self-awareness as a necessary condition for productive use of the joint interview. One of these comments was phrased entirely in individual terms and stressed the need for the partners to develop a clearer picture of their own personality problems before they are seen together. All the others singled out an interactional aspect of self-awareness. They suggested that joint interviews were useful only after each partner had gained a beginning awareness of his own part in the marital conflict. Several stated that the partners may often need to be seen individually at first.

Although most practitioners might agree that some self-awareness is certainly a condition favorable to the use of joint interviews, not all would necessarily see it as a prerequisite. Weisberg, for example, makes clear that couples she has regarded as candidates for treatment primarily through joint interviews had "no recognition of need for help with individual problems. In fact, a lack of capacity and of tolerance for self-examination was apparent in many" (53, p. 11).

Individual Characteristics Considered Unfavorable

Most of the respondents who discussed the individual characteristics of the partners focused on traits unfavorable to the use of joint interviews. Their comments suggested five conditions—all aspects of ego functioning, broadly defined—that might bar use of the modality. Nearly a quarter of these comments concerned fear of exposure. The rest were almost evenly divided among limited capacity to tolerate discomfort, rigidity of defenses, limited capacity to control hostility, and presence of severe pathology.

Limited Capacity of Both Partners
To Tolerate Pain, Pressure, and Criticism

Limitations in the capacity to tolerate pain, pressure, and criticism were seen by a few respondents as a bar to the use of joint

120

interviews.[2] These caseworkers wrote in rather general terms. Some thought it essential for the client to be strong and secure enough to be able to work with the partner in the interview in spite of the inevitable pain. They spoke of using joint interviews when they do not pose a threat to either partner or when the client has "some capacity to tolerate critical interpretation."

On the other hand, there were those who believed joint interviews were indicated precisely when the clients *were* in certain ways vulnerable and insecure. As one of these respondents put it: "Individuals who are too vulnerable to examine personal problems and their relationship to the family problem may be able to use multiple-client interviews to improve their role in parenting or in [being a] husband or wife." Such clients were seen as possessing "egos not strong enough to probe with more intensive treatment." The Akron agency study group agreed with this, stating that they "found that couples with very week egos and characterological difficulties often benefited from joint appointments" (1, p. 7).

Both of these viewpoints clearly grant that some minimal capacity to tolerate pain and pressure is essential for any kind of interview, as it must indeed be for living in the community at all. They differ, however, in the areas of pain that they pinpoint. On the one hand, there is the individual who can bear to speak of both his personal and his marital problems in the partner's presence. Such an attitude offers a favorable condition for joint interviews if the marriage is the current focus of concern. On the other hand, there is the person who cannot cope with the pain of looking at his personal problems, but can work on the marital difficulties provided his partner participates. Some of the respondents referred to the weak egos of such clients as the reason for their fear of individual treatment. However, they did not describe the factors that for this type of partner make the joint interview bearable if it focuses on the marriage rather than on the problems of each individual. To arrive at such a description, it would be necessary to give a clear account of the kinds of ego strength that are needed for productive participation in interviews. Furthermore, it would be necessary to formulate more clearly than is now possible the relationship between individual ego strength or weakness, on the one hand, and the nature

---

[2] Of the seven respondents who wrote on this point, four wrote from extensive experience with joint interviewing for both diagnosis and treatment; the other three had used the method mainly for diagnosis.

of the marital balance, on the other. Further study of these two questions would throw greatly need-d light not only on the elements of personal pathology and m :tual fear, but also on the positive elements in the marital balance that often shield and support the vulnerable individual even in an endangered marriage.

The remaining four groups of conditions unfavorable to th : use of joint interviews might all be described as impediments to the individual client's tolerance of pain, pressure, or criticism. In that sense they define, rather loosely, some of the factors that heighten or lessen the strength of the individual in the face of stress and pain.

Great Rigidity of Defenses [3]

At least some flexibility of individual defenses was seen by some respondents as a prerequisite for the use of joint interviews. All the rest stated their views negatively and spoke of rigid defenses as a contraindication to joint interviews. Some barred joint interviews altogether when they saw the clients' capacity for change and insight as limited and confrontation therefore as serving only as a further defeat and as a reinforcement for defenses. The rest also regarded defensiveness as a contraindication to joint interviews, but perhaps only a temporary one. Thus the use of individual interviews concurrently with joint interviews was proposed for the client who is "unable to move from a fixed point of perception as long as the stimulus for his perception [the spouse] is present with him." Such fixedness was thought typical at some time for all individuals in treatment, as specific areas of sensitivity and pain come to light. The tendency of an individual to "repeatedly deflect away a problem" was also mentioned as a contraindication to joint interviewing.

A different kind of defensiveness was cited by a group who avoided joint interviews when these are being used to resist working out "what needs to be worked out individually." This comment does not deal with the question of whether all problems amenable to help could be worked out in joint interviews, but it is a useful reminder that the interviewing modality is a tool, not an aim, of treatment.

Considering these rather generalized statements on defenses, it is

[3] All but one group of those commenting within this category were thoroughly experienced in joint interviewing for both diagnostic and treatment purposes.

important not to overlook the fact that respondents did not necessarily see all strongly entrenched defenses as a bar to the use of joint interviews. (If they had, they could not have advised the use of such interviews until fairly late in treatment.) On the contrary, a great many workers pointed out the remarkable values of joint interviews for couples and families who distort and project a great deal or displace their problem onto children or in-laws (see p. 66). These observations, together with the burgeoning use of joint interviews with psychotic patients, suggest that the predominance of certain specific defenses may actually serve as an indicator *for* the use of joint interviews rather than as a bar to the approach. Here, it would seem, lies yet another field for further clinical exploration and research.

Particular attention was given to the consideration of defenses in relation to the use of joint interviews by the study group formed by the St. Louis Jewish Family and Children's Service and four other agencies (9). One of their self-imposed tasks was the rating of twenty-two defense mechanisms and personality traits suggested by their research committee as indicators for the use of joint interviews as the primary treatment modality.[4] The ninety-five workers participating in this phase of the study were substantially agreed in citing projection on the part of either spouse as strongly indicating the use of the joint interview.[5] Although these workers found it very difficult to agree on constellations of traits that would offer criteria for the use of joint interviews, a majority of them concurred in the view that joint interviews should be used as the primary approach when the husband's defenses are basically passive and withdrawing while those of the wife are mainly active and aggressive. On the other hand, this group saw a more restricted usefulness for joint interviews than did some of the other respondents in the study. For example, they unanimously regarded reaction formation, aggressive acting out, regression, and identification with the aggressor as defense mechanisms and personality traits presenting strong con-

---

[4] Joint interviews were defined in this study group report as "those in which the worker meets with two or more members of the nuclear family by plan." However, all the criteria but one were based on the worker's perception of the *couple*. For this reason, the criteria offered by this report are discussed in this chapter on joint interviews rather than in that on family interviews.

[5] This was also pointed out by the Akron study group (1) and by many other respondents more fully reported on elsewhere (*see* pp. 66–67). The study group of the Glen Ellyn agency (7) stressed the modification that joint interviews were indicated when both partners project responsibility onto the spouse but have at least "some capacity to listen" to one another.

traindications to the primary use of joint sessions. As for other defense mechanisms and personality traits, there was substantial agreement among this group that detachment, sexual or vicarious acting out, repression, counterphobia, overcompensation, and conversion were also contraindications. The participants' reasons for the ratings were not sought in the study group's questionnaire and are therefore not stated in the group report. Furthermore, their degree of certainty about these contraindications was not spelled out in relation to differences in the amount of reality stress on the couple or in the nature of treatment goals. It is conceivable— and further exploration might prove or disprove the point—that marital treatment in the face of extreme reality stress or severely limited goals might call for the use of joint interviews even in the presence of some of these factors.

Anxiety or Fear
about Exposure to the Partner
or the Partner's Presence

Fear or anxiety about the partner's presence in the interview was cited more than any other individual characteristic as a bar to the use of joint interviews. Surprisingly, all but one of the brief comments within this subcategory came from respondents thoroughly experienced in the use of joint interviews. They did not suggest which ego functions might be especially needed for such interviews but had to be presumed lacking when there was fear or anxiety about the partner's presence. Implied, however, in the general statements about fear of revelation or exposure seemed to be such traits as lack of capacity for coping with hostility and frustration (one's own or the partner's) and difficulty in trusting or in communicating constructively. Thorman, in the Indianapolis Family Service Association study of fifty couples treated by joint interviews as the primary approach (48), brought out one aspect not included among these comments. He stated that "individual interviews were rarely used, but when they were it was for the purpose of overcoming resistance on the part of one marital partner who was finding it difficult to engage in the discussion of their marital conflict in the presence of the other partner" (48, p. 16). The pivotal concept here is "resistance"—a forcible reminder that apprehension about joining with the partner in the interview may

124

be an unfavorable condition for such interviews for the moment, but should be explored by the worker not only for diagnostic reasons, but also in order to be handled and overcome if both parties wish to save the marriage. It should not be forgotten, however, that fear of threat or exposure may also refer to realistic conditions of vindictiveness, physical violence, and the like, in which case they would constitute no ego weakness.

Although a feeling of being threatened and pressured by the presence of the partner was the main point made by these respondents, only one type of stress relating to the partner's presence was singled out for comment. One respondent stated that joint interviews were contraindicated when "there is such ego fragility that exposure of hostile feelings would be devastating to the individual and the family." [6] It is conceivable that many other pressures might be felt. Sexual factors, for instance, might be an important ingredient in a partner's anxiety about the spouse's presence or absence, since sexual anxieties and frustrations must surely play a considerable part in marital difficulties. Crouter, for example, in her discussion of Weisberg's paper on joint interviewing (53, p. 32) cites three cases with severe sexual problems in which individual interviews had only meant fruitless, excited accusations about the partner's abnormality. In this failure Crouter saw an indication for joint interviews and found that "a teaching and management oriented approach that had failed in individual interviews succeeded in joint interviews in lessening the excitement and the anxiety about abnormality." She surmises that joint interviews may also have helped because they removed the topic of sexuality from the "secret" individual interview to the "open" joint interview.

Mention was made at the start of this section of ego functions that may be needed for joint interviews but lacking in situations in which there is fear or anxiety about the partner's presence. It is possible that the ability to discuss sexual problems in the partner's presence requires not only certain qualities in the worker (see pp. 157 ff.) but also certain kinds and degrees of ego capacity from each spouse, especially from those for whom reticence is a cultural norm. Just what these ego capacities are is a matter for further study and description.

[6] *See* p. 126 and pp. 140 ff. for a discussion of the actively hostile client or couple. It is understood, of course, that excessive fear of the partner's hostility implies problems with the individual's own anger.

Little Capacity To Control
Hostility and Aggression

Problems in coping with hostility have already been mentioned as a possible contraindication to the use of joint interviews (p. 125). However, in the previous context the focus was on the individual who could not face hostility from another. Now interest is centered on the individual whose own aggression and hostility are beyond his control for the time being. Both sections deal with the *individual* partner who finds it difficult to cope with hostility. (On pp. 140 ff. will be found a discussion of criteria for joint interviews with *couples* whose *interaction* is characterized by excessive conflict.)

A lack of controls on hostility and aggression was mentioned by a number of respondents as a condition unfavorable to the use of joint sessions. All were experienced in both the diagnostic and therapeutic applications of this type of interview. They barred its use when a partner makes destructive use of his spouse's participation in the interview, when he uses information obtained in joint interviews vindictively, or when one partner cannot control his hostility and aggression and the spouse may be further disillusioned or hurt. A further contraindication cited referred to the one spouse who so devastatingly depreciates the other that the result would be a serious loss of self-esteem by the partner or perhaps his withdrawal from treatment altogether. Another respondent singled out the situation in which there is violent acting out by one of the partners and when "it is unwise to use joint interviews because all you get is a demonstration of their anger and bitterness."

In contrast to this convergence of opinions on hostility as a contraindication to the use of joint interviews, several comments were received from workers who were convinced that joint interviews could be of real value for two types of enraged partners: those who are both unable to express their hostility directly and those who can both use the structure of a formal interview as a method of controlling their anger (see pp. 141–142). The comments cited in the present section dovetail quite satisfactorily with this point of view since they refer only to those individuals who need to build the capacity for responding to such controls and for establishing their own. Vesper and Spearman would not even rule out a combination of joint and individual interviews for partners who behave very destructively or antisocially as long as they both have some ability to relate to the worker and the worker can accept very limited goals and communicate a genuine belief in their capacity to improve (49, p. 583).

Severe Pathology

The respondents who mentioned severe pathology as a contraindication were evenly divided between those who were experienced in the use of joint interviews for diagnosis only and those who had also used them for treatment. All saw such pathology as a definite bar to the use of joint interviews, not merely as an unfavorable condition.[7] They were joined in their conviction by the Akron study group (1). This unanimity is of particular interest because of the extensive literature to the contrary (23, 52, *et al.*).

Nowhere is the ego likely to be more fragile than in the psychotic patient. Yet it is precisely with this group that a great deal of joint and family interviewing has recently been attempted. This does not invalidate the concern of the respondents who would avoid such practice, because they were all working in family agency settings, whereas the work with psychotics in multiple-client interviews has taken place in psychiatric settings and usually has involved psychiatrists as therapists. What is most important in the context of this monograph is the possible conclusion that ego strength alone may not be a reliable criterion for or against the use of an interview modality, provided a suitable setting and competent staff are available. The balances within the marriage and larger family must also be taken into account. Some authorities, such as Scherz,[8] see the ego defects outweighed as a criterion for choice of approach by the couple's wish to stay married and their willingness to come in for treatment. Vesper and Spearman, on the other hand, bar casework treatment of any kind if both partners are significantly impaired in reality-testing (49, p. 584).

CONDITIONS RELATED TO
THE PARTNERS' INTERACTION

The category of interactional characteristics attracted not only the largest proportion of criteria comment but also by far the greatest

---

[7] However, several mentioned the usefulness of joint interviews with highly suspicious partners, as reported elsewhere (*see* p. 82).

[8] Private communication to the author, October 8, 1965.

number of disagreements. It should therefore be viewed as an area of concentrated interest, controversy, and ferment in the thinking and practice of caseworkers.

Characteristics of the Interaction Considered Favorable

Five groups of conditions related to the partners' interaction emerged from the responses as offering favorable ground for the use of joint interviews. They included willingness to come in together, presence of communication problems, increase in constructive mutuality, preponderance of interactional problems, and past use of individual interviews for attacks on the partner.

Willingness To Come in Together

The couple's wish to come in together proved to be the subcategory attracting the most comment within this major topic. In fact, over a sixth of all comments on criteria for the use of joint interviews stressed this indicator. This is hardly surprising since the couple's attitudes toward the marriage and toward working on the marital problem, and their ability to share some goals, are all reflected in some measure in their wish to be interviewed either jointly or separately.

A little less than a third of those commenting on a couple's attitudes about coming in together saw joint interviews as definitely contraindicated, at least for the time being, in situations in which the partners were adamantly set against such interviews or even reluctant to engage in one. Most of these respondents used such general terms as "unmotivated," unready," or "resistive" or saw the partners as anxious and threatened by the prospect of the experience.[9]

Greater specificity about the possible characteristics of such resistance or anxiety was reflected in the comment that such a couple may have problems with regard to closeness and may be fearful of being trapped or overwhelmed. In that case it was thought important to deal with the resistance before holding a joint session. When one

---

[9] These points recall those made about partners with fear or anxiety regarding the spouse's participation in the interview (*see* pp. 124–125), but differ from the earlier individual focus in that they are phrased in terms of interaction.

partner refuses altogether to come in for treatment, some respondents advised against continuing to attempt a joint interview, but not against attempts to help with the marital problem. In one illustration, a worker experienced in joint interviewing decided to work with the wife alone because the husband stiffly refused "outside interference." This approach enabled the wife to effect through her own progress a "shift in the marital balance which was ultimately more gratifying to both than their previous relationship." [10]

Almost twice as may respondents as spoke of contraindications discussed attitudes that indicated that joint interviews *should* be used. Like their colleagues who had seen resistance as a contraindication to the method, they used a couple's readiness or willingness as a criterion for the caseworker's decision, but they did not intimate the extent to which the worker's readiness for a joint interview might be a factor in such a decision. Some dissident voices were raised, however. One respondent expressed regret about those occasions when she had met the partners' request for a joint interview but in retrospect had found that the timing had been poor. Another interpreted the worker's assent to the demand for a joint session early in contact as initial willingness to be controlled by and to acquiesce in the wishes of the applying spouse.

Clearly there are few exceptions among these respondents to the general position that the choice between joint and individual interviews rests largely on the couple's attitude. Almost all of those discussing criteria *for* the use of joint interviews specifically mentioned that they usually saw partners jointly if the couple requested this. Even those who explained that they routinely offer joint interviews —or at least one joint interview—to couples who come with a marital problem usually added that they held them only if the clients were willing. This was a contrast, as some noted, to past practice in many agencies where individual interviews had been routinely scheduled for each spouse even if the clients inquired whether they could not come in together or bring the children too. However, this situation has been changing profoundly as agencies have become increasingly impressed with the values of joint and family interview-

---

[10] This case illustration is not intended as a statement on the validity of individual interviews for marital counseling. Some practitioners would deny that marital counseling is possible with only one partner and would see this as a process of individual help that may or may not help the marriage. For a full discussion of ways to engage the reluctant partner, *see* the chapter by Haberman in the full project report (26).

ing. As one respondent reported, requests for joint sessions may now be given serious consideration because they are seen as revealing of the clients' attitudes about their problems and their ideas about treatment. Another caseworker went even further in her comment on client preference as a criterion for choice of approach. She saw the presence of services ranging from individual to group treatment as providing a chance for the clients to request the kind of experience they wished: "This may not be the final method of treatment, but it will give valuable clues as to what kind of help the couple want."

An especially interesting experiment in using the criterion of willingness was undertaken by one of the agencies participating in the project. They offered some troubled couples the choice of waiting indefinitely for individual interviews or being seen in regular joint interviews immediately. In their view, this approach enabled them to begin treatment when motivation was at a peak, and also helped the clients to feel that the agency was interested rather than rejecting.

Although *readiness* and *willingness* were the words most used in describing the essential ingredient in the couple's attitude, these terms were not usually elucidated, except in the one instance when a worker spelled out some of the reasons for which couples may refuse individual interviews. No one, strangely enough, enlarged on the reasons why a couple might *want* to be seen together, beyond the implication that some requested joint sessions because they saw their problems as marital. However, the Baltimore study group mentioned the fear of losing control or fear of what the partner might say as two possible reasons for the couple's refusing individual sessions but accepting joint interviews (2). One respondent enlarged on the "valuable clues" mentioned earlier that may be inherent in a couple's request for a specific type of interview. She suggested honoring the request for a joint session and then observing the purpose it serves for them and the way in which they tend to use the worker.

This comment suggests the usefulness of looking for certain highly specific indicators early in the contact, even if the clients do want help jointly: What makes for the couple's willingness to be seen together? Is it their interest in maintaining the marriage? Is it fear of what the partner will say? Is it one partner's wish to show up the "bad" spouse? Is it to prove that nothing can be achieved? Is it to support each other through a new and threatening experience? Is it to control the process? The list can be greatly increased. It clearly suggests that generalized criteria that now enable the worker to decide on an initial joint interview will be supplemented in time by far more specific criteria developed on the basis of diagnostic observations gained from such a session.

Clients, however, are not the only interview participants who may be ready or unready for joint interviews. Obviously the worker's readiness also needs to be placed in the picture, although respondents did not generally attempt this. An initial joint interview will yield valuable clues not only to the couple's ability to carry on joint interviews, but also regarding the worker's capacity to engage in them with that particular pair. What some of the characteristics and skills of the worker need to be, in the view of respondents, will be discussed later (see pp. 157 ff.). Here the point is mentioned merely to emphasize that throughout the worker must be remembered as a variable part of the treatment formula. No "objective" criteria regarding clients can ever be valid if they are not seen in conjunction with the worker's attitudes and skills.

With the exception of the comments on suggesting waiting list priority for couples willing to be seen together, an interesting contrast may be noted between the reluctance of most of the respondents to structure the situation and the position of such writers as Satir (42), Bell (14, 15), and Bardill and Ryan (12). Writing in the context of total family group treatment, these authors hold that it is the worker's role to decide who should be seen together and that it is his conviction and approach that will insure the participation of all these members. This viewpoint was barely represented among the responses, but lack of experience with the use of joint interviews could not have been the reason for this more eclectic stance, since most of the fourteen respondents who barred use of the modality with unwilling couples had extensive experience in all the uses of joint interviewing. They were therefore not likely to have shrunk from this approach for lack of familiarity or confidence. Their hesitation must have been due to reasons they did not specify. Quite possibly these may have included conviction about the clients' right to self-determination and about the special responsibilities of family agencies whose function is affected by the nature of both their client population and their sponsorship. No doubt these and other factors would need to be taken into account and would also be illuminated by some future studies of the comparative usefulness of flexibility and structuring in such situations. Some agencies have tried to steer a middle course between agency demand and couple willingness by acceding to an applicant's initial refusal of a joint session for intake, if it could not be overcome, but pressing for a joint session at the next meeting or as soon as possible thereafter.[11]

Presence of Problems
in Communication [12]

The presence of problems in communication was cited in 14 percent of the criteria references, almost as frequently as the couple's wish as a reason for the use of joint interviews.

At first sight it may seem strange to cite problems in communication as offering conditions favorable to the use of joint interviews. Ease in communication between the partners would obviously be the truly favorable indicator for use of any shared sessions. However, if this highly desirable condition were made a prerequisite for getting help, there might be few candidates indeed for marital treatment. In view of this, it is heartening to note that a total of thirty-eight respondents pointed out a wide range of communication problems that may seem severe and yet inclined these workers to use joint interviews. Nevertheless, it was the issue of communication that revealed the first sharp disagreement reported in this monograph. In fact, the disagreement count was higher for communication than for any other topic on the total criteria list (see Appendix Table 3). Actual comments in this area fall into three groupings: breakdown of communication, impaired communication, and changing communication patterns. Almost a quarter of all those who commented on communication saw a standstill in communication as indicating the use of joint interviews. This opinion no doubt reflects a growing interest on the part of these experienced joint interviewers in overcoming communication barriers by skillfull use of the multiple-client session. However, most of the comments were quite general and included a wide range of situations in which there had been failure in or breakdown of communication. Usually they did not state whether joint interviews were thought suitable as the exclusive, or only as an occasional, method under these conditions.

[11] Private communication from Mrs. Frances Scherz to the author, October 8, 1965.

[12] It should be noted throughout that the workers tended to use the term *communicate* in the sense of verbal communication.

On the whole, the communications dilemma of these couples was not clearly defined by the respondents, although mention was made of partners who lack communication skills but greatly want to understand each other. The remaining comments affirmed a general belief that communication could and should be developed, and reference was made to the fact that the wish for mutual understanding could also be used to show a couple *why* they had failed to communicate effectively. Beyond this, no specific reasons were offered for the hope that casework intervention could lead to improved communication.

In spite of this general vagueness, there was no doubt that an experienced group of caseworkers saw failure in constructive verbal communication between the partners as a possible indicator for the use of joint interviews. This put them into disagreement with a smaller number of respondents, most of whom were also extensively experienced in the diagnostic and therapeutic uses of joint interviews. The latter group generally concurred in the belief that nothing can be accomplished in a joint interview when communication is poor and when it is held "before the clients can talk together." However, a somewhat modified and doubting stand was taken by the respondent who saw partners separately if they seemed unable to express their feelings when together but who was not yet sure that this really facilitated their treatment. A different kind of failure in communicating was highlighted by a comment opposing joint interviews when the partners are extremely verbal—a reminder that the liberal use of words does not always add up to effective communication, as every writer knows.

The Glen Ellyn study group (7) concurred with these dissidents. They asked for real ability on the couple's part to express feelings and to hear each other before undertaking joint interviews. Unlike many project respondents, however, they included openly hostile exchanges as demonstrating such ability, seeing them as the only way in which some partners may know how to communicate even while they may want to learn better ways.

These opposing views put the burden of proof on different sides of the casework exchange. Those who would bar joint interviews for couples who cannot communicate ask that the partners be at least minimally able to express and hear expression of feelings. Those who would use joint interviews when communication has broken down state no specific requirement of the couple, except for the respondent who asked for a wish on the part of both to understand each other better. The second group therefore seems to put the major burden of proof on the worker, at least by implication, while the first asks the couple to bring more to the interview. This is a fascinating cleavage of opinion that may well be clarified by controlled experimentation followed by careful evaluation of process and results.

Impaired but Improvable Ability To Communicate

Nearly another quarter of all the respondents who wrote about impaired communication thought joint interviews appropriate when communication between the partners needed improvement. Their comments encompassed those situations in which communication on a specific subject could be improved and those in which couples were being treated primarily through joint interviews and could still hear each other or work toward the immediate goal of re-establishing communication. An illustration from experience showed the use of joint interviews from intake through treatment for a family who had "a good deal of warmth . . . and basic trust" and when "there still was . . . a fair level of communication . . . although communication of deeper feeling was certainly part of the problem."

Arrival at a Point of Change in Ability to Communicate

The criteria discussed so far have all been expressed in fairly static terms. Additional indicators become evident as the focus shifts toward examination of the changes that may signal the introduction of joint interviews. Thus joint interviews were seen as indicated to bring about communication when treatment becomes mainly educational. Another comment suggested a place for joint interviewing after the passive partner who could not express feelings in a joint interview had been encouraged to do so in separate interviews. At that point the respondent suggested that with the client's permission his ideas might be presented to the spouse in a joint interview. Further positive indicators were seen in those situations in which individual conflicts had eased and the principal problem seemed to be lack of communication or a decrease in communication and in

134

those in which, by contrast, it had been somewhat restored or newly established. Several respondents agreed with this last point and took their cues from "a beginning tendency toward realistic communication" or from the fact that they judged the couple as able to share feelings or concerns they had previously been unable to communicate to each other. As one respondent acknowledged, such criteria as these constitute a great challenge to skill since they depend on the caseworker's gauging "the point at which there is some receptivity on the part of each partner to the other's thoughts and ideas."

Since the essence of casework is communication, it may seem puzzling that most of the references to this topic were nonspecific. It was not possible to identify from the responses the difference between couples whose verbal communication could and could not be improved. Nor was it clear why six of the respondents asked for good communication capacity before using joint interviews while the other thirty-two did not. An implication runs through all this material that negative or hostile communication is more constructive if expressed verbally rather than nonverbally, but this was not actually stated, and the process of expressing anger in words and then being able to cope better with its causes, effects, or both, is not yet fully understood. Some light may well be shed on the whole problem of communication not only by fuller understanding of psychological blocks, but also by further exploration of the mechanics of communication itself, as already foreshadowed in the work of Satir and Weakland (42, 52).

Meanwhile, the issue, as already noted, rests largely with the worker's confidence that he can enable others to communicate because of his own skills in breaking through communication barriers. Just what goes into such an interchange is a matter for further study. Undoubtedly one of the factors involved relates to the worker's ability to gauge when and how far the partners are becoming able to hear each other. The responses suggest that the clues for gauging or helping to create this readiness may include both changes in the individual (modification of internal conflicts) and changes in the marital relationship (decreasing or reawakening communication). The individual's receptivity, in other words, may depend on his experience of and reaction to the complex balance between the conflicts and satisfactions within his marriage. Much further study would be needed to determine whether one could generalize and say that a change in the previously existing ratio of conflicts and satisfactions may indicate the need for a change in type of interview [13] and that the direction of change in approach should depend on whether the immediate goal is enhanced or restored communication or a focus on the individual's intrapsychic problems.

Increase in Constructive Mutuality

Common sense would suggest, as do some of the comments, that the presence of constructive mutuality or some increasing signs of movement toward such a state would favor the use of joint interviews. Some lessening of conflict, some tightening of mutual bonds, an increase in self-control, a lessened need to be destructive, and an awareness of positives in the marriage were all singled out as evidence of such developments and as appropriate reasons for switching from individual to joint interviews. A possible reason for such new control was suggested by the view that joint interviews would be indicated after both partners "have released hostile feelings to the point where they can begin to use themselves more positively."

At the same time, the absence of these favorable conditions and even the presence of stalemate or escalation in the marital conflict were not necessarily seen as barring use of the joint interview. In fact, this approach was urged for evaluation of the interaction in situations in which problems were not being solved or the conflict seemed to be increasing. Such use of joint sessions for diagnostic purposes, then, could lead to a change of direction or focus in treatment while their employment under more favorable conditions would help to consolidate gains already made and would thus provide a means of further growth.

Paradoxically, the joint interview was also recommended for exclusive use precisely with those couples who have long been emotionally distant from each other. For them, it was thought, individual interviews might imply a false promise that the worker could fill the emotional gap left by the partner. This comment suggests that joint interviews for treatment may be strongly indicated for specific reasons even in the absence of contructive mutuality. Thus, the "favorable conditions" under consideration in this monograph

---

[13] This viewpoint seems to be supported, at least to some extent, by those respondents who discussed the use of joint interviews for periodic evaluation, highlighting and consolidating gains, supporting constructive agreement, and testing out a sense of improved mutual feeling (p. 85).

are not, on the whole, to be considered prerequisites for the use of joint interviews. They are mainly signals to alert the practitioner that such interviews might be appropriate. However, the true absence of any mutual goal was cited as a possible contraindication to joint interviewing because this or any other treatment modality would be likely to fail in helping the couple to achieve mutuality under such conditions.

It would be interesting to learn whether joint interviews might prove worthwhile with certain couples even when they seem to lack any real sense of mutual belonging, as may be the case in some forced marriages, for instance. Conceivably, in some such situations their joint facing of this fact might lead them into one of two constructive directions. Either it might free them to realize what the positives were that drew them together and to assess whether these are important enough to them to hold out hope of further mutual growth and happiness, or it might cause them to resolve residual doubts and to decide responsibly to move toward separation or divorce.

Mainly Interactional Concerns

Willingness to come to the agency together, attitudes toward communication, and the extent of constructive mutuality are all specific criteria involving the interaction between the partners. However, a few respondents departed from specifics and instead mentioned the primacy of interactional problems in general as a favorable condition for the use of joint interviews.[14] Speaking in global terms, they advised the use of this approach when either the conflict or the presenting problems seemed centered more on the interaction than on the disturbance of one or both individuals. By far the greater number suggested the primacy of personal problems as a contraindication to the use of joint interviews (see pp. 145 ff.). However, both groups phrased their comments in terms of the *comparative* prepon-

[14] From a strictly logical point of view it is redundant to discuss the preponderance of interactional or intrapersonal concerns as further categories, since in one sense this generalization includes all of the more specific subcategories. However, a considerable number of respondents phrased their replies in these general terms and used the preponderance of either type of concern to pinpoint the need for a specific modality. In order to reflect the workers' own thoughts and phrasing, these generalized comments are therefore grouped together and discussed either in this section or in that on unfavorable conditions, depending on their focus on either interpersonal or intrapsychic problems.

derance of either tendency. This in itself shows that interactional thinking was an important factor even among those who singled out the primacy of intrapersonal problems.

It is important to emphasize, in this context, that there can be no assurance that any problem is primarily intrapsychic or primarily interactional. There are only problems seen by a given worker, client, or clients to be primarily of one kind or another. A worker committed to an exclusively individual approach may not recognize interactional problems as primary at any time. Another may recognize them as such in a given situation, but may feel better equipped to work with his client through individual interviews. Thus even the caseworker's or the client's view of what is primary may not automatically lead to choice of a modality, and even that choice may be deceptive. A practitioner may, for example, hold a joint interview but use it to give individual attention alternately to each of the partners, never concentrating on or handling interaction at all. Furthermore, the worker's orientation and his consequent views regarding goals of treatment are likely to have a deep influence on the type of interactional factors that he will see as allowing or barring the use of joint interviews. Thus, the St. Louis study group (9, p. 8) stated a belief that joint interviews were to be considered as the primary treatment modality only in situations in which each of the mates could function at least minimally as a marital partner and parent and adequately as a breadwinner and homemaker. Ideally, they thought, both should be equally strong in role functioning if this approach were to be used. This view was not developed further in the report or offered by any other group. However, its author explained that the emphasis on equal strength in role performance as a criterion for joint interviewing was based on the group's view of role functioning.[15] They saw it as a continuum progressing from inadequate through minimal to adequate performance. Within the range of adequate functioning, one partner might be considerably stronger than the other in some aspects and weaker in others. This suggests that the study group participants regarded a good deal of ego strength on the part of both partners as essential if joint interviews were to be used primarily. All this suggests that the goals generally considered by this study group in their treatment of marital interaction were geared to a level that may not hold true

---

[15] Letter of October 1, 1965, from Margaret Milloy of the Jewish Family and Children's Service, St. Louis, Mo.

for all caseworkers. Quite possibly, such differences in goals may be due to differences in client population as well as in worker orientation. The Indianapolis study, for instance, stands in vivid contrast to the St. Louis group's views. It found (48, p. 17) joint interviews as a primary treatment modality to be highly effective with some inadequate partners functioning at a limited level. Their role performance and decision-making were seen as particularly improved through use of this technique.

Use of Individual Interviews
To Attack the Absent Spouse

One respondent experienced in use of the joint interview for treatment suggested that this should be used "to eliminate the client's use of the individual interview to attack the partner." This point was amplified by another comment recommending joint sessions if the partners have been using material from an individual interview against each other. "It is difficult," it was said, "to deal with this kind of behavior in individual interviews without revealing material which came out in the interview with the other person, but in a joint interview it can be handled." Clearly, conditions of this kind are especially unfavorable to the use of individual interviews and offer a possible opportunity for—but not a guarantee of—movement in joint interviews in which such attitudes and maneuvers can be handled in the presence of the partner. This point of view is buttressed by Haley's insistence on trying joint therapy when individual treatment has failed or when a sudden onset of symptoms coincides with a marital conflict, when the patient's improvement might lead to divorce or else to the eruption of symptoms in the spouse (27).

Characteristics of the Interaction Considered Unfavorable

The use of joint interviews with partners in intense or open conflict emerged from the responses as one of the areas of greatest controversy and ferment. The practitioners who took part in the project did not see the presence of conflict in itself as a criterion. Instead, they considered the degree and nature of the conflict as offering a basis for differentiating those who could from those who might not be able to benefit from joint interviews. Differences of opinion were great, however, on the implications of various levels of conflict intensity for choice of approach. Among these divergencies of view, the worker's capacity for coping directly with embattled couples was seen as at least as decisive a criterion as the couple's own characteristics and potentialities.

Extreme Mutual Hostility and Destructiveness

The overriding majority of comments on interactional contra-indications to the use of joint interviews referred to very hostile and destructive partners and presented extreme hostility as a condition highly unfavorable to joint interviewing.[16] Only a few, however, spelled out the type of anger they had in mind and whether they saw it as a habitual or transient interactional phenomenon. Among these, an important warning was issued that joint interviews may be unproductive if either partner is basically hostile in his orientation to the other sex. Such a situation was described as likely to make it hard for the caseworker to remain empathically neutral and as equally likely to cause the attacked partner such pain and humiliation that he may withdraw into silence or resist continued contact. The wisdom of using joint interviews was further challenged in situations in which a couple has reached an intense peak of mutual hostility or when one partner sees the other as a "primitive instrument either to give direct punishment or to deny gratification." Presumably these two situations represent, respectively, a temporary interactional difficulty and a deep-seated intrapsychic difficulty. Apart from these more specific points, some respondents confined themselves to generalized opposition to joint interviews if the partners are extremely hostile, destructive, or punitive toward each other or if the situation is too explosive. Others addressed themselves to the effect of the partners' combat on the actual interview. They felt that with some couples, "mutually destructive behavior is too severe to be controlled by the caseworker" and that their constant fighting may make it impossible for the worker to function as a treatment

---

[16] Only one of the twenty comments on this point came from a respondent with only occasional experience with joint interviewing; sixteen were extensively experienced in their use for diagnosis and treatment and three in their diagnostic uses.

person. A further view suggested that couples who show only negative reactions in joint interviews may make use of this approach inadvisable because their behavior precludes "any possibility of exploring each spouse's personal role in the situation."

These comments highlight the burden placed on the worker who finds himself caught between two warring partners and feels unable to control the situation or to act therapeutically. His ability, actual or potential, to cope in the face of such onslaught is as pertinent to the choice of modality as are the clients' capacities. If he can find ways of dealing with the impact on himself of the partners' mutual fury, he may be able to retain interview control and to further treatment of the partners. This requires not only some emotional stamina but also diagnostic alertness to group-level phenomena. One respondent group, even though citing the worker's ineffectiveness in the face of combative couples as a bar to joint interviewing, nevertheless questioned whether "there might not be other techniques for breaking through," in view of their feeling that "this continuation of combat in the interview situation may be a form of resistance and manipulation of the worker by both partners acting as a unit."

This recognition of the possible importance of collusion, which is also supported in the literature (46 *et al.*), acts as a counterweight to the concern, quoted earlier, that the worker may find himself unable to explore individual contributions to the marital problem. At times it may be even more fruitful to explore the shared than the individual contributions of the partners to the perpetuation of their marital difficulties. Seen in this light, great hostility and aggression on the part of the couple can prove to be conditions favorable to the use of joint interviews when the worker's skills permit. It would be interesting to know whether the respondents who counseled against joint interviews for the couple who continue fighting, are not motivated to resolve their conflicts, or derive major gratification from its continuation would see the concept of collusion as a possible tool for opening up the fruitful use of this modality with such couples.

There is an intriguing difference between the approach just mentioned and the view of those respondents who valued joint interviews in work with extremely hostile couples. Of the latter, none had in mind the collusive couple who need to be confronted with their maneuver. Instead, almost all were clearly referring to

141

couples whose anger was great, but not so great that it could not respond to the controlling influence of a third party. In this sense, these respondents were speaking of a different type of couple from that discussed earlier. They were focusing on those capable of using the chance to ventilate hostile or conflicted feelings in a "safe and contained situation." Reference was also made to the need to use joint interviews with couples who have been fearful of expressing hostility and who need "the support and control of the objective person to do so."

Some of the points discussed in this section are reinforced by the evidence cited in Thorman's report of the Indianapolis Family Service Association experiment (48). He found joint interviews especially helpful as the major treatment method with "perfectionist" families (48, p. 7), because they helped, among other things, to alleviate the anxiety of these families about feelings of love and hostility. The report also noted that, on the other hand, caseworkers experienced great difficulties in treating "egocentric" couples. Their volatility, hostility, and extreme narcissism often tempted workers to close the case prematurely or at least to switch from joint to individual interviews, even though Thorman questioned whether comparable difficulties would not be encountered in individual sessions.

One might well wonder why caseworkers would be concerned about "protecting" couples from repeating in the office the behavior they doubtless practice at home. Light is thrown on this issue by those who stated that "the presence of a third person helps to control the nonconstructive flow of hostility and keeps the focus on the meaning of it." Some stressed that joint interviews should be used only "when the worker feels . . . able to structure the interviews . . . in such a way as to protect each partner from destructive attack that would reinforce negative defenses."

These comments highlight the fact that conditions are favorable to the use of joint interviews when they promise some possibility that habitual patterns will be revealed and opportunities offered for dealing effectively with those that are destructive or futile. In this sense, the stress is not on protecting the partners from each other as much as on protecting them from wasting the opportunity for help. Fighting may be nothing new to the couple, but examining the meaning of their hostility may be one way to modify that pattern. Destructive attack may be familiar but, as the phrasing of the comments makes clear, it is not the sharpness of the attack alone that must be weighed. Even more important are diagnostic clues that might suggest whether the attack will lead to opening up the problem or to closing it off even further as a result of the spouse's defensive reaction. Another factor calling for "protection" during the interview may result from the undercutting of habitual defenses that is likely to develop during treatment and may temporarily leave one or both partners more rather than less vulnerable to attack and pain. This point may have been implicit in some of the comments already quoted. Most useful in this context is Weisberg's differentiation among three forms of fighting: defensive, obstructive, and eroticized (54, p. 4). She sees joint interviews as appropriate for couples who are fighting defensively or obstructively. The former may be helped to understand the anxieties probably underlying their stance and relating to closeness to the partner or the worker or to the possible effects of revealing themselves as individuals or as a couple. The latter may need to evaluate, together with the worker, their mutual goals and concepts of help before the eventual modality for continuing treatment is selected, since their obstructionist fighting may express either basically poor motivation for or merely misconceptions about the helping process. Even eroticized fighting, in Weisberg's view, may not automatically rule out the use of joint interviews, depending on the balance of health and pathology in the individuals and in the marriage (54, p. 4).

The Akron study group, which chose partners in hostile interaction as their special topic,[17] singled out two kinds of combativeness as contraindications to joint interviewing. They barred use of the modality when "competition for role or for control is too great a part of the major problem," or when physical violence is close to the surface. The other twelve indicators they offered for or against the use of joint interviews did not refer at all to either the presence or the nature of the hostility between the partners. They related instead to the adequacy of the couple's preparation for joint interviews, their readiness, their attitudes toward the marriage, their capacity for communication, the need for clarifying attitudes and the reality situation, and the extent of pathology.

---

[17] In this report, joint interviews were not seen as the exclusive approach. The Akron agency usually also used individual interviews concurrently, with family interviews added if necessary.

No doubt these criteria are also relevant to noncombative couples, but the need for adequate preparation was stressed as being of particular, even primary, importance in work with hostile couples. The study group participants reported that they offered help in planning the content of, and even the expected conduct in, the interview. Again, then, the worker's capacity for offering such preparation and for facing and handling couples who are furious with each other and may also show great anger toward him becomes a criterion as important as the couple's responsiveness.

Severely Sadomasochistic or Inequitable Interactional Patterns

In addition to the problem of mutual hostility, some thoroughly experienced respondents identified other interactional patterns that may contraindicate the use of joint interviews, at least for a time. They referred to situations in which the partners want "total adaptation" from each other or when one is so dominant that the other is relegated to a completely passive role even in the interview. Similarly, the sadomasochistic constellation was mentioned as one that poses grave problems for the use of joint interviews. When such a relationship is expressed verbally, one respondent stated, the interview may be "used as a major source of negative satisfaction which seems to obscure totally the underlying desire for positive satisfaction." While Scherz (43), for one, shares this point of view, the Akron study group (1) thought that joint interviews *could* be used with such couples if their need for punishment is not too great.

These observations point to indicators that hinge mainly on the degree of interactional deadlock. However, a closer look suggests a factor even more decisive than the degree of difficulty, namely, the extent of openness of the marital system to the worker's intervention. Unlike the earlier comments on interactional problems that had inclined caseworkers to use joint interviews, the responses now being examined concern marital interactional patterns that are so extreme as to preclude the effectiveness of a third agent— the worker—since the presence of both spouses together only evokes the accustomed interchange of negative or inequitable satisfactions. This, then, is the specific difference between the dominant-passive marital patterns described by the St. Louis Jewish Family and

Children's Service study group (9) and those of the couples just discussed. The interactional patterns of the latter appear to be so deeply entrenched that they are seemingly impervious to the worker's intervention in the interaction and therefore appear to contraindicate joint interviews. Yet, again appearances may be deceiving. The worker needs to be alert to the possibility that the behavior of these sadomasochistic and other pairs, like that of overtly hostile partners, may represent a form of resistance to and manipulation of the worker by both partners acting as a unit. Whether such possible patterns of unconscious collusion could be interrupted by being pointed out and handled in joint interviews, or whether they require concurrent or exclusively individual interviews, is a matter for further clinical study and evaluation. Already the work of Weisberg (53) suggests that joint interviews may be indicated and effective with couples manifesting character disorders and character neuroses for just this reason: because they allow handling of the partners' complicity.

Predominance
of Intrapersonal Problems

A substantial group of respondents implied in various ways that a predominance of intrapersonal problems suggests the need for individual interviews. Most of them used highly general terms to indicate the conditions that would bar joint interviews except for such occasional purposes as review or diagnostic clarification. They spoke of situations in which "problems of interaction are subordinate" to the individual pathology of one or both partners. One worker was more specific in barring joint interviews "when the neurosis or character disorder of one individual consistently produces conflict to which other family members are reacting, and the caseworker cannot break into the family 'merry-go-round.' "

Only a few workers were more specific. Some suggested that marital interaction was best dealt with in joint interviews but that the need for temporary use of individual interviews may arise in situations in which transient intrapersonal problems became acute for one or both partners. The illustrations they offered included "blocking" on the part of a spouse, the need to tackle problems besetting one of the partners only, or the necessity for extra help for one spouse during a crisis. Other respondents focused on situations with more lasting obstacles to concentration on the marital interaction. Their comments included the view that joint interviews with extremely narcissistic clients are unwise because they will be used to serve the individual's unhealthy defenses, and because such individuals tend to do poorly in joint or group interviews.

The great difficulties in using joint interviews with narcissistic clients were also acknowledged, as already mentioned, by Thorman's report on the Indianapolis Family Service Association experiment (48), which used the Voiland typology (50). However, this report did not take the position that narcissism is necessarily dealt with any more effectively in individual interviews either, because the presence of extreme narcissism was seen as posing special problems for any type of treatment. In fact, it indicated that some of these problems do yield in the face of confrontation, thus suggesting that joint interviews may be regarded as the most appropriate medium with such families if "competence in interpersonal relationships" is the goal of treatment (48, p. 19).

A comparison of the responses, the literature, and the views of consultants suggests that the issue of intrapersonal difficulties as a possible bar to the use of joint interviews is an area of substantial difference and fluidity of opinion. Certainly respondents did not see all forms of self-absorption as a true contraindication to the use of joint interviews. On the contrary, some caseworkers held that joint sessions are the very tool needed in situations in which "the person is preoccupied with himself and bogged down . . . to the exclusion of the feelings of others." They thought that two such partners "stuck in preoccupation with individual hurt and deprivation" would "not be able to move beyond this to consideration of the problems of the relationship" unless joint interviews were introduced.

It would seem, then, as if respondents saw some kinds of self-preoccupation as being best corrected through the use of joint interviewing, while other conditions, including the lack of an adequate sense of personal identity, were described by some as constituting a genuine, if perhaps temporary, bar to joint sessions. One might perhaps speculate that such immature couples experience an initial focus on the marital relationship as a threat because they feel their still highly insecure sense of individual identity may be jeopardized by the demands for some emotional closeness implicit within that relationship. Thus a few replies from practitioners

146

highly experienced in the approach stated that individual interviews should be offered, at least at first, to couples who are immature or who manifest significantly different levels of maturity, because such individuals have not adequately worked through their emancipation from their family of origin. This viewpoint was shared by the Cincinnati Family Service study group (3), whose members concurred in the view that joint interviews might be called into play only after some individual work with partners in this plight. It was also buttressed by Jolesch as a result of her work with twelve young couples revealing "delayed maturation." She found it necessary to see them individually until a relationship had been established with each partner and enabled each to examine his individual role performance and self-image to some extent. After progress in these areas, she used joint and individual interviews in various combinations (32). One of the respondents, however, hesitated to rule out joint interviews for such couples, even at the beginning. She thought it possible to use them from the start, concurrently with individual sessions designed to work on the emancipation issue.

The issue of maturity is not far removed from those of dependency and self-worth. Acute problems with regard to both were seen by Scherz as possible temporary contraindications to the use of joint interviews.[18] At times, she suggested, a crisis about self-esteem may call for individual treatment until the hurt has been lessened. Similarly, she saw a need for concurrent joint and individual treatment when strong dependency needs are a focal part of the problem. Weisberg, on the other hand, mentions "excessively interdependent" partners (53) as good candidates for joint interviews, because they allow direct handling of their interaction.

Depending, then, on the basis, the degree, and the effects of the intrapersonal problem, it was seen as serving to contraindicate joint interviews or, by contrast, to call for their use so that the marital relationship might be used as a means for healing not only its own wounds but the partners' intrapsychic hurts as well. This emerging view of the interactional and the intrapsychic focus as mutually supplementary promises to become a "third force" bridging the gap between the proponents of exclusively individual interviewing and those who want to use multiple-client sessions for exclusive focus on the interaction and transactions. This approach, reflected in the

---

[18] Views expressed in a letter to the author, dated October 8, 1965.

responses, has also been developed in the psychiatric work of Sager (41) and in the casework approaches of the Midwest Seminar and the Midwestern Regional Committee on Family Diagnosis and Treatment (11, 19). It deserves further thought and study that may well foster the development of a body of concepts and a type of practice that can overcome the false bifurcation between the treatment of the individual seen as a sacrosanct whole and the treatment of partners, families, or groups of individuals seen as interacting units only. It is perhaps time that the healing professions took up the philosophers' habit of challenging false dichotomies. Their workaday material affords them an endlessly rich and subtle basis for such investigations.

Lack of Readiness
To Work Together

Responses related to the couple's lack of readiness for working together were concentrated in three quite different areas. They described joint interviews as inappropriate when partners do not want to maintain the marriage, have no sense of mutual belonging, or have no wish to share goals and work on their marital difficulty.

Lack of desire to maintain the marriage. Almost all respondents who chose to speak on the question of separation or divorce in this context saw the situation as unfavorable to the use of joint interviews if a couple has already decided to separate or if the question of separation has arisen during joint treatment. In such an event, the partners were seen as needing individually "to clarify where they are and what they really want." A dissenting opinion mentioned the possible use of joint interviews with couples who are heading for separation. It urged that at least one joint interview be used, even when separation seems to be the goal, because of the value of the couple's saying so "responsibly in each other's presence." They can then move more freely toward the next phase of whatever help they need and can use.

Several workers did allow for joint interviewing when partners are separating, if the problems to be considered are such practical ones as planning for the children. However, none mentioned joint interviews as a means for discussing the decision itself or for exploring whether separation is really the appropriate goal or represents a questionable step for the couple. Considering the great

148

public concern over the divorce rate, it certainly seems striking that there was not more comment along these lines.

On the whole, then, respondents appeared to look on joint interviews as a symbol of the wish to continue the marriage and on encouragement of joint sessions as a way of possibly conveying the idea that "the worker is encouraging reconciliation." It would be interesting to learn whether this attitude, apparently widespread in family agencies, would necessarily be borne out by workers in other settings, as, for example, in family courts. In any case, it no doubt reflects, as does the paucity of comment on this topic, a stance also noted by Helgason (28), who reports that respondents hesitated even to appear to want to influence a couple's decision about the future of the marriage.

No sense of belonging together. A number of respondents, all well experienced in the use of joint interviewing, concurred in the view that this method was contraindicated when "there is no common meeting ground between the partners." Each one of them described a different aspect of the couple's relationship: their lack of a sense of belonging to each other, the depth of the impasse between them, or the total or almost complete absence of positives without which joint interviews "may be destructive." It would be interesting to know whether these same respondents saw individual interviews as an approach that can overcome such deep emotional isolation or alienation, but no comment was offered on that score.

Supporting the same position by implication, but approaching it from the positive side, some recommended the use of joint interviews for couples who show "a large degree of mutuality about a problem" and "common areas of gratification." One respondent used the phrase "family ego" to describe the ability of such families to "balance or limit their emotional demands against the demands of reality, and so to maintain some kind of family functioning despite the stresses of their conflict." She saw this ability as rooted "in some sense of belonging together despite their difficulties" and regarded joint interviews as appropriate as a regular treatment modality with such families.

No wish for sharing goals or for mutual involvement in working on the marital problems. All but one of the responses received on this issue reflected the conviction that joint interviews are indicated with couples "if they are, at least in part, both ready to work on the marital problem" or on some common practical problem or point of information. One comment stressed that the absence of any mutual goal may render any marital treatment technique ineffective. Mention was also made of the fact that anxiety about the marital relationship might spur the partners to involve themselves in treatment, while another view stressed that the couple needed to "have enough hope in common" for joint interviews to be helpful. Two of the study groups (1, 7) spoke similarly in terms of *degrees* of willingness rather than asking for the total presence or absence of an attitude. One (7) saw the need for at least a minimal wish to work on the marriage if joint interviews were to be used. The other (1, p. 4) cited "some foundation for a mutual commitment" as an indicator for the use of joint interviews. Only one respondent disagreed with the rest. He stressed that the need for joint interviews is all the more evident when there is inadequate involvement of both partners.

It seems unlikely that there is a deep disagreement here since neither group has defined what is adequate involvement or what constitutes minimal readiness to work on the marriage. Possibly it is the factor of hope that links both types of comment. Those partners who cannot become adequately involved in treatment on their own may feel "some hope in common" in the very fact of a joint effort. Again, it appears that the global level of description of this criterion needs to be replaced by more specific indicators before workers can agree on whether a given couple would or would not benefit from joint interviews.

An attempt at such refinement was made by one of the respondent groups in another context. In this instance the group was discussing couples in which "only one partner is really investing in counseling" even though the spouse is "also present." To attempt joint interviews exclusively with such a couple, they felt, "might mean losing the case, because the 'present' partner is blocking the caseworker from getting to the 'available' one. To see the less motivated partner on a less frequent but supportive plan . . . may mean a more effective casework service."

This stress on compatible goals, although only briefly mentioned, is in direct opposition to the views of Gullerud and Harlan (25), who include the lack of such goals as one of their seven criteria *for* the use of four-way interviews. This contrast suggests the possibility that the four-way interview involving two workers may be especially suited for developing common goals with couples lacking them at the start. This approach to the problem might well be explored further.

Feelings or Information
Unacknowledged to Partner

Although a number of highly experienced respondents suggested that a spouse be seen alone if he feels unable to share a specific feeling or a secret in the partner's presence, only one gave an instance of what might be considered a valid secret: an extra-marital affair, abandoned as the marriage improved. The rest suggested a range of reasons for individual interviews: One partner may have a painful personal problem, unrealistic expectations of himself or his partner, or some specific information that cannot at the time be discussed in front of the spouse, at least in his view. A few simply felt that individual personal material in general should be dealt with in individual interviews, even if this only meant expressing disappointment with a previous joint interview. If a client is ready to work on a specific personal problem or wants a chance to look at his own feelings and problems in separate interviews, then, in the view of some of the respondents, joint interviews should be suspended until there are new indications for them.

It seems clear that the extensive past practice and knowledge of social workers along individual lines have led to criteria about the uses of the individual interview that are more refined and specific than is currently possible for multiple-client interviews.

Past Failure To Use
Joint Interviews Productively

The situation that received the least comment was that in which past joint interviews had proved fruitless in general or, more specifically, in terms of constant mutual blame and attack. Such past failure was noted as a signal for a shift to individual interviewing, at least for a time. This position is in line with the thinking that a stalemate with one approach may be solved by introduction of another, provided the alternate is selected carefully rather than merely out of desperation. It does, however, pose a paradox, at least with regard to the mutually blaming couple, since a great many respondents see projection as a mechanism that lends itself especially to handling by means of joint interviews.

CONDITIONS RELATED TO THE RELATIONSHIP BETWEEN THE CLIENT OR COUPLE AND THE WORKER

Since the effectiveness of casework depends in large measure on the relationship between the client or couple and the worker, no interviewing approach can succeed if this basic link is not established. Respondents who commented on this issue focused mainly on aspects of the casework relationship that are of particular importance for multiple-client interviews. They also hold true for the partners being seen in separate interviews with the same worker.

Altogether, about one respondent in eight discussed the implications of the worker-client or worker-couple relationship for the choice of interview modality, mostly citing conditions unfavorable to the use of joint interviews. While the presence of trust in the worker was mentioned as a condition auguring well for this approach, these comments were consolidated with those on lack of trust as an unfavorable condition.[19] As a result, all criteria in this area are phrased as contraindications.

Characteristics Considered Unfavorable

Respondents' comments on unfavorable conditions centered in the main on the client's or couple's inability to share the worker because of special needs or because of rivalry or inability to understand the worker's role. The least discussed subcategory was the one for inability to trust the worker—a problem that would also be of primary importance in individual interviewing. All three of these topics will be weighed in turn.

Inability To Share the Worker,
Owing to Special Needs

Almost half of the comments on the relationship between the couple and the caseworker focused on the couple's inability to

---

[19] For explanation of procedures *see* footnote 1, p. 118.

share the worker as a result of special needs (other than rivalry or failure to understand the worker's role). At first sight they seem to overlap considerably with the statements that described the predominance of intrapersonal problems as a bar to joint interviewing, because such problems as narcissism, dependency, and lack of self-esteem are cited in both categories. However, in the former section the spotlight was on these qualities as intrapsychic problems basic to or provocative of the marital conflict and requiring treatment before the marital interaction can be handled fruitfully. In the present discussion, these characteristics are taken as contraindications to the modality because they interfere with the proper development or use of a relationship between both partners and the worker even though they may not necessarily constitute the basic ingredients of the marital difficulty. Almost all the respondents describing these special needs were extensively experienced in all phases of joint interviewing. Their seeing them as contraindications to use of this approach therefore did not represent a wariness of the modality but rather a move toward more refined criteria. The greater the extent of experience with any given type of interview, the greater the worker's awareness of its uses and also of its limitations.

Over half the comments on special needs were very general and emphasized the advisability of individual interviews when a partner needs additional attention and support, either temporarily or for an extended period. Such an interval, as one group put it, should then enable the partner to use "the support or the gratification from this relationship to move toward better functioning within the marriage." This group further illustrated what they meant by the otherwise undefined concept of "support" by mentioning their efforts to help the partners "understand and accept their own strengths and those of the mate."

The remaining comments focused on the various forms that special needs of one partner might take. Individual interviews were seen as indicated for the more disturbed partner who may need the atmosphere of empathy and the lack of the partner's provocation. The presence of excessive dependency needs was mentioned as another contraindication to joint interviews—a view that would be challenged, among others, by the report from the Indianapolis Family Service Association (48) on their work with "inadequate" families through joint interviews. A further plea was made for

153

initial individual interviews for partners who must first gain more self-confidence and a greater sense of self-worth before they can use joint interviews productively.

Especially interesting in this context is the observation that the more deeply upset spouse may not be the only one requiring separate attention. Individual support may also be needed by the "so-called stronger member of the family if he is to permit and accept expression by the more passive members within a joint or multiple interview." This support given in individual interviews running concurrently with joint sessions was seen as possibly supportive "through the meeting of dependency needs, possibly through ventilation of hostility or long-felt resentment, sometimes simply through an acceptance of this partner's strength with permission *not* to use it as well as to use it."

A few mentioned the extremely narcissistic client in his relationship to the worker. They agreed that his wish for joint interviews should be regarded as a contraindication to their use because such clients often "consider the caseworker as their ally" or because they simply cannot envisage the needs of the other or might use the interview "to manipulate the caseworker and the other partner to their own selfish whims." The latter statement, of course, carried an implication of difficulty for the worker, which will be further explored in the section on worker skills.

To summarize briefly, then, it seems clear that respondents did not see any of these special needs, with the possible exception of narcissism, as conditions permanently unfavorable to the use of joint interviews. They merely pointed to them as calling for individual interviews in certain circumstances so that joint interviews, either concurrently or later on, might be rendered more fruitful.

Inability To Share the Worker,
Owing to Rivalry or
Failure To Understand his Role

The capacity to share the worker is a condition that is especially important for multiple-client interviews and for individual interviews with a worker who also sees the spouse in separate sessions. No wonder, then, that it attracted considerable comment and provoked some sharp divergences of view centering on the importance of rivalrous feelings as a bar to joint interviews.

Rivalry. Roughly two-thirds of those mentioning the prevalence of rivalry or, on a more general level, inability to share the worker saw such an attitude as a contraindication to joint interviews. They could see no value in attempting joint interviews "when a couple is so grossly competitive for the worker that no progress is made," when they are for a period unable to share the worker, when the "personality structure of one partner is such that he cannot tolerate sharing the worker with another," or when one partner tries to "monopolize the relationship by 'tattling' while yet keeping the partner out of the therapy."

The foregoing view is in direct contrast with that of a number of respondents who saw in the joint interview a most suitable instrument for handling rivalrous feelings. They seemed to agree with the group who stated that joint interviews "can be helpful in demonstrating the caseworker's interest in both clients" in situations in which "two clients are rivaling for the attention of the caseworker." All but one of them specifically mentioned that joint interviews were useful in such situations for demonstrating the worker's equal interest in both clients. The remaining respondent went beyond the direct experience of nonpartisanship to comment on the opportunity offered in such situations "to show the client this association with sibling rivalry and to help work out rivalrous feelings."

Since most of those commenting were experienced in the use of joint interviews, it is difficult to assess the reasons for this disagreement. As so often, whenever there is a sharp divergence of opinion, a resolution may well be sought in one of two directions—through refinement of the criteria involved or examination of the impact of the worker's own attitudes. The capacity for sharing the interview with more than one participant is as much a challenge to the worker as to the clients. His own sense of rivalry, of being pressured, and the like needs to be taken into account, as well as that of the couple in treatment.

One point from the literature should also be considered. Hunnicutt (30, p. 3) comments on the fact that many family agency clients fall into the general category of character disorders. "Their parental and sibling experiences may have been such that they are suspicious, distrustful, and rivalrous, feeling that they do not get as much as others, that parents do not have enough love and interest to go around. For them especially, the worker can provide a healing experience with a parent figure who can share love and attention, who can deal comfortably with their distrust and jealousy." Whether such a healing experience could also be provided in the presence of both partners and could speed their learning to give each other attention and support is worth exploring.

Failure to understand the worker's role. The ability to move away from seeing the worker as a referee was also mentioned as a prerequisite for use of the joint interview. While this might be regarded as an ego function related in a general way to the capacity to move beyond a fixed point of perception (see p. 122), the quality of the worker's relationship to the partners and the quality of their response to his particular style and attitude are also crucial in helping the clients to shift this stance. Often some direct explanation of the worker's role in relation to the partners and the conflict between them can facilitate the reorientation needed.

Inability To Trust the Worker

Most of the respondents speaking about trust of the worker or the partner spoke from a conviction that joint interviews should not be used, as one put it, "when one spouse is still overly fearful of revealing behavior to the other spouse and is afraid either of the worker's revealing behavior in the joint interview or of revealing it himself." Only one respondent demurred. She mentioned the possibility that joint interviews might be needed when a client is uncomfortable in a one-to-one interaction with the caseworker and needs the protection of the spouse. This clearly represents a situation in which the client is more fearful of exposure to the worker than to the partner. One reason for such fear is identified by Weisberg (53), namely, the fear of seduction or of stimulation in individual interviews. In such a situation, as the respondent mentioned, the use of joint interviews should perhaps lead to an individual interview—or even a whole period of individual contact.

Of the remaining comments, just one was geared to the couple's readiness to allow the worker into their interaction. All other respondents seemed to feel that an individual contact with the worker is needed before joint interviews are held, in order to create a sense of trust and to establish an adequate relationship with the worker. (On the other hand, a total of twenty respondents spoke, in another context, of starting the contact with joint interviews immediately at intake as long as the partners are willing. Under certain conditions, these respondents even continued joint interviews throughout treatment. Clearly, then, these workers did not necessarily believe that the only way to create trust in the worker is through the one-to-one contact.)

The paucity of comment on this aspect of the casework relationship possibly reflects the difficulty at this stage of understanding just what may be the conditions essential for a constructive triadic therapeutic relationship as distinct from a dyadic one. Pollak, for one (35), has stressed that there can be no real multiple-client session unless the clients allow the worker into their interaction. Whether this depends on trust or hope on the clients' part or on other elements, a fruitful relationship of the worker with a couple can only be maintained as long as both partners find it at least minimally acceptable and effective or minimally promising or rewarding.

CONDITIONS RELATED TO
WORKER SKILLS AND CHARACTERISTICS

Throughout the discussion of individual and interactional characteristics as criteria for the use of joint interviews, it was noted that certain characteristics or skills on the part of the worker seemed to be implied. It is somewhat surprising, therefore, that only 6 percent of the total volume of comment on joint interviews was directly concerned with this topic. In fact, fewer direct comments were offered on worker characteristics as they affect the decision to use or reject joint interviewing than on any other topic except the question of reality factors and objective characteristics.

Those comments that were received concentrated on two major areas: the worker's personal qualities and his specific skills. These two are so closely interwoven in practice as to be almost inseparable except for purposes of analysis. Moreover, one worker's natural qualities might be developed as conscious skills in another.

Worker Skills and Characteristics
Considered Favorable

The caseworker's comfort with the particular type of interview, his perceptiveness and flexibility, his capacity to handle complex transference and countertransference reactions, and his good sense of timing were the main criteria on worker skills and characteristics emerging from the responses on joint interviews. These offerings were evenly divided between conditions that would favor and those that would hamper the use of joint sessions. In addition, some relevant criteria were mentioned by respondents replying in other contexts.[20]

Essential Personal Qualities

A sense of comfort with the technique as well as perceptiveness and alertness, especially to nonverbal forms of communication, were mentioned as essential for the worker who wants to use joint interviews. As one confessed: "I am more familiar with the use of the one-to-one relationship, particularly in the area of feelings and attitudes, and so I am able to facilitate movement by this method." Conversely, there were several who remarked on their increasing comfort with joint interviews and on their increasing confidence in the type of discriminate use that resulted from more practice with them.

One group of caseworkers, in the context of a different question, stressed that joint interviews make especially heavy demands not only on the worker's knowledge and skill, but also on his self-discipline. It would be interesting to know whether this emphasis is the result of discomfort with the modality or may perhaps reflect some situations and problems specific to the joint interview as compared with the individual session. To identify such problems and situations might be one of the tasks for future study or research so that the necessary attitudes might be more consciously developed. Doubtless, being comfortable with the treatment approach chosen and being self-disciplined in its use are as crucial to individual as to joint interviewing. However, the elements necessary for such comfort and discipline in joint sessions are likely to differ from those essential for individual sessions because the former involve the simultaneous presence of both marital partners.

Another worker quality suggested by one of the project's consultants is important for all forms of treatment but may perhaps be conveyed differently in different types of interviews. The point

[20] Results of an intensive analysis of some of these questions are given in the main project report (38, 39).

in question has already been documented by Chance (18) and Ripple (37): A sincere therapeutic optimism on the caseworker's part is a vital force for success in casework treatment. A couple's capacity for involvement in treatment may depend on their seeing a glimpse of hope for their marriage. At times they may be discouraged enough to depend for that glimpse on the caseworker. Whether joint interviews might stir such hope in a special way and whether their impact in this respect would therefore differ from that of optimism conveyed in individual interviews remain to be tested. It is worth speculating that the worker who can feel and convey this therapeutic optimism, even though he is experiencing the partners' destructive interaction in the same interview, may be offering a more powerful impetus for change than the worker in individual sessions because the couple can no longer maintain that he does not really grasp what goes on between them.

Essential Knowledge and Skills

The capacity to handle complex transference and countertransference reactions. The Akron study group (1) suggested that joint appointments might reduce the danger of transference or dilute its effect, but many writers and practitioners would question this and would rather concur with Sager (41) that the transference situation is likely to be different but still highly important and potentially useful. Jolesch, for instance, stresses that the joint session with immature couples tends to develop a transference situation in which the worker represents a parent figure who is strengthening them in their efforts toward emancipation (32).

Consistent efforts to understand and control transference reactions in the joint session were seen as essential both by Sager and by the study group participants. Sager recommends frequent consultation for this purpose whenever joint interviews are used. At the same time, as a respondent pointed out, there can be great value in the heightened countertransference evoked by joint sessions, provided that it is examined and controlled, thus helping to clarify the way in which the couple functions and the effect they may have upon each other. The dangers of uncontrolled countertransference were highlighted by a comment referring to the anxiety that may be provoked as a worker is plunged into a familial conflict similar to that within his own family of origin. Without much skill,

159

self-awareness, and plain fortitude, a caseworker will be unable to cope with such a situation in a therapeutic fashion and may see joint interviews as contraindicated.

Another aspect of countertransference was revealed in a respondent's warning against joint interviews with clients who will manipulate worker and partner to their own whims. This suggests a criterion in relation not only to the client but also to the worker; unless he can recognize and handle manipulative maneuvers, his job in the joint interview or in any interviews with such clients may be frustrated to the point of contraindication. One might add that this holds true also of maneuvers or problems of which the client may not be at all aware. The caseworker must, as a respondent pointed out, be "alert to the use of transference as an obstruction to communication with the other spouse," and such a phenomenon may be a signal to "examine the problem of overidentification on the part of the worker or the degree of deprivation on the part of the client."

Sexual and cultural aspects of the countertransference were not singled out as conditions relevant to the joint interview by any of the respondents, but one of the study group reports (2, p. 10) commented on their crucial role.[21] They stressed the importance of the counselor's understanding of sexuality and ability to discuss it "in a way that will be helpful to the client" and "connect his actions with his feelings" (2, p. 10). This involves, as they point out, "not only . . . accurate anatomical facts but a sensitiveness to the emotions involved and aroused . . . . This requires a counselor discipline born not only of training . . . but a full recognition of his or her own impulses and biases in relation to sex. Only as she has come to terms with her own sex needs and uses and an integration of her own experiences in marriage will she or he be completely free to help another" (2, p. 11).

These points were not made by the study group with the joint interview particularly in mind, but they are cited here on the assumption that they are even more relevant when more than one client—and members of both sexes—face the worker, especially in a society in which discussion of sexual matters in mixed company is not part of the usual pattern. Also relevant here is Blood's examination of some of the specific transference problems that may

[21] The Towson report is one of the group of reports submitted as contributions to the Baltimore Interagency Study Group report (2).

arise if a male counselor sees the wife alone or the partners separately (17). The sexual rivalries, resentments, frustrations, and longings that he discussed in relation to individual sessions are likely to be stirred all the more, and further complicated for all the participants, by the triadic structure of the joint interview. The worker's ability to recognize these reactions in himself and his clients and to deal with them appropriately will be crucial not only to the success of the joint session but probably also to the continuation of the treatment contact.

The comments from Towson also brought out that an understanding of the basic cultural pattern of marriage within the community is essential for the worker because it "sets the ideal standards by which most of the clients judge success or failure." Within these cultural patterns, they stressed, "the counselor must be aware of the differences related to religious and ethnic background" (2, p. 9). Although the study group made no special reference to joint interviewing, these remarks seem especially relevant to this topic and to the issue of countertransference, because the worker facing a couple may be the only representative of his culture and feel outnumbered in the interview (22, 35)—a reaction that would bear watching. To point out the general lack of comment on cultural factors is not to overstate their importance but rather to make room for them as one of many facets of the complex joint interview situation.

Thorman's report on marital treatment suggests further that transference and countertransference reactions may be fairly predictable, given a knowledge of the type of family with whom the caseworker is dealing (48, pp. 9–13). Complications involving these reactions, he indicates, are least likely in the treatment of "perfectionist" families and more likely in work with the "inadequate" and the "egocentric" and "unsocial" families—with especially acute difficulties involving the last two groups. He does not attempt to outline a typology of caseworkers, but if some future inquiry studied this topic further, it might well become possible to arrive at a body of more refined knowledge regarding the mutual impact of worker personality types and family constellations on each other. One of many possible ways of approaching such a study might be to examine the assignment practices that develop naturally in agencies large enough to allow specialization among their workers.

A good sense of timing. A fine sense of timing was stressed as a necessity by a respondent who saw "the immediacy of decisions regarding the timing of . . . intervention in the interaction" as an added difficulty in such sessions. It would have been interesting to know the views of other respondents on this issue: Is there a basic difference between the timing skills needed for joint and individual interviews? Do chances for well-timed intervention in the interaction recur less frequently than chances for well-timed interpretation or demonstration in individual interviews? It remains to be seen whether exceptionally skillful timing is essential for the use of joint interviews or is mainly a factor in speeding such treatment.

An observation of Pollak's may provide a relevant illustration (35, p. 219). He notes that a dramatic improvement in communication may often be followed by stagnation in treatment. This, he believes, can result from the couple's having to face the depth of their problems and the extent of needed change at a time when secondary gratification from the marital difficulty may still be considerable. Obviously, the chances of withdrawal from treatment are high at this point unless the worker can promptly help the partners to recognize and deal with the ambivalence resulting from this clash of motives. Skill in assessing and handling this difficult situation is essential in cases of treatment by individual interviews also. However, the need for appropriate timing in the handling of ambivalent feelings may be even more crucial in the presence of both partners since discouragement in joint interviews may reinforce a sense of despair about the marriage that may be experienced more powerfully when it is shared than when it is suffered fleetingly in individual sessions. At the same time, the partners may react by forming an alliance against the caseworker and be led in the process to rediscover more productive kinds of reciprocity.

Additional Worker Skills Cited
in Response to Other Questions

A variety of further worker skills necessary for joint interviewing were mentioned in different contexts among the wider group of questionnaire replies. Several cited as essential include an ability to focus on interaction and to use the interaction therapeutically from the start. While one respondent stressed the ability to participate in the three-way process, not merely to observe, another gave a cogent illustration of therapeutic participation by urging "skill in promoting interaction which points up the mutuality of a problem." Skidmore supplements this point by asking for casework skill in introducing relevant material without betraying confidences (47).

Other respondents identified further skills and qualities that would enable the worker to be a therapeutic participant in joint interviews. These included the ability to identify positives; the capacity to "universalize marital difficulties in order to reduce guilt, shame, or inferiority feelings as these may interfere with communication in the interviews"; the ability to encourage direct communication between the spouses rather than merely between one or both partners and the worker; and the acumen to gauge when probing should be limited and when the couple needs protection against uncontrolled expressions of their mutual anger or aggressiveness. While several of these skills (as well as an ability to use humor, cited by one lone respondent) are clearly important for individual as well as joint interviewing, the presence of the partner was thought to lend a new dimension with which the worker must be able to cope. A capacity to maintain control of the interview's direction, as indicated, was also seen as essential. This was illustrated not only with reference to control of the couple's excessive anger but also in relation to the worker's ability to be appropriately aggressive, if needed, and to protect the participants against one partner's monopolizing the session. Problems of this kind may call for a capacity to foresee the futility of one course and to choose another. This was highlighted by a respondent group who warned that the worker must be able to help the couple move from superficialities to consideration of deeper problems. Otherwise the momentum is forfeited and "the couple may be lost to treatment." Although reference is occasionally made both by respondents and by authors (43) to the possible acceleration in time and comparative effectiveness of joint as compared with individual interviewing, joint interviews are no miraculous shortcut to success but depend for their outcome on the caseworker's skill in knowing how to use the unique opportunities afforded by the technique.

Worker Skills and Characteristics Considered Unfavorable

In the earlier discussions of extremely rivalrous and hostile partners it was noted how difficult a situation such couples often pose for the caseworker and how practitioners' attitudes may vary regarding the best approaches to use with them. This predicament is reflected in the few comments on worker attitudes that represent conditions unfavorable to the use of joint interviews. Almost all of these focused on the worker's ability to remain neutral or to cope with two sets of demands, defenses, and hostilities at the same time. Only one mentioned the need for comparable skills in situations in which two workers are interviewing a couple together.

Inability To Remain Neutral

All of those commenting on the question of the worker's neutrality, regardless of level of experience, concurred in the view that the worker's capacity in this respect is essential for the use of joint interviews. They felt that joint interviews were contraindicated "if the caseworker feels strongly identified with one spouse" or even "when there is a danger of appearing more identified with one client." None of them mentioned a factor referred to by Skidmore (47) and no doubt taken for granted by many, namely, the need to be able to feel equally comfortable with a male client and a female client.

The respondents tended to describe the worker's ability to refrain from alliances in terms of personal attitude, with only one mention made of the possibility that self-awareness and skills can be developed to overcome this problem at least in some instances. One such comment did suggest, however, that the use of joint interviews from the start tended to minimize the likelihood of developing a preference for one partner.

Difficulty in Coping
with Two Sets of Demands,
Defenses, and Hostilities

Those commenting all concurred in the view that joint interviews were contraindicated in situations in which "it is too difficult to balance the degree of touching on the defenses of the two partners" or when the worker is not able to handle hostility from more than one client at a time. This point was further clarified by the suggestion that the worker should be able "to hear out an argument long enough to have the material to clarify what they do to each other and how each reacts so that he can diagnose and let them also see what happens and how they feel." No mere tolerance of hostility, then, is required of the worker, but rather a capacity to use this tolerance in the service of treatment. All those mentioning this point had extensive experience in joint interviewing. Their statements round out the impression, gained in the section on hostile partners, that the worker's capacity for dealing with the couple's anger is at least as crucial for the choice of interview modality as is the state of mind or stage of conflict of the partners themselves. This capacity for dealing with the onslaught of many conflicting demands and feelings from the partners is also stressed as important in some current articles (10, 24, 33). Some of these same authors (24, p. 139) stress the consequent need for the worker to know how to pay selective attention, how to hold to a focus among the many possible issues raised in each session, and how, at the same time, to use himself with great freedom.

Difference in Levels of Skill among Participating Workers

The sole respondent who mentioned using four-way interviews specified that these were contraindicated when "caseworkers are at different levels of casework development and the less experienced worker may be placed in a disadvantageous position with his own client." This view is also expressed in an article by Gullerud and Harlan (25), who suggest that the two workers be "of equal rank" [22] to keep the atmosphere "informal" and "democratic." However, they stress as most important of all the workers' capacity to communicate with freedom and without competitiveness. They suggest that the two workers be of opposite sexes so that each partner may have a worker of his own sex to help him with problems of sexual identity and role and so that the eventual four-way interviews may allow the two workers to symbolize a parental pair. It would be interesting to learn whether such symbolism is useful or desirable in the view of other practitioners, and how administrators would weigh the expenditure of casework time used in this fashion

---

[22] Ryan and Bardill (40) describe quite a different situation: the use of joint interviews with field instructor and student as a teaching device—clearly a situation involving vastly different levels of skill. Although the aim is teaching, the result may still be therapeutic if the co-interviewers co-operate freely and uncompetitively.

as compared with the "split" case or the joint interview with one worker.

Role of Agency Administration
in Relation to Worker Skills

This discussion would not be complete without reference to an issue never mentioned by the respondents but touched on by several Research Committee members and consultants: The development of any type of skill, including that for joint or multiple interviewing, depends in part on the interest of agency administration in helping workers to learn new skills and use them for service. Even the worker naturally attracted to such methods may hesitate to try them without special training or encouragement. One reluctant to move beyond the one-to-one situation—especially if he was trained exclusively in that tradition—will be unlikely to develop such skills without administrative help and encouragement. Even given such encouragement, not all workers are likely to engage in joint or multiple interviewing as a regular part of their practice. The exent to which these methods will actually be used will depend on many factors, including the degree of specialization practiced by staff members in the agency. Agency needs and requirements and administrative policy, although not mentioned in the responses, cannot be overlooked in a discussion of worker skills as criteria for joint interviews. Worker skills and attitudes are as much subject to change, growth, or regression as those of clients. Administrative orientation and support are crucial factors in such change, and they can play a crucial role in helping workers to develop new skills and to utilize them for service.

CONDITIONS RELATED TO REALITY FACTORS
AND OBJECTIVE CHARACTERISTICS
OF INTERVIEW PARTICIPANTS

Out of all the responses on criteria for or against the use of joint interviews, only five referred to reality factors, and even within this small group one is controversial. No respondents mentioned either objective characteristics or cultural factors as criteria. However, one of the study groups (9) examined objective characteristics as indicators. Since all three topics are dealt with only briefly, they will be examined together.

Reality Conditions as Criteria

Only two reality factors were mentioned as criteria and both were phrased as contraindications. They were as follows:

Need To Discuss
Confidential Material
with One Partner Alone

Private factual material, such as psychological test results on one partner, was regarded by one worker as a definite indication for an individual interview "because there is value to a client's self-esteem in having . . . these results presented to him alone."

Joint interviews were also seen as contraindicated when "the spouse must limit his expectations due to post-shock residue suffered by his partner." Closely related to this is the comment that joint interviews should not be used when "one spouse needs help in understanding and adjusting to difficult and irreversible psychotic behavior in the other spouse." Such a situation may, of course, require long-term treatment, but it is the element of knowledge limited to one partner that calls for its inclusion here. In any case, the word "irreversible" begs to be defined, and there is evidence in the discussions on this topic (see p. 127) that in recent years the presence of severe disturbance has been seen by several practitioners in psychiatric settings as the very signal for the use of joint interviews.

Unavailability of Both Partners
at the Time Feasible for Interviews

Availability of both partners and the worker was stated as an obvious prerequisite for the use of joint interviews.[23] Such availability, as an illustration showed, may be barred if the absent spouse is already in treatment elsewhere, especially if that facility is not open to the partner. Such a situation may be unavoidable, but shows how eligi-

---

[23] John Bell (14, 15) believes that a family usually manages to be available if the worker makes clear that this is essential and that his attention will center on all of them as a unit.

bility requirements and criteria for the best treatment modality may at times war against each other.

Objective Characteristics as Criteria

The study group of the St. Louis Jewish Family and Children's Service (9) took an especially keen interest in objective characteristics as criteria for the use of joint interviews as the primary treatment approach. Almost all the ninety-five participants in this study ruled out the family's income, the husband's occupation, employment of the wife, and the partners' educational levels as significant factors in the decision to use joint interviews primarily. However, one respondent not linked with this study group cited a related factor as highly significant. She advised the use of joint interviews for couples from very deprived backgrounds.

As for the age of the partners and the length of their marriage, three-quarters or more of the study group participants did not consider these important for deciding on the most suitable approach to treatment. Those who disagreed tended to prefer couples under the age of 30 who had been married less than eleven years.

Sixty-three percent of the participants listed the presence or absence of children as not being significant in their choice of the primary treatment modality. Those who disagreed showed a general tendency to favor family interviews when children were between six and twelve years of age.

Respondents took a different position regarding the significance of the success or failure of previous agency contact, the nature of the presenting problem at that time, and the previous use of joint interviews. All these factors were seen as significant by over half of the participants. The report does not specify, however, what effect such knowledge was thought to have on the decision about alternative treatment approaches. Similarly, almost all of the participants rated presence of severe psychosis or neurosis as highly significant to a decision, but did not divulge whether they would see joint interviews as indicated or contraindicated by such a diagnosis.

Cultural Factors as Criteria

In view of the growing interest in cultural factors, it is striking to find them totally omitted from the comments of respondents on criteria. The comments of the Baltimore study group (2), which stressed the need for alertness to cultural factors, did not go into specifics of cultural situations that might favor or bar the use of any particular type of interview. This is clearly an area in which further study might provide helpful clues. Taking as an instance the groups in which the father traditionally reigns supreme, it would be useful to explore whether joint interviews might be indicated for such couples because they would reassure the husband that no secret mutiny would be encouraged or because they might help him to pioneer necessary changes as a voluntary act of leadership. Or would such families be unable to work in joint interviews with the necessary freedom? And what of the matriarchal family, the overprivileged, the severely deprived? A good deal is now being written on the last of these groups (21, 44, *et al.*). No doubt additional studies of these and many other cultural groups will add to the caseworker's skill by alerting him to such additional considerations as customary patterns of family openness or conflict.

Conditions Related to the Family as a Whole

It is curious to note that none of the specific criteria offered regarding joint interviews referred to the family as a whole although many related to the clients as individuals or as a marital pair. However, among the workers who commented on the values of joint interviewing, there were four who suggested that this is useful when the parents see their phobic or "problem" child as the presenting difficulty although the source of the problem may turn out to be essentially marital. This highlights the view that joint interviews can in some situations help those parents who have been unable to face the fact of their marital conflict and have displaced their concerns and reactions onto the children. Such situations may therefore be seen as a variant of the principle that projection can be handled well in joint interviews.

Needless to say, projections of this kind may also call for other varieties of multiple-client interviewing. The following chapter on criteria for the use of family interviews will offer some discussion of this point and will suggest other criteria regarding the family as a whole that may be important as a basis for selecting or rejecting family interviewing as the treatment of choice.

SUMMARY AND CONCLUDING OBSERVATIONS

A review of 275 criteria comments from 205 separate question responses forms the basis for this analysis. Intensive consideration of their total range revealed the possibility of organizing them in a way that would be logical and systematic and would yet allow room for all the fascinating divergences of view presented.This scheme forms the backbone of the chapter's textual organization and is summarized in Appendix Table 3. It grew directly out of the workers' comments, and great pains were taken not to superimpose any preconceived ideas on the material they had offered. Analysis of all these responses together suggested thirty-four criteria for joint interviewing, a list substantially longer than any offered in the literature, at least to the author's knowledge. It also revealed some solid areas of agreement, in spite of the great variety and complexity of the criteria cited, the general fluidity of the field, and the presence of sharp disagreement in certain areas.

Out of these thirty-four conditions relevant to the decision to use joint interviews, only nine received any comments disagreeing with the majority view. Moreover, the total amount of disagreement constituted only about 8 percent of the total number of references to criteria.[24] All except a small minority seemed to agree, at least by implication, that joint interviews have a valid part to play in the diagnosis and treatment of marital problems as long as the use of such interviews is closely geared to the needs of the individual partner and the couple or family as a whole, to the capacity of the worker, and to such considerations as diagnosis and timing. On the other hand, not one respondent suggested that the existence of marital difficulty was in itself a signal for the worker to insist on the use of joint interviews from start to finish, although a few expressed a preference for this approach in the treatment of marital problems. Workers also generally agreed in their view that partners with good ego strengths would make good candidates for the use of joint inter-

[24] The source questions were open-ended and deliberately phrased to encourage respondents to write as spontaneously as possible, to raise the issues they themselves thought most relevant, and to express them in their own words. The amount of consensus among the replies therefore cannot necessarily be taken as an accurate reflection of the true extent of support or dissent with regard to any given position. However, since most of the respondents were thoroughly experienced in the uses of the joint interview, it is significant to note how much agreement did emerge and how clearly areas of disagreement were delineated even in the course of a study mainly geared to probing the range of workers' views.

views—or, presumably, for any other treatment modality. The presence of certain ego defects and rigidities was thought to make joint interviews inadvisable, but even very limited capacity to bear frustration or pain was seen as no bar to joint sessions in situations in which the nature of the marital balance permitted such interviews. Furthermore, the presence of certain other ego weaknesses and the exaggerated use of defenses, such as projection and distortion, were thought to be good reasons for the introduction of that modality.

The couple's willingness to be interviewed together and an at least minimal wish for continuation of the marriage were two further indications in favor of joint interviews on which there was general consensus. The approach was also seen as an appropriate way to plan for the children of separating couples and to enable partners to state their wish for separation responsibly to each other.

When personal pathology was believed to predominate over interactional problems, workers again agreed in their statements that joint interviews should not be used, with the single exception of a reference to the opportunity these offer to rescue a spouse from self-absorption. Throughout, there seemed to be a tendency to regard changes in the marital balance as cues for a possible change in interviewing modality.

In relation to worker skills and characteristics, no respondent disagreed with defining as prerequisites for the use of joint interviews (a) experience and skill in joint interviewing, (b) a capacity to remain neutral and to handle countertransference, and (c) a sense of ease with the co-interviewer (in the case of four-way interviews). No doubt, however, most would also have agreed—if asked—that this approach could be used by the professional novice if he has been provided adequate in-service training and if he receives supervision.

Thornier by far was the problem of hostility, but the apparent disagreements on this topic proved in the end to represent differential indications for the use of different modalities for couples showing different types of hostility. More specifically, joint interviews were seen as appropriate for those who held in their anger and could use a safe place to express it; individual interviews as appropriate for those who were excessively destructive toward each other or whose anger evoked a too extremely defensive reaction or proved too much for the particular worker to handle. Two other forms of prob-

171

lematical interaction—the sadomasochistic and the dominant-passive—were seen as permitting joint interviews as long as the pattern was not so extreme that it precluded the possibility of therapeutic three-way interaction. In fact, the dominant-passive partnership was described by some as especially suitable for the use of joint interviews under such conditions.

Disagreements emerged most sharply among respondents in the areas of marital co-operation, communication, and capacity to share the worker. Some saw the couple's readiness to attack the marital problem or to share goals as essential for the use of joint interviews, while others saw the modality itself as a possible instrument to create such readiness.

Respondents were strongly divided on communication. Some thought good ability to communicate a necessary condition for the use of joint interviews, while others felt that a lack of communication was the signal for introducing them. Similarly, some respondents thought it essential that partners be uncompetitive and not too needful to share the worker in the interview, while others saw the joint interview as a tool to help the partners overcome their rivalry. As for immature couples, there was some hint of disagreement regarding the most appropriate approach, with most respondents leaning toward initial use of individual sessions.

Striking by their comparative or total absence were reality criteria, such as socioeconomic and cultural factors, and criteria relating to sexual problems of the partners.

While examination of the relevant literature introduced several reservations and disagreements into all this material, nothing can obscure the fact that joint interviews are being used with increasing discrimination for an ever wider range of problems. The thinking of leading theoreticians and practitioners in the field [25] shows a clear trend in this direction, provided that such use is based on a sound diagnostic understanding of the family as a whole and a valid assess-

[25] Casework leaders and practitioners extensively experienced in the multiple-client interview approach who read this chapter in draft form and gave individual consultation to the author include Dr. Dorothy Aikin, Mrs. Frances L. Beatman, and Gertrude Einstein of the FSAA Research Committee; Mrs. Gertrude L. Leyendecker of the Community Service Society of New York City; Mrs. Margaret C. Lovell of the Family Service Organization of Worcester; Mrs. Frances H. Scherz of the Jewish Family and Community Service of Chicago; and Mrs. Doris C. Wolfenstein, Jewish Family Service Bureau, Cincinnati, Ohio. At an earlier stage the emerging criteria were also discussed with a number of others, including Dr. Hilda M. Goodwin of the University of Pennsylvania.

ment of the worker's capacities. This type of interview is not seen as being employed exclusively, however. At different points diagnostic understanding may call for the occasional or extended use of other modalities ranging from individual to family interviews and group treatment, either exclusively or in varying combinations with each other or with joint interviews.

The areas of greatest change and ferment are, without a doubt, represented by those criteria on which there was lively disagreement among the respondents. It is probably fair to say that most of the casework leaders consulted in person, and most of those in the literature standing for a flexible approach, are, in every one of these controversies, on the side of thoughtfully expanding the use of multiple-client approaches. While they recognize, as do many of the respondents, certain highly specific contraindications to the use of joint interviews in marital treatment, they place their hope of better service for families on use of joint interviews in most cases. In work in the marital area, they see such interviews as useful for breaking deadlocks in and barriers to constructive interaction. Whenever the respondents are in disagreement, these authorities tend not to ask for productive or peaceful interaction as a requirement for the use of joint interviews. Instead, they express confidence that casework with the couple jointly can be used to demonstrate that mutual silence, fear, anger, struggle for control, and the like can be halted or modified with skilled help.

What is most needed now is refinement of understanding. Practitioners need to know more about the ingredients of ego strength and weakness, about communication principles and techniques, about the possible impact of worker attitudes and demands on the partners' capacity to share goals and to overcome their competitiveness, and about the implications of these factors for choice of treatment modality. They also need a clearer articulation of the implications for choice of approach. Fortunately these are already beginning to emerge, however tentatively, from a system-level view of the marital and family unit and of the worker-couple group. Some attempt will be made at the end of the next chapter to restate, from such a perspective, the conditions relevant for making a choice among joint, family, or individual interviews in the treatment of marital problems under varying circumstances. Eventually these refinements and clarifications may well resolve some of the current sharp divergences of view. They are certainly likely to enrich the whole field of casework knowledge far beyond the immediate problem of interview selection.

BIBLIOGRAPHY

Study Group Reports

1. AKRON, OHIO, FAMILY AND CHILDREN'S SERVICE SOCIETY OF SUMMIT COUNTY, *Joint Interviews as a Method of Treatment with Marital Partners Where There Is Hostile Interaction*
Study group participants: Mrs. Martha Van Valen (Leader), John C. Freeman, Christian C. Heim, Ronald Kerkhoff, Mrs. Annette Mc-Gunnigal, Margaret Minich, Mary C. Monsour, Rosemary Nagy, Mrs. Emily J. Roth, Mrs. Edith Weigl.

2. BALTIMORE, MD., FAMILY AND CHILDREN'S SOCIETY; JEWISH FAMILY AND CHILDREN'S SERVICE; also TOWSON, MD., CHILDREN'S AID AND FAMILY SERVICE SOCIETY: *Practices and Methods of Different Agencies in Handling Marital Relationship Problems*
Family and Children's Society study group participants: Ellen Power, Mrs. Mary Rauh, Albert Tarka.
Jewish Family and Children's Service study group participants: Mrs. Pauline Graff, Mrs. Elsie Seff, Mrs. Anita Weiss.
Children's Aid and Family Service Society study group participant: Mrs. Dorothy Melby.

3. CINCINNATI, OHIO, FAMILY SERVICE OF THE CINCINNATI AREA: *The Relationship of Emancipation to Marital Conflict*
Study group participants: Mrs. Pauline Cohen (Leader and Recorder), Mrs. Margaret B. Ballard, Mildred Bateman, Sarah Benedict, Mrs. Gretchen Bode, Mrs. Madge Cone, Mary Elizabeth Dodson, Ruth L. Lampley, Mrs. Sarah Lusby, Lois Margot Marples, Mrs. Marilou McCreadie, Janet Rae McKee, Mrs. Jean Powers, Mrs. June B. Ruger, Mildred Ryan, Mrs. Frances Wise, Mrs. Roberta Wooten.

4. CINCINNATI, OHIO, JEWISH FAMILY SERVICE BUREAU, *Family Diagnosis and Treatment as Related to Marital Counseling*
Study group participants: Morton R. Startz (Leader), Anne Billinkoff, Miriam H. Dettelbach, Mrs. Paula Edelstein, Mrs. Ruth Goldberg, Rose L. Greenstein, Margarete Hirsch, Helen Lampe, Jacqueline Lancaster, Michael Meyer, Mrs. Miriam O. Smith, Mrs. Bernice Temin, Mrs. Miriam Tsevat, Mrs. Doris Wolfenstein.

5. DETROIT, MICH., JEWISH FAMILY AND CHILDREN'S SERVICE: *Treatment of Couples Where the Man Is Passive and the Woman Dominant*
Study group participants: Rose Kaplan (Leader), Mrs. Rose H. Buchhalter, Mrs. Ida Kost, Mrs. Mildred Littman, Mrs. Hilda Lucas, Mrs. Lillian Weisberg.

6. FLINT, MICH., FAMILY SERVICE AGENCY OF GENESEE COUNTY, *Marital Research Study of Interaction*
Study group participants: Lorraine Lull (Leader), Mrs. Catherine B. Farner, Mrs. Ruth E. Spurlock, Mrs. Fonda M. Williams; Warren Kennison, M.D., Psychiatric Consultant.

7. GLEN ELLYN, ILL., FAMILY SERVICE ASSOCIATION OF DUPAGE COUNTY, *Criteria for Use of Joint Interviews in the Treatment of Marital Couples*
   Study group participants: Margaret Bates (Leader and Recorder), Frances Barry, Mrs. Marjory Casey, Sema Levinson, Mrs. Anne Ross, Juanita Thorn, Margery Whitcomb, Don Yohe; Mrs. Frances Scherz, Jewish Family and Community Service, Chicago, Consultant.

8. PHILADELPHIA, PA., FAMILY SERVICE OF PHILADELPHIA: *Casework Intervention in Marital Conflict Where the Man Is Passive and the Woman Is Dominant*
   Study group participants: Mrs. Mildred Rosenstein (Leader), Mrs. Hilda Cassert, Mrs. Matilda Mick, Mrs. Bernice Mopsik, Jacob Rubin, Evelyn Stiles, Mrs. Lois Taber, Anna Wiggins.

9. ST. LOUIS, MO., JEWISH FAMILY AND CHILDREN'S SERVICE, *Some Criteria Used by Family Caseworkers in Their Decision to Use Joint Interviewing as the Primary Method of Treatment*
   Study group participants: Michael A. Solomon (Leader), Mrs. Winifred Gross, Margaret Milloy, Mrs. Clara Rosenthal, Mrs. Charlotte Schwarzenberger.
   Outside study group participants in second phase of study: 54 staff members from Family and Children's Service of Greater St. Louis; 16 staff members from Family and Children's Bureau of Columbus, Ohio; 8 staff members from Family Service Association of Cleveland; and 20 staff members from Family Service Bureau, United Charities of Chicago.

General References

10. ACKERMAN, NATHAN W., BEATMAN, FRANCES L., and SHERMAN, SANFORD N. (eds.), *Exploring the Base for Family Therapy,* Family Service Association of America, New York, 1961.

11. AIKIN, DOROTHY, "A Project on Family Diagnosis and Treatment," *Social Work Practice, 1963,* Selected Papers of the National Conference on Social Welfare, Columbia University Press, New York, 1963, pp. 3–18.

12. BARDILL, DONALD R., and RYAN, FRANCIS J., *Family Group Casework: A Casework Approach to Family Therapy,* Catholic University of America Press, Washington, D.C., 1964.

13. BEATMAN, FRANCES L., "The Training and Preparation of Workers for Family-Group Treatment," *Social Casework,* Vol. XLV, No. 4 (April 1964), pp. 202–208.

14. BELL, JOHN ELDERKIN, *Family Group Therapy,* Public Health Monograph No. 64, U.S. Government Printing Office, Washington, D.C., 1961.

15. ———, "A Theoretical Position for Family Group Therapy," *Family Process,* Vol. II, No. 1 (March 1963), pp. 1–14.

16. BLANCK, RUBIN, "The Case for Individual Treatment," *Social Casework,* Vol. XLVI, No. 2 (February 1965), pp. 70–74.

17. BLOOD, ROBERT O., JR., "Transference and the Marriage Counselor," *Marriage and Family Living,* Vol. XX, No. 4 (November 1958), pp. 373–378.

Conditions Considered Favorable or Unfavorable: Joint Interviews

18. CHANCE, ERIKA, *Families in Treatment*, Basic Books, New York, 1959.
19. COMMITTEE ON FAMILY DIAGNOSIS AND TREATMENT OF THE MIDWESTERN REGIONAL COMMITTEE OF THE FAMILY SERVICE ASSOCIATION OF AMERICA, *Casebook on Family Diagnosis and Treatment*, Family Service Association of America, New York, 1965.
20. CROUTER, JUNE, "Discussion," in *Second Jackson Memorial Institute*, Family Service Association of Cleveland, Cleveland, Ohio, 1963, pp. 29–36.
21. GEISMAR, LUDWIG L. and LA SORTE, MICHAEL A., *Understanding the Multi-Problem Family*, Association Press, New York, 1964.
22. GIOSEFFI, WILLIAM V., "Culture as an Aspect of the Total Personality," *Social Casework*, Vol. XL, No. 3 (March 1959), pp. 115–119.
23. GRALNICK, ALEXANDER, "Conjoint Family Therapy: Its Role in Rehabilitation of the In-Patient and Family," *Journal of Nervous and Mental Disease*, Vol. CXXXVI, No. 5 (May 1963), pp. 500–506.
24. GREENE, BERNARD L., BROADHURST, BETTY P., and LUSTIG, NOEL, "Treatment of Marital Disharmony: The Use of Individual, Concurrent, and Conjoint Sessions as a 'Combined Approach,' " in Bernard L. Greene (ed.), *The Psychotherapies of Marital Disharmony*, Free Press, New York, 1965, pp. 135–151.
25. GULLERUD, ERNEST N., and HARLAN, VIRGINIA LEE, "Four-Way Joint Interviewing in Marital Counseling," *Social Casework*, Vol. XLIII, No. 10 (December 1962), pp. 532–537.
26. HABERMAN, ELINOR, "Reaching the Reluctant Partner," in Dorothy Fahs Beck (ed.), *The Treatment of Marital Problems*, Family Service Association of America, New York (in preparation).
27. HALEY, JAY, *Strategies of Psychotherapy*, Grune & Stratton, New York, 1963.
28. HELGASON, ARTIE, "Counseling in Relation to Separation and Divorce," in Dorothy Fahs Beck (ed.), *The Treatment of Marital Problems*, Family Service Association of America, New York (in preparation).
29. HOLLIS, FLORENCE, *Casework: A Psychosocial Therapy*, Random House, New York, 1964.
30. HUNNICUTT, HELEN, *Joint Interviewing as a Method of Treatment in Marital Counseling* (unpublished paper).
31. JACKSON, DON D., and WEAKLAND, JOHN H., "Conjoint Family Therapy: Some Considerations on Theory, Technique, and Results," *Psychiatry*, Vol. XXIV, Supplement to No. 2 (May 1961), pp. 30–45.
32. JOLESCH, MIRIAM, "Casework Treatment of Young Married Couples," *Social Casework*, Vol. XLIII, No. 5 (May 1962), pp. 245–251.
33. LEADER, ARTHUR L., "The Role of Intervention in Family-Group Treatment," *Social Casework*, Vol. XLV, No. 6 (June 1964), pp. 327–332.
34. MUDD, EMILY H., and GOODWIN, HILDA M., "Counseling Couples in Conflicted Marriages," in Bernard L. Greene (ed.), *The Psychotherapies of Marital Disharmony*, Free Press, New York, 1965, pp. 27–37.
35. POLLAK, OTTO, "Entrance of the Caseworker into Family Interaction," *Social Casework*, Vol. XLV, No. 4 (April 1964), pp. 216–220.

36. ———, and BRIELAND, DONALD, "The Midwest Seminar on Family Diagnosis and Treatment," *Social Casework*, Vol. XLII, No. 7 (July 1961), pp. 319–324.

37. RIPPLE, LILIAN, ALEXANDER, ERNESTINA, and POLEMIS, BERNICE W., *Motivation, Capacity, and Opportunity: Studies in Casework Theory and Practice*, Social Service Monographs, Second Series, No. 3, University of Chicago Press, Chicago, 1964.

38. RONALL, RUTH E., "The Caseworker's Objective Characteristics and Background as Factors in the Treatment Process," in Dorothy Fahs Beck (ed.), *The Treatment of Marital Problems*, Family Service Association of America, New York (in preparation).

39. ———, "The Caseworker's Personality and Skill as Factors in the Treatment Process," in Dorothy Fahs Beck (ed.), *The Treatment of Marital Problems*, Family Service Association of America, New York (in preparation).

40. RYAN, FRANCIS J., and BARDILL, DONALD R., "Joint Interviewing by Field Instructor and Student," *Social Casework*, Vol. XLV, No. 8 (October 1964), pp. 471–474.

41. SAGER, CLIFFORD J., "The Treatment of Married Couples," in Silvano Arieti (ed.), *American Handbook of Psychiatry*, Vol. III, Basic Books, New York, pp. 213–224.

42. SATIR, VIRGINIA M., *Conjoint Family Therapy: A Guide to Theory and Technique*, Science and Behavior Books, Palo Alto, Calif., 1964.

43. SCHERZ, FRANCES H., "Multiple-Client Interviewing: Treatment Implications," *Social Casework*, Vol. XLIII, No. 3 (March 1962), pp. 120–125.

44. SCHLESINGER, BENJAMIN, *The Multi-Problem Family*, University of Toronto Press, Toronto, Canada, 1963.

45. SHERMAN, SANFORD N., "Joint Interviews in Casework Practice," *Social Work*, Vol. IV, No. 2 (April 1959), pp. 20–28.

46. SHOLTIS, HELEN S., "The Management of Marital Counseling Cases," *Social Casework*, Vol. XLV, No. 2 (February 1964), pp. 71–78.

47. SKIDMORE, REX A., and GARRETT, HULDA VAN STEETER, "The Joint Interview in Marriage Counseling," *Marriage and Family Living*, Vol. XVII, No. 4 (November 1955), pp. 349–354.

48. THORMAN, GEORGE, *Casework Treatment of Marital Disorders—A Clinical Research Approach*, Family Service Association, Indianapolis, Ind., 1964 (mimeographed).

49. VESPER, SUE, and SPEARMAN, FRANKIE W., "Treatment of Marital Conflict Resulting from Severe Personality Disturbance," *Social Casework*, Vol. XLVII, No. 9 (November 1966), pp. 583–589.

50. VOILAND, ALICE L., and ASSOCIATES, *Family Casework Diagnosis*, Columbia University Press, New York, 1962.

51. WATSON, ANDREW S., "The Conjoint Psychotherapy of Marriage Partners," *American Journal of Orthopsychiatry*, Vol. XXXIII, No. 5 (October 1963), pp. 912–922.

52. WEAKLAND, JOHN H., "The Double-Bind Hypothesis of Schizophrenia and Three-Part Interaction," in Don D. Jackson (ed.), *Studies in Schizophrenia*, Basic Books, New York, 1960.

53. WEISBERG, MIRIAM, "A Caseworker's Experience in Joint Interviewing with Marital Partners," in *Second Jackson Memorial Institute,* Family Service Association of Cleveland, Cleveland, Ohio, 1963, pp. 1–24 (mimeographed).

54. ———, "When Difficulties Relate to Marriage—Techniques in Joint Interviewing," Paper presented at the Biennial Conference of the Family Service Association of America, Detroit, Mich., November 11, 1965 (mimeographed).

5

Conditions
Considered Favorable or Unfavorable
to the Use of Family Interviews

If criteria for joint interviewing are still in a state of evolution and experimentation, the issue of family interviews in marital treatment is even more beset by searching and controversy. Chapter 3 showed a substantial body of opinion that family sessions do have value under certain conditions in the treatment of couples in conflict. What, then, might be some of the specific conditions that would rule children or other relatives into or out of interviews made necessary by the marital partners' unhappiness? Are severe psychopathology, excessive mutual anger, or entrenched habits of mutual projection or scapegoating in the family indications for or against the use of family sessions? Does the worker need any special skills or personal qualifications to be able to use family interviews effectively as compared, say, with the skills needed for joint interviewing?

This chapter will be concerned with answering such questions as these on the basis of respondents' comments and related material. Other sources that will be drawn on include the only study group report that focused specifically on family interviews—that from the Jewish Family Service Bureau in Cincinnati (1)—a recently revised report concerning criteria for this approach as evolved by the Jewish Family Service of Philadelphia (19), and insights gained from consultations and from some of the relevant literature. As before, a family interview will be defined in this context as one in which a worker meets with at least three members of the nuclear or extended family, including the couple. Usually the family interviews

179

mentioned by respondents included all members of the nuclear or extended family living under one roof, but there may be fewer participants or more, if grown children or other relatives are included.

The basic organization of this chapter will be the same as that for criteria regarding joint interviews, but discussion will concentrate mainly on conditions thought unique for family interviews. At the chapter's end a tentative effort will be made to use the perspective of a system-level view of the family to restate some of the current thinking on possible criteria for both joint and family interviewing, with the stage of the marital conflict, the phase of treatment, and the family's relationship to the wider society acknowledged as relevant factors in addition to the characteristics of the treatment system participants. It must be stressed, however, that these formulations are not as yet validated by any formal research. They represent an effort to clarify the concepts that seem to underlie some current practice, so that the efficacy of such practice may be tested more precisely. There is much that they leave undefined and unexamined. Family interviewing, for instance, is defined only in terms of the participating membership in the sessions, even though the variety of treatment styles and orientations (see 26) is great and both are bound to influence the selection or rejection of the modality for given purposes.

At the time when the respondents were writing, family interviewing was still in its infancy in all but a few agencies, and the actual number of respondents thoroughly experienced in the use of this approach was quite small, as Appendix Table 1 shows.[1] Furthermore, the project's focus on marital treatment no doubt encouraged many participants to focus their comments on the use of joint interviews. About one out of six commenting on the question of the use of multiple-client interviews for treatment indicated that they would definitely not use family sessions at all in treating marital problems, even though they had found this type of inter-

[1] It consisted of (a) 12 respondents and respondent groups, comprising 29 individuals, who had used this approach extensively for diagnosis and treatment, (b) 14 respondents and respondent groups (31 individuals) who had used it extensively for diagnosis only, and (c) 68 respondents and respondent groups, representing a substantially larger number of individuals, who undertook to comment in spite of only occasional experience. Because of the sparsity of comment from those experienced with the modality, no tabular summary of family interview comments was undertaken to parallel Appendix Table 3 on joint interview criteria.

view helpful in the treatment of parent-child difficulties.[2] For these various reasons, the volume of criteria comments was much smaller for family than for joint interviews. However, in spite of this, a surprisingly large number of categories and subcategories of criteria were covered by these comments. In fact, the range of themes exceeded that for joint interviews. Furthermore, although some respondents had not had sufficient experience with family interviews to comment at all, many with only occasional experience with the approach expressed vivid interest in the use of family sessions, a stance that has since been mirrored in practice trends.

On the whole, all respondents seemed to concur with the view that the theoretical approach of caseworkers should always include the family as a whole.[3] However, they did not believe that a family-centered approach need always lead to the use of techniques actually involving the presence of the whole family during treatment sessions. This is also the view of those leading theoreticians and practitioners (3, 5, 18, 35) who include considerations of diagnosis and timing among their criteria, in contrast to those who make the locus of the problem within the family their sole criterion for choice of approach (6, 11, 12, 14).

Conditions Related to the Characteristics of Family Members as Individuals

Although the past education of many experienced caseworkers is likely to have placed considerable stress on an understanding of individual psychodynamics, it is interesting that only a very small proportion of the criteria comments on family interviewing was based on an assessment of individual rather than interactional characteristics of family members.

Individual Characteristics Considered Favorable

Respondents who looked to clients' individual characteristics for clues saw family interviews, like joint sessions, as indicated when

[2] Since then, their use of family interviews has increased substantially.

[3] For some comment on the intertwining of individual and family difficulties, *see* Aikin (5), Mitchell (33), Jewish Family Service of Philadelphia (19), Sherman (47), and Boszormenyi-Nagy (14).

one or more family members find individual interviews too threatening. Such individuals may be able to participate in treatment when the focus is kept on their role functioning. They may even be helped to use treatment more effectively through the presence of other family members less highly defended than themselves. In particular, children who feel unable to speak freely alone were cited as often becoming able to express themselves if other family members are present to support them and to give implicit or explicit permission for such expression. In their case, apprehension about individual sessions is less likely to spring from ego weakness or even from a poor relationship with the worker than from the natural effect of their dependent status and their view of the importance of family loyalty.

None of the respondents mentioned that family interviews might be indicated because the couple feared joint rather than individual interviews. However, such a situation is likely to arise, especially when the marital problem has been concealed behind or displaced onto problems concerning the children. What the respondents' comments did imply was that family interviews may be indicated when the elements of mutual emotional support are still present or even outweigh those of conflict in the marriage or family. In such situations, the participation of other family members serves to strengthen the individual at his most vulnerable points. When family participation has precisely the opposite effect or cannot touch the suffering individuals, family interviews may be contraindicated, as will be evident in the next section. At the same time, as a respondent pointed out, the family session itself may sometimes be indicated because it can help to bridge the gap between members who need to overcome their mutual distrust.

Individual Characteristics Considered Unfavorable

As in the case of joint interviews, individuals persistently or temporarily dominated by intrapsychic problems or preoccupations were regarded by respondents as poor candidates for family interviewing. Their difficulties were described as including severe personal pathology, extreme narcissism, immaturity or dependency, and strong fear or anxiety about the presence of other family members in the interview. Existence of a problem not shared by the group and a need for special individual support were also cited as contraindications to the use of family interviews. Respondents did not indicate whether the presence of these adverse clues in only one family member would be sufficient to preclude the use of family interviews.

Since each of these categories had also been seen as contraindicating the use of joint interviews, the only criteria that will be discussed here in any detail are the two unique to family interviewing.

Excessive Anxiety or Fear about Exposure to or the Presence of the Others in the Interview

Fear and anxiety about exposure to the partner have already been listed in the chapter on joint interviews as a contraindication to use of multiple-client interviews. However, an important qualification of this principle was added with reference to family interviews. When family interviews seem contraindicated because they threaten to be "devastatingly painful, some individual interviews can bolster up a suffering client so that he can tolerate additional family sessions." This comment, as has been true of so many others in the context of joint interviewing, suggests the more general principle that it is not the sheer presence of such anxiety or fear in the individual client that should determine the worker's course of action. Rather, it is the intensity of the client's emotion and the degree to which this feeling can be modified within the time available.

The worker's anticipation of or response to such possible anxiety or fear may be another factor worth examining. Those agencies pioneering in the use of multiple-client approaches have generally found that both the worker's apprehension and the clients' fears about family sessions need not necessarily bar use of the approach, provided agency policy makes available the training and encouragement necessary for workers to venture into this field (8) and to handle constructively their own and their clients' reluctance, if any.

Severe Psychopathology

Most of the few commenting on severe disturbance saw it as a bar to family sessions, either on a generalized basis or because of a specific area of intense difficulty. Among the contraindications mentioned were inability of a family members to accept negative criticism, due to a severely paranoid state, and inability to tolerate the attacks of other family members in the session, because of individual pathology or such weakness in ego functioning and reality-testing that family sessions would be too threatening. However, some dissenters favored using family sessions when there is evidence of psychosis or prepsychosis or, more specifically, when mental illness of the mother may have caused disorganization and conflict in the home and in all family relationships.

These apparently divergent responses may possibly dovetail on particulars. The same holds true of the literature on this point.[4] Mitchell would exclude from family interviews those individuals whose " 'fixed personal psychopathology . . . prevents participation in the family interviews' " (32, p. 68). Ackerman, who uses family sessions with psychotics, outlines a whole series of specific contraindications. He would not use this type of interview when the rigidity of defenses in some members is so great that their breaching "might induce a psychosis, a psychosomatic crisis or physical assault" (4, p. 112). Furthermore, he would rule it out when one parent suffers from a form of psychosis that "critically dominates and invades the emotional life of the entire family" or is "afflicted with a systematic, progressive paranoid condition or is a true psychopath, incorrigibly criminal or sexually perverse" (3, p. 6). Scherz, in one paper, suggests that family interviews might be contraindicated in the presence of acute depression (42). In another she states that "family unit treatment is the choice and can be worked with in a non-institutional setting" in treatment of "families with a psychotic equilibrium . . . often characterized by double-bind communication that is pervasive and shows a psychotic core with some areas of adaptation" (43, p. 10).

The crux of these statements would seem to lie in the differentiation between fixed patterns and progressive, organized disease, on the one hand, and on the other hand, patterns that allow, for enough adaptation so that some threat to the psychic equilibrium can be accommodated. The implication, to be confirmed, refined,

[4] The ample psychiatric literature on family group treatment of schizophrenics is not quoted here because the project responses were derived from practitioners in family agencies with functions and facilities markedly different from those of the psychiatric setting.

or ruled out by further work, is clear: It is the degree of flexibility, reversibility, and openness remaining, even within the psycho-pathological framework, that constitutes the criterion for or against family interviewing. To this one might further add the tendency of the family interviewing system to maintain, bolster, or hamper the individual in his ability to function despite intrapsychic difficulty.

CONDITIONS RELATED TO
THE INTERACTION AMONG FAMILY MEMBERS

The vast majority of all comments offering criteria for family interviewing, as well as most of those unique for this approach, proposed indicators based on the interaction among family members. Even those who spoke more from a theoretical orientation than from personal knowledge made family interactional patterns their major criterion for weighing the advisability of family interviewing.

Interactional Characteristics Considered Favorable

It seemed to be the challenge of problems often left unsolved by casework treatment in the past that most impressed respondents with the need for family interviews. This technique was seen as indicated for families suffering from general interactional friction but lacking adequate awareness of their mutual feelings and provocations. It was also thought appropriate when interactional friction is evident in the parent-child relationship and in relation to in-laws. Even though the difficulties concealed by these conflicts may involve, basically, a marital conflict, some partners may find family interviews a more tolerable avenue for entering treatment. In addition, family interviews were recommended for families in a state of chaos, for those willing to involve themselves in treatment, and for those sharing some strengths despite conflict.

Most of these conditions cover extremely difficult problems in mutual awareness, communication, suspiciousness, and anger. They even extend to mutual distortion and projection, to acting out, to inequitable relationships within the family, and to the repetition and ramification of marital conflict. Yet they are not cited as bars to the use of family interviews, but rather as signals *for* their use.[5] Only a few of the subcategories of comment referred to conditions that promised comparatively smooth sailing: a readiness on the part of family members to come in together, to become involved in treatment; the presence of at least some shared gratifications, values, and goals; and some excess of co-operation over conflict. Yet the majority of clues *unique* to the approach actually did not refer to families beset by excessive anger, character disorder, mutual suspiciousness, and chaos. Instead, they referred to situations in which the whole family was involved in the marital problems or in which the focus was definitely off the marital pair, but on the children or in-laws. They also encompassed those families whose members were willing to come and be involved in treatment or were generally concerned about family interaction. All this suggests that respondents were most clear about the use of family interviews for interaction when the situation was most like a parent-child problem and least like a marital problem.

These general observations provide needed perspective for the discussion to follow, which will concentrate mainly on those categories of comment that include observations unique to family interviewing.

General Interactional Friction
in the Presence
of Inadequate Awareness
of Mutual Feelings and Provocations

Respondents saw family interviews as indicated when family members show major concern about interactional problems, when they are disturbed by the marital or familial friction but inadequately aware of its ingredients and of their own contribution, even though all members are "adding to the problem in their own way." Some respondents affirmed the view that family interviews are properly concerned with the interaction and relationships among *all* family members, or with their common concerns —as in a family crisis—while strictly marital issues are best dealt with by other means, as long as they have not yet entangled the other members to any great extent. Moreover, there are always

[5] Only one group of respondents ruled out family interviews when the partners are too competitive.

those families whose members lack either the wish or the energy to examine their personal problems (44), but are willing to define their problems as interpersonal, perhaps because they depend on the family for emotional or physical survival and are, in that sense, "captive" to the family either by age or need (28).

Many aspects of inadequate mutual awareness were cited as reasons for the choice of family interviews: the failure of family members to realize what they really feel about each other, their failure to recognize the trigger points that usually set off conflict among them, and the need to examine the validity of their mutual expectations or assumptions. Often in such situations, children were seen as the ones who may pinpoint the parents' difficulties or "interpret a sibling's statement or behavior to help a parent face a marital conflict." Conversely, some respondents pointed to the need for this approach when one or more members, far from avoiding or denying their participation in the problem, are excessively anxious or guilty about their contribution as they see it. They believed that family sessions or a group setting might enable such individuals to "gain reassurance, to recognize that the family's problems are of multiple origin, and thus to become free to work more actively toward a solution."

An interesting variant on this theme of enhanced awareness was offered by the respondent group who mentioned families in which there are children from previous marriages. They saw family interviews as particularly indicated in such situations "because the family's coming together provided a visible and concrete demonstration of their physical unity, that could be used to highlight their emotional distance or unreadiness to become members of this group." One might add that this point has importance far beyond the issue of mutual awareness, since the high frequency of divorce means that there is a high incidence of second marriages in which two sets of children are brought together into the new family unit.

It may be worth pointing out here that the members' lack of awareness of their interactional patterns, seen as a cue for the use of family interviews, did not necessarily suggest to all the respondents that awareness of these patterns would always result from the interview. Family group sessions are indicated in such situations, in the view of one of the respondents, because the worker wants "to focus on the *effect* of the clients' behavior, so that it can

187

be corrected, rather than analyzing it so that insight can be developed into the causes of it."

Interactional Friction in the Relationship between the Parents and the Children

When the focus is on problems of the children, many respondents saw family interviews as being uniquely indicated. Often in such situations, parents were thought to be unable, at least for a time, to face or even to realize the presence of marital conflict. Yet these partners may be able to admit the reality of family problems, provided that "the symptom of dysfunctioning is in the child." In some of these families, as respondents noted, the child may be seen as a source of conflict, especially when one partner refuses to become involved in coping with the child's problems. In such a situation, family interviews may be called for in order to involve the reluctant partner. In other families, some or all of the children may be used as pawns or allies in the marital conflict, whether family members are aware of it or not. However, a minority defined criteria more narrowly. They insisted that family interviews should be used "very selectively . . . and usually in those situations in which the parents were expressing their marital difficulties through their children *and this fact had been established with the parents present*" [italics mine]. One respondent group went even further and suggested that not only the parents but the children, too, should be "consciously and actively involved in the marital situation" if family interviews were to be used.

Some respondents, as well as the Cincinnati Jewish Family Service Bureau study group (1), showed particular interest in the choice of family interviews when adolescent children were part of the family problem. Like many authors in the field (12, 31, 43), this study group recommended the use of family interviews when adolescents and their parents are beset by problems in their relationship. Their examples linked such difficulties to marital conflict although they certainly did not suggest that all adolescent problems are necessarily a reflection and displacement of such difficulty. They pointed out, for instance, that the "oedipal attachment of son to mother, daughter to father, may cause competition and resentment to arise between the marital partners." One might add

188

that the quality of each parent's attachment to each child and the unresolved oedipal attachments of the parents to their own parents may also contribute to the current marital and familial conflict. Such oedipal attachments on the children's part make it essential, they suggested, to diagnose and treat the total family (including the other children in the sibling system) through some family interviews and to help the family "work through this task in a healthy way."

As a means of helping some of the family members to a more positive relationship, this study group also recommended "occasional modifications of family interviewing, such as pair interviewing of father-son or mother-daughter." They also mentioned the couple with a sense of failure in their marriage or in their children as one that may scapegoat the children. In addition, they highlighted the resentment that may be caused in the parents individually and also between the parents if one or both feel threatened by the success of a teen-ager or by his developing sexuality. The scapegoating of the adolescent in such cases may serve "as a way of avoiding an examination of the marriage or of their own attitudes around sexuality." Lastly, this group took note of the fact that a couple "may be forced to turn toward each other for need satisfaction (previously satisfied by the child) and may find something missing" when the child reaches adolescence. Or else they may feel that they are "losing control of their child and . . . that they will not hold together as a family." Thus, in spite of the child's normal maturational problems in separating from the parents during adolescence, this group saw a need for family interviews to include adolescents, at least when their problems are associated with or aggravated by difficulties between the parents.

The distinction between problems of adolescents that are basically related to emancipation and those that are basically related to the parents' conflict may be an important one. This becomes strikingly evident in relation to two sets of responses that would otherwise appear to be mutually contradictory: One group of practitioners spoke of seeing the family interview as indicated in work "with delinquent children whose acting out has proved to be a symptom of marital disharmony." Another respondent was most emphatic in stating that family interviews should not be used with sexually or socially delinquent children "because they need to hold firm to the alienation pattern. Since the struggle is one toward

189

separation, it appears contraindicated at this time to do anything to enhance feelings of community between the affected individuals." Thus the delinquent behavior (presumably in families that do not support it) is related back to problems of emancipation rather than to the parents' marital troubles.

Wynne, with striking clarity, developed a criterion that seems appropriate here. He sees exploratory family therapy as being especially indicated when parents "share in the adolescent's ambivalence and confusion about his separating from them and going ahead with new extra-familial roles." In such a situation, he sees the problem as one in which "the difficulties continue to be reciprocally shared" within the family (50, p. 297). When the "active, continuing residue" of trouble resides chiefly in one family member, he would choose individual treatment for its alleviation (50, p. 297). This brings confirmation, from psychiatric experience, of the point made by Scherz that since parents and adolescent are simultaneously engaged in parallel and intermeshing maturational tasks, there are likely to be aspects of this struggle that would call for other modalities in addition to the family session (41).

Thus, she urges that the adolescent may need to be seen alone concurrently for the sake of developing "self-responsibility" while the parents may need to be seen together as a pair in addition to participating in family sessions if they need strengthening in the face of maturational tasks posed for them at that juncture (41). The crucial criterion, accordingly, would seem to be the nature of the current entanglement rather than the historical source of this involvement, whether it is the marital or the emancipatory struggle that requires attention. Even from this standpoint, awareness of the cause of the difficulty would still be of great value for the planning of treatment direction and goals, but does not seem to be the determining factor in choice of approach.

No discussion of the inclusion of children in treatment sessions can overlook the unease expressed by some practitioners regarding the wisdom of such a step in the course of marital treatment. A good many respondents, as already noted, disapproved altogether of the use of family interviews for treating marital problems. Their stance quite possibly expresses, in stronger form, at least two deep concerns that also ran through many other responses. These related to the whole issue of marital privacy and to the possible dangers of exposing children to problems in their parents' interaction. Some did stress that children were usually well aware of at least some of the parents' difficulties and actually found it a relief to have the matter brought out into the open. However, not one respondent attempted to state just what aspects of the marital conflict might be aired under what circumstances in front of children at which stage of development. Even the study group that spelled out the possible connections between adolescent problems and marital conflict (1) did not discuss just how far the parents' troubles should be aired in front of the children. They also did not state whether any of the difficulties they had mentioned were to be definitely included or excluded at any time as subjects for family discussion in the sessions. Thus there appeared to be a general uncertainty about the content appropriate for family interviewing in a marital context. Should the full range of parental pain, of deep mutual disappointment or inadequacy, be made evident in family interviews? Or is there an essentially private, intimate core to marriage that cannot be exposed to children without radical loss even if one grants, with Grosser and Paul (24), that all can gain if the aura of parental omnipotence is thoughtfully dispelled? Clearly the answer to these questions must rest on the worker's own feelings and philosophy about marriage. This, in turn, will determine both the utilization and the choice of modality.

Little seems to have been written on this point, although Ackerman (2) and some others do acknowledge the marital entity and its disorders as a special component of the family system, entitled to receive treatment as such.[6] A clear statement even seems to be lacking, both in the responses and in the literature, about the wisdom of including children in a discussion of the parents' sexual problems. A somewhat vaguely sensed gentlemen's agreement seems to be implied that sexual problems of the partners will not be taken up in front of the children. Yet sexuality is not the only form of intimacy in marriage. Furthermore, in some subcultures, even in our society, parents neither have nor expect privacy in sexual matters. In such a context, children may have been fully exposed to the phenomenon of adult sexuality, so that their inclusion in family interviews may actually be indicated in some instances—if the worker can handle the situation and refrain from trying, inappropriately, to impose his own value system on the family.

[6] Mrs. Frances H. Scherz, in a private communication dated October 8, 1965, concurred in this view.

191

Concern was shown both by respondents and in the literature about the possible effects of family interviews not only on the roles and status of the partners as mates and parents, but also on the role of the children as children. Might family sessions be contraindicated because they may tend to spread rather than to illuminate or heal the marital conflict? Might they seem to place on the children the responsibility for effecting changes in the behavior of their parents?

Framo addressed himself quite sharply to this question in a recent paper (20, p. 190). He asks whether "therapists are subsidizing the family pathology by implicity or explicity calling on the assistance of the children in 'marrying' their parents, thereby again parentifying the children." He then goes on to stress that the co-presence of all in the interview actually demonstrates to the children that the therapist is assuming the responsibility for the therapy. In this way, the children are helped to be "children again," freed of the vainly assumed task of trying to mend the parents' marriage. This point suggests that family interviews may be indicated in the course of marital treatment in situations in which the children have been trying to cement the parents' relationship, whether voluntarily or as a result of conscious or unconscious parental pressure. Needless to say, it will depend on the worker's use of their presence whether they will really become free to begin to relinquish this burden or will become even more deeply caught up in the parents' minuet of pain.

Interactional Friction
in the Relationship with In-laws

Only one respondent mentioned that in-laws might need to be included in the sessions with the partners or in family sessions when the focus of treatment includes the relationship with them. She did not indicate whether in-laws should always be included when they are part of the problem. Conceivably, there might be many situations in which their inclusion in the marital conflict might be mainly a reflection of the partners' immaturity, failure to form a real union, or search for allies. In such situations, an important goal would be to help the partners achieve appropriate psychological separation from their families of origin, without cutting them off, as Sherman has shown (46, p. 220), from finding "a more mature and different kind of closeness to them," in keeping with a firmer sense of individual and marital identity. Whether this goal would best be reached with or without inclusion of the extended family may well have to depend, as was seen in the context of adolescent problems (pp. 188–190), on the extent of the emotional collaboration of the partners' parents in the marital problem. Here again, Wynne offers a possibly crucial criterion when he identifies those involved in the "shared entanglement" as those who may need to be included in the family session (50, p. 306). This criterion seems to go beyond the early—since abandoned—concept of involving the "key figures" in the family problem (42, p. 211). It allows for inclusion of those whose role within the family may not be visible, at least at first, but places them within the psychosocial boundaries of the family's web of significant relationships even if they may be geographically outside the family (7).

Existence of a State of Chaos

With chaotic families, too much in turmoil to focus on intrapsychic problems, family interviews were thought to enable the worker to fasten on "one major area at a time with the efforts of the entire family pooled to obtain a solution." Some might question whether the possibilities of co-operation in such families will necessarily be greater in family than in joint interviews, especially if the children are young. However, it is conceivable that the parents might be too unsure of themselves as partners and carriers of responsibility to be able to use a joint session at the start. Scherz has pointed out how often such families show a lack of role differentiation among their members and has cited this as a contraindication to seeking to resolve issues of task allocation through separate interviews with individual members. At the same time, she has warned that hurt self-esteem and rivalry for affection may be so great in chaotic families that family treatment may have to run concurrently with some individual or joint sessions, or may even have to be preceded by some preliminary individual treatment (43).

By taking the profusion of problems and the family's disorganized approach to them as a signal for a family interview, the worker no doubt hopes to enable the family to use their neglected or unacknowledged resources. He acts on either the knowledge or assumption that something has been keeping the family together in spite of individual vulnerability and shared disorganization. The family interview, timed early in contact, may thus enable the worker to recognize some elements of cohesion, or at least to use them to bolster the goal of growth, even before they can be identified. Diagnostic as well as therapeutic reasons, then, would seem to underscore the wisdom of using family interviews in such situations.

This topic, although barely touched on, is of great importance, especially for work with multiproblem families.[7] It is of importance even for families plagued by few external problems and certainly not in a state of chaos. In such families, nevertheless, as respondents pointed out, members may be so "preoccupied with each other's shortcomings that the caseworker can find no positives to work with in individual sessions." Some respondents saw family sessions indicated in such situations, since they might enable the worker to spot and use positives that could become evident only when the family members were seen together.

It is arguable that in apparently disintegrating situations—such as those of chaotic or extremely hostile families—the very choice of the family interview may have great therapeutic potential. By acting as if the family's chaos and anger were a reason *for* getting together, and as if the getting together could bear some fruit rather than merely exhibit the family's distress, the worker conveys to the family a powerful sense of his therapeutic optimism. The choice of this approach may, therefore, be indicated all the more in such situations and may help to convey to the family the possibility of social rapprochement as well, since the worker's acceptance of them, although not of their ways, represents a reaction they have not usually encountered from outsiders.

While these effects are possible, they cannot be assumed to be universal. In fact, the Jewish Family Service of Philadelphia (19), in evolving their criteria for the use of family group treatment, suggested that family interviews would be indicated when survival problems were not so prevalent as to preclude attention to relationship problems. This view, juxtaposed with the approach discussed previously, points to the possibility that family interviews

[7] *See* Schlesinger (45) regardng the rising interest in the use of family interviews with such families.

may serve different purposes and may therefore warrant different indicators for families in very divergent social situations. In communities where the demands for help with individual survival problems are high, agencies may adapt the family interview process to meet them. When the help needed is primarily with relationship problems, the techniques of family interviewing developed in a particular setting may be geared specifically to helping families survive *as families.*

Willingness for
Treatment Participation and
Presence of Some Joint Strengths
despite Conflict

High motivation for treatment and some degree of family cohesion were seen as helpful for any treatment modality, but some of the points made had special bearing on family sessions. When family members previously absent from treatment would like to participate, they should be included in family sessions, according to some respondents. Yet diagnostic skill was thought to be called for even in weighing a request for family treatment. One mother's wish for a family interview, for instance, was not granted because it was taken by the worker as an attempt to "maneuver the treatment plan" because of rivalry with the daughter, who was receiving group therapy. Mitchell similarly cautions about "the applicant [who] comes because he has heard that we work with the famliy as a whole" (32, p. 67). She suggests that in encountering such an applicant, the worker guard against falling in with the use of projection as a defense. Only if the client is capable of realizing some of his own share in the problems would it be advisable, in her view, to start work with the family group immediately. It is conceivable, however, that the known availability of family sessions may increasingly lead applicants to request this service because they see it as a natural approach or intuitively sense a need for it.

Some respondents acknowledged that families may be reluctant about coming in together even though they may truly want treatment. Parents may be fearful of "loss of face or the loss of adult status as a parent in the eyes of the children," and therefore unwilling to have them included. This concern was underscored by the study group of the Jewish Family Service Bureau of Cincinnati (1). They believe that parents concerned about only one child "might see the inclusion of other children [ostensibly well] as a threat to their [parental] adequacy and an indication that the worker might be looking for more individual problems." The group therefore suggested that the worker point out that each family member "contributes his share to improving, or continuing the damage to, the total family situation," so that the rationale for the family interview will be clear to all.

No comment, interestingly enough, was offered to suggest that the children might urgently want to come in for a family interview in situations in which the parents are in conflict. The wish for a total family interview was thus stated exclusively in terms either of the worker's judgment or the parents' concern. The latter may reflect, in turn, the partners' reluctance because of fear of loss of face, their interest in understanding the impact of their conflict on the children, or their wish to give the children a chance to express their feelings.

This failure to mention the wishes of the children at all as a criterion may well be another reflection of the genuine difficulty posed for caseworkers by the issue of marital conflict and its treatment, even partially, via the family interview approach. Parent-child problems or difficulties of children outside the home allow an easily acceptable and logical basis for the family's concerted effort. But should the worker even appear to turn to the children as he weighs the choice of approach for amelioration of the marital conflict? Unless the children's wishes are consulted only in relation to the imapct of the parents' difficulties on them, it is possible that parents may sense in such a move a deep threat to the privacy of their marriage, to their own sense of identity, adequacy, and responsibility as adults. In this sense, more is involved than the problem of status. The danger is that the partners will feel that they have abdicated as adults and partners if a familial approach is used in a situation they see as strictly marital. It is probably this danger of which the respondents were speaking who, before they would use family interviews at all for treatment, asked that both parents and children be fully aware of their involvement in the marital conflict.

The treatment of marital problems, as distinct from their diagnosis, may therefore be handled largely through the use of joint rather than family interviews even by pioneers as thoroughly committed to the family approach as Ackerman. In an article on marital treatment, he states that "the psychotherapy of marital disorders is viewed as the focused treatment of a component of family disorder. It is a phase of family therapy, adapted to and specialized for the specific features of a marital problem" (2, p. 163).

Interactional Characteristics Considered Unfavorable

Not one of the interactional factors seen as contraindicating family interviews was unique to that approach. However, some criteria relevant only to family interviewing were found among the comments on families involved in destructive interaction and those in which the partners no longer wanted the marriage. The rest of the responses mentioned families who lack all sense of belonging together as poor candidates for the use of any type of multiple-client interview. One may perhaps suppose that some families in this latter group may be close to the same point in the conflict spiral as those who have decided to separate. These would be the families in which the partners' wish to rebuild satisfactions within the marriage and family has been obliterated by a confirmed pattern of dissatisfactions within or greater satisfactions outside the marriage. On the other hand, families with no sense of cohesion may also include those that lacked free mutual assent from the start, as in the case of some forced marriages.

Two types of consideration not mentioned by respondents were cited by Ackerman (3) as representing a bar to family interviewing: the presence of deceitfulness deeply rooted in the group or exhibited by one or both parents and the existence of a "valid family secret." It would be interesting to know what kinds of secrets caseworkers might consider legitimately kept out of the family arena.

Destructive
or Highly Explosive Interaction

Considering the great diversity of comment on the use of joint interviews with very hostile partners, it is surprising that only four respondents discussed the appropriateness of family interviews for such couples. Those who saw family interviews as contraindicated in such situations focused on the destructive rather than on the merely hostile elements in the family interaction. They ruled against family interviews when destructive motivations pervade the family or when the members are actually gratified by their mutually destructive defensive maneuvers. In doing so, they stressed the excessive degree of the family's hostility or aggressiveness. One presumes they would allow use of the modality if they did not fear an uncontrolled and destructive outburst, due either to the family's feelings or to the worker's inability to set controls.

One respondent pointed out that beginning workers are often needlessly afraid that family interviews will be used destructively, and added that this had not been true in her experience: "I think that treatment may fail if the worker does not know how to handle these offerings, but I have never yet found that families introduce any material in front of me with which they are not already quite familiar." Her criterion, in other words, seemed to be the worker's skill in handling a family in conflict, rather than the symptoms of the family conflict per se. However, she saw family interviews as indicated only "about once or twice, and more for diagnostic purposes than treatment, when the main problem is a marital problem," with occasional family interviews later in treatment to check on the effect of changes in the marital relationship, especially on the children.

Some of the leading writers in the field confirm the view that an understanding of the basis or aim of the family's hostility might aid the worker in his choice of approach (32, 35, 44). Scherz sees consistent and major gratifications derived from destructive defensive maneuvers as a contraindication to family interviewing. In addition, Ackerman and Mitchell (4, p. 111; 32, p. 68), have both suggested that the presence of a concentrated focus of malignant, destructive motivation represents a contraindication to family therapy. Taken together, these views would seem to differentiate between different aims in the discharge of extreme family hostility. One is the ventilation of anger and frustration out of a need to express, to be understood, to bring about some change. This does not bar the use of family interviews. The other is the wish to vent extreme hostility in order to gain negative gratifications that will further reinforce the present family interactional patterns. The aim may even be to destroy the partner or family member, in either a psychological or a physical sense. Such aims would vitiate the use of family interviews.

It is conceivable that a highly skilled worker may become able to hold family sessions even when they might at first serve as a source of negative gratification for some or all of the clients. As the nature of such destructive satisfactions, motives, and interactional patterns becomes better understood, it may become feasible to strengthen the members not as yet caught up in this type of spiral and even to make vivid, in family interviews, the realistic possibility of less damaging substitute gratifications. However, Ackerman's and Mitchell's use of the word *malignancy* acknowledges this issue to be one of profound difficulty. Further study is needed, particularly to clarify whether family interviewing focused on some facing of the members' destructiveness might run the risk of stimulating homicidal or suicidal tendencies, especially in highly suggestible individuals. The definition and diagnosis of destructive motivations, and knowledge about their reversibility or irreversibility and about the socially feasible ways of dealing with those who possess or share them, must await further study.

Individual motives are not, however, the only ones at work in the discharge of anger in family sessions. Since the status quo of the family system is threatened by such behavior, excessive fighting, as Scherz has shown, may be an expression of resistance at the family level. She therefore urges that family interviews not be abandoned at such a point. Great benefits may be expected if such angry family resistance can be worked out in the sessions, just as the initial passive, withdrawing reactions of some members may turn out to have been a prelude to active participation and productive change (43). In such situations, the conflict may not necessarily have advanced to the point of serious question about the marriage. However, even for couples who have reached the final phase in the escalation of conflict and who no longer find the marriage worth maintaining, the inclusion of children in some of the separation counseling [8] may be indicated. It is conceivable that family interviews at such a point may help the children toward acceptance of the parents' decision, may relieve their guilty fear that they are to blame, and can help them acknowledge that they still need both parents. By the same token, family interviews help the partners pay attention to the children's needs at a time of great marital stress. They can be aimed at helping the parents to refrain from using the children

[8] For more detailed discussion of separation counseling *see* Helgason (27).

against each other, at enabling the "victimized" partner to avoid pressing the children toward contempt or hatred of the other parent, and at highlighting for the latter his responsibility to the children.

CONDITIONS RELATED TO THE RELATIONSHIP BETWEEN THE WORKER AND THE FAMILY

All the comments on the worker's relationship with the family related to conditions considered unfavorable rather than favorable to the use of multiple-client interviews, such as clients' inability to share the worker or to have a good relationship with him. None was unique for family interviews. They will therefore not be discussed again here except to state that special needs of individual clients in relation to the worker have already been touched on in the section on conditions for family interviewing as they relate to the family members as individuals (pp. 181–185).

One may perhaps wonder whether the relationship of a worker with a whole family really does not harbor any factors influencing the choice of approach except those that are identical with the criteria regarding joint interviews. Common sense suggests that the worker has to deal with more people in a family interview and has feelings about this modality that differ from his feelings about others. There must surely be more to be understood about a situation in which the worker is in an extreme minority position, one in which, even though he is endowed with social and professional power, he may yet find himself feeling threatened by the family's moves to absorb, reject, or ignore him.

The family's readiness to allow the worker into its interaction was cited long ago as a necessary condition for family treatment (5, 34). Seen as an expression of the autonomous working of the marital or familial system, such readiness may be thought an essential condition for both joint and family interviews, although it need not be complete and is likely to vary in degree in the course of the contact. However, if the family's refusal to let the worker in is viewed, at least in part, as involving the reaction of its members to a particular worker, its clarity as a contraindication to these approaches will fade. True, a worker excluded from the clients' interaction in joint or family interviews may be shut out so that the status quo can be maintained. However, he may also be kept out of the interaction in joint interviews to preserve some sense of their marital privacy, but may be allowed by the same pair to enter into their interaction with their children in family sessions. Should such a development occur, it might reflect a defense of the marital situation and perhaps also a wish to legitimize the request for help by attributing it to children's problems. However, it may also be due to the presence of realistic or transference elements in the parents' appraisal of the worker's aims and role perception as he tries to enter into the family system. Even if the worker is shut out of the total family interaction, the reasons again might not be exclusively homeostatic in a negative sense. He may, for instance, exhibit a sense of values or personal mannerisms of speech or dress [9] that run so counter to the family's standards or ideals that they reject him as a helper. On such a basis, the parents may even fear him as an identification model for the children. It would be essential, in such a situation, to distinguish the indications against the use of family interviews altogether from those unfavorable to continued assignment to a particular worker, if the difficulty cannot be worked out. In other words, the system that needs considering here is not only the marital or familial one; the worker-family temporary treatment system also needs to be understood. Family treatment can be advanced through further attempts to explore and define the factors that enable one worker to form a working alliance with a family for therapeutic purposes but bar another from doing the same.

CONDITIONS RELATED TO
WORKER SKILLS AND CHARACTERISTICS

Much of the controversy about family interviewing for marital problems centers on the capacity of workers to handle so complex a situation therapeutically.[10] Worker comments, as far as they were unique to family interviews, stressed mainly the factors of transference and countertransference and the need for perceptiveness and special training on the worker's part. Otherwise, the references were geared, as in the case of joint interviewing, to the worker's sense of comfort with the approach, his alertness, his ability to handle hos-

9 *See also* Ronall (36).
10 *See also* Ronall (37).

tility from several people at once, and his capacity for remaining neutral. Only the reference in the joint interviewing material to the need for comparable skill, if two workers were co-operating in the interviews, was omitted in the comments on family interviews. Those worker skills and characteristics that were cited by the respondents as uniquely necessary for family interviewing could all be described as desirable worker traits. Consequently, the present section, unlike all the others, will not be subdivided into two separate parts for conditions favoring or barring the use of the modality.

Ability To Handle
Complex Transference
and Countertransference Reactions

Respondents thought it important in any interview situation that the worker be able to understand and handle transference and countertransference reactions at a level appropriate for casework. However, there was some conviction that the predominant use of family interviews from the beginning might leave the worker "less likely to develop irrational reactions to one family member" or "to have a favorite to the extent that it might interfere with treatment." In other words, a worker who finds it hard to avoid these pitfalls in individual interviews may find family interviews indicated on this basis. On the other hand, it was noted that "some workers, plunged into a type of family interaction similar to what they themselves experienced as children, may become so anxious that it affects treatment. In some instances, it might be better for them to avoid the family session." In others, it is presumably implied, workers may be helped to deal with their feelings and reactions in this predicament.

Several, speaking from extensive experience, pointed out further that the impact of family interviews on the worker is probably greater than the number of participants alone would justify. They attributed this, at least in part, to the fact that the worker may feel overwhelmed, as if plunged back into a childhood in which he was chronically outnumbered. Group therapy of unrelated individuals, of course, may pose a similar problem for the therapist, but there is a distinct ingredient present in the family interview because of the fact that the family members have been and continue to be a group outside the interview. They are of vital real-life importance to each other and are better able than a group of unrelated individuals to co-operate in accepting or rejecting the worker. They also have developed norms, goals, and an integrated life style of their own that may be congenial, alien, or even inimical to the worker's. In any case, he is bound to react to their group values and aspirations, and will need to be aware of these reactions and respectful of the family's right to their own goals and standards, within socially viable limits, if treatment is to be successful.

These various considerations suggest that the volume and intensity of realistic and irrational reactions on the part of the worker may actually be heightened by the family interview situation. The approach therefore implies the need for a worker especially capable of discerning and coping with them. Many of the leading authors in the field bear out this point. Leader thinks it highly unlikely that the worker could avoid countertransference reactions in the family interview since the greater number of participants increases the number of roles into which they may cast him, and therefore the likelihood of his reacting unrealistically (30). Quite possibly, unconscious hostility in the worker may be aroused even more in family than in joint or individual sessions if his negative reactions relate not only to the individuals but to the total family style or system. Unless the worker can realize and handle such reactions on his part, he is likely to reinforce the whole system's tendency to withstand change. Pollak has already made clear how such a reaction may strengthen that part of the client that is opposed to treatment (34).

Although countertransference will arise in any interview situation, its character might be expected to vary, then, with the number and kind of participants in the interview. While individual sessions run the risk of further fragmenting the family, the family session may also pose this possibility if the worker's conscious or unconscious needs should prompt him to intensify the rift between the partners, to encourage unconstructive forms of rebellion or defiance on the part of the children, or to expose parental inadequacies to the children, beyond the family's ability to handle the challenge. Lack of capacity to handle such reactions within himself may not only lead to defeat of the worker's conscious aim of preventing or arresting the dissolution of the family; it may, conversely, lead the family to consolidate their existing system all the more, partly as a defense against the worker.

The presence of the children in the interview, then, is likely to call forth many long-buried fears and needs in the worker, some of which may hark back to feelings about his own childhood siblings. This may heighten the temptation to form collusive alliances with one or more family members. Anxieties arising from such countertransference reactions (as well as other factors) may push the worker toward either premature confrontation or premature alleviation of the family's pain, as his own needs for quasi-defiant challenge or speedy easing of discomfort come powerfully to the fore.

Clearly no worker can be expected to be fully aware and fully in control of feelings of such depth and complexity even most of the time. However, for most effective use of family interviews it does seem essential, on the basis of both the responses and the relevant literature, that the practitioner be ready to pay special attention to the more unfamiliar countertransference phenomena, as well as to the better-known aspects (40, pp. 485–490). This includes Mitchell's interesting concept of "cross-transference," a term that covers the worker's reactions not only to the actual people important to each client in his current life, but also to the client's "introjects" of early childhood (32). One respondent recalled that the interference of tranference and countertransference factors in multiple-client interviews had been underestimated when she first participated in the Midwest Seminar on Family Diagnosis and Treatment. Later, however, there had been "a return . . . to psychiatric evaluation and consultation," partly through a renewed awareness of treatment problems caused by these phenomena. This suggests that a supplementary criterion may need to be highlighted if the use of family interviews is under consideration: administrative provision of adequate facilities for checking and weighing countertransference reactions, as well as powerful realistic ones, and, perhaps, for counteracting in this way the problems attendant on the worker's minority position in the interview. Whether the agency should provide such facilities through individual or group supervision and observation, through casework and psychiatric consultation, or through provision of two or more therapists for family sessions are points to be further explored.

In contrast to countertransference, no transference phenomena were cited by respondents as either easing or hampering the use of family interviews, although some thought transference reactions became "diluted" in multiple-client sessions. This was a point of view also evident in the literature of the early 1960's, although subsequent accumulation of experience has caused a shift of views in this respect. Writing in 1963, Freeman and his co-authors (21), like the respondents, saw the role of transference as altered in the family interview. They attributed this to the fact that treatment goals in family interviews differ from those in individual sessions. Instead of aiming to change one or more individuals in the group, family group treatment, in their view, attempts to change those aspects of the family system that foster dysfunctional behavior. In line with this goal, these authors see the counselor in family interviews as an agent who "deliberately de-emphasizes the transference relationship by avoiding . . . unilateral interaction with individual family members." They contrast this sharply with the spotlight on transference in individual interviews as a "means of effecting insight leading to intrapsychic change" (21, p. 169).

Freeman and his associates were not necessarily stating that the transference reactions are *ipso facto* diluted in the family interview, as project respondents had suggested. They claimed, instead, that the family interview makes possible the minimizing of such reactions by the counselor because it offers an opportunity for "avoiding unilateral interaction" with family members individually.[11] In 1965 Scherz also stressed that transference reactions are minimized in family interviews because members tend to express intense feelings toward each other rather than the worker. However, she thought this most likely to hold true if family interviews are used from the start, or at least quite early in the contact, since strong transference reactions must be expected during a period of individual treatment (43). Yet another point of view is possible: The worker's special style, skills, and interests may be even more influential in the emergence and handling of transference reactions than these authors would allow. The extremely passive worker, for instance, is likely to encourage more transference reactions, if only by default.

One may perhaps question whether the concepts of transference and countertransference, which are linear and which were forged in the crucible of individual psychoanalysis, are fully appropriate for discussing treatment of the circular, even spiraling, relationships

---

[11] However, the worker cannot necessarily avoid the possible transference and countertransference fantasies in such situations.

and events related to the family system. However, these are the terms constantly used both by the respondents and by writers in the field. Suffice it to say, then, that transference and countertransference in family as in joint sessions are likely to differ in some important respects from these same phenomena as they emerge in exclusively individual treatment, and hence may require different handling.

Sufficient Alertness and Perceptiveness

Constant alertness and perceptiveness to the vulnerabilities and strengths of both the individual family members and the family system were implied as necessary throughout the responses on family interviewing. One comment suggested that "almost anything" could probably be handled in family sessions if the worker is able to "empathize, to understand, to expedite growth, and to build on healthy functioning." Since every one of these qualities is essential for all interviewing, one may assume that this highly experienced respondent saw them as being needed in particular depth or intensity in the family session. Here the worker is beset by so many impressions, so many emotional pulls, that the maintenance of focus, let alone of constructive empathy and therapeutic optimism, requires a constant state of awareness and of multidirectional diagnostic alert.

The presence of children adds further new dimensions to this requirement. At each developmental phase children present special needs that may further tax an already strained marriage and that must be taken into consideration in deciding direction and focus. For instance, the perceptiveness that allows the worker to see the children's provocative role in the marital conflict must also guide him to recognize when its demonstration in the interview would be harmful or would have to be handled with special care. There may be situations in which the children's growing realization of the precariousness of the marriage may also increase their fright and guilt about their own provocations to such an extent that they may be inhibited in developing even the necessary amount of self-assertion. Thus, in family as distinct from joint interviews, the worker must be perceptive not only about the timing and method of ventilation or of control in relation to the worker-couple system but

206

also in relation to the worker-family system as a whole. Furthermore, he needs to be alert to the shifting alliances, the possible tendency to "gang up" on one or more members, as some respondents showed. Only in this way can he hope to avoid being drawn into collusive alliances himself. The danger of such involvement may seem to be numerically and dynamically greater in family than in other interviews. However, it may well be that it is less, since the interview structure makes this pitfall all too evident and allows family members to take the worker to task. In joint or individual sessions the worker may be in unwitting collusion with an absent and therefore invisible member.

Special Training and Skills

The importance of specific help in learning to work with the whole family group was stressed by several who suggested the need to provide special training or supervision for this purpose. Here, as in the case of joint interviews, the orientation of agency administration is likely to make the difference between exploration or bypassing of this approach by practitioners and between offering and failing to offer such service in the face of possible apprehension on the part of clients or workers.

Even among agencies concerned with developing worker skills in family interviewing there is unlikely to be any full consensus regarding the qualities uniquely essential if a practitioner is to use this treatment modality successfully, both in general and in relation to marital problems in particular. Most, in fact, are likely to see the presence of such qualities and skills as being less important than the willingness to acquire them. However, it seems worthwhile to explore briefly whether there were any skills or requirements that either the respondents or leading writers saw as being especially needed for family interviewing in such a context and therefore worth cultivating in the course of special training.

One of the study groups (1, p. 6) saw the worker as generally much more of an enabler than an active participant in family interviews because "the family members themselves were much more of a 'therapeutic work group' than in individual therapy." In fact, they thought it likely that workers may react by feeling displaced and useless and may therefore resort to more activity than the situation calls for. This may relate to Bell's point that the worker should not assume a role that rightly belongs to a family member (13), and also to Pollak's stress on the worker's ability to share the therapeutic task (34). Although Klein (29) also stresses the catalytic role of the worker, the bulk of current literature seems to favor a view of the worker as intervening much more actively in family interviews. As one of the consultants put it: One tries to promote the family members' ability to meet each other's needs, but when they become bogged down, the worker has to enter in actively.

It may be necessary, then, for the worker to know how to be an active intervener or an educator and enabler in the presence of all the members at once. In addition, he needs, more than ever, a clear sense of primary focus so that the main feasible treatment goal at any given time may not be submerged through excessive attention to the many other possible goals seen as desirable for the whole family. For these purposes, as Leader has made clear, he needs to be able to take the full impact of a family's "latent and manifest" feelings without being so totally thrown off course or "sucked into the maelstrom" that little energy remains for appraisal or hope (30, p. 331). Perhaps stamina rather than skill would seem to be the proper word for these qualities. However, knowledge and skill can provide the basis of minimal security from which such strengths and perseverance may develop. Beatman and Mitchell have variously sketched a broad outline of the necessary knowledge (8, 33). It should encompass an understanding of the basics of individual and group psychology, group process, family dynamics, and the relations between family and society.

The vital intervention seen as essential by Ackerman, Aikin, Leader, and Pollak (4, 5, 30, 34), among others, calls for a high degree of versatility on the worker's part, especially if one agrees with Scherz that different types of families may require different types of stance and activity on the part of the worker (43). Such intervention seems to require, for that matter, a good deal of courage, since the worker must be ready to accept the perhaps temporarily explosive consequences of his intervention (30). A willingness and ability to express and expose personal and professional values, if indicated, is also likely to be called for in exchanges with the family (43), with an extra dimension presumably added by the presence of the children, who belong to a different generation from that of the worker and their parents. Flexibility may be a tame word indeed to express the quality needed in a worker who must be capable of strong activity and yet willing not to dominate but to share the therapeutic task (34). The study group of the Jewish Family Service Bureau of Cincinnati (1) thought such sharing an essential ingredient of family interviewing and of the evolution of the treatment contract in family sessions. However, they did not spell out whether this sharing necessarily applied to long-range as well as intermediate goals, or whether its extent might be affected by the age of the children or by any other factors.

A great deal, clearly, remains to be added to this emerging profile of unique qualities and skills needed for family interviewing.[12] As yet, the role of such objective worker characteristics as age and stage of personal development is unclear. The special educative skills needed in this context also should be spelled out. However, basic to all the worker's equipment for family interviewing in marital treatment is the ability to care about and relate to the family as a whole—intellectually, clinically, and emotionally—without losing sight of the crucial place and role of the marital pair within the whole. This is the orientation that will enable him to use most effectively the special social structure of the family interview for the special ends it may uniquely serve. Especially for those originally trained in the one-to-one approach, this structure seems to demand an exacting and new dimension of awareness on the part of the worker. Even when he is manifestly communicating, for the moment, with a single participant in the session, the worker is at the same time communicating implicitly with all the rest as well, as Sherman has pointed out (47). In the family interview, he needs to be aware of the therapeutic implications of all these levels of communication at once. One might perhaps go further, using the Palo Alto school's concept of congruence (49), to say that his conscious aim of helping all the participants is likely to be frustrated unless his manifest exchanges with one participant and his implicit exchanges with the others are congruent with his aim of helping the family as a whole. Furthermore, when treatment is leading the couple to question their marital partnership as a continued goal, the worker must be alert to the changes that such developments will cause in his relationship to and role with all the members of the family.

[12] For a full discussion of worker characteristics and skills as factors in the treatment of marital problems, *see* Ronall (36, 37). She also offers a discussion of skills necessary in family interviewing.

In conclusion, one might add that a fruitful source of information on worker qualities essential for family interviewing might be derived from follow-up studies with the families themselves—those who stayed and benefited, those who stayed without benefiting, and those who withdrew.

CONDITIONS RELATED TO REALITY FACTORS
AND TO OBJECTIVE CHARACTERISTICS
OF INTERVIEW PARTICIPANTS

Age of Children

Although the age of children in the family was thought to be relevant to the choice of approach, its implications are still a subject of disagreement. One respondent group indicated that they would not include children under ten in family interviews. Another doubted the usefulness of such sessions with preschoolers. Satir, who will see the marital pair rather than the whole family if the children are four years old or younger, still includes all the children for at least two sessions for diagnostic purposes (38, p. 137). The stress on verbal fluency as a prerequisite for a child's participation in treatment is shared by Bell (12).[13] One may wonder, nevertheless, whether nonverbal communication may not be of more than diagnostic significance. There may be times when nonverbal communications within an interview including very young children might be used to fill a therapeutic need of the child as well.

One study group (1, pp. 3–4, 5) shared some of these doubts about the inclusion of preschoolers when the problem is stated to be marital. However, they did feel that older children "can often serve as a catalyst. . . . As the children talk about their feelings concerning a marital strain, the parents may be impelled to move beyond their initial resistance to an examination of the marriage and its problems." Moreover, they were convinced that all the family members together need to be told that the marital problem affects the whole family and that "each individual family member

---

[13] Bell also believes that children under 9 cannot verbalize well enough to contribute to or benefit from family sessions, but he qualifies this by stating that the use of "other modes of communication" might allow inclusion of the very young.

contributes his share to improving or continuing the damage to the total family situation." Such interpretation, they felt, will do much to prevent the parents' seeing the inclusion of children as a threat to their own adequacy.

In summary, respondents failed to agree on any hard and fast age criterion for the inclusion of children in family interviews. Their decisions seemed to rest largely on the purpose of the interview, the extent of the marital conflict, and the worker's ability to use or observe nonverbal forms of communication. One might add that if small children are to be present, the worker needs to have a special ability to communicate with the young and to include them in the session.

Chronic or Congenital Illness
or Handicap

One special situation that may or may not be associated with marital difficulties was cited by the respondent who suggested family interviews for families who needed to gain "understanding and acceptance where there is chronic illness or congenital handicap of a member." Whether or not these are to be total family group interviews that include the patient was not spelled out by the respondent, but deserves further exploration. In any case, the point is apt and probably equally relevant for other acute situations such as mental illness, birth of a defective child, a death in the family, and the like. Any of these may lead to or intensify marital strain and might benefit from family sessions for the sharing of relevant information and for dealing with the members' varying, shared, and discrepant reactions.

Inadequate Office Space
or Worker Coverage
To Provide Family Interviews

Cramped office quarters were said to have hampered the use of family sessions by some who also stated that shortage of staff time had prevented their interviewing families in their own homes. Probably this difficulty is most relevant to large family groups and might be overcome if crowded quarters did not increase the worker's anxiety unduly.

Conditions Considered Favorable or Unfavorable: Family Interviews

The Jewish Family Service of Philadelphia points out (19) a further realistic requirement: A worker must be available if such treatment is to be offered. Here agency administration plays a crucial role since the availability at appropriate hours of staff competent to use a particular type of interview depends not only on past training but also on the agency's in-service training program and on its over-all policies, office hours, and priority allocations. A realistic problem is also posed by the possible difficulty of finding workers able to work during evening hours to accommodate employed family members.

CONSIDERATIONS RELATED TO THE TIMING OF FAMILY INTERVIEWS

Considerable interest was shown by respondents in timing family interviews appropriately in the course of a contact, combining them with joint interviews, individual interviews, or both. Unlike some authors (6, 11, 12, 13), none of the respondents adhered to the concept of exclusive family interviewing, nor did they offer any other immutably structured sequence of techniques. In fact, their convictions as to timing appeared to be subordinate to the conditions they regarded as favoring or barring the approach for other reasons. For example, some who generally favored a family interview as part of the intake process would refrain from using it if the client's fear or reluctance were great. Thus the comments on timing do not represent criteria but rather some possible patterns of preferred sequence of approach, to be chosen or modified in the light of all the conditions already discussed in this chapter.

Intake or Assessment

Respondents were divided in their views about the advisability of family interviews at or close to intake. In line with their recognition of the many diagnostic values of this modality, they saw its possible usefulness during this initial period. Treatment considerations, however, operated in two opposing directions. One set of comments and one study group (1) stressed the need for early family interviews to establish the character of the casework relationship with all the family and to involve the children in an

212

understanding of the treatment plan. They saw this as the most "natural" way to begin treatment and hoped that it might help to move the family from seeing the worker as a mere referee, because his concern with and caring about the whole family would be demonstrably evident from the start. Others, however, favored some individual interviews so that the caseworker might first establish a working relationship with the partners or might give the pair an opportunity to talk freely of anything, without being inhibited by the children's presence.

These two main arguments against the use of family interviews at intake appear to reflect two quite divergent approaches. The first may hark back to the days when the one-to-one relationship was seen as the model of all casework treatment. It is therefore likely to be modified by increasing familiarity with the approach and its underlying orientation. The second recalls the many problems already noted as workers weighed the wisdom of including children in any phase of marital treatment. Even Satir, a pioneer in the almost exclusive use of family interviewing, states that her first interview is held jointly with the partners and without the children, to acknowledge their role as family leaders and mates as well as parents. She departs from this rule only if the couple cannot bear to look at their marital relationship at all (38). (Conversely, one respondent suggested exclusion of children when a couple is so absorbed in their marital difficulties that they never even mention the children and seem temporarily unable to function as real parents.)

Perhaps one might say that, in this early phase, the worker's choice of family interviews is bound to be dictated in large measure by the area of diagnostic concern, the worker's orientation and work style, the family grouping or subgrouping regarded as essential or relevant to the treatment contract, and, consequently, the boundaries within which the marital problems exist or have ramified. Since all of these factors will vary, the choice of approach must also be flexible. Clearly, many of the conditions seen as possible contraindications to family interviewing for the treatment of marital problems need not be a bar to a session aimed mainly at diagnostic assessment, although all the therapeutic implications of bringing children into the interviews, even if only for diagnostic purposes, need to be carefully weighed in relation to the total family's situation, capacities, and needs, as must also the implications of excluding the children altogether from contact with the worker.

Periodic and Occasional
Review and Refocusing

As in the case of joint interviews, some respondents recommended the use of family interviews at periodic intervals for a joint review of progress. They were seen as indicated particularly for gauging and handling the effect of changes in the marital relationship on the children, especially when these were showing marked upset or other reactions to changes in the marital relationship and in the family balance as a result of treatment. Such interviews were also seen as useful when treatment gains for the whole family needed highlighting and reinforcing, the partners had made no progress in joint interviews, family relationships were deteriorating, workers seeing family members separately needed to counteract a sense of dilution about the family as a whole, and hostility had been aired enough in individual sessions to allow constructive communication in a family interview.

Many of these same circumstances were also thought to suggest the need for a change of focus,[14] which in turn may be introduced or reinforced by a change in approach, as was seen in Chapter 3. Whether the movement will be away from or toward family interviewing will depend in large part on the worker's style and skills, the family's needs and capacities, and the current phrase of both conflict and treatment.

One might speak broadly of two cycles of focus in marital treatment that may include family interviews.[15] Either of these may include some concentration on individual difficulties and growth via individual interviews. One of these cycles moves from overriding concern about parent-child problems to tackling the marital difficulty, a change of focus that may be expressed by a move away from family and toward joint interviews as the preferred approach. On the whole, this would appear to be the most common cycle in the

[14] For a fuller discussion of changes in focus in the course of marital treatment in general, *see* Froscher (22).

[15] Other cycles not including family interviews may involve moves from individual to joint sessions as the partners develop more identity and maturity. They may also include a move from joint to individual sessions as the marriage improves, if intrapsychic problems then become the focus.

214

experience of the respondents. Its rationale, perhaps most succinctly expressed by Bowen, lies in the conviction that if marital treatment is to be truly effective, the parents must stop making a project out of the children and start to make one out of their marriage.[16]

The second type of cycle moves from direct work on the marital situation to direct intervention in the family system as a whole. Such a move toward family interviewing, as already noted, may be indicated when entanglement of the children or in-laws in the ramifications of the marital conflict needs to be understood and handled or when neglect of the children's needs calls for correction.

Termination

When individual sessions have been the rule, family interviews were suggested to dilute the casework relationship prior to termination. Although respondents did not mention any other indications, several of those offered for the joint interview at or near termination would also seem to apply to family sessions. They may be called for to facilitate a joint review of progress made and of plans for the future. The worker, when about to leave the family system, may need to clarify for all simultaneously the standing offer of renewed service in case of need. Ideally, a final family interview focused on termination may be indicated as the last of several family sessions during treatment, as a means to reinforce the boundaries of the family system now being restored to its fuller autonomy without the worker. It may serve to reassure the family that its boundaries are defined enough and the system resilient enough to accommodate not only ongoing dealings with the world outside, but also temporary inclusion of a therapeutic agent.

CONSIDERATIONS RELEVANT TO CHOICE OF MODALITY TENTATIVELY RESTATED FROM A SYSTEM-LEVEL PERSPECTIVE

Up to this point, the views of the respondents and of some authors regarding the criteria for using joint or family interviews

---

[16] Based on staff recollection of a point made in an unpublished paper given by Dr. Murray Bowen on February 9, 1963, at a Symposium on Family Dynamics and Family Treatment sponsored by the Mental Health Institute in New York.

in the course of marital treatment have been explored separately for the two modalities. It is now possible to make a preliminary attempt to restate, from a system-level perspective, their views regarding the selection of either modality or both.

There can be little doubt that the married partners represent the most basic and pivotal subsystem within most intact American families, the subsystem with leadership responsibilities. If their conflicts are severe enough to lead to separation or divorce, the nature of the family system will be profoundly altered. It would therefore seem reasonable to assume that families beset by serious marital conflict should be offered treatment mainly involving the marital dyad, since that would represent the most critically dysfunctional subsystem and the one most crucial for recovery of the whole family. However, the dynamics operating within human beings and their interlocking relationships are so complex that the system or subsystem most in need of treatment may not necessarily be either the one most disrupted or the one through which treatment might best be initiated or accomplished.

Although various modalities including joint and family interviews are bound to be diagnostically useful to the worker as he tries to understand the operations of the marital and family system, his choice of a particular type of interview for *treatment* has to depend on a variety of considerations, among them the changing parts played by the various subsystems within the family system in the course of treatment, his changing understanding of these, his skills and personal qualifications, and the avenues for therapeutic change that might be opened for or closed to the family if at any given time their total system or some specific subsection were to be directly involved in treatment.

A variety of difficult questions arise in the course of weighing these factors: Is the marital conflict confined to the couple or has it extended to involve the children and others? Is that conflict basic to the family's problems, or is it being provoked because of strife or pain springing mainly from other segments of the family's life? Even when the marital conflict does represent the core problem for the family, the choice of modality is by no means obvious: Are the partners able to face this conflict directly or have they displaced it onto other problems, such as difficulties with children or with in-laws? Can such displacement, if any, be tackled directly at a given time, to allow direct treatment of the marital difficulty?

216

Or would such an approach be likely to precipitate premature withdrawal from treatment or deterioration of the marriage? Is the displacement temporarily necessary for the partners because of the family's present phase of development or the urgency of other pressures? If so, a temporary concentration on such problems within the family as friction with children or in-laws may offer the partners a more acceptable area for initial intervention. As the feasibility of improvement in family relationships is demonstrated in areas slightly less vulnerable than the marital one, the partners may become able to lower their defenses enough to begin work on the marital problem itself. Before this avenue can be chosen, however, the worker must weigh the alternative: Might inclusion of the children unduly prolong the parents' displacement of the marital difficulty and thus further undermine the marriage? Might it tend to increase the children's exaggerated sense of responsibility for causing or healing the parents' problems and thus weaken the family system and shake the foundations of the children's growth?

The answers to these questions clearly depend not only on the nature of the family system and its participants at a given time and on their probable response to inclusion in treatment, but also on the worker's orientation and on his skill in using a multiple-client situation for purposes of furthering disentanglement as well as enhancing cohesion, as appropriate.

Basic Considerations
Regarding System
and Subsystem Interrelationships

One might propose that the means of intervention in marital treatment needs to be selected with a view to at least four aspects of the relationship of the family system and its subsystems to the marital and familial conflict: (a) It is important to consider and define the system of entanglement, the extent to which the whole family system, its subsystems, or individual members may be actively or passively enmeshed in the marital conflict.[17] (b) It is necessary to determine which system or subsystem is most endangered by the conflict and whether it should be treated directly or not. This involves deciding whether direct treatment should, at a

[17] For a more detailed discussion of the concept of entanglement *see* Wynne (50).

given time, be geared mainly to helping the participants to change their dysfunctional system, to supporting them in optimal functioning without attempting change, or to supporting the endangered system to sustain it while members belonging to different or overlapping subsystems within the family may be undergoing direct treatment geared to change. (c) The worker must assess which system or subsystem may be the one most crucial for the whole family's survival and recovery and whether this system should be treated directly. (d) Perhaps most important of all, the worker must strive for clarity as to whether the total family system or one or more of its subsystems may offer the most promising avenue for therapeutic intervention at a given time.

A number of more specific system-level considerations are also urgently relevant. They involve factors that will be discussed later, such as the stage of family life cycle, the stage of the marital conflict, the environmental situation, the phase of treatment, and what the worker can bring into the specific treatment system. In view of this multiplicity of considerations, it is all the more important for the worker to identify and work with the most promising system or subsystem, so that in the end the most endangered and the most crucial systems can be affected. At times this strategy may appear contraindicated if only the area of most conspicuous turmoil is considered. It is therefore urgent that his original assessment be constantly re-evaluated so that intervention techniques suggested by the worker's initial impression and reactions and by his general orientation may be revised in the light of further contact.

It follows from this view that the specifics of the interactional difficulty are not as important for the worker's decisions as is the role of these factors within the family and the treatment systems. Individual vulnerability and even severe psychopathology need not bar joint or family interviewing if the marital or family system holds enough elements of mutual support to bolster the individual, ease his defenses, and reduce his sense of disloyalty about discussing marital or other family matters. They become bars to these approaches only when these supports are missing or have been eroded in the course of conflict, or when the intrapsychic problems are so intense and so rigidly structured that there is no room for opening up or adapting to outside influences or for seeking better rapport. In that case, individual sessions may offer the necessary corrective experience within a nonentrenched relationship and may thus open up the possibility of progress in multiple-client sessions later on. Excessive fighting or acting out also need not rule out joint or family sessions unless this behavior emanates from consistently destructive motives that wipe out the possibility of a promising therapeutic point of entry in family interviews.

Before the worker can be sure that the prevailing motivation is destructive and that he is being genuinely excluded by the family rather than by his own apprehensions about coping with their particular behavioral patterns, he will do well to probe for a clearer picture of the dangers that the family's concerted resistance may be attempting to ward off (23) and for the values it may be trying to protect and preserve. If he can gain some understanding of these underlying concerns, he may be able to ease their fear of admitting him into the interaction or help them realize that the alternative to his admission and to treatment is the even more threatening realistic danger, posed by their exclusion of constructive changes, to the family's survival as a unit and as a haven for at least minimally healthy individuation of its members. In some situations, of course, the partners' or older children's more realistic recognition of their individual and shared needs, capacities, and opportunities may convince them that they cannot satisfy each other or make room for each other's growth. In that case, the partners may decide against continuing the marriage, or older children may prepare to leave the home. Such developments would call for the worker's use of whatever type of interview would be the most helpful in clarifying their decisions and dealing with the consequences of these for the individuals concerned and for the whole family.

This combined concern with family entanglements and with the identification and therapeutic use of the currently most endangered, most crucial, or most promising system or subsystems for intervention is reflected, although not necessarily always made articulate, in the efforts of the respondents and of a majority of the writers to use, in the course of marital treatment, whatever combination of interviewing modalities seems most appropriate. Eventually this trend may lead to greater use of family interviews concurrently with joint and/or individual sessions even in the treatment of marital problems. This is likely to be true especially as some success in treatment may call for temporary shifts in modality so that the system or subsystem essential for consolidating or

219

sustaining the changes achieved may be involved directly in the contact. Such a focus may be temporarily essential if relapse into the status quo ante is to be prevented and reinforcement of the new system modifications encouraged. Conversely, a shift in interviewing modes may also be necessary because system interferences from other subsystems or from intrapsychic pressures within one or more members may prevent progress with a given group of treatment participants. This may call for direct and temporarily exclusive treatment of the interfering system or subsystem. In other situations, it may require concurrent sessions with the interfering individuals or subsystems on the one hand, and with all the regular treatment participants together, on the other.

The worker considering therapeutic entry into the marital or family system or a shift in modality will always need to bear in mind the pivotal role of the marital subsystem. When direct strengthening of the marriage is feasible, when the partners' satisfactions within it can be increased or their dissatisfactions and disillusionment at least minimized, when possible problems of separateness and closeness can be clarified and eased, the benefits are likely to spill over into the rest of the family system. The parents' more appropriate role functioning is likely to free the children for roles more befitting their age and sex than the roles into which they have been pressed by their entanglement in the conflict. The achievement of such effects, of course, may require multiple decisions regarding the modalities best suited to working through the repercussions and temporary dislocations attendant on such change.

Any possibility of therapeutic gain also implies the risk of damage as a result of treatment. Thus recognition of the assets of the marital and family systems must carry with it an awareness of their particular limitations. Viewing the family system as a whole, the worker will need to weigh the possible cost of treatment or of treatment failure against the likelihood and extent of possible gains. Thus he may, for instance, as Carroll and his associates have pointed out (16), need to assess whether he would be justified in disturbing an unhealthy marital balance if little would seem to be gained for the partners by a changed relationship. Whether he moves toward or away from therapeutic intervention with a goal of considerable change, the worker will have to choose that modality, or those modalities in combination, that will best enlist the participants who will be necessary for and affected by the chosen treatment approach, whether it be remedial, sustaining, or preventive.

All the criteria discussed so far need to be considered not only in relation to each other but also in the context of the intermediate and long-range goals of treatment. This involves an assessment, as already intimated, of the family's stage in the maturational cycle and the marital conflict, of its relationship with the outside world, and of the worker's capacities and orientation.

The Family's Maturational Phase

Treatment goals are evolved in relation not only to the tasks made necessary by the partners' unique problems but also to those that normally arise in the course of the family life cycle and may or may not be complicated by the marital difficulty. Since the composition of the family varies in the course of its life, different combinations of family members may need to participate in sessions variously designed to help them cope with tasks typically presented at given stages of family maturation. Considerable departure from any such "typical" interviewing patterns may, of course, be advisable for specific families for all the reasons already discussed in this and the previous chapter.

Two stages of the family maturation often marked by marital conflict are those concerned with the major emancipatory tasks. One of these occurs when the young couple is struggling to establish their own new-family identity while yet striving to reforge into the new form the old ties with their families of origin. The other develops when the same couple faces the need of their now adolescent children for appropriate emancipation. Whether interviews at these stages should include all the participants in the family drama together, or whether the different generations should be seen separately is still a point of controversy among family therapists who differ on the comparative importance of working the problems through jointly (41) or of reinforcing the process of individuation by means of noninclusive interviewing modalities (see Chap. 4, pp. 146–147).

Other family life stages, such as those of preparing for the first child, nurturing the young, helping children to branch out into the wider world of peers, school, and so on, may variously call for strengthening of the marital dyad or for concentration on parent-child or intersibling involvements or on the family system as a whole, while the tasks facing the partners in the "empty nest" or in retirement are again more likely to call for major concentration on the marital dyad. At other points in the family's life cycle that concentration may have to be diluted through interviewing modes appropriate to the right admixture of closeness and separateness as vocational pressures of either mate or severe problems of ill-health or advancing age in one of the partners require the other spouse to find at least some interests and satisfactions not dependent on the preoccupied or incapacitated spouse.

The Stage
of Marital Conflict

Because of the pivotal role of the marital dyad, the family life stage at any given point can never of itself determine the choice of interviewing technique without careful evaluation also of the point the couple seem to have reached in their marital conflict. Unless this is taken into account, the acuteness or the ramifications of that conflict might render useless or even harmful a modality that might otherwise have been logical.

A basic link between the question of criteria for choice of modality and the concept of conflict escalation can be found by scrutiny of the relative attractions and rewards inside and outside the family system, in the manner of Cartwright's analysis of groups involved in a process of planned change (17). Such scrutiny can help the worker understand which subsystem or which aspects of the total family system still hold out enough hope of gratification or actual gratification for the partners to promise some benefits from therapeutic intervention and from further bolstering of these assets.

Cartwright stresses that a group is attractive to its members to the extent to which it satisfies their needs and that its influence over its members is commensurate with its attractiveness for them (17). Clearly, marital partners and children old enough to have any option are likely to be willing to work for restoration of the family if its attraction for them has only been somewhat impaired. However, few married couples come to an agency at that early point in the conflict spiral. At the other extreme are those for whom the rewards of the system have become so minimal that they are no longer interested in working to revive it. For such groups joint or family interviews may prove impossible because the members refuse to participate even though the worker may be able to envisage ways in which such sessions could prove helpful, either in holding out some overlooked satisfactions or in planning for separation or divorce.

Midway between these two points of minimal and maximal family disintegration lie all the other typical phases of the conflict spiral—the latent but increasingly dissatisfying stage, the point of "trigger and clash," the spread of conflict, and the search for allies and for alternate sources of gratification (9). Again, Cartwright's concepts (17) imply some helpful pointers for treatment: If the family members perceive the therapeutic goals in joint or family interviews as important, then such sessions may become an instrument for rebuilding family satisfactions. If the partners and family members find the values, attitudes, and behaviors expressed in the worker-family interaction to be deeply relevant to basic although possibly unrecognized satisfactions they derive from participation in the family itself, then such sessions may help them to widen or deepen hitherto shrinking areas of gratification. A positive spiral may thus replace the negative one. Such sessions may be indicated particularly because the worker's entry into the system introduces the long view. He has seen many other families go into the throes of conflict and emerge from them with improved solutions or attitudes. This helps him to stimulate or revive the partners' and family members' interest in working on their shared problems, because he offers realistic hope that increased family cohesion, growth, and strength can emerge for this family, too, from such a process.

At times, then, joint or family interviews may be indicated to reverse the direction of the conflict spiral. In other situations they may, oddly enough, be needed to bring on a new phase of that same spiral. This may be especially true of the points between latent conflict and its triggering into open clash. When the family has been held captive by pseudomutuality pressures, for instance, during the latent stages of marital conflict, the family interview may be needed to bring conflict into the open so that it can be dealt with. In such cases, a temporary escalation of conflict may be a necessary prelude to the development of positive trends and may have to be fostered actively.

The Family's Relationship to the Wider Environment

Constant clarification of the issue of treatment priorities entails a view of the family not only as a system with its own components, but also as a system affected by and sometimes affecting the wider network of social, economic, and other systems in the world outside. When special pressures, opportunities, or dangers arise from beyond the family, the worker may need to weigh whether the married couple, or perhaps the whole family, may need to be seen together so that together they may learn ways of coping more effectively with the environment. They may need to be bolstered with respect to the partners' right to a life-style or sex role patterns that may run counter to prevailing norms but may work well for them. In other instances the worker may need to see the whole family together so that he may reinforce the parents as they try using their increased capacities for co-operation as a couple to help the total family resist, escape from, or join with others to transform a destructive environment. Similarly, joint or family interviews may be called for to strengthen the relevant subsystem or total family system for confrontation of other issues that the environment may present or the members may need to bring to outside attention and that call for maximal mutual support among themselves. Preparation for and mobilization of the couple or whole family for referral might be one familiar illustration of this type of situation.

Worker Capacities

In addition to all the foregoing factors related to the family system and its components, the worker's assets and liabilities as a therapeutic participant must be carefully weighed in selecting the optimal membership of the treatment system. In order to be and remain an effective therapeutic agent within the family and its subsystems, the worker needs not only some of the same skills and qualities that stood him in good stead for individual interviewing; he also requires a cluster of those capacities that equip him to become part of a treatment system that includes two or more members of the same family. Such capacities are most likely to be developed when the agency administration's over-all policies encourage caseworkers to face what is still for most of them a new professional experience. Without such backing, the worker would find it difficult indeed to withstand and use constructively the multiple stresses of multiple-client interviewing and to use with the necessary flexibility the skills and qualities needed for this taxing approach. Nor is he likely, without agency backing, to risk having to tolerate the temporary dislocations or even momentarily explosive results of his intervention in the family system and the discomfort of inevitable treatment errors on his own part.

Furthermore, he needs to be capable of openness to a present and open alien system without being so open that his differentness from the family is obliterated and his efforts are nullified by the partners' or family members' efforts to manipulate or reject him or to absorb him into their system. Such openness calls for an ability to cope simultaneously with people of both sexes and of different age and maturity levels, and for a capacity to feel and convey a realistic sense of hope for the family group and its members even when they confront him as a group with their overwhelming sense of present troubles and past failures. If there are points within the marital conflict spiral or within the family life cycle that are especially threatening to the worker because of his own experience with and within family systems, his choice of modality must be influenced by this knowledge and by the assistance available to him for coping with this stress. The type of interview most appropriate for the family at a given time may become the least appropriate if it renders the worker incapable of functioning as a therapeutic agent within the treatment system.

The caseworker's philosophy and therapeutic orientation also play a decisive role in the choice of modality and in its eventual effectiveness. If the pursuit of individual problems in growing and in relating to others is his central concern, the worker is likely to see individual treatment and some resolution of these problems as the eventual treatment goal and to regard multiple-client sessions as a possible prelude rather than a major means of interviewing (see 48, Part II, study No. 6). If, like Satir (38), he believes it most essential for the worker to recognize and affect the nature and operation of the basic family rules, then his goal will favor

225

multiple-client approaches that involve the whole system of rules, its makers and sustainers.

Clarifying Effects
of the Complex System-Level View

It must be evident from the foregoing that a system-level perspective provides no simple approach to the selection of interviewing modalities in marital treatment. Rather, it urges consideration of what may at first seem an unnecessarily complex set of factors. It involves not only an assessment of the family system and the treatment system viewed horizontally, with their subsystems' varying impacts on each other; it also entails a longitudinal system-level view of the varying circumstances of the family life cycle, the course of the marital conflict, and the treatment process.

Although indeed complex, all these perspectives together should help the worker to remain alert to the full range of considerations and feelings relevant to his understanding of the complex interlocking of factors in marriage and family life and to his responsibility for helping the partners decide on priorities in treatment. As a result, his focus may be greatly sharpened, his clarity as to the best area for therapeutic intervention at a given time greatly increased, and his choice of approach made more relevant to the partners' and family's immediate needs.

The concentration in this chapter on criteria regarding the use of joint and family interviews in marital treatment, with some implied criteria about individual interviews in this context, should not be taken as opposition to the use of other modalities. The next chapter will discuss rather briefly the new or revived interest of caseworkers in the use of couples' groups, multifamily groups, and other variants of the multiple-client approaches in treating marital problems. As will be mentioned there, the principles just outlined with reference to the choice of joint and family interviews can be explored for their relevance to all these approaches as well.

SUMMARY OF CURRENT VIEWS AND FURTHER QUESTIONS

Since family interviewing is still evolving as a treatment modality, it is not surprising that there are many uncertainties and differences of opinion, even among experienced practitioners, regarding its specific uses. Nevertheless, important areas of consensus do emerge from the responses regarding criteria for its use with couples with marital troubles who wish to maintain their marriage.

Areas of Wide Agreement

The use of family interviews for diagnosis, as noted in Chapter 2, has become increasingly accepted. From them workers gain an understanding of both the problems and the positives in the marital and family situation and a sense of the possibilities for greater family fulfillment and growth. As for treatment, joint interviews are regarded as the core of marital treatment by most respondents, although not by all the writers. In the main, respondents see family interviews as a useful auxiliary method, indicated when family members other than the partners have become entangled in or cannot easily be disentangled from the marital conflict or are actively provoking conflict. They also see them as useful preventive measures to show the children that something is being done about the strife and to reassure them, when this is valid, that their parents, like themselves, want the family kept intact.

It is clear that respondents regard adequate training in family interviewing as an important prerequisite for its use. The worker's personality and skills emerge from the comments as further crucial factors if family interviews are to yield their unique values. The worker must be able—or able to learn—to feel some comfort with this type of session, to be alert and perceptive, and to relate to all the family without forming inappropriate alliances with individual members. He should have the capacity to understand, tolerate, and use therapeutically the realistic and irrational impact of the family on himself, and may need special stamina in handling multiple hostilities.

Granting the many over-all values of family interviews for diagnosis and treatment, respondents yet see many contraindications to their use evolving from specific considerations of individual need and vulnerability, family interaction, and family-worker relationship. All of these, once again, are weighed also in the light of the worker's characteristics and skills. Thus the lack of necessary special skills in family interviewing was viewed as contraindicating the use of family interviews, but the modality was not unanimously ruled out even when the partners are moving toward dissolution of the marriage, because family sessions in such cases were seen as an opportunity for helping the members to deal with the consequences of that situation. When the partners wish to stay together, the contraindications mentioned were not chiefly concerned with the presence, per se, of such negative factors as great personal rigidity, needfulness, or self-preoccupation among individual family members, or with their apprehension about participating in an interview with all the others. Instead, these factors seemed to be viewed as barring use of the modality only if they were excessive enough, and if the family balance was precarious enough, to allow them to impair the effectiveness of the family session. Since many of the contraindications offered were cited by the workers most experienced in family interviewing, one sees a confirmation of the common trend that greater refinement of criteria is likely to follow more use and knowledge of a given therapeutic instrument.

Areas of Disagreement

It would be neither valid nor desirable at this stage in the development of the family approach to minimize the differences of opinion that necessarily beset this rapidly developing field. Some of these exist in relation to the use of interviews with families including adolescent children. Moreover, some practitioners ask that parents, or even the offspring too, be aware of the children's involvement in the marital conflict if family sessions are to be used. Others set no such requirements. Severe psychopathology, excessive fighting, and rivalry for the worker were symptoms on whose significance for the choice of family interviews there was also disagreement. The worker's role is also under cross-fire. Although this emerges more clearly in the literature than in the responses, some see him mainly as a catalyst to the family as a therapeutic work group; others ask a capacity for active intervention or direct teaching. A third view sees all these roles as needed, but at different times or with different types of families.

A System-Level Perspective

While respondents seldom described their criteria in system terms, a tentative effort has been made in this chapter to restate their views and those of various authors from this perspective. This venture yielded some general principles that may help to guide the worker in choosing joint or family sessions in the course of marital treatment. With respect to family interviews in particular, this approach suggests that all the members may need to be seen together if all are entangled, actively or passively, in the marital conflict. This would be indicated at least for purposes of recognizing both the difficulty and the fact that the parents are trying to deal with it in a constructive fashion. However, system-level considerations make clear that the extent of entanglement is not in itself a decisive guide for selecting those who should be included in the interview. The total family should become the system of intervention for treatment only if it represents the most promising area for intervention, support, or prevention at a given time and if such treatment at least would not further endanger the most jeopardized or weaken the most crucial subsystems within the family.

Areas Requiring
Further Attention

Many areas requiring further practice and study await clarification. Of prime importance among them is the respondents' almost pervasive sense of malaise about including children at all in situations in which a marital problem is being treated. This seems to relate to the core issues of subsystem strengths and promising points of entry and suggests the urgent need for further development of the system-level view. It calls for a clearer spelling-out of the nature and requirements of marital privacy for specific types of families and of the role of children in the maintenance of various patterns of marital balance (10). It may well be that there are differences in what is felt as unique and essential to the marriage, depending on the basic type of marital relationship a given couple has established.

The effect of the various treatment modalities on the relative strengthening or weakening of the family and its subsystems also needs to be evaluated constantly. Perhaps further attention should be given to the possible indications for the use of family interviews and family subgroup interviews in situations in which two sets of children from previous marriages, as well as the newly

229

married pair, need to be helped in integrating into a new family unit.

A common problem as to choice of approach, left undiscussed in the responses, is posed by those families in which one partner clings to the spouse who has already decided to abandon the marriage. Many applications for help to family agencies are made at precisely this point in the marital conflict and pose difficult questions as to the wisdom and the possible results of including the children or even both partners in the same interview.

Other questions abound: What is a "valid" family secret? Are family interviews necessarily barred if the family should close the worker out, or could this maneuver be handled at the family level? Should children below the age of easy speech necessarily be excluded from treatment sessions? Need the positive or supportive elements in the family outweigh the negatives if family sessions are to succeed, or might the presence of even a few such elements sometimes offer the possibility of sufficient therapeutic leverage? If so, what are these elements in what situations? Are there any topics, such as the parents' sexual problems, for instance, to which children should not be exposed in the sessions except in specified circumstances? Might family interviews be used to hold out more constructive substitute gratifications, even to those who are now barred from them, because they use such sessions only for negative gratification? Are there any dangers in a family's becoming aware of the full intensity of their mutual destructiveness? How can these be recognized and avoided? What techniques are appropriate when the children need both parents but the parents need to separate? The list is incomplete and no doubt every practitioner experienced in family therapy could add to it.

BIBLIOGRAPHY

Study Group Report

1. CINCINNATI, OHIO, JEWISH FAMILY SERVICE BUREAU, *Family Diagnosis and Treatment as Related to Marital Counseling.*
Study group participants: Morton R. Startz (Leader), Anne Billinkoff, Miriam H. Dettelbach, Mrs. Paula Edelstein, Mrs. Ruth Goldberg, Rose L. Greenstein, Margarete Hirsch, Helen Lampe, Jacqueline Lancaster, Michael Meyer, Mrs. Miriam O. Smith, Mrs. Bernice Temin, Mrs. Miriam Tsevat, Mrs. Doris Wolfenstein.

General References

2. ACKERMAN, NATHAN W., "The Family Approach to Marital Disorders," in Bernard L. Greene (ed.), *The Psychotherapies of Marital Disharmony*, Free Press, New York, 1965, pp. 153–168.
3. ———, "The Future of Family Psychotherapy," in Nathan W. Ackerman, Frances L. Beatman, and Sanford N. Sherman (eds.), *Expanding Theory and Practice in Family Therapy*, Family Service Association of America, New York, 1967, pp. 3–16.
4. ———, *Treating the Troubled Family*, Basic Books, New York, 1966.
5. AIKIN, DOROTHY, "A Project on Family Diagnosis and Treatment," in *Social Work Practice, 1963*, Selected Papers of the National Conference on Social Welfare, Columbia University Press, New York, 1963, pp. 3–18.
6. BARDILL, DONALD R., and RYAN, FRANCIS J., *Family Group Casework: A Casework Approach to Family Therapy*, Catholic University of America Press, Washington, D.C., 1964.
7. BEATMAN, FRANCES L., "Intergenerational Aspects of Family Therapy," in Nathan W. Ackerman, Frances L. Beatman, and Sanford N. Sherman (eds.), *Expanding Theory and Practice in Family Therapy*, Family Service Association of America, New York, 1967, pp. 29–38.
8. ———, "The Training and Preparation of Workers for Family-Group Treatment," *Social Casework*, Vol. XLV, No. 4 (April 1964), pp. 202–208.
9. BECK, DOROTHY FAHS, "Marital Conflict: Its Course and Treatment as Seen by Caseworkers," *Social Casework*, Vol. XLVII, No. 4 (April 1966), pp. 211–221.
10. ———, "Variations in Treatment in Relation to Type of Marital Interaction," in Dorothy Fahs Beck (ed.), *The Treatment of Marital Problems*, Family Service Association of America, New York (in preparation).
11. BELL, JOHN E., *Family Group Therapy*, Public Health Monograph No. 64, U.S. Government Printing Office, Washington, D.C., 1961.
12. ———, "Recent Advances in Family Group Therapy," *Journal of Child Psychology and Psychiatry*, Vol. III, No. 1 (January/March 1962), pp. 1–15.
13. ———, "A Theoretical Position for Family Group Therapy," *Family Process*, Vol. II, No. 1 (March 1963), pp. 1–14.
14. BOSZORMENYI-NAGY, IVAN, and FRAMO, JAMES L. (eds.), *Intensive Family Therapy: Theoretical and Practical Aspects*, Hoeber Medical Division, Harper & Row, New York, 1965.
15. BOWEN, MURRAY, "Family Psychotherapy," in "The Family as the Unit of Study and Treatment," Workshop, 1959, Stephen Fleck (Chairman), *American Journal of Orthopsychiatry*, Vol. XXXI, No. 1 (January 1961), pp. 40–60.
16. CARROLL, EDWARD J., et al., "Psychotherapy of Marital Couples," *Family Process*, Vol. II, No. 1 (March 1963), pp. 25–33.
17. CARTWRIGHT, DORWIN, "Achieving Change in People," in Warren G. Bennis, Kenneth D. Benne, and Robert Chin (eds.), *The Planning of Change*, Holt, Rinehart & Winston, New York, 1966, pp. 698–706.

18. COMMITTEE ON FAMILY DIAGNOSIS AND TREATMENT OF THE MIDWESTERN REGIONAL COMMITTEE OF THE FAMILY SERVICE ASSOCIATION OF AMERICA, *Casebook on Family Diagnosis and Treatment,* Family Service Association of America, New York, 1965.

19. EINSTEIN, GERTRUDE, *Report on Family Group Treatment Project at Jewish Family Service,* Jewish Family Service of Philadelphia, 1964 (mimeographed).

20. FRAMO, JAMES L., "Rationale and Techniques of Intensive Family Therapy," in Ivan Boszormenyi-Nagy and James L. Framo (eds.), *Intensive Family Therapy: Theoretical and Practical Aspects,* Hoeber Medical Division, Harper & Row, New York, 1965, pp. 143–212.

21. FREEMAN, VICTOR J., et al., " 'Family Group Counseling' as Differentiated from Other 'Family Therapies,' " *International Journal of Group Psychotherapy,* Vol. XIII, No. 2 (April 1963), pp. 167–175.

22. FROSCHER, HAZEL B., "Special Tasks of the Middle and Ending Phases of Treatment," in Dorothy Fahs Beck (ed.), *The Treatment of Marital Problems,* Family Service Association of America, New York (in preparation).

23. GEHRKE, SHIRLEY, and KIRSCHENBAUM, MARTIN, "Survival Patterns in Family Conjoint Therapy," *Family Process,* Vol. VI, No. 1 (March 1967), pp. 67–80.

24. GROSSER, GEORGE H., and PAUL, NORMAN L., "Ethical Issues in Family Group Therapy," *American Journal of Orthopsychiatry,* Vol. XXXIV, No. 5 (October 1964), pp. 875–884.

25. HALEY, JAY, *Strategies of Psychotherapy,* Grune & Stratton, New York, 1963.

26. ————, and HOFFMAN, LYNN, *Techniques of Family Therapy,* Basic Books, New York, 1967.

27. HELGASON, ARTIE, "Counseling in Relation to Separation and Divorce," in Dorothy Fahs Beck (ed.), *The Treatment of Marital Problems,* Family Service Association of America, New York (in preparation).

28. KEMPLER, WALTER, "Experiential Family Therapy," *International Journal of Group Psychotherapy,* Vol. XV, No. 1 (January 1965), pp. 57–71.

29. KLEIN, ALAN F., "Exploring Family Group Counseling," *Social Work,* Vol. VIII, No. 1 (January 1963), pp. 23–29.

30. LEADER, ARTHUR L., "The Role of Intervention in Family-Group Treatment," *Social Casework,* Vol. XLV, No. 6 (June 1964), pp. 327–332.

31. MacGREGOR, ROBERT, et al., *Multiple Impact Therapy with Families,* McGraw-Hill Book Co., New York, 1964.

32. MITCHELL, CELIA B., "Integrative Therapy of the Family Unit," *Social Casework,* Vol. XLVI, No. 2 (February 1965), pp. 63–69.

33. ————, "The Use of Family Sessions in the Diagnosis and Treatment of Disturbances in Children," *Social Casework,* Vol. XLI, No. 6 (June 1960), pp. 283–290.

34. POLLAK, OTTO, "Entrance of the Caseworker into Family Interaction," *Social Casework,* Vol. XLV, No. 4 (April 1964), pp. 216–220.

35. ————, and BRIELAND, DONALD, "The Midwest Seminar on Family Diagnosis and Treatment," *Social Casework,* Vol. XLII, No. 7 (July 1961), pp. 319–324.

36. RONALL, RUTH, "The Caseworker's Objective Characteristics and Background as Factors in the Treatment Process," in Dorothy Fahs Beck (ed.), *The Treatment of Marital Problems,* Family Service Association of America, New York (in preparation).

37. ———, "The Caseworker's Personality and Skill as Factors in the Treatment Process," in Dorothy Fahs Beck (ed.), *The Treatment of Marital Problems,* Family Service Association of America, New York (in preparation).

38. SATIR, VIRGINIA M., *Conjoint Family Therapy: A Guide to Theory and Technique,* Science and Behavior Books, Palo Alto, Calif., 1964.

39. ———, "Conjoint Marital Therapy," in Bernard L. Greene (ed.), *The Psychotherapies of Marital Disharmony,* Free Press, New York, 1965, pp. 121–133.

40. SEARLES, HAROLD F., "The Contributions of Family Treatment to the Psychotherapy of Schizophrenia," in Ivan Boszormenyi-Nagy and James L. Framo (eds.), *Intensive Family Therapy: Theoretical and Practical Aspects,* Hoeber Medical Division, Harper & Row, New York, 1965, pp. 463–495.

41. SCHERZ, FRANCES H., "The Crisis of Adolescence in Family Life," *Social Casework,* Vol. XLVIII, No. 4 (April 1967), pp. 209–215.

42. ———, "Exploring the Use of Family Interviews in Diagnosis," *Social Casework,* Vol. XLV, No. 4 (April 1964), pp. 209–215.

43. ———, "Family Treatment," Paper presented at the Biennial Conference of the Family Service Association of America, Detroit, Mich., November 11, 1965 (mimeographed).

44. ———, "Multiple-Client Interviewing: Treatment Implications," *Social Casework,* Vol. XLIII, No. 3 (March 1962), pp. 120–125.

45. SCHLESINGER, BENJAMIN, *The Multi-Problem Family,* University of Toronto Press, Toronto, Canada, 1963.

46. SHERMAN, SANFORD N., "Intergenerational Discontinuity and Therapy of the Family," *Social Casework,* Vol. XLVIII, No. 4 (April 1967), pp. 216–221.

47. ———, "The Sociopsychological Character of Family-Group Treatment," *Social Casework,* Vol. XLV, No. 4 (April 1964), pp. 195–201.

48. SMITH, NEILSON F. (ed.), "Family Phenomena, Problems, and Treatment: Some Family Agency Studies" (A Terminal Progress Report on the Project, "Casework on Marital Problems: A National Experiment in Staff Development"), Family Service Association of America, New York, 1968 (mimeographed).

49. WEAKLAND, JOHN H., "The 'Double-Bind' Hypothesis of Schizophrenia and Three-Party Interaction," in Don D. Jackson (ed.), *The Etiology of Schizophrenia,* Basic Books, New York, 1960, pp. 373–388.

50. WYNNE, LYMAN C., "Some Indications and Contraindications for Exploratory Family Therapy," in *Intensive Family Therapy: Theoretical and Practical Aspects,* Ivan Boszormenyi-Nagy and James L. Framo (eds.), Harper & Row, New York, 1965, pp. 289–322.

6

Expansion of the Circle
of Treatment Participants
and Related Experimental Approaches

Recent years have seen increased use of a variety of approaches aimed at direct handling of the marital or family interaction but not necessarily confining interview participation to one worker or to the married couple or the immediate family alone. Therapeutic teams, married couples' groups, multifamily groups, multiple-impact therapy, and treatment of the social network are modalities that have been attracting attention. Not all of these are new, but they have been viewed in a new light in family agency practice. In addition, technological advances have made possible the use of various devices such as one-way screens and audio and video tape to dramatize the interactional process or to enhance treatment and allow the student therapist a more direct experience of the treatment process than is possible through verbal reports. Although these devices may be helpful for many different forms of treatment, they have appealed in particular to those interested in joint and family interviewing and related group approaches to marital and family problems.

Hardly any of the approaches just cited were in use in most of the participating agencies at the time this project began, although a few agencies were experimenting with the use of several workers at once and with couples' groups. Nevertheless, all these modalities and the devices used to enhance their effectiveness warrant some consideration in this monograph because of their great practical and conceptual relevance to the issues involved in treatment of

234

marital problems. They combine some of the special features of group therapy with the unique characteristics of interviews allowing the worker to intervene directly in the marital or family system. They must therefore be considered here briefly, even though they are still experimental and marked by controversy and by a dearth of information about their possible limitations and drawbacks, their long-range effectiveness, or the special worker, client, or family characteristics that would augur the likelihood of their success or failure. Even reports in the literature are still far too sparse for any full clarity, let alone consensus, regarding these approaches. Nevertheless, the project responses that did come in on this topic reflected sufficient excitement and enthusiasm on the part of the few who had ventured into these areas to warrant consideration of these modalities.

Since such responses were few in number, the format of the present chapter differs from that of the rest of this monograph in that it is based on consultations and on the literature far more than on caseworkers' responses. It is intended mainly to convey whatever may seem conceptually stimulating and relevant to marital treatment among these rapidly developing endeavors. Quite possibly a more serious study of their results and implications may lead to a re-evaluation of the division between family casework and group work (37) and to a reconsideration of the relevance of the accumulated experience and literature of social group work for the treatment of marital and family problems.

Consistent with the focus throughout this volume, the present chapter omits discussion of the details of technique and deals only with the special values of these modalities and criteria for their use. It also omits discussion of group treatment that involves only persons unrelated to each other, since, although a probe on group treatment was included among the source questions, respondents cited no values from such treatment that would not also be attributable to couples' groups and multifamily groups (see p. 6). Source materials for the chapter include comments submitted by respondents who answered the project questions on multiple-client interviews, a supplementary query in March 1965 focused specifically on couples' groups, and one study group report from the National Experiment in Staff Development, a program that was a direct outgrowth of this present project (16). Occasional articles in the literature, some unpublished agency reports, views of consult-

235

ants experimenting in this field, and information gleaned through workshops were also drawn on.[1]

Respondents' comments covered such topics as the values of using several therapists or couples' groups in the course of treatment of marital problems, with a few comments offered on possible criteria for the use of more than one worker. Discussion of these topics has been supplemented from other sources. However, the criteria cited for the use of couples' groups and the comments on all issues related to multifamily groups, multiple-impact or network therapy, and technological aids have been derived almost without exception from consultations, workshops, and perusal of the literature rather than from the respondents.

For the purposes of this chapter, a couples' group is defined as one in which two or more married couples participate in the session with one or more workers, while a multifamily group is one in which two or more groups, each consisting of at least the married pair and one or more of their children or other relatives, are seen simultaneously by one or more workers. Multiple-therapist sessions may involve two or more workers of the same or different sexes, as stated in the context.

INCLUSION OF MORE THAN ONE CASEWORKER

Originally, agencies seemed to resort to the use of two caseworkers simultaneously in interviews with one couple primarily in order to improve treatment impact and co-ordination in situations in which the partners had been seen individually by separate workers. However, the use of two or more workers has also been found to ease the observational load on the individual therapist and to modify the special emotional pressures besetting both the clients and the individual worker in joint and family interviews, couples' groups, and multifamily groups. Respondents, like many authors (2, 22, 23, 28), saw such a procedure as helpful diagnostically and therapeutically, and even as benefiting the agency itself.

---

[1] For consultation the author is indebted to Mrs. Margaret Lovell of the Family Service Organization, Worcester, Mass., and to Dr. Dorothy Aikin of the University of Chicago School of Social Service Administration. Workshops attended were focused on married couples' groups. They were headed by Mrs. Elsa Leichter of the New York Jewish Family Service, who also acted as consultant, and by Dr. Helene Papanek and Capt. Anthony A. Gottlieb, M.D.

Inevitably, certain pitfalls need to be taken into account, as incipient experience shows (23) and as will be made clearer in the discussion of criteria for the use of therapeutic teams. However, the following are tentatively seen as assets derived from the simultaneous participation of two or more workers in the interview.

Special Values
of Therapeutic Teams

Improved diagnosis and worker objectivity. Respondents and authors both mentioned the diagnostic values of having one worker's observations balanced against the other's (2, 35). Some respondents used periodic four-way interviews for this reason. Because one worker can pick up what the other misses, personal biases of both workers and clients become clearer (2), and the workers are likely to see the couple or family more realistically, especially since the momentarily less active worker can note the reactions of the overtly nonparticipating family members as well as the interaction of those engaged in the immediate interview give-and-take (35). As compared with situations in which the partners are seen by separate workers in individual interviews, overidentification with one client and competition between workers are reduced. Needless to say, this latter value is partly a function of the ability of the two workers to work well together.

Enrichment of treatment potential. The division of labor made possible by having more than one worker can, if it works well, ease the difficulties of treatment for both clients and workers (18). Leichter and Schulman (28) describe, for example, how one of them focuses more on broad group themes in multifamily sessions while the other responds more frequently to individual feelings. Others (2, 9) suggest that one worker can be using confrontation while the other is giving support. Thus the likelihood of mistimed confrontation attempts is reduced since the temporarily less active worker may spot the need to redirect the discussion (2). Additional impact on or support for the couple or family may be expected when one worker's comments reinforce the other's (20). Moreover, if the co-workers are of opposite sexes, no adult interview participant can feel outnumbered by the other sex—a factor that may be especially important in marital conflict when issues of relationship between the sexes may be dominant. When the partners are being seen in

237

concurrent individual sessions with separate workers and in a couples' group with two therapists, the presence of an individual's own therapist may hasten the therapeutic process because it exerts "gentle pressure" on the individual to bring out in the group intense feelings that have so far been expressed in separate sessions only (22, pp. 91–92).

Some of the remaining arguments in favor of the multiple-worker approach rest on the need for relief from the special pressures exerted on workers in joint and family interviews and in groups of couples or families. The presence of another therapist is seen as reducing the sense of pressure on the individual worker and as increasing his tolerance for taking or listening to expressions of intense hostility (2). It should also help the therapists to be more aware of countertransference reactions and therefore in better control of them, since each is in a position to spot such stirrings in the other's attitudes or behavior in relation to the clients (35).

Better co-ordination of treatment and treatment planning. The respondents who described using four-way interviews focused on their values for better co-ordination of treatment and treatment planning in situations in which the partners are undergoing primarily separate treatment experiences. They used such sessions periodically to co-ordinate treatment planning and the direction of change for the partners and, near termination, to review progress made. An example given of the latter use involved a situation in which two workers from separate agencies co-operated in joint sessions when eligibility requirements necessitated the treatment of a student spouse and his nonstudent wife in different settings.

An especially difficult problem was highlighted by the respondent group already mentioned, whose members had attempted treatment of a number of couples by placing one partner in a group and the other in individual sessions with another worker. With this approach the movement of the partners had proved very uneven. Some of those in individual treatment had dropped out, while the group members "tended to hold each other to the contract." Four-way interviews with the two partners, the group leader, and the caseworker were therefore set up "to refocus on the marital relationship and redefine some goals."

Leichter and Schulman, treating parents in a couples' group and their daughters in an adolescents' group, found it possible to integrate these two treatment experiences by jointly seeing single-family

238

units at various points in treatment as well as at the beginning and end. They see the coming together of both the therapists with all or some of the individual members of the family group as helping the child's therapist to "integrate for himself the changes in the parents," with the result that his overidentification with the child is diminished and he becomes able to help the child use positive changes in the parents for her own growth (29). Although this may seem to be a gain for the child rather than for the marital relationship, the elements associated with the progress of each are closely interwoven here since the parents' growth so often occurs in the course of their facing and working through marital problems.

Increased opportunities for learning new ways of relating, communicating, and problem-solving. The presence of two or more workers in the joint or family session inevitably gives rise to some differences of view and possibly to some tensions between the therapists. Several authors agree that the couple or family benefits from seeing the team handle or resolve their differences (30) and that the team's actions can thus become a helpful example for members in conflict. They see the good realtionship between the therapeutic team members as helping to reassure and free all the participating family members as they explore their own mutual relationships (18, p. 201; 23). In addition, the family may be particularly helped, as Pollak has stated (35), if the team's behavior and attitudes reveal new ways of coping with intimacy and with the need to check sexual fantasies about interview participants.

Enhanced opportunities for staff development and other agency gains. MacGregor and his associates, as well as Ryan and Bardill, stress that new lines of communication are opened up between staff members as a result of the shared experience in treating families. They also laud such sessions as a vehicle for training (30, 36). Whether casework hours are saved by such means is subject to differences of opinion (20, 28), since the time of two workers is required for the sessions and since practitioners differ regarding the need for joint worker conferences under such circumstances.

Criteria for Use
of Therapeutic Teams

Little clarity or unity of view seems to exist as yet on criteria for the use of therapeutic teams. Some respondents suggested their feasibility when "two workers have similar methods of work or respect for each other's work." Among the authors on this topic are those who believe that workers will best be able to work together comfortably and to communicate freely, with minimal competitiveness, if they are of equal rank (20). Others think that such difficulties can be worked through (28) and that mutual respect and the capacity to accept differences and to refrain from domination are more crucial than differences in background, skill, or experience.

It is clear from the foregoing that unresolved difficulties in the team's working relationship are likely to be detrimental to treatment. They may certainly be expected to have a negative effect on the clients' learning by identification. Whether some of the difficulties inherent in such relationships can be worked out will depend on the workers and on the assistance offered to them by the agency administration. Some of the problems may be relatively simple, such as irritation owing to the co-worker's interruptions at points conceived as crucial by the teammate (23). Others may be profoundly complex, as outlined by Hock and Donley (23), who describe the working through of feelings about sexuality, closeness, and exposure of inadequacy between a married male and an unmarried female co-worker. Whether the time and effort needed for working through such problems are justified by the therapeutic gains for the clients is probably a matter for individual consideration in each case of therapeutic partnership. In any case, it seems essential that the team relationship be free of competitive conflict and that each worker's responsibilities be clearly delineated.

Turning finally to indicators related to client needs, Gullerud and Harlan suggest three criteria for use with couples initially seen by separate workers (20). They would use the approach when more diagnostic information on the marriage relationship is needed, there has been an impasse in individual sessions, and the partners are ready, after individual treatment with workers of their own sex, to look at their relationship and modify their interaction.

INCLUSION OF SEVERAL COUPLES

Special Values

Couples' groups seem to have developed in response to the treatment challenge presented by partners who could not tolerate individual or joint sessions or made no progress in them. A sense of hope, almost of exhilaration, pervades some of the informal comments of practitioners who have described this approach. This excitement has even found its way into print in Berne's description of two therapists who found such a group "the greatest invention since the wheel" (5, p. 213). Project respondents were more staid in their comments. They singled out four unique values of the couples' group: enhanced diagnostic and therapeutic productivity, better maintenance of focus on the marriage, aid against stereotyping of the opposite sex,[2] and aid for couples who had benefited in individual treatment while their marriage failed to improve. In the present section, these and additional values not mentioned by respondents will be seen in the context of views offered by consultants, workshop sessions, and the literature.

Enhanced diagnostic and therapeutic productivity. Respondents saw simultaneous work on marital and group interaction as more productive than either approach alone. Moreover, diagnostic appraisal of the marital interaction was thought eased by the spouse's presence in the group and by the fact that the number of participants in any given couples' group involves precisely half the number of marriages represented by the same number of clients participating in a group without their own spouses. Since partners are emotionally involved with each other from the start, their co-presence also makes for lively and spontaneous behavior early in treatment, and thus speeds results (33).

Enhanced motivation and holding power. The power of a group —especially a group of married couples—to hold its members in treatment was acknowledged by various sources. One author stresses that attendance at these groups was exceptionally good, perhaps because of a particularly strong unity of purpose (8). Another emphasizes the optimism released early in treatment by the cathartic effect of fervently expressing aggressive emotions about marital friction in the presence of the partner and of others, without punishment and in a climate of understanding (6). An especially interesting example of the holding power of such groups was reported to the author by Arnold Mendelson of the New York Jewish Family Service, who was treating a group of married couples, each of which included at least one spouse with a criminal record. They termi-

---

[2] This can also be a gain in traditional group treatment. Here the added factor is experience of it in the partner's presence.

nated as a group after 110 sessions, or about two and a half years—a remarkable record in view of the usual difficulty of holding such couples in treatment.

Taken together, these experiences seem to confirm what Lovell has stressed, namely, that couples' groups can offer multiple reinforcement for the positive side of clients' ambivalence about treatment and may thus serve even to win and hold the reluctant partner.[3] This latter effect is also acknowledged by Janowicz (24), who describes the use of couples' groups to enable both the ambivalent wife and the hesitant worker to allow involvement of the seemingly unmotivated husband.

As Lovell sees it, the tendency to withdraw from contact seems lessened in couples' groups as compared with treatment in individual or joint sessions. Socially isolated couples are helped to overcome their alienation from others in a setting in which their marital problems are acknowledged. Group members are encouraged, by virtue of the clear and specific marital focus, to search for links with each other. They may, as Burton and Kaplan found with couples including at least one alcoholic partner, discover such a link in their sharing of a common suffering, thus experiencing a powerful impetus for treatment (10). It is possible that the staying power of couples in these groups may also be increased because members from outside the family have become witnesses to the treatment contract. Furthermore, hope grows from the vicarious experience of progress, regression, and renewed progress for different couples and from the fact that one couple's period of despair may coincide with another's emergence from such a state to a level of greatly improved mutual feeling and functioning. If this is true, it would be another argument in favor of selecting couples with at least some heterogeneity of interactional patterns and degree of alienation so that phases of conflict and treatment may vary within the group.

Better maintenance of focus on the marriage. In spite of the numerical size of couples' groups, the marital focus is reported easier to maintain in these than in the joint interview, when the worker may be tempted to see the clients mainly as two separate individuals. In the couples' group, in which all have come for help with the marital difficulty, the focus on the marriage may be more readily

---

[3] Personal communication to the author.

maintained since digressions will be seen as dysfunctional by most participants. Thus problems specific to the marital interaction, such as communicational difficulties rooted in problems about separateness and closeness, can be worked on especially readily, as one respondent stated.

Increased provision of support. Respondents and others seem agreed that group participants gain a special and meaningful kind of support from other group members. Self-esteem and mutual esteem are enhanced by witnessing that others also have severe marital difficulties and yet are likable people. In fact, the Worcester Family Service study group, in their follow-up contacts with participants in four couples' groups, found this realization of shared problems and feelings and of lessened isolation to be the single most important contribution reported by clients as stemming from these couples' groups. Apparently this new awareness was also most conducive to better acceptance of problems, freer communication, the development of more realistic expectations, and heightened self-esteem (16). In addition, peer support and acknowledgment of gains made seems more believable than support from the therapist who is paid to help. Thus individual and mutual confidence are further enhanced. Boyer (8) goes so far as to say that this shared experience in the group may help to cement the marriage because the group becomes so important that the partners would not wish to separate since they would then lose the group.[4] This almost suggests that, in his view, the group's hold on its members may temporarily be stronger than the marital axis. Further exploration would be necessary to establish this, but the point seems again to reinforce the view that the group buttresses the positive side of the partners' ambivalence about the marriage, perhaps partly because of the lesser ambivalence about the group experience. Group members tend to respond supportively to change in one of the members (27). Under the therapist's direction, they themselves may also become healing persons (33).[5]

Provision of increased perspective. Partners seeing themselves in the context of several other marital partnerships under conditions

[4] Boyer does not accept separated partners in his couples' groups.

[5] Dreikurs' child guidance centers in Chicago, mentioned by Carroll (11), seem to be based, at least in part, on this principle of mutual healing. There a group of twenty to thirty parents, already enrolled in treatment, act as co-therapists and socializing agents for families newly applying for help.

243

of unusual openness may gain a clarifying perspective on themselves, their partners, and their mutual relationship. Often they discover that they really belong more to each other than to anyone else. Another effect unique to such a group is the highlighting of inappropriate reactions between partners. Leichter (27) gives a most telling illustration of this in a situation in which the group responded appropriately and supportively to change in a husband while his wife reacted either as before or else with enormous anxiety. She could not escape the knowledge that her reactions were totally out of line with those of all the rest of the group. This realization was an important step in treatment.

Contrasts in communicational patterns may also become strikingly evident. Partners who listen and respond with understanding to other group members often find that they never hear each other out. Their ways of communicating with each other are highly "condensed," to use Leichter's phrase. The live contrast enables them to see the need for deciphering and clarifying their mutual communications.

One might also speculate that the lessening of cognitive dependence on the parents' marriage, discussed in Mayer and Zander's study on disclosure of marital problems (31), might be yet another effect of couples' group experience, because each couple can draw on unusually intimate knowledge of a range of marital patterns.

Provision of new types of corrective experience. No amount of insight will lead to improvement of the marital situation unless the partners are able to improve their feelings and/or behavior in relation to each other. This requires actually practicing the new ways of relating and interacting. The couples' group provides a unique arena for such testing in a favorable environment. The reality of the group experience also helps to modify unnecessary stereotyping of the sexes, as some respondents pointed out. It illuminates much more tellingly than words some of the generally accepted differences in attitudes between the sexes (6) and provides important opportunities to identify with group members of one's own sex (22). Respondents stress, furthermore, the opportunities for confronting and correcting distortions and projections between partners. This also occurs in joint and family interviews, but in the group it may come from as many sources as there are participants, with a proportionally stronger impact. Moreover, as the

244

Worcester study suggests (16), confrontation through peer reactions is likely to arouse less defensiveness and to be tolerated more readily than the therapist's challenge, because the peer group members all have marital problems and are therefore less threatening to each other's self-esteem. In the view of this study group, partners with character disorders seem to be benefited especially, since they cannot easily avoid having their acting out or manipulative behavior pointed out by their peers in the presence of their spouse. They are thus pressed into trying more rewarding behavior in a situation especially structured for testing it out.

The Worcester group also found that couples' group treatment helped many participants to move from narcissism to a genuine interest in others and an ability to be helpful to them, which in turn enhanced the giver's self-esteem. Such an effect is likely in other forms of group treatment but has special value in this context since it is witnessed or even shared by the partner.

The unique opportunities in couples' groups for exposing repressed feelings related to the marriage (8) make freer communication possible between the partners. In contrast to individual treatment, they learn to communicate with each other rather than with the therapist (33). This could be accomplished in joint sessions also, but the group affords a wider range of possible approaches to the improvement of communication. As Hastings and Runkle have shown, a passive partner attacked by the spouse, and usually suppressing his reactions, may begin to express his feelings to another member. This member, in turn, may translate this feeling to the partner and freer communication between the spouses may then be tried or accomplished (22). Some obsessive neurotic couples, according to Flint and MacLennan (17), become able to allow themselves more feeling and to derive support from others. This expression of emotions between partners in the context of the group may hasten change, particularly when one partner has proved able to withstand an onslaught of the spouse's negative feelings. This was suggested by Lovell, who described a wife's attack on her husband in the group and declaration that she no longer loved him. The husband expressed hope for their future in spite of this. That proved to be a turning point for the wife, who came to realize that she had not only been denying her partner a wife but herself a husband.

Negative reactions even to consciously desired change in the mate

245

are common in marital treatment. The couples' group offers unusual flexibility and versatility in dealing with this phenomenon. As members perceive the partner's reaction to incipient change in the marital balance, their attention may switch from the changing partner to the anxious, resistant partner, as Leichter has shown (27). Such a move can also be accomplished by the worker in joint or even in separate interviews, but in the couples' group it is the manifold addition of challenging and supportive elements within the group situation that may be a crucial factor in maintaining the thrust toward change, bringing out the underlying anxieties or aggression regarding the change and, at best, sustaining the couple through the process until a better marital balance is finally reached.

Easing of worker's task. In spite of the complexity of the couples' group situation, several factors were cited as easing the worker's task. For example, a worker is less likely to fluctuate between elation and depression since movement and regression occur at different times for different couples. The worker's therapeutic optimism is therefore more readily maintained. Members are also less likely to compete with the worker than in joint interviews, since they may share the leader's role at various times. Papanek also sees less pushing of the therapist into the role of judge (33), while others stress that the leader is seen more realistically and that transference feelings, although strong, are "split up" along a broader front and can therefore be dealt with better (6, pp. 145–146). Views differ as to whether the worker is more or less active in couples' groups than in other situations. All stress, however, the importance of allowing the mutually corrective group forces to do as much as possible, with the therapist intervening only when necessary—e.g., to point out the underlying conflict.

Criteria for Assignment
to Couples' Groups

It is too early for clear indications or contraindications to have evolved regarding the use of married couples' groups or for generalizations from experience with respect to their pitfalls or inherent risks. However, some broad groupings of views seem possible.

Past treatment experience. When individual interviews have helped the individual partners without improving the marriage,

Papanek suggests the use of couples' groups (33). Opinion is divided as to whether previous treatment experience is a prerequisite for admission to a couples' group. Lovell, for one, considers such experience helpful but not essential.[6] She notes that problems may arise if the switch is away from individual treatment, because of loss of the special relationship with the worker.

Type of couple. Many references are made in the literature to types of couples who respond especially well to this approach or who make progress after other approaches have failed. Into this latter group Boas places couples in symbiotic "zipper" relationships (6). Although other forms of group treatment may also help to diminish the symbiotic ties (27), Boas thought couples' groups to be especially helpful in this context because they afford the possibility of direct confrontation of one partner by other participants in the presence of the other partner (6). In addition, the partners may also be helped by the "vitalizing" effects of the group as it expands their life experience (29).

Flint and MacLennan (17) list marital constellations for which short-term couples' groups have proved beneficial. Included are relatively withdrawn couples who communicate little but feel some dissatisfaction about this and mildly neurotic individuals with a basically sound marriage that has been disturbed by misunderstandings and misinterpretations. Long-term couples' groups, they suggested, are indicated for immature couples who show feelings of inadequacy and confusion about their sexual identification. This was also true for mildly depressed, inadequate people trying to satisfy dependency needs through their marriage. Chronic, well-defended paranoid schizophrenics were thought good candidates for such groups by these authors, as were sadomasochistic couples engaged in mutually provocative acting out that can be exposed and explored in the group. Lovell also confirmed the value of this approach with sadomasochistic couples, but felt that the dynamics of the process were not yet adequately understood.

On the other hand, increasing experience throws light on some types of couples who should not be assigned to couples' groups. For example, Flint and MacLennan (17) report lack of success with couples when one partner is passively hostile and the other needs to feel intellectually superior. These authors apparently could not

[6] Personal communication to the author.

prevent group attacks on the more arrogant partner, who made the others feel helpless. Neubeck (32) would exclude those who are exhibitionistic, wish only to impress the group, and tend to overwhelm it. One respondent kept out couples she expected to drop out, because she feared adverse effects on the remaining group members.

Gottlieb bars couples who just go through the motions of trying, those in which one partner has already decided against the marriage, and couples only one of whom is really sick—e.g., when a wife has had repeated postpartum psychoses.[7] Further contraindications noted in the literature include a lack of tolerance for open communication, inability to relate to others, and lack of resources for change (33). To this list the Worcester study would add the presence of psychosis in one partner and the inadmissibility for certain couples of any risk of community exposure (16). Their further findings imply that couples whose difficulties would seem alien to the rest of the proposed group should be screened out. These couples should be included in a group in which they would sense at least some community of feelings, although the specific problems and life styles within the group need not by any means be homogeneous. When participation in a specific group is likely to confirm a couple's sense of isolation and hopelessness, the group experience might well increase their difficulties instead of healing them. When this seems clear beforehand, it may be advisable to plan for the couple's inclusion in another group or to use a different modality altogether (see footnote 11, page 260). Lovell has pointed out two other conditions that may bar the approach: primacy of intrapersonal concerns and the existence of a secret, as in the case of prominent community members. She also felt that immature couples might need to be toughened through joint interviews—if they were not too competitive—before they could accept the confrontation and directness likely to occur in the group.[8]

Group composition. A strong bid was made by some practitioners for group composition rather than type of couple as the decisive criterion (see 8, pp. 21–22). The Family Service Organization of Worcester found, for example, that individual and joint interviews used at intake yielded no real criteria for selection, but that excessive homogeneity in the group was likely to threaten its success. A

[7] Opinion expressed when speaking as leader of a workshop.
[8] Personal communication to the author.

group composed principally of repressed couples, for instance, is unlikely to open up enough for treatment to get going. This view is also borne out by the workshops and by Hastings and Runkle (22). In this context it is worth noting that some think it beneficial although not essential for the whole group if at least some group members are in concurrent individual treatment. Boyer describes such a group member as becoming a possible model of less defensive reactions (8). Hastings and Runkle, however, imply the generalization that marital partners whom they describe as suffering from very severe neurotic character disorders, such as the couples constituting their group, would all need to have concurrent individual treatment (22).

Questions Awaiting Exploration

In view of the relative absence of negative reports in the literature regarding the use of couples' groups, many issues come to mind as worth exploring: What kind of intake would be most appropriate for selecting couples to participate in a couples' group? [9] Is any special preparation in the group or by other means needed to make such treatment maximally productive from the start? Is such treatment—alone or in combination with other modalities—faster or more lasting than the joint or individual approach? Does the approach work better with certain marital constellations; socioeconomic, ethnic, or cultural groups; or individual personality types than with others? Might it have to be ruled out in a small town or suburban setting where potential group members would have ongoing relationships with each other in their daily lives? Are irrational reactions between members and the worker different and differently dealt with as compared with other modalities? Is there a greater or lesser tendency toward uncontrolled behavior in the couples' groups? Are special problems or dangers posed by the possibility of the group's consolidating its deviances vis-à-vis the therapist, or by its ganging up against a couple or individual? If so, what group approaches are best suited to deal with such events, or do they indicate the need for other modalities? Are the inhibited likely to egg on the impulsive, and may the latter provoke

---

[9] Dillon (14) reports that couples with marital difficulties, unlike parents with problem children, were unwilling to attend group intake out of feelings of shame and a sense of marital privacy.

repressive efforts by the former at other times? Do secondary gains derived from the support and excitement of the group experience tend to prolong treatment or pose special problems near termination? As practice grows, answers to these and other as yet unformulated questions should become available, and with them greater clarity regarding the indications and contraindications for the use of couples' groups.

INCLUSION OF SEVERAL FAMILIES

Like couples' groups, multifamily groups have come into being to remedy some lack that practitioners saw with regard to other approaches. Leichter and Schulman felt an "incompleteness" in other forms of family or group treatment (28, p. 59) and devised this new structure to meet it. Their use of this approach is, to the best of the author's knowledge, the only instance of its kind in a family agency setting cited in the literature on such experiments.[10] Although their initial focus was on problems between children and parents, the multifamily group also had to work on the marital relationships of the parents that began to emerge as a primary theme and focus later in treatment. It therefore seems appropriate to consider this approach here even though it would probably not be chosen when the marital problem has not ramified severely or when problems with children are not in evidence. Only those values that are relevant to the treatment of the marital conflict and do not duplicate the assets of couples' groups will be discussed in this context. All those discussed are drawn from Leichter and Schulman's recent informative description of dynamics in the multifamily group (28).

Since the multifamily group throws the spotlight on the individual family unit, each family system comes into focus in a variety of ways and is thus open to challenge and therapeutic intervention from both the therapist and the group members (28). One may assume that this allows unique opportunities for dealing with the ramifications of the marital conflict.

Children were found to become catalytic agents quite early in the sessions because adults outside the family felt less threatened

---

[10] Curry (13) reports on work in a psychiatric setting with five family units at a time, each including a hospitalized psychiatric patient.

by them than by other participants and could allow them to touch "the child in the adult" (28, p. 62). The children participating were also found to be amazingly perceptive about the dynamics of other people's families. This unique contribution of the multi-family group clearly can work toward opening up and handling feelings stemming from marital conflict and its ramifications. It is also likely to have preventive values in that it allows children to realize from direct contact with several families that adults are not all-knowing and all-powerful (28), but are capable of both regression and growth.

To the extent that the multifamily group frees the children to be more childlike, as the authors found in the interaction between the "sick" and the "well" children (28, p. 65), the group also presses the parents toward tackling their life tasks as partners, parents, and achievers. On the other hand, in a family in which the parents were preoccupied with each other almost to the ex-clusion of the children, Leichter and Schulman observed that the multifamily approach pressed the partners into awareness of the children's needs (28).

Above all, the multifamily group deals with the whole family. It handles directly not only the marital axis, as do joint interviews, family interviews, and couples' groups, but also the specific family system in the context of other such systems. Any resistances to marital improvement that exist in the sibling subsystem or in the relationship between one or more of the children and one or both parents are therefore open to direct handling in the group. Al-though this is also true in family interviews, the added values of reinforced motivation, support, control, and challenge from many group members would seem to be as operative here as in the couples' group. They help to sustain the whole family system as it suffers the pangs of change.

At this stage it is not possible to identify the criteria for the use of multifamily groups beyond the interest of both worker and clients in attempting this approach, nor have the special skills and qualities required of the worker or workers been spelled out. How-ever, as some of the unique values of this and related approaches become clearer, the conditions favoring or barring their use are also likely to become more definable. Meanwhile, exciting practice, research, and testing lie in store for those interested in contributing toward such answers.

INCLUSION OF THE WIDER SOCIAL NETWORK

The experience gained from tapping possible sources of mutual healing within families and within groups composed of suffering couples or families led some therapists to search for more lasting wellsprings of mutual assistance and gratification that might be opened up for dysfunctional families within their own environment. Thus psychiatrists both in a medical and in a family agency setting have recently attempted to help seriously endangered schizophrenic patients by involving them and their immediate families in sessions together with some or all of the members of their social network (38, 39, 40). This represents an attempt to see the suffering family together with those whom they are willing to contact and who "maintain an on-going significance in . . . [their] lives" (39, p. 1). The aim is to strengthen the network to cope with the current crisis and to release continuing supports in order to forestall future crises or make provision for them. At the same time, the authors found this approach especially suited to the modification of intrafamilial symbiotic ties, since it provides simultaneous opportunities for the members to build valid closer ties with other network members. This aspect of the approach is of particular interest in the context of marital treatment, even though treatment of the social network has not yet been tested systematically, and may not be suitable in situations in which the presenting problem is a marital one.

Reaching even beyond the circle of close relatives and friends, some programs recently developed in work with the disadvantaged have involved participants recruited from entire neighborhoods in semieducational, semitherapeutic meetings to acknowledge and solve shared problems. Such recognition on the part of social agencies of the importance of the wider social network for many families may in itself have important therapeutic implications. This possibility is underscored by the all-too-brief experience of Project ENABLE, jointly undertaken in 1965 by the Family Service Association of America, the Child Study Association of America, and the National Urban League, with the help of federal funds from the Office of Economic Opportunity.

The eight hundred parent education groups sponsored by ENABLE in sixty-two communities were not concerned primarily with intimate familial or marital problems, although these were brought up not infrequently by participants. In the main the issues tackled spontaneously in these sessions had to do with the problems involved in raising children in a severely deprived and endangering environment, and with obtaining better or more relevant service from community institutions. At least three hundred neighborhood action projects resulted.

Even though all family members serving in a parental role were encouraged to attend, it proved difficult in many cases to involve the fathers and father surrogates. The men tended to view the sessions and child-rearing issues as a whole as related principally to women's concerns, while the women welcomed the chance to be away from home on their own. Nevertheless, as a secondary result of this neighborhood approach, a number of referrals were made by ENABLE staff to family agencies for casework help with marital problems. These proved to be substantially more effective than had been true of referrals of comparable families before the ENABLE neighborhood groups were formed. These clients were reported to show greater confidence in family agencies and to make better progress than was typical in general of referrals from these neighborhoods. One might speculate that the strengths and resourcefulness released and developed by neighborhood network co-operation, even in a semieducational context, can also become usable on behalf of greater personal, marital, and family fulfillment. For the disadvantaged especially, the sense of dignity and hope encouraged by such network groups and by agency sponsorship of their self-help and legitimate protest efforts may at times be a *sine qua non* of marital treatment or any other treatment of intrafamilial problems.

RELATED EXPERIMENTAL APPROACHES

The burgeoning interest in multiple-client approaches has been accompanied by a general upsurge in experimental effort, some of which represents radical departures from past therapeutic practice in office sessions or home visits. Many of these endeavors have been developed in response to parent-child rather than marital problems as such, but even these are of interest here because they so often involve at least some dealing with the marital difficulty. Since all of these evolving approaches have some conceptual rele-

253

vance to the issues of this monograph, they will be listed and discussed here briefly. However, no attempt will be made to evaluate their over-all effectiveness at this early stage, although some of them were undertaken with careful follow-up plans and research evaluation in mind (30).

Increased Concentration
of Contact

Many families in need of service live far away from suitable facilities while others seek help but baffle the therapist by the apparent diagnostic and therapeutic impenetrability of their interactional patterns. The challenge of these obstacles from within and outside the family has evoked a variety of interesting responses.

Multiple-impact therapy, an approach developed at the University of Texas (19, 30), represents one attempt to deal with both sets of obstacles simultaneously. It was designed to provide treatment for intact and willing families whose adolescent children were severely endangered and facing the possibility of hospitalization, delinquency, or severe neurotic difficulties, and whose home areas lacked adequate facilities for help. The therapists operated on the principle that the "self-rehabilitating forces in the family" could be used in crisis situations precipitated by adolescents' problems and that "comparatively small changes in the attitudes and behavior of parents . . . [may be] followed by dramatic improvements in the behavior of their children" (19, p. 32). Furthermore, they believed that total cure need not be the goal and that improved communication, improved awareness of the effect of attitudes and behavior on others, and greater "attention to unrewarding patterns of behavior and interaction" (19, p. 35) could be stimulated by two full days of highly concentrated diagnostic and treatment sessions with some half-day or full-day follow-ups after two or more months. These sessions involved the various members of the multidisciplinary therapeutic team, alone and in combination, in a sequence of intensive interviews with family members in joint, family, family subgroup, and overlapping individual sessions, as the situation seemed to demand. The investigators reported especially good results with adolescent behavioral problems including "uncontrollable" children and children with school phobia, but indicated that this approach was less successful with anxious or neurotic boys and girls.

An adaptation of the multiple-impact approach is currently being used by MacGregor in relation to an urban population in Chicago and has also been given some trial and evaluation at the Family Service Association of Indianapolis (41). That agency used a two-hour diagnostic procedure involving a team of three case-workers in interviews with the whole family and also with the parents alone. These two conferences were followed by a discussion between team and family of the family's responses to a questionnaire on family relations. A diagnosis was then formulated in writing by the team. Treatment of the diagnosed problems was offered in a subsequent full day of sessions in the general style of the Texas approach (30), with a follow-up session scheduled for six months later. Careful study of the cases involved in this kind of experiment should cast light on the effectiveness of concentrated casework treatment in relation to certain family problems and, one might hope, to the marital relationship.

In contrast to the multiple-impact approaches described thus far, heightened concentration and impact of treatment were sought by some therapists through more direct familiarity with and role in the patients' daily life. Thus Bowen (7) went so far as to have four families, including at least the parents and the hospitalized schizophrenic patient, live in the hospital ward for up to two-and-a-half years, in order to treat the whole family. Two of these resident families also included well siblings who participated in the treatment for as long as two years. Conversely, Hansen (21) moved in with one family to live in their home for intensive and strenuous on-the-spot treatment. In another variation, the staff of a residential institution for disturbed boys arranged for groups of the boys' parents to spend periodic weekends living with staff members and their families at the institution for treatment purposes.

In varying degrees, all these approaches seem to be aimed at making the most of the added diagnostic information made available by such concentrated association. When they succeed, the relevance of treatment is heightened for all the participants. An increased and benign impact on the dysfunctional marital and family system is thus made possible through the concentrated assault on destructive defenses in a context in which elements of shared strength and realistic hope can at the same time become available simultaneously to all participants.

Still another form of contact concentration—or even saturation —intended to achieve maximum therapeutic impact, but with minimal emphasis on the diagnostic aspect, is the marathon group, in which the therapeutic contact of a group of participants with one or more therapists is maintained continuously for a period of twenty-four hours or even longer. George and Peggy Bach have adapted this approach to marital couples' groups with a husband-wife team as therapists. Their marathon sessions feature the teaching of the art of intimate communication, loving, and fair and effective fighting.

Integration of Separate Group Approaches for Different Family Members

At times another multiple-client modality may be used to implement the treatment aims also sought through a group approach. Westman, Carek, and McDermott (42) see the partners in groups of the same sex. After three to six months they combine both groups every six weeks or so, with sometimes one, sometimes the other, therapist as leader. Since they are essentially oriented to the partners as individuals, their use of the joint meeting is mainly as a stimulant and diagnostic aid. They see it as loosening repressions or weakening impulse control in relation to the spouse, and then handle these feelings in subsequent one-sex group meetings. They also value these gatherings for their revelation of different aspects of the spouses' personalities, especially in relation to peers of the opposite sex and their own spouse (42). Leichter and Schulman use single-family interviews as an integrative device to mold together the separate treatment processes of parents and children in couples' groups and adolescent groups respectively (29).

Auxiliary Technical Aids

The use of one-way screens and audio or video-tape recordings need not be confined to marital treatment or, for that matter, to group sessions. However, these devices have been variously used as auxiliaries in the teaching, supervision, or implementation of family treatment and at least one of the video-tape reports involves a specific focus on marital treatment (1). All these approaches will be touched on here briefly, because all have potential relevance to marital treatment and some have already been used in a manner designed to take full advantage of the special opportunities offered in multiple-client interviews for the recognition and treatment of interactional problems.

The only respondent who reported use of any such device found audio tape useful for enabling the marital partners to recognize with some objectivity their inappropriate mutual reactions in joint sessions. Those authors who describe the use of videotape (1, 34) for playback and discussion with the family or couple in treatment are equally emphatic about its value for revealing the family's pattern of multiple and often contradictory communication channels. Alger and Hogan (1) make heavy use of this technical aid to give the marital pair an opportunity to clarify messages that were lost or left contradictory in the original session, thus utilizing the video tape for teaching better ways of communicating. Because the insights gained from self-observation are direct rather than the result of the therapist's interpretation, these authors see them as powerful motivating agents for change. The individual or couple sees such change as freely sought and in no sense the result of pressure by the therapist. In addition, resistance and mutual blame seem lessened since the actual facts of the interaction are usually clear. Criteria so far offered (34) suggest as candidates for video-tape methods those families whose interaction needs clarification, who have communication difficulties, and who can respond to such "objectification." However, some practitioners caution against this approach with seriously depressed individuals or families.

ASSETS OF TREATING
MARITAL OR FAMILIAL INTERACTION IN
THE PRESENCE OF SEVERAL COUPLES OR FAMILIES

In what way do the advantages and limitations of couples' groups, multifamily groups, and certain variants of the joint and family interview differ from those of the more traditional group approaches in which participants also meet in groups but are unrelated to each other? How do they differ from joint or family interviews in which no outsiders other than the worker are present? How do these different approaches compare as agents for the achievement of constructive change in the light of some evolving concepts regarding group processes?

Assets in Comparison with
Treatment of Individual Partners
in Groups of Unrelated Persons

In more traditional group treatment, no two group participants are members of the same family, and the group is used as a medium to help the individual client. Similarly, in network therapy the network may be seen largely as a vehicle for aid to the individual patient and his family. In multiple-couple and multifamily groups, in contrast, the targets of change are the couple or family respectively, rather than the individual, although greater individuation is an implicit goal of treatment even in these settings. Furthermore, since the various couples and families participate specifically because of their problems in relation to their own partner or family, the focus on the marriage or family is more readily and directly maintained.

The co-presence of strangers and relatives in these groups adds several factors that are absent when strangers alone participate. In the first place, both the positive and negative impacts of each session are likely to be much more direct on important home relationships since family members live with each other between meetings. This may make for greater explosiveness in some situations and for greater control in others, owing to the knowledge that behavior outside will be reported back to the group. At best, treatment gains made and reinforced by partners and family members in the wider group are more likely to be maintained in the home because the couple or family have learned and practiced them together under therapeutic guidance. In traditional group treatment, the group member may improve and may then become an agent for change within his family, but this interactional and integrative process is beyond the worker's direct intervention.

A second difference of vital importance relates to the opportunities afforded in multiple-couple or multifamily groups for simultaneous reality-testing with strangers and with important family figures. Various blind spots and distortions, both mutual and individual, are revealed and worked out in the presence of family members and in relation to them as well as to other group members. Thus the reality-testing directly benefits not only the individual client but his interrelationships with partner and children.

Inevitably, however, the presence of these intimate life figures imposes certain restraints on the nature and extent of the reality-testing possible in the group. It bars, for instance, insistence on the usual group treatment norm of greatest possible frankness in the expression of positive and negative feelings experienced in the group (3, pp. 103–104). Deep hurt, withdrawal, disapproval, or retaliation between sessions may be the actual or feared reactions of partners or children to revelations made by a spouse or parent in the group. Marital privacy and the developmental needs of children may require restraint in relation to certain subjects, at least at certain times. In this apparent limitation of multiple-unit groups lies one of the approach's unique features: It allows the wider reality-testing also offered in traditional group therapy, but adds the opportunity to apply in the same context the resultant learning to the relationship with partners and children and to test out the realistic need for restraint, protectiveness, or openness in relation to them. Finally, the presence of the partner and of the children eliminates a substantial cause for anxiety and suspicion on their part regarding the nature of the exchanges within the group.

Assets in Comparison with
Joint and Family Interviewing
without Other Couples
or Families Present

Compared with the joint or family interview, couples' and family groups offer the advantage of a wider social perspective. They open up varied possibilities for experiencing and testing out different attitudes, life styles, and ways of resolving problems. Partners or families may thus experience an increase in tolerance and flexibility directly as a result of the encounter with other group members or with members of the therapeutic team, as distinct from the joint or family interview in which the partners and families are exposed only to each other and the worker. In the expanded groups, contact with adults or children from other families and the patterns of interaction among them may cause otherwise untapped feelings to emerge. When this leads to an increase in defensive reactions, these can be handled by the worker or team in the presence of the added supports provided in group experience (see below). In those cases in which the encounter leads directly to greater tolerance and flexibility, the added gains can be utilized immediately to further the change process.

In addition to the wider perspective and range of experience offered by these groups, they seem to make available an exceptionally wide range of supports for the participants. Since all need an accepting climate in these sessions, they also tend, as a gesture of reciprocity, to grant it to others. This encourages the release of multiple forms of support for group members and helps to sustain them through the pains of treatment, to increase their sense of closeness to the group, and to offer a counterweight to the strongly ambivalent feelings that may be aroused in the process of change in the marriage or family.

Another new ingredient provided by couples' or multifamily groups relates to the unique opportunity they offer for a couple or family to evaluate their own situation in comparison with that of others. Because of prevalent privacy norms, most people know little about the marital and familial problems of other couples. They tend to think that other families have fewer difficulties. As their own conflict escalates, couples may thus tend to become increasingly unsure about continuing the marriage and increasingly hopeful about the rewards possible outside it.

The encounter with other couples or families in the group session exposes them to the reality of other families in turmoil. To many couples this experience may, for the time, reveal the extent of other partners' difficulties. As they learn of problems they might not have imagined or situations that may seem even worse than their own, their difficulties may seem less unbearable by comparison.[11] As their perception of their own relative deprivation changes,

---

[11] When group participation, on the other hand, leads a couple to feel confirmed in their sense of isolation and hopelessness, their problems are likely to mount unless the worker is quick to help them deal with these feelings, either within the group or in the context of another treatment modality used concurrently with the group or in its place.

the couple's ambivalence may be lessened in favor of continuing the marriage. In this sense, the perspective provided by couples' and multifamily groups may be a great potential aid to partners in an advanced stage of conflict and undecided about the future of their marriage.

Still another contribution of these groups is perhaps derived from the small-scale antidote they provide to the prevailing pattern of social alienation. Here couples or families may, together, experience intimacy not only with their own but with other families. For many the need for such human contact is great, but modern society often affords few opportunities to fill it. It may well be that some meeting of this need, plus the presence of the many other added supports mentioned, together account for much of the holding power of the couples' or multifamily group as compared with other approaches.

A further asset of the expanded group in comparison with the more limited one seems to be its capacity to increase incentive for change, especially for those for whom the rewards within the family have been eroded by conflict. In the first place, groups of couples and families seem to offer each other a particularly strong sense of belonging and opportunities for participatory leadership, both of which are considered by Cartwright as important prerequisites for the achievement of change through group approaches (12).

Second, his stress on the attractiveness of a group—its capacity for meeting members' needs, if it is to exert influence for change—is equally relevant. Often the marriage or the family may for the moment hold so few gratifications that joint or family sessions may serve to underline rather than to modify the members' unhappiness. The couples' or multifamily group, on the other hand, introduces the warmth and interest of social contact free of the intensity of the long-term linkage involved in family ties. Thus the wider group may temporarily be more attractive than the joint or family session alone and yet more essentially meaningful to its members than a nonrelated group.

Third, there can be little doubt that both couples' and multi-family groups also meet Cartwright's requirement that group attitudes, values, and behavior be relevant to the reasons that attracted its members in the first place if the group is to exert influence for change (12).

Since family systems tend to resist change, the group combining several couples or families offers the possibility of creating a climate in which family change may become acceptable and feasible because of the pressures and pulls of the newly developing group norms and rewards. These pressures arise from the group's shared perception of the need for change and thus assure that some pressure for change will come from within the group (6). At the same time the presence of others who are not directly involved makes available multiple supports to deal with the resultant strains for the particular couple or family. Added to the strengths existing within individuals, partners, and families, these positive forces may prove powerful in combating intrafamilial difficulty and even the sense of social alienation. They represent, in a sense, a search for allies—not to extend the conflict (4) but rather to heal it.

SUMMARY AND CONCLUSIONS

The author has undertaken in this chapter to suggest briefly the nature and potential of the now rapidly expanding repertoire of alternate and auxiliary therapeutic approaches relevant to the treatment of marital difficulties. It was only a few years ago that the traditionally tight bonds of the one-to-one therapeutic relationship between one worker and each spouse separately were relaxed enough to permit the inclusion of the partner and other family members in the same interview. More recently, the circle of those included in treatment has, on occasion, been further expanded to include additional caseworkers, other couples, other families, and even in some instances persons from the families' wider social network. Experimentation with related approaches has also moved on apace to test out new patterns of treatment concentration, new combinations of modalities, and the use of auxiliary technical aids. Reports from those directly involved in the ferment of these varied pioneering efforts reflect not only the excitement and exhilaration of the search, but also a clear conviction that significant values are being realized by opening up the usually reticent inner family circle to a process of mutual sharing of problems and solutions with other couples and families.

Relying mainly on the literature and on consultations and only secondarily on the small number of responses related to this area, the author has attempted to suggest something of the potential significance of these new and revised modalities and to state some of their possible assets in a preliminary way. Some views regarding indications and contraindications, especially in relation to couples' groups and videotape recordings, were also reported, but on the whole, criteria regarding all the approaches discussed in this chapter are still in the process of evolving.

Granted the conceptual importance and the relevance of these various approaches for the treatment of marital problems through multiple-client modalities, the reader has nevertheless been cautioned that, in the main, these developments are too new and untested for their hidden risks and dangers to have become fully evident. Much further experimentation, conceptual effort, and systematic research evaluation are seen as necessary before guidelines for the optimal use of each can be formulated. It is possible that some of the principles outlined in Chapter 5 with regard to the choice among individual, joint, and family sessions may also prove relevant for choosing among these other approaches, but as yet the available clinical data are inadequate for any approach to be tested. Meanwhile, these exciting and rapidly proliferating ventures deserve close watching and open-minded evaluation not only in relation to the treatment of marital problems but also for their over-all therapeutic potential.

BIBLIOGRAPHY

1. ALGER, IAN, and HOGAN, PETER, "The Use of Videotape Recordings in Conjoint Marital Therapy in Private Practice," unpublished paper presented at the Annual Meeting of the American Psychiatric Association, Atlantic City, May 13, 1966.

2. BARDILL, DONALD R., and BEVILACQUA, JOSEPH J., "Family Interviewing by Two Caseworkers," *Social Casework,* Vol. XLV, No. 5 (May 1964), pp. 278–282.

3. BECK, DOROTHY FAHS, "The Dynamics of Group Psychotherapy as Seen by a Sociologist: Part I, The Basic Process, and Part II, Some Puzzling Questions on Leadership, Contextual Relations, and Outcome," *Sociometry,* Vol. XXI, Nos. 2 and 3 (June and September 1958), pp. 98–128 and 180–197.

4. ————, "Marital Conflict: Its Course and Treatment as Seen by Caseworkers," *Social Casework,* Vol. XLVII, No. 4 (April 1966), pp. 211–221.

5. BERNE, ERIC, *Transactional Analysis in Psychotherapy: A Systematic Individual and Social Psychiatry,* Grove Press, New York, 1961.

Expansion of the Circle of Treatment Participants

6. BOAS, CONRAD VAN EMDE, "Intensive Group Psychotherapy with Married Couples," *International Journal of Group Psychotherapy,* Vol. XII, No. 2 (April 1962), pp. 142–153.
7. BOWEN, MURRAY, "A Family Concept of Schizophrenia," in Don D. Jackson (ed.), *The Etiology of Schizophrenia,* Basic Books, New York, 1960, pp. 373–388.
8. BOYER, CLAYTON L., "Group Therapy with Married Couples," *Marriage and Family Living,* Vol. XXII, No. 1 (February 1960), pp. 21–24.
9. BRODY, EUGENE B., "Modification of Family Interaction Patterns by a Group Interview Technique," *International Journal of Group Psychotherapy,* Vol. VI, No. 1 (January 1956), pp. 38–47.
10. BURTON, GENEVIEVE, and KAPLAN, HOWARD M., "Group Counseling in Conflicted Marriages Where Alcoholism Is Present: Clients' Evaluation of Effectiveness," *Journal of Marriage and the Family,* Vol. XXX, No. 1 (February 1968), pp. 74–79.
11. CARROLL, EDWARD J., "Family Therapy—Some Observations and Comparisons," *Family Process,* Vol. III, No. 1 (March 1964), pp. 178–185.
12. CARTWRIGHT, DORWIN, "Achieving Change in People," in Warren G. Bennis, Kenneth D. Benne, and Robert Chin (eds.), *The Planning of Change,* Holt, Rinehart & Winston, New York, 1966, pp. 698–706.
13. CURRY, ANDREW E., "Therapeutic Management of Multiple Family Groups," *International Journal of Group Psychotherapy,* Vol. XV, No. 1 (January 1965), pp. 90–96.
14. DILLON, VERA, "Group Intake in a Casework Agency," *Social Casework,* Vol. XLVI, No. 1 (January 1965), pp. 26–30.
15. EINSTEIN, GERTRUDE, "Report of Family Group Treatment Project at Jewish Family Service," Jewish Family Service of Philadelphia, Philadelphia, 1964 (mimeographed).
16. FAMILY SERVICE ORGANIZATION OF WORCESTER (MASS.), "Observations on Clients' Reactions to Group Treatment of Marital Problems," in Neilson F. Smith (ed.), "Family Phenomena, Problems, and Treatment: Some Family Agency Studies" (A Terminal Progress Report on the Project, "Casework on Marital Problems: A National Experiment in Staff Development"), Family Service Association of America, New York, 1968 (mimeographed).
17. FLINT, ARDEN A., JR., and MacLENNAN, BERYCE W., "Some Dynamic Factors in Marital Group Psychotherapy," *International Journal of Group Psychotherapy,* Vol. XII, No. 3 (July 1962), pp. 355–361.
18. FRAMO, JAMES L., "Rationale and Techniques of Intensive Family Therapy," in Ivan Boszormenyi-Nagy and James L. Framo (eds.), *Intensive Family Therapy: Theoretical and Practical Aspects,* Hoeber Medical Division, Harper & Row, New York, 1965, pp. 143–212.
19. GOOLISHIAN, HAROLD A., and RITCHIE, AGNES, "Multiple-Impact Therapy," in *Casework Papers, 1961,* from the National Conference on Social Welfare, Family Service Association of America, New York, 1961, pp. 31–43.
20. GULLERUD, ERNEST N., and HARLAN, VIRGINIA LEE, "Four-Way Joint Interviewing in Marital Counseling," *Social Casework,* Vol. XLIII No. 10 (December 1962), pp. 532–537.

21. HANSEN, CONSTANCE COLLINGE, "An Extended Home Visit with Conjoint Family Therapy," *Family Process,* Vol. VII, No. 1 (March 1968), pp. 67–87.
22. HASTINGS, PHILIP R., and RUNKLE, ROBERT L., JR., "An Experimental Group of Married Couples with Severe Problems," *International Journal of Group Psychotherapy,* Vol. XIII, No. 1 (January 1963), pp. 84–92.
23. HOCK, ROBERT A., and DONLEY, JOAN L., "The Impact of the Resolution of Co-Leadership Conflicts in the Treatment of a Married Couples' Group," unpublished paper presented at the 24th Annual Conference of the American Group Psychotherapy Association, New York, January 28, 1967.
24. JANOWICZ, RUTH, "Methods and Goals of Group Therapy in a Family Service Agency," paper presented at the National Conference on Social Welfare, Cleveland, Ohio, May 1963 (mimeographed).
25. KLAPMAN, HOWARD J., and RICE, DALE L., "An Experience with Combined Milieu and Family Group Therapy," *International Journal of Group Psychotherapy,* Vol. XV, No. 2 (April 1965), pp. 198–206.
26. LANDES, JUDAH, and WINTER, WILLIAM, "A New Strategy for Treating Disintegrating Families," *Family Process,* Vol. V, No. 1 (March 1966), pp. 1–20.
27. LEICHTER, ELSA, "Group Psychotherapy of Married Couples' Groups: Some Characteristic Treatment Dynamics," *International Journal of Group Psychotherapy,* Vol. XII, No. 2 (April 1962), pp. 154–163.
28. ———, and SCHULMAN, GERDA L., "Emerging Phenomena in Multi-Family Group Treatment," *International Journal of Group Psychotherapy,* Vol. XVIII, No. 1 (January 1968), pp. 59–69.
29. ———, and SCHULMAN, GERDA L., "The Family Interview as an Integrative Device in Group Therapy with Families," *International Journal of Group Psychotherapy,* Vol. XIII, No. 3 (July 1963), pp. 335–345.
30. MACGREGOR, ROBERT, et al., *Multiple Impact Therapy with Families,* McGraw-Hill Book Co., New York, 1964.
31. MAYER, JOHN E. (with the assistance of Mary Zander), "The Disclosure of Marital Problems: An Exploratory Study of Lower and Middle Class Wives," Community Service Society of New York, New York, 1966 (mimeographed).
32. NEUBECK, GERHARD, "Factors Affecting Group Psychotherapy with Married Couples," *Marriage and Family Living,* Vol. XVI, No. 3 (August 1954), pp. 216–220.
33. PAPANEK, HELENE, "Group Psychotherapy with Married Couples," in Jules H. Masserman (ed.), *Current Psychiatric Therapies, 1965,* Vol. V, Grune & Stratton, New York, 1965, pp. 157–163.
34. PERLMUTTER, MORTON S., et al., "Family Diagnosis and Therapy Using Videotape Playback," *American Journal of Orthopsychiatry,* Vol. XXXVII, No. 5 (October 1967), pp. 900–905.
35. POLLAK, OTTO, "Disturbed Families and Conjoint Family Counseling," *Child Welfare,* Vol. XLVI, No. 3 (March 1967), pp. 143–149.
36. RYAN, FRANCIS J., and BARDILL, DONALD R., "Joint Interviewing by Field Instructor and Student," *Social Casework,* Vol. XLV, No. 8 (October 1964), pp. 471–474.

37. SAX, PATRICIA, "A Discussion: What Is Family-centered Casework?" *Social Casework*, Vol. XLVIII, No. 7 (July 1967), pp. 426–428.

38. SPECK, ROSS V., "Psychotherapy of the Social Network of a Schizophrenic Family," *Family Process*, Vol. VI, No. 2 (September 1967), pp. 208–214.

39. ———, and MORONG, EUGENE, "Home-Centered Treatment of the Social Network of Schizophrenic Families: Two Approaches," paper presented at the American Psychiatric Association Convention, Detroit, May 1967 (mimeographed).

40. ———, and OLANS, JEROME, "The Social Network of the Family of a Schizophrenic: Implications for Social and Preventive Psychiatry," unpublished paper presented at the Annual Meeting of the American Orthopsychiatric Association, Washington, D.C., March 21, 1967.

41. THORMAN, GEORGE, "Application of Multiple Impact Therapy in a Family Service Agency: A Preliminary Report," Family Service Association, Indianapolis, Ind., March 1968 (mimeographed).

42. WESTMAN, JACK C., CAREK, DONALD J., and McDERMOTT, JOHN F., "A Comparison of Married Couples in the Same and Separate Therapy Groups," *International Journal of Group Psychotherapy*, Vol. XV, No. 3 (July 1965), pp. 374–381.

7

Summary and Implications

The preceding chapters have surveyed a wide range of views regarding the use of joint interviews, family interviews, and other related multiple-client approaches in the treatment of marital problems. To bring into consideration the full spectrum of current opinion, the sources tapped have included both intensive content analyses of responses from caseworkers and local study group reports collected as part of a larger project. More than that, they have also encompassed, to the extent feasible, a review of relevant literature and consultations with leaders in the field. The project of which this analysis is a part has involved a general conceptual exploration of workers' views on the treatment of marital problems rather than formal research in any usual sense. Its major findings are reported separately (9). The innovations in practice covered in the present volume have been singled out to receive intensive attention in this separate supplementary monograph because of their exceptionally fertile implications for both practice and theory. The purpose throughout has been to piece together from a content analysis of the diverse views of respondents and from the writings of professional leaders a composite picture of the values of these modalities and the criteria for their appropriate use, to reassess and restate their conceptual and practical implications, and to present them in a way designed to encourage further exploration of them through systematic research.

The monograph has not attempted to cover all aspects of joint and family interviewing in relation to marital problems. It has omitted, for instance, issues related to the details of method and technique, since these were not raised in the questions submitted to the participating caseworkers. Consideration of group therapy of unrelated individuals has also been omitted since respondents said little to describe the specific assets of this approach in the treatment of marital difficulties. A brief look has been taken, however, at the possible contributions made in this area by the use of therapeutic teams, couples' groups, multifamily and social network groups, some further experimental multiple-client approaches, and the use of certain technical aids. Although still largely untested and unevaluated, these approaches are significant and stimulating in relation to the attempt in this monograph to conceptualize further the contribution of multiple-client approaches to the treatment of marital problems.

In each area the main intent has been to reflect the views of project participants, to set them in the larger context of the literature, and to spell out some of the concepts that seemed implicit in them. A special effort has been made to point to possible gaps in present knowledge and to highlight those concepts that may advance current understanding of the family as a system and the impact of treatment on that system. It should be understood that the responses and study group reports go back to the period between 1963 and early 1965, when most family caseworkers were only beginning to experiment with multiple-client sessions other than joint interviews. By contrast, much of the literature cited is of more recent vintage. Participating caseworkers therefore did not have the same chance as the authors who published later to report changes and refinements of opinion that arose as a result of increased experience and comfort with these modalities. Respondents' disagreements and omissions must be viewed in this light. At the same time, one must not forget that it was precisely the readiness of these practitioners to have their views, including their beginning impressions and doubts, examined at a specific point in time that made possible whatever perspective this monograph may have to offer on more recent work in these and related modalities, the areas needing further study, and the need for further conceptualization of practice.

Although the use of multiple-client interviews is still surrounded by the excitement, controversy, and caution natural in relation to comparatively new approaches, some broad areas of agreement and disagreement have stood out clearly in relation both to their values and to possible criteria for their use. A brief initial overview will serve to summarize the main issues of consensus and dissent, the areas understressed or omitted, and the concepts tentatively offered as describing, at the system level, some of the ways in which multiple-client interviews bring about and sustain change in the process of marital treatment. This will be followed by a glimpse of their possible implications for practice, theory-building, research, and professional education and training.

AN OVERVIEW OF RESPONDENTS' COMMENTS

Areas of Wide Agreement

Diagnostic Values

Except for one agency group opposed in principle to all multiple-client approaches, all respondents commenting were enthusiastic in their affirmation of the many diagnostic values of joint interviews. As for family interviews, a minority of respondents declared themselves unwilling ever to use this approach in relation to marital problems. Those who utilized it at all concurred with the users of joint interviews in affirming the unique values of both these modalities for diagnosis.

All aspects of marital and familial interaction were seen as illuminated by multiple-client sessions, which allow direct observation of the individual members in interaction with each other. Thus their family and sociocultural patterns and some aspects of their reality situation are revealed (in home or office visits), as are individual and collective reactions to the agency, the worker, and treatment. All this material was seen as conducive to more accurate and relevant diagnosis, both of the marital and familial difficulties and of the individual and family strengths available for coping with them. Speedier treatment was thought by many to result from such a comprehensive approach. Use of multiple-client and individual interviews to complement each other was especially favored since together they provided an interrelated view of the individual's feelings and thoughts as well as of the couple's or family's interactional patterns. Those who used family interviews for diagnosis when working with marital difficulties lauded them particularly for illuminating the ramifications of the conflict, the subtler aspects of the marital relationship in an enlarged social context,

269

and the family's place and view of themselves within the larger society.

Treatment Values

Use of multiple-client interviews in the course of marital treatment was generally viewed as offering the marriage or family as a whole as an arena for direct therapeutic intervention and for mobilization of mutual strengths and co-operative effort. This was seen, in turn, as contributing to a more effective use of agency service by both clients and workers, because the partners' and the total family's needs tend to be clearer to the worker when he sees the members together than when he faces them one by one. Even if he is inclined to overlook needs, to overidentify with one member, and so on, the others are likely to pull him up short if they are present in the interview.

It should be made clear that none of the respondents saw multiple-client interviews as totally replacing the individual interview. Unlike some of the writers in the field, they were convinced that the marital and family situation, the needs of individual members, the requirements of diagnosis and treatment at a particular time, and the personality and skills of the worker should all be weighed in relation to choice of approach. In their own practice, they had found that this usually pointed to the use of at least two types of interviews in combination. Most respondents saw joint interviews as the major tool in the treatment of marital problems. However, they also allowed for individual sessions when these were indicated because of temporary or persistent needs of one or both partners or when individual interviews could be used to prepare the clients for later multiple-client sessions. Such situations include the spouse with severe intrapersonal difficulties that precipitate conflict with other family members and require individual treatment. Individual interviews were also seen as appropriate if the partners are highly immature and need to develop more as individuals before they can use joint interviews effectively. In addition, they were thought necessary for partners who need to ventilate their anger in the spouse's absence before they can make use of joint interviews for tackling their marital difficulties. "Strong" partners can be given support in individual sessions that may enable them to express some of their concealed feelings of anger or would-be dependency

270

and consequently to become able to allow the spouse more room for growing stronger.

When individual interviews are being used as the main treatment modality, multiple-client interviews help co-ordinate the direction and speed of individual treatment and aid in the evolution of treatment goals and areas of concentration acceptable to both partners. Distortions and problems common when one worker and one spouse meet exclusively in the partner's absence may thus be largely avoided. In this fashion, the development of overdependence on the worker or of significant secondary gratifications from the relationship with him is minimized; moreover, growth of the individual partner is less likely to take place at the expense of the marriage and family.

Granting this readiness to use a combination of multiple-client and individual interviews, most respondents were clearly enthusiastic about the values of joint and family interviewing for the direct handling of interactional difficulties. They saw in these approaches valuable opportunities for helping couples who are involved in repetitive, constant, or spreading conflict, whose marital difficulties are affecting other aspects of their lives, and who are unable to resolve their sexual or role problems or to recognize the "trigger actions" that precipitate their conflict. They also saw them as providing an opportunity for more adequate mutual communication of emotions and for the development of less defensive behavior and feeling in relation to each other. Mutual projection and distortion and the tendency to scapegoat a family member or otherwise to displace the basic marital difficulty can also be modified through such sessions.

Although similar results may at times be the indirect outcome of individual treatment, the multiple-client interview was seen as accomplishing such ends directly (when successful), because the worker can become a direct therapeutic factor in the live interaction. Because family members observe him and may identify with him, his intervention may also serve to support constructive experimentation on their part with new attitudes and behavior during the interview and, later, at home. The partners' problems with each other can thus be worked on directly and their individual and mutual strengths jointly recognized and mobilized. In this respect, joint and family interviews offer especially striking opportunities since such mutual strengths and positive elements are often

271

undetectable when the clients are not seen together. These effects may be further enhanced if two or more therapists participate in treatment, for multiple and often simultaneous challenge and support to family members are then possible, and opportunities for modeling constructive ways of handling differences are increased.

Apart from the provision of opportunities for promoting greater mutuality and more constructive means of behaving and of solving problems together, the values attributed to multiple-client sessions seem to operate in two major directions. On the one hand, they enable the worker to encourage fuller expression of feelings and thoughts among family members when this is necessary for ventilation, confrontation, or better understanding and more realistic mutual accommodation. On the other hand, they enable the worker to provide the couple or family with a structure within which controls may be placed on excessive expression of anger or acting out, which may have been escalating rather than moderating the conflict. Both effects (of expression and constraint) may be needed simultaneously in situations in which clients need to express long-pent-up feelings but may fear being overwhelmed by their own impulses. For all these needs, the multiple-client interview offers a suitable structure and, in a sense, a teaching ground that may help families to apply at home what they have practiced together at the office.

Some pioneers in the field see such benefits as deriving also from the use of couples' and multifamily groups, which they regard as offering certain added advantages. Among these advantages are multiple forms of mutual support from within the group and an enlarged arena for viewing family life and for practicing new kinds of interacting and problem-solving. Furthermore, hope is enhanced since regression on the part of some group members is counterbalanced by the progress of others. Only the future can reveal the extent to which these claims can be substantiated.

While recognizing these many advantages, respondents also acknowledged that use of multiple-client interviews exerts special pressures on the caseworker. Outnumbered, he must temporarily become part of and affect an unfamiliar system, yet avoid unconstructive alliances. There seemed to be general agreement that his reactions—both realistic and unrealistic—to a couple or a whole family group are likely to be highly complex and difficult to handle. Special training for such work, together with agency provision for ongoing supervision or consultation, was therefore recognized as essential. Some saw the use of multiple therapists as another way to lighten this load through sharing the labor and stress.

Criteria for Choice of Modality

Some areas of substantial agreement emerged not only in relation to the values of multiple-client interviews but also with regard to criteria for their use, even though the latter issue typically called forth lively disagreement. Implicit throughout the responses was the conviction that no single criterion is in itself enough to determine the appropriate modality. Such a choice must always depend on several interdependent factors related to the couple and family, the worker's personality and skill, and considerations of diagnosis and timing. Granting this principle, there was wide agreement that joint sessions are indicated in the treatment of marital problems when the couple does not refuse and the partners do not present interactional difficulties so extreme as to obliterate the mutual supports or strengths within the marriage needed for the therapeutic effectiveness of this type of interview. Similarly, those who approved the use of family interviews at all in the treatment of marital problems saw them as indicated when the values of revealing or undoing the entanglement of other family members in the conflict were not nullified by the arousal, in the process, of even greater threats to the marriage and family or to the individual members.

Although considerations of diagnosis and treatment indicated the use of some type of multiple-client interviewing as close to intake as possible, no respondent used a family interview (as differentiated from a joint interview) at intake in situations in which the problem had been initially presented by the applicant as one of marital difficulty.

When serious psychopathology on the part of a spouse was clear, there was division about the advisability of multiple-client sessions. However, there was implied consensus that the marital or family system cannot benefit from direct treatment as a unit unless the disturbed spouse can be helped to refrain from major destructive acts against either system. When this level of control cannot be achieved, the issue of hospitalization or separation is bound to arise and may require individual, total family group, or subgroup interviews to deal with the effects of the marital rift and to contain the conflict.

Areas of Wide Disagreement

In this rapidly developing field, disagreements are a necessary concomitant of exploration, experimentation, and growth in perspective. There can be little doubt that they reveal the growing edge of the profession and that highlighting these differences should encourage further work to clarify the full reach and realistic limits of multiple-client modalities in the treatment of marital problems. On the whole, leaders in the casework field seem to favor carrying these approaches further into the arena of direct handling even of severe conflict, provided the worker is equal to the task.

Family Interviews

As might be expected, the area of greatest uncertainty and difference of opinion concerned the use of family interviews for any purpose whatever when the focal difficulty relates to the marriage. About one out of six of those commenting on the use of multiple-client sessions for treatment opposed the use of family interviews in this context at any time. Among the rest, some advised early use of at least one family interview to diagnose the total situation and to pave the way for later sessions, should they be needed.

Should children or in-laws be included in the sessions when they have become entangled in the marital problem? Most of the respondents thought this a valid criterion for using such sessions, but some were wary lest such inclusion encourage further displacement or the diversion of the couple's attention away from their marital difficulties. Deep concern about the effect of family interviews on the children and the marriage was also reflected in divided opinions. Some advised the use of family interviews to help couples and children express previously concealed negative and angry feelings, so that they might face the falsity of their "perfect" family front as a necessary preliminary to treatment. Others were fearful of the possible exposure of the children to more of the marital problem than they had already recognized or could tolerate. Still others believed that children were relieved to have previously concealed conflict brought out into the open. Closely connected

274

with these issues was another divergence of views. Some barred family interviews unless the parents were already aware of the children's involvement in the marital problem, while others preferred to exclude the children if they were not already aware of being caught up in the conflict. Still others took the fact rather than the awareness of involvement as their criterion.

In all these situations, the uncertainty of many workers was clear regarding the effect of family interviews not only on the children but also on the marriage itself, since there was no clarity as to which topics might be legitimately open to all the family and which might be essentially private to the marriage. Even among those who chose to include the children in some sessions, there was no unanimity as to whether children of certain age groups should be excluded. This seemed to depend on the purpose of the interview, the extent and intensity of the conflict, and the worker's ability to observe or use nonverbal forms of communication, especially with very young children.

Joint Interviews

Further differences of opinion were largely, although not exclusively, related to joint interviewing. One difference concerned the wisdom of relying on the applicants' wish for joint interviews as a criterion for using that approach, as compared with structuring the intake process to include such a session. A second focused on the role of joint interviews as tools either to create or merely to utilize the clients' commitment to treatment. A third related to the dispute concerning the saving of treatment time through the use of multiple-client sessions. Many believe this possible, but not all agreed.

A persistent theme of disagreement centered around differing views of certain conditions as prerequisites for joint interviews or as objectives to be attained through them. The most extensive disagreement on this score concerned communication: some workers saw a measure of ability to talk together as essential before joint interviews can be introduced, while others saw this approach as capable of nurturing communication when it had vanished. Similarly, each partner's beginning awareness of his share in the marital conflict, the existence of some mutual goals, and some ability to share and trust the worker were all seen as prerequisites for joint interviews by some and as conditions fostered by the use of the joint interview by others. In other words, there appears to be a close similarity between workers' views of the clues that predict a couple's capacity to use a specific type of service and the outcomes anticipated from that service—a pattern that was also true of prognostic clues generally (9).

Disagreement as to the advisability of joint interviews was also evident in reference to particular marital constellations. With excessively hostile and rivalrous couples, partners with quite different levels of role functioning, and couples showing an excessively sadomasochistic or dominant-passive mutual adaptation, joint interviews may be appropriate if the interactional pattern is not so destructive that the risks involved in the interview would outweigh possible gains. With reference to very young couples, the literature suggests the use of individual interviews until each partner has matured enough for joint sessions—although others think the goal of emancipation well served by joint interviews from the start. Extreme psychopathology or extreme dependency on the part of one or both partners also gives rise to opposing counsel, with some avoiding the use of the joint session as unconstructive, while others use its special structure in order to help modify these difficulties.

The Worker's Role and Relationship

As for the more technical aspects of multiple-client sessions, differences of view centered on the role and skill of the worker and on the intensity of transference manifestations. Comparable skills and similar rank were thought to be prerequisites by some if two workers are to participate in multiple-client sessions, while others thought readiness to co-operate and mutual freedom of communication the really crucial factors. The worker's role was seen as mainly catalytic by some, and highly active by others, but most conceived of a range of roles depending on treatment needs and the worker's capacity. Finally, respondents were inclined to regard the transference as diluted by the use of multiple-client interviews. This was the prevalent view when these types of sessions first came into vogue. However, greater experience has more recently suggested to many practitioners that irrational reactions to the worker

276

are at least as strong under these circumstances—if not stronger—but may take unfamiliar forms.

Choice of Treatment Modality

In general, there seems to be little disagreement among the great majority who do use joint or family interviews in marital treatment regarding the possibility of using such approaches when family cohesiveness and some willingness to accept treatment exist and when conflict is not so excessive that the web of constructive mutual supports within the marriage or family has been seriously disrupted. In situations in which the conflict has not ramified to any significant extent beyond the partners and when the family system is still reasonably integrated, with some positive communication and motivation in evidence, consensus seems to favor joint interviews as the major approach, although often in conjunction with other modalities. Work on the core marital difficulty is likely to be more direct and effective under such circumstances and may therefore obviate the need to involve the children in ongoing treatment.

When conflict has spread to embroil the total family system in the marital conflict or when the parents are as yet ready to discuss only their parent-child problems, the family interview is seen as particularly indicated. However, disagreement as to choice of approach mounts as the intensity of the family conflict increases and as demands on the worker or workers are heightened for this and other reasons. Some of this disagreement rests on differing views about possible practitioner skill: A few believed that the worker can use multiple-client sessions to create or revive communication, mutuality, and the like even after they have seriously broken down. Others thought this impossible and advised use of these types of interview only in the earlier stages of conflict when communication and mutuality are still present to some degree.

Disagreement about the choice of modality also focused on situations in which intrapersonal problems of one partner were predominant. In such situations, some believed that joint or family interviews would be unwise, even in the presence of a measure of family integration. When intrapsychic pressures experienced by one spouse are great or are expressed in ways severely disruptive of the marital and family system, that spouse may be unable to use existing supports from within the family. In that case both partners may first need individual strengthening. Once the intensity of the personal problem is eased, joint or family interviews may again be indicated to strengthen the marital axis or to deal with conflict ramifications among all the members of the family group.

Home visits proved still another moot issue related to choice of treatment modality. Some favored such visits to couples or families, especially for diagnostic purposes. Others saw them as encouraging acting out or misrepresentation.

Areas Understressed or Omitted

A few themes were striking by their omission or by the sparsity of comment on them. Foremost among these—and crying out for attention—were the possible values and pitfalls of multiple-client interviews in dealing with the sexual or financial difficulties of the partners. Since one or both of these concerns looms large indeed for the majority of applying couples, these topics need active consideration if worker and clients are to start from a mutual agreement on problems and goals.

Similarly urgent but little discussed in the responses on multiple-client interviews was the possible applicability of these approaches to the needs of couples either on the verge of separation or divorce or already living apart. About one-quarter of all marital applicants to FSAA member agencies are already separated at the time of intake (7) and many more must be assumed to be weighing such a step. This stark statistic represents a desperate need for service in which multiple-client interviews could be useful, whether for reevaluation of the need to separate or for the working through of separation plans.

Comments on other reality factors were similarly sparse. What of the difficulties of finding a time when worker and clients are all available or a place where geographically distant but emotionally involved family members can meet? Do socioeconomic and cultural factors have a bearing on the use of multiple-client interviews? With the revival of social work interest in the social sciences and the involvement of agencies in the urban crisis, similar responses written today would undoubtedly reflect more concern with the wider social network and with environmental pressures generally. However, such issues were given scant attention in the replies related to multiple-client interviewing. The special uses or dangers of the various modalities in relation to families from given socio-economic, cultural, religious, national, and ethnic backgrounds were not mentioned, for example, nor were such factors cited as criteria for or against the choice of any type of multiple-client interview. Similarly, possible value clashes between worker and clients were not discussed, despite their implications for the advisability of undertaking treatment in the first place or for clarifying or modifying family values. The potential of multiple-client approaches for the resolution of role conflict, the enhancement of self-esteem and mutual esteem, and increasing the family's coping capacity outside its own circle also warrant consideration beyond what they received. Parental privacy and the validity (or lack of validity) of family secrets are other important topics that loom large by implication but have not been adequately examined.

It is perhaps not surprising that many of these issues have been sidestepped in the past. They involve highly charged areas where social and familial requirements and resources may be out of alignment for a time. However, investigation and experimentation may show that they are not beyond mutual reconciliation through the use of imaginative approaches.

DISTINCTIVE CONTRIBUTIONS OF MULTIPLE-CLIENT INTERVIEWS TO SYSTEM CHANGE

An attempt has been made throughout this monograph to restate at the system level at least some of the concepts and processes that respondents described mainly in terms of personal dynamics and interaction between individual family members. Fundamental to this effort has been the assumption that the family can appropriately be described as a system in the sense that a change in one of its parts will almost inevitably produce change in the others (40), usually in a direction designed to reinstate the previous equilibrium or to achieve a new equilibrium through appropriate modifications of the components. In a real sense, therefore, treatment of the marital relationship must involve treatment of a system of interaction. As such, its conceptualization must take into account how the forces for both re-equilibration and change can be understood and handled so that the partners and other family members may be helped to participate effectively in necessary modifications of their own marital and family system.

It should be made clear that the focus in this conceptualization is entirely on the specific contributions of multiple-client, as distinct from individual, interviews, and does not attempt to encompass all their assets for treatment. Before the distinctive values of these methods can be identified, it is necessary to stress certain broad principles.

Within this structure the worker and all participating family members are directly and mutually exposed to each other's impact, with the result that the worker is placed in an especially strategic position for intervening directly in the system. Here he has the benefit of constant feedback between therapeutic impact on and diagnostic assessment of the marriage or family as a unit, as well as similar feedback with regard to individual members. By his direct contact with all members of the system, multiple points of entry and influence are opened up to him and multiple points of resistance revealed directly and made available for prompt and differential handling. When the worker's handling may threaten the balance between necessary family cohesion and anchorage on the one hand and necessary individuation and personal growth on the other, he is kept mindful of the need for the dovetailing of changes to keep the balance viable. Insofar as family members actually learn to provide for each other the climate experienced in the interview and develop more realistic and flexible norms and family patterns, the preventive effect of multiple-client interviews can be far-reaching indeed.

The following brief summary will recapitulate, in system terms, the potentialities for treatment inherent in the special structure of the multiple-client, as distinct from the individual, session. For sharpened focus, it will exclude consideration of couples in the process of weighing or undertaking dissolution of the marriage. Worker characteristics necessary for multiple-client interviewing and criteria for choice of modality are also discussed elsewhere. Instead, this summary will highlight, first, how such sessions may help to establish and maintain the worker's relationship with all system participants. Second, it will show how such a relationship may be used to enhance their motivation for change, increase their awareness of the nature and effects of the dysfunctional system, aid them in bringing about change and in removing obstacles to it,

and assure enough cushioning in the process to safeguard both
the system and its members.

Facilitation of the
Worker's Entry into the System
and Development and Maintenance
of a Direct Relationship
with All System Participants

Treatment is possible only because the family is not a fully
closed system with tight boundaries. Under the pressures of pain,
frustration, fear, and hope, it can admit an outsider into its inner
privacy provided he is seen as a competent and acceptable but
temporary helper who will respect its autonomy and withdraw as
soon as he is no longer needed. The structure of the multiple-client
session exposes both partners *and* all the family members simultaneously to the worker. They therefore have an opportunity to assess
jointly whether his personality, attitudes, and behavior are at least
minimally acceptable, effective, and relevant to their difficulties,
needs, capacities, and goals. The marital couple are likely to consent to this therapeutic intervention only as long as these conditions are fulfilled. On the worker's awareness of these conditions
and on his success in meeting them depends the maintenance of
the casework relationship with them as a pair. Their consent de-
termines, in turn, the worker's access to the children and other
family members.

Since all participants are simultaneously exposed to each other,
the possibilities of misunderstanding the worker's role and aims
in the interview are minimized and can be directly handled in the
group when they occur. Any efforts by one or more participants
to reject the worker or to nullify his influence are readily visible in
this setting and can therefore be handled promptly. Similarly, any
tendency on his part to take sides unconstructively is also visible
and evokes reactions that should enable him to realize and correct his error. Thus all participants can directly experience the
worker's concern and respect not only for the family members
as individuals but also for the marriage and the family as a unit
and for the right of the group to autonomy in choice of directions.
Moreover, the worker is constantly experiencing the effects of his
impact. He can see whether he has been pushing too hard for change

or not hard enough or has given premature or false reassurance. Since his therapeutic intervention can thus be kept closely geared to the tolerance of the system participants and the elasticity of the total system, he is better able to mainain the treatment relationship with the group as a whole.

Simultaneous Enhancement of the Motivation of All System Participants for Change

Exposed together to the worker's therapeutic optimism and to his willingness and ability to involve himself in an unfamiliar family system, the partners or family members are able to confront as a group the problems that led them into treatment. In the multiple-client session they can recognize together the multiple effects of these problems and can become directly involved as a group in tackling them. This simultaneous enlistment of all members who share in the difficulties in a joint effort to resolve them provides an added impetus for involvement in treatment. It may also allow the participants to revive and experience together previously submerged positives. As these emerge they can, in turn, be highlighted and reinforced by the worker so that they promote a process of positive instead of negative escalation. Since all participants shared in its development, the treatment contract with the worker is more likely to suit the realistic goals of all and therefore to command their adherence even in the face of setbacks. In couples' or multifamily groups, motivation for treatment may be additionally enhanced by the fact that other couples or families have been witnesses to the common contract.

Simultaneous Recognition of System Characteristics and Effects by All System Participants

Spurred and bolstered by shared hope and by the worker's judicious balancing of challenge and support, the participants can maintain a consistent focus on the current realities and effects of their system. As the worker questions some of their dysfunctional ways and highlights their strengths (and as other systems are directly observed in couples' or multifamily groups), at least some of the participants may become able to recognize latent patterns as they become manifest. They may thus identify incongruent communication patterns; dysfunctional family themes and myths; destructive alignments and splits and related scapegoating; restrictive, inappropriate, or unclear role configurations; excessive mutual cohesion or separateness; failures in reciprocity; and covert and inappropriate rules and norms. Joint maneuvers to ward off real or felt threats may become evident, as will structural instabilities within the marital system and unrealistic but shared perceptions and myths regarding the conditions essential for survival of the particular family as a unit. An increased awareness of individual behavioral patterns and of their effects on other participants may also emerge. Although not all families or family members can be involved in an examination of such latent patterns and their sources, many are likely to respond to a demonstration of their current effects. Similarly, changes in the system that may occur in the course of treatment can be jointly experienced and recognized.

Simultaneous Exposure
of All System Participants
to the Worker's Treatment Initiatives
and Encouragement
of System Modifications

The simultaneous exposure of all system participants to the worker and to each other in a therapeutic context makes it possible for all to witness and directly experience the impact of the worker's varied treatment initiatives. As dysfunctional patterns, values, and norms are manifested directly in the interview, the worker can promptly challenge them either verbally or by his behavior. He can also refuse to act within the terms and roles prescribed for him by the dysfunctional family system, thus demonstrating that new approaches need not destroy the ability of the members to function together as a group. At the same time he fosters increased communication about here-and-now experiences, points of friction, and possibilities for more constructive mutuality and improved reciprocity. He both encourages and demonstrates new ways of relating and coping as well as revised patterns for expressing or controlling the expression of feelings. He supplies elements needed in but missing from the family system and in so doing affords opportunities, through identification with him, for new social and emotional learning. In the presence of all, he legitimizes new norms and expands members' perceptions of the range of permissible and worthwhile behavior, thus stimulating all system participants simultaneously to modify the basic norms controlling their family interaction.

While he is providing distance and perspective through sharing his knowledge of other systems and their consequences, he also helps the partners and other system participants to call on previously untapped inner and group resources to implement the process of system change. At the same time he also promotes and creates a safe milieu for testing within the interview the kinds, amounts, and directions of change that can be tolerated by the group. If two therapists participate, this process of selective challenge and support can be carried forward co-operatively in a way that may ease not only the clients' pains but also the individual worker's tasks. If multiple couples or families are treated together in the same group, the members can experience alternative patterns of family interaction through direct observation of other families rather than through the worker's indirect reports.

Throughout this complex process, the co-presence of all offers opportunity for maximum dovetailing of individual changes so that there will be minimal jeopardizing of the balance between the members' needs for individuation, growth, and self-reliance and their shared requirements for living as a couple or family unit in a way that will provide anchorage, cohesion, and need-satisfaction for all. Change is also furthered all along the way as the couple or family members are encouraged to face and meet each other's needs more adequately, to plan for new satisfactions together, and to strengthen, both within and outside the family, ties that are more appropriate to the age and sex of the participants than those of previously existing alliances.

Simultaneous Attention
to the System's Relationship
to the Larger Environment

The marital or family system may be threatened not only from within but also through the impact of external forces affecting the whole society, specific groups within it, or the individual or family in particular. In such stress situations, multiple-client interviews can play a vital part in helping the partners and other family members to move from the role of victims or outcasts to that of conscious agents when this is possible, or to work on shared acceptance of the immutable when it is not. Together with the worker, they can examine the role of given environmental factors in precipitating, maintaining, or exacerbating the marital and family difficulties and can come to a joint decision regarding the most fruitful and realistic avenue for change or for consolidation of forces. Thus the worker may use the sessions for directly bolstering the partners and other family members against outside criticism in situations such as those involving marital role reversal, when the family's life-style may be unconventional but may legitimately meet members' needs. In other cases, interview participants may join in assessing their situation and deciding whether to act alone, as a group, or in concert with others outside the family in modifying the environment or their reaction to it.

Inasmuch as the multiple-client interview engages the partners or family members together in learning new ways of relating to outsiders and using outside help, it can be of value to them as they deal with other agencies and institutions, join with others to effect necessary changes locally or in the wider society, or struggle through the vicissitudes of such effort.

Because of the perspective made possible through the worker, the client participants can develop some shared understanding of the needs, strengths, excesses, and deficiencies of their particular marital or family system and of the ways in which the environment might help, in part, to meet, utilize, soften, and counterbalance these characteristics. To the degree that this shared assessment is accurate and generally acceptable to the members, the family is likely to set more achievable goals and to pursue them more vigorously together. As a result, they will benefit as a group from the sense of hope, self-esteem, and solidarity that comes from coping with a problem together, achieving a decision, sharing in an accomplishment, and becoming active rather than passive in relation to the environment. When members of the family's immediate social or wider neighborhood network are included in the sessions, further beneficial changes can flow from the broadened base of mutual concern and assistance and from the lessened sense of isolation and alienation.

All these modalities, in varying degrees, can also provide a means for dealing with the repercussions of environmental changes, including possible alterations in mutual relationships, status, and the like that could threaten the marital balance in new ways.

Early Attention to
Obstacles Hindering Needed Change

Multiple-client sessions make possible comparatively early detection and handling of obstacles to change, whether these arise from the nature of the family system or in response to its actual or imminent modification. Thus resistance, evasion, sabotage, individual and shared ambivalence, and dysfunctional family myths can be jointly recognized and tackled. Any moves by participating individuals or subgroups to reinstate former dysfunctional patterns can be seen and countered. Temporary chaos or dislocations due to change and the development of discrepant rates and directions of movement that threaten successful system modification can be acknowledged and handled within the group. When individual pathology emerges as the major precipitant of marital conflict and as a serious obstacle to progress in such sessions appropriate handling can follow.

Provision of Multiple Supports
for Facilitating and Sustaining Change

Whether families are facing the pangs and risks of system modification or have already accomplished some change, some inner or outside bolstering is needed to strengthen them and enable them to sustain these adjustments so that they may become part of a newly modified system rather than a prelude to relapse into old patterns. The need for hope and buttressing can be experienced together and met with immediate encouragement and highlighting of the rewards of change, with reinforcement of the members' maturational strivings, and with identification or mobilization of multiple supports. In couples' or multifamily groups, the direct experience of simultaneous progress and retrogression as observed among participant families may offer additional hope to both worker and participants, encourage their patience and perseverence, and foster a growing realization that the status quo is likely to

286

be more destructive than the evolving changes. Most important, perhaps, is the opportunity for the couple or family together to practice modified ways under therapeutic conditions that foster optimum results and therefore encourage transfer to the daily life situation. Once this transfer is accomplished and sustained, the modification of the system can be said to have been achieved.

IMPLICATIONS FOR PRACTICE

As experience with multiple-client interviewing grows, some important implications latent in the special social structure of these approaches are becoming evident. Not all of these implications are as yet widely recognized, but they all deserve further probing if the full potentials and limits of the multiple-client approach to marital treatment are to be realized.

As casework practice in general has been evolving over the past two decades, several changes have affected the development of multiple-client approaches and some have been directly inherent in their use. These changes relate variously to the merging of diagnosis and treatment, to increased concentration on the present, and to the emergence of new facets of the worker's role. At the same time, the growing range of available modalities has provided widened choice and opportunity, stimulated some beginning development of differential criteria for the use of each approach, and cast a clearer light on the issue of marital treatment within a family treatment context.

Increased Merging
of Diagnosis and Treatment
and Growing Stress on Current Factors

Since multiple-client sessions make marital and familial interaction immediately available for both observation and intervention, diagnosis and treatment tend increasingly to merge in practice. The same development has also been conducive to increased concentration on the present and on current interactional patterns, with correspondingly less exploration of the past. At the same time, the past is not neglected when it appears relevant to present difficulties. There are even some hints that multiple-client interviews may become preferred tools for the exploration of marital and familial as distinct from individual history.

Changes in the Role
of the Worker

There can be no doubt that the worker's role is also changed radically whenever joint or family sessions are used instead of individual interviews. With an increased number of interview modalities available to him, the worker's ability to use authority constructively becomes even more essential and inescapable than in individual interviews. It is he who must take the final responsibility for choices and shifts of interviewing modality as well as for the content of treatment. As he temporarily enters a social system in conflict, he must realize the implications of his relationship for all the participants even when he is temporarily engaging only one client. Moreover, he himself becomes subject to the typical processes and pressures of an established system trying to absorb, cope with, or eject the outsider. He must enter the system and allow enough influence on himself so that he can understand the couple's or family's customary patterns, critical excesses, and omissions. Yet he needs to resist absorption into or manipulation by the system. Therapeutic needs require that he remain free to assume whatever role the moment requires—enabler, intervener, challenger, interpreter, bridge, upholder of reality, and so on. He must be able to use whatever the special social structure permits to help provide the needed elements, affording opportunities for ventilation of feeling or for control of feeling or behavior, as indicated. Clearly, then, with the growth of multiple-client approaches, the role of the worker has shifted from helping with feelings *about* interpersonal conflict to direct demonstration and help in *dealing with* conflict involving central figures in the clients' lives. It is this need for multiple worker roles and functions that has given rise to experimentation with the use of multiple therapists.

Increased Range and Reach
of Approaches Utilized

Growing familiarity with the varying uses of individual, joint, and family sessions increases the worker's range of choice with

288

respect to modality. As these approaches become more widely known, clients will also be able to express their preferences in this context. Moreover, the greater variety of interviewing approaches seems to offer opportunities for service to clients who were often left untouched by the individual approach, especially couples or families whose members may suffer from character disorders, an excess of mutual anger, or a lack of communication, mutual or self-esteem, or capacity for co-operation. Couples' and multifamily groups and even more inclusive modalities, although still new, may further extend the range and reach of marital and family treatment since they combine some of the advantages of joint and family sessions with the added bonus of modifying the widespread sense of marital and social isolation and alienation.

Reshaping Criteria
for Choice of Approach

The use of multiple-client sessions is highlighting the fact that negative feelings or functioning within the family are less crucial for the choice of modality and for its possible benefits than is the nature of available interlocking mutual supports and positive elements. When these do offer a web of constructive supports, the marital or family bond may, in fact, become an important treatment tool. As experience with these group approaches grows, workers are increasingly able to face and identify the specific advantages and disadvantages of each. They can also be more realistic about the risks involved in use of all or any of them and about the penalties of failure, as compared with the gains that might be expected. A reinterpretation of the concept of "key members" to be seen in treatment is also emerging. While only those actively contributing to the problem might have been included in the past, those helping, overtly or covertly, to maintain the family system that perpetuates the problem may now be asked to participate. Indeed, some of the special values of multiple-client sessions may lie precisely in the direct approach possible to those who are maintaining the old structure.

All these considerations are making possible some tentative refinement of criteria for the use of these modalities. As multiple-client interviews illuminate the interrelationship between the pivotal marital subsystem, the total family system, and its individual and subsystem components, it becomes more likely that the best area for therapeutic intervention at a given time can be more accurately identified. As has become evident in the present analysis, such identification depends on delineation of the extent of family members' entanglement in the marital problem, on recognition of the system or subsystem (s) most endangered by the marital difficulties, on the system or subsystem(s) most crucial to the family's recovery, and, to an important degree, on pinpointing the system or subsystem(s) that might represent the most promising area for intervention. Thus the apparently enormous complexity and multiplicity of factors to be weighed in choosing, using, and possibly combining appropriate modalities can serve to sharpen the focus on that particular system or subsystem that calls for treatment priority or concurrent attention at any given time.

In addition to considerations based on current system and subsystem interrelationships, the choice of approach should also be influenced by recognition of the family's phase of development, stage of marital conflict, and phase of treatment. All these cast further light on the modality or modalities indicated if remaining satisfactions within the marriage and family are to be enhanced and excessive conflicts moderated in the long run.

New Perspectives
on Treatment of Marital Problems
as a Segment of Family Treatment

Workers deeply committed to the concept of family treatment have long debated the legitimacy of either carrying on or systematically investigating marital treatment as such. Some have feared that concentration on a segment of family functioning might lead to fragmentation of the worker's perceptions of the family as a whole or to a move away from family-focused treatment to marital counseling as a separate treatment modality. This apprehension is lessening, however, as leading therapists acknowledge marital treatment as a legitimate and basic component of family treatment. Furthermore, the choice of focus is increasingly seen as flexibly determined by a multiplicity of highly specific factors, among them the needs of individual family members, the characteristics of the specific marital and family system, the emerging pattern of relationship between the worker and the couple or the worker and the total family group, the family's place within its maturational cycle, the stage of marital conflict, and the course of treatment. Furthermore, the direct treatment of marital interaction, in joint interviews or couples' groups, need not be seen as separate from family treatment at all if the choice of such a treatment course leaves room for shifts in modality as needed and is based on the conviction that the selection of the pivotal marital subsystem for treatment best serves at that time the interests not only of the marital pair but of the family as a whole, along the lines outlined in the discussion of criteria.

As shifts in the focus of treatment become necessary, some typical sequences in treatment modality seem to recur in many instances. These may variously reflect a turning of attention from the parent-child to the marital problem, or vice versa, a move toward dealing with the marital problem and its ramifications as personal difficulties become modified through treatment, or a new concentration on intrapsychic difficulties as the marital difficulties are relieved enough to allow the shift in focus.

Need for Attention
to Neglected Areas

Family rules encompass what may and may not be talked about and by whom. If in multiple-client sessions the caseworker seems to join in a conspiracy of silence on matters related to sex, money, personal values, or national, religious, cultural, or racial issues, as the response omissions suggest may be true in some instances, he may be unwittingly reinforcing some destructive or self-defeating family norms. He may also be increasing the gap between his own and his clients' conception of the problem. Caseworkers need to explore further what factors should influence their decision as to when and where and in the presence of whom to encourage or discourage the discussion of such topics.

Workers also need to re-evaluate the role of sociocultural, economic, and ethnic factors in the lives of client families and in their relationship to the worker and the agency. The potentially therapeutic uses of value clashes between worker and clients also need further investigation as a treatment tool. Similarly, new ways of dovetailing the agency's services more closely with the strengths, resources, and limits of the client family and its environment will no doubt become increasingly evident as clinical knowledge gained in multiple-client sessions is used to enrich administrative inventiveness.

Also comparatively untapped in the realm of practice are the potentials of multiple-client approaches for counseling in cases involving separation and divorce. Although the couple's paths will part, the need to plan for the children, to help the partners and children through this difficult period, and to evolve optimal ways of handling visitation rights may well provide the impetus for some joint or family sessions.

New Possibilities
for Prevention

As caseworkers equip themselves with a wider variety of approaches, some exciting possibilities for prevention are opened up. Joint or group sessions may be offered, for example, at critical points in the family life cycle: to engaged couples, to young married couples who are about to become or have just become parents, and to families in which the children will be leaving home. Such services could play a part in the mental health field comparable to that of the prenatal clinic in medicine. They would require of the worker some specialized knowledge of the specific tasks and developmental strains of each particular family life phase. In addition, they would call for a public image of family agencies as a natural, unstigmatized resource for help on family growth and its strains. Similar preventive effects might be expected for the children in cases in which agency services are provided to couples who are ending their marriage and who need to help their children cope with this painful transition at a time when the parents themselves may feel highly conflicted.

IMPLICATIONS FOR THEORY-BUILDING

Casework theory as well as practice is being deeply affected by insights born of the use of multiple-client sessions, although the knowledge reflected both in the responses and in the literature is still piecemeal. Implications for theory-building with regard to at least four broad areas seem to flow directly from the structure and processes unique to these modalities. They concern a need for (a) the forging of links between individual and system-level concepts, (b) the clarification of the applicability of certain specific concepts to marital treatment, (c) an improved conceptualization of the nature and life-history of marital or familial relationships, and (d) an improved understanding of the treatment process itself. Above all, what is still missing is a language for describing system-level events clearly and succinctly. Perhaps some help from the linguists might be in order, for other cultures may possess some of the terms needed. Hindustani, for example, which springs from a culture with an age-old extended family system, has simple verbs describing such phenomena as the formation of collusive ties among family members. A search for such words may suggest English counterparts.

Improved Linkage
of Individual Psychodynamic
and System-Level Concepts

Some links and parallels between individual psychodynamic concepts and family system concepts are already at hand, although in varying stages of theoretical development. For example, every important new phase in individual and family development confronts the organism and the system with parallel and yet different forms of challenge. These challenges relate at one and the same time to personal capacity for human relationships and to social role; to individual value perception and control and to family norms and values; to personal capacity for realistic and goal-directed activity and to family goals; to the individual's defenses, rational and irrational, against real or misperceived dangers, and to group-level defenses in the face of threatened change; to personal exercise of flexibility in the use of skills and defenses and to family system structures that allow flexible responses and behavior.

Many other linked concepts are relevant: Individual integration is linked to marital and family equilibrium, as is suggested by the possibilities of adjustments in family equilibrium to accommodate both individuation and mutuality. The concepts of individual and group continuity have much in common, including the relevance of the concept of transference if this is applied to the carryover of both past individual and past system experience. Also to the point are such concepts as that of family boundaries and their openness or closedness, both in relation to individual members within the group and to the larger system beyond, and, finally, the dual concepts of individual ego strength and group strength and mutual support within a family system.

Close examination of treatment situations and family life phases in which these parallel processes are simultaneously at work is likely to illuminate these interrelationships and the points of complementarity and stress between them. Such improved understanding should, in turn, help workers assess their comparative responsibility toward the individual client and the family as a whole, especially at points when the interests of the two may seem poles apart, as, for example, when only one partner wishes to end the marriage.

Improved Linkage of Subsystems to the Total Family System

Greater clarity is also needed regarding the relationship between the family's subsystems and the viability and adequacy of the whole. Although theoretically the marital subsystem might seem central to the whole family system and the prime source of its leadership, the actual hierarchies and constellations among the family subsystems may differ from this model. Clinical information derived from multiple-client interviews should greatly enrich our theoretical understanding of such linkages and their effect. What happens, for example, when one parent and one child, instead of both the partners, form the dominant axis in the family? What is the effect on the total family when the partners are so intensely involved in the marital subsystem that they neglect their parental roles? What is the role of the sibling subsystem and how do its patterns relate to the marital subsystem? All these issues require further theory-building if the whole family and its subsystems are to be properly understood and the fullest possible benefits are to be gained from family-level treatment.

Improved Linkage of Family System Concepts with Those for Larger Social Systems

Multiple-client interviews give an intimate glimpse into each family's unique way of combining into a system the ingredients made available by their own members and by the subculture and wider culture of which they are a part. A knowledge of these ingredients is essential if the worker's diagnostic evaluation and treatment suggestions are to be realistic in terms both of internal family well-being and total family survival. What, for example, is the worker's responsibility when the larger culture rewards persistence and success and the family culture values pleasure and immediacy? What are some of the typical reciprocal pressures and influences between the family system and the wider society in situations involving different ethnic, religious, cultural, national, and socioeconomic groups? What modifications, if any, might be called for, or even possible, on either side? What resources can either offer the other? Further understanding of these issues should be of general benefit to marital treatment—perhaps especially so in situations in which parents or children have come into conflict with the environment.

More Systematic Examination
of Particular Concepts
and Their Application

Many of the terms used rather globally by the respondents could be illuminated in all their specificity by examination of actual interviews. The value of the role concept for treatment, for instance, could be clarified: Did the worker attempt to assess the areas of role failure or role conflict and their effect on the family's coping capacity? How did he approach these role problems in treatment? What role modifications, if any, helped to re-establish equilibrium? How and when did the caseworker help the couple to accomplish them? Do patterns of role functioning and of role complementarity between marital partners tend to be characteristic of all their relationships or to be closely geared to specific roles? What, if any, are the effects of improved role perception and role functioning on personal and mutual feelings and attitudes as well as on performance?

The meaning of many other concepts could also be sharpened by such studies, with eventual benefit for theory-building. The process of family involvement in treatment needs to be further conceptualized, for example. Communication patterns and family-level defenses need to be classified and interrelated. The difference between a resistive and a healthily protective defensive maneuver should be clarified, together with the kinds of evidence that would enable workers to distinguish between them. Greater precision is also needed in the use of such terms as "marital equilibrium," "marital balance," and the like. Do these concepts require revision in the light of greater understanding of the relationship between individual ego strengths and weaknesses and marital or familial positives and negatives? At what points might the requirements for maintenance of equilibrium run counter to the need for individuation and personal growth? Quite possibly, some of the disagreements among caseworkers may be resolved as these concepts are defined more precisely on the basis of clinical experience. As the variables involved are specifically identified and descriptively defined, clinical material will become increasingly productive as a base for exploratory studies that may lead to clarification of theory.

Improved Conceptualization of
the Marital History and of
the Nature of Normal and Abnormal
Marital and Family Relationships

Sociologists have recently begun to integrate some data about individual psychodynamics into their theories, while psychodynamic thinkers are turning to some sociological concepts to round out their insights. New concepts are thus becoming available to both groups for better understanding of both the normal and the dysfunctional family. Currently available resources that might well be cultivated include small group theory (14, 18, 35), descriptive and analytical sociological methods (28), and psychoanalytic theory focused on marital interaction rather than on the individual problems of the partners (24, 46). These concepts, systematically applied to the study of clinical material, may well open up a deeper understanding of the ways in which different families succeed or fail in resolving conflicts between the system's push for equilibrium and the individual's need for growth. Such knowledge should be of great aid in directing treatment to the areas most fruitful for intervention. It may also shed light on the way in which a system as a whole can grow and change.

In relation to the marriage seen longitudinally, a good deal may well be learned from careful study of the marital career of couples.

This focus may throw light on the structural instabilities in marriage, the sources of breakdown, and the natural history of conflict. What can be attributed to normal maturational stresses and what to faulty patterns of system development and maintenance? A clearer understanding of the marital life cycle in all its aspects should sharpen treatment focus and offer valuable clues for prevention.

Improved Conceptualization
of the Treatment Process
in System Terms

Since many changes in theory have grown out of new developments in practice, a close examination of interview material could also do much to advance a system-level conceptualization of process. For example, some of the factors already described as seemingly operative at the system level in multiple-client sessions need substantiation, modification, or negation through actual study of interviews. The same applies to the experimental use of concepts from learning theory and from the social sciences. To what extent are workers actually making use of such concepts as conditioning, family rules, congruence of communication, life style, and the like, and what is the impact of their use? Whether such studies must be mainly descriptive or whether more formal analysis and validation will be possible remains to be seen. In any case, they will make an essential contribution to further understanding of the way in which the group process may be used to further therapeutic ends. They could also clarify the different effects of various worker orientations and roles on the family system and the goals of treatment.

IMPLICATIONS FOR FUTURE RESEARCH

Many of the unanswered questions raised earlier in this chapter need careful clinical investigation and the thinking through of underlying casework concepts and values before formal research can be productive. However, some issues can be investigated systematically, even at this stage, by careful research procedures. A few of these topics may be suited to investigation by experimental methods involving control or comparison groups. At this stage, however, a larger number seem more appropriate for careful study based on the systematic evaluation of clinical material (8; 20; 27, p.7). Some issues suited to each approach will be suggested briefly, but no attempt will be made to detail the serious methodological problems involved in tackling these difficult explorations.

Relative Advantages and Disadvantages of Various Interview Modalities

Carefully conducted descriptive, comparative, and control-group studies could throw light on the outcomes of multiple-client sessions as contrasted with those of other approaches. For example, comparison of case samples could perhaps show whether the use of some multiple-client interviews really resulted in better co-ordination of treatment direction between the partners than was the case when individual interviews were used exclusively. Thus interviews with three sets of similar couples and workers might be reviewed: those seen mainly in multiple-client sessions, mainly in individual interviews, and in individual interviews with periodic multiple-client sessions. Answers might be sought to the following questions: In which group were there fewer discrepant or un-co-ordinated developments between the partners? Were such developments spotted or prevented earlier in one or the other group? Did the length or effectiveness of treatment differ substantially among couples seen by the same worker but in different types of sessions?

The same case material could perhaps be used also to throw light on other claims for the eclectic approach, such as its avoidance of certain known pitfalls of the exclusive use of individual interviewing. It would be possible to examine whether there was a difference among the groups in the tendency, if any, of some clients to become too dependent on the worker, in the tendency to seek or find secondary gratifications from the relationship with the worker, or in the comparative ability of both clients and workers in these groups to see each other and to understand their respective roles without excessive distortion?

Other special assets of the multiple-client approach might be similarly probed by close attention to already available case material or by the use of control groups when feasible. Thus the respondents' sense of more effective involvement of the partners in the multiple-client session as compared with individual treatment might be tested, first, in relation to the relative success of joint or individual interviews at intake and, second, in relation to their use for ongoing treatment. Case studies and follow-up investigations could compare couples who dropped out after intake with those who continued. As for those who remained in treatment, it would be fruitful to compare some couples seen in individual interviews with others treated jointly by one worker and with yet others seen by two workers simultaneously. If the worker succeeded through the use of any of these approaches in aiding the partners to develop some mutuality, it might be possible to identify the factors that contributed to this outcome and some that worked against it.

The transfer of treatment gains is another issue warranting research attention, since many practitioners see multiple-client interviews as offering a unique contribution in this respect. Examination of cases in which client reports indicate that treatment gains in joint interviews and perhaps also in family interviews were well transferred to the home might be compared with cases in which transfer was inadequate or failed to take place entirely. What were the differences in the worker's attitudes and handling of the interviews, the families' situations, and so on? Do they shed light on the differences, if any, between successful and unsuccessful transfer of gains to the home? Follow-up interviews might reveal whether and to what extent such transfer was well maintained after closing and how this record compared with the success of couples seen mainly in individual interviews.

Occasional reference in the responses to the importance of good timing on the worker's part raises again the question of comparison with individual sessions, but with another emphasis. Is good timing, as some respondents indicated, more essential in multiple-client than in individual sessions? Do missed opportunities have greater negative impact here than in individual treatment? Joint or family interviews could be analyzed to assess the effect of missed opportunities for confrontation, control, and support and for the fostering of co-operation, mutual communication, and mutual awareness. Such cases could then be compared with others seen in individual treatment by the same worker, when opportunities for helping the client face a problem, restrain his impulses, and gain better awareness and insight and for appropriately supporting him were also identifiable and missed. What was the possible effect of such omissions in either group of cases? Does such study bear out the possibility that skillful timing and response are even more important in the multiple-client than in the individual interview? May the missing of such opportunities in an interactional situation be taken as tacit acceptance of or support for destructive or unhelpful behavior and attitudes? Clarification of such questions should throw needed light on some of the special assets and pitfalls of multiple-client interviewing.

A further question worth exploring is that of the usefulness of at least some joint interviews in situations in which the partners wish to dissolve the marriage. Both worker and clients may too readily assume that the structure of joint interviewing symbolizes the couple's wish for continuation of the marriage or the worker's interest in their reconciliation. Perhaps an examination of the experience of workers in domestic relations courts would cast light on this assumption. What use do they make of the joint session? Do they employ it readily with couples who are separating in an effort to smooth the process, minimize bitterness, and help with the children? Are the clients who apply to such courts generally willing to engage in joint interviews? If so, with what results? What has been the experience of caseworkers in agencies that have made similar attempts? Venturesome testing of the limits of the method's utility in this and in other respects can further increase the range of choices available to the practitioner and hence his helpfulness to couples in conflict.

Criteria for Choice of Modality

Inevitably clarification of the values of various multiple-client approaches will lead to refinement of criteria regarding their use. However, direct research on this issue is also needed, especially since many practitioners question the wisdom of using family interviews in the context of marital treatment and are uncertain about criteria for shifts in modality. To a lesser extent, the use of multiple-client interviews with severely disturbed, excessively rivalrous, or competitive partners or with very young couples were also doubtful areas.

When family interviews have been used for diagnosis in cases of marital difficulty, one might search for the effects of such interviews on the children, the parents, the relationship between them, and the later course of treatment. Such findings might serve to indicate the need for freer or more limited use of the approach for diagnosis. When family interviews have been used for treatment in situations in which the marital conflict has been concealed by other problems, an examination of interview content could show what was actually learned about the marital situation and what was accomplished with it in these sessions. How did this learning and tackling affect the children? the parents? their relationship? the course of treatment? In what areas were these effects evident? Were they helpful? Were they detrimental to the family, the marriage, or any of the individuals? In what way? Have all cases in which family interviews have been used for the treatment of marital problems presented open or latent parent-child conflict or involvement in the problem? Would the workers have chosen this approach in the absence of this particular type of conflict? What was discussed in such sessions? What was the effect—if any —of discussing certain topics, such as sex, money, or parents' feelings of inadequacy? Clearly, a fuller assessment of the accumulated practice wisdom gained on these topics would help in the refinement of criteria for the use of family interviews and would further clarify their values for marital treatment.

An especially thorny problem is posed by the criteria for shifts in modality since for ethical reasons caseworkers would hesitate to hold the interviewing mode constant for one couple regardless of the situation while varying it with another couple according to the family's needs. Control groups could therefore not be used. However, a study of decision paths and critical decision points and of reasons for the choices made where the road forks should be productive, even without the use of control groups. As part of such a study, workers could systematically record when and why they chose a specific approach at a particular juncture, what happened, whether or not they were satisfied with the decision, and why.

Three possible subcategories of cases might be studied in this way and compared: (a) couples who came for help with their marriage, (b) those who came because of difficulties with the children, and (c) those presenting both types of difficulty from the start. In these situations special attention could be given to the point at which the parent-child problem became recognized as springing from marital difficulties, or marital concerns were eased and children's problems came into focus. What happened at these points? Was there a shift in type of interview? Did anticipation of the penalties of failure affect the choice of approach? Did the shift help or hinder? What, in the worker's view, were the dynamics involved? A systematic cumulation of corresponding information on a large number of cases should promote the refinement of criteria.

The controversy over the use of joint or family interviews in families in which one partner is severely disturbed may also be aided by well-focused descriptive studies. It might be worthwhile to examine records, tapes, or films or to observe treatment in family agencies where these modalities are being used to advantage with gross pathology. The special pitfalls likely, the possible safeguards needed, and the special techniques that are helpful can then be identified, together with the dovetailing of family strengths with individual need, as observed and encouraged by the worker. All this should further the development of criteria for or against the use of multiple-client approaches when one spouse is exceptionally disturbed.

As for the very young and immature couple, this same approach could be used to compare the progress of those seen first in a course of individual sessions with those seen from the start mainly in joint interviews. Such a comparison could throw light on the question of personal maturation when this is seen as a necessary preliminary to marital growth. Was direct work on personal growth really necessary for marital progress? In what specific areas did such growth become evident? Was it accomplished in both sets of circumstances? How and why was it accomplished or not? Was either method clearly preferable to the other and in what respects? In what way, if any, did the attitudes, age, sex, or other characteristics of the worker influence the outcome?

Premature Withdrawal
from Treatment

Since a high proportion of clients with marital problems withdraw after brief contact with the agency (9), efforts to study dropout losses should be especially rewarding. Through follow-up study it could become clear which clients withdrew because they had received the help they needed and which stayed away out of disillusionment with the service, the worker, or the prospects of a change in their marriage. It would also be possible to test whether multiple-client interviews reduced the dropout rate as compared with individual interviews or changed the couples' or families' explanations for dropping out. Did these interviews exert pressures to keep the family in or out of treatment? What were these pressures? Is there any evidence that dropout patterns may be linked to the phase of treatment, that some couples may terminate contact at the first twinges of actual or anticipated change, while others flee at the period of chaos that may follow therapeutic impact, just before improvement might be expected? Are these outcomes affected by differences in the alertness of the worker to the need for retaining the consent of both partners if constructive contact is to continue with them as a couple or with the whole family group?

Those partners who stayed and benefited and those who withdrew could be interviewed regarding the factors that did or did not induce them to try treatment and to stay with it. Such studies could be made in relation to joint interviews, family interviews, and also multicouple and multifamily groups. It would be of special interest, for clarification of concepts, to compare the clients' impressions with those of the workers in each situation.

It would also be interesting to determine whether any other over-all patterns are associated with premature withdrawal from treatment. Do certain kinds of families generally drop out at similar points? Does the dropout pattern seem to vary with the type of worker? Examination of cases that failed or closed prematurely might also be undertaken to identify possible clashes of norms that were not used therapeutically by the worker and the family.

The Caseworker's Role in Outcomes

The crucial role in treatment of the worker's qualities and skills has been stressed throughout this monograph and in the over-all project report (9). Research is urgently needed if the worker's special roles and their uses are to be more clearly understood and more effectively taught as they apply to the use of multiple-client interviews for marital treatment. Descriptive case analyses and observation of interviews through one-way screens, films, and the like should be helpful in clarifying many questions: What was the full range of worker roles in given cases? Might there be identifiable clusters of worker roles needed in relation to certain types of couples or families? Can patterns of idiosyncratic reaction to and by the worker be predicted, as some suggest, in relation to specific family types (48)? Does the "worker type" also have to be included in the prediction?

Unusual skills in multiple-client interviewing for marital therapy would certainly reward intensive study whenever they can be identified. Some highly skilled and gifted workers can be remarkably effective in joint interviews with couples whom others are unable to see together. This has been found true in relation to partners unable to talk together or showing extremes of hostility, passivity, and dominance, or manifesting a sadomasochistic interaction. There are even instances of treatment success in joint interviews with couples who at first seemed to derive only destructive gratifications from them. Observation and analysis of the work of such practitioners may reveal some of the qualities and techniques that make the difference between modification and stalemate—or worse. Full confirmation of this relationship would, of course, require careful study of the comparative results in similar cases carried by workers with various approaches and personalities.

Values of Newly Emerging Interview Modalities

Developments in the use of more than one worker, couples' groups, multifamily groups, and other modality variations suggest further areas for research designed to clarify the values of and criteria for these various approaches. As a simple beginning, the gross dropout rates might be examined and compared with those for other modalities. On a more complex level, analysis of tape recordings or other process records might be undertaken for couples' groups, for instance, to determine whether the marital focus is indeed especially well maintained in this approach. For example, at the end of each session the worker (or workers) might check what problems were discussed, what supplementary methods were used, and which ones did or did not accomplish their end. It would also be interesting to examine, through case study and follow-up, the differences between couples who accept and those who reject couples' groups, between those who are accepted for such groups and those who are screened out, and between those who do well in them and those who drop out or do not benefit. Couples might also be asked directly for their observations of the process, the critical turning points, and the nature of their discussions at home between sessions.

Relevance of Past Research
to These Needs

Does recent or current research in social work and related fields suggest answers to these various questions? So far, little formal research has focused on the relative advantages and disadvantages of these modalities, the criteria related to them, the worker's role in outcomes, or the reasons for premature withdrawal from marital treatment. Neither has the applicability of newly emerging concepts been formally tested in most casework settings on any significant scale. Most of the published research on family interviewing has been carried out in hospital, clinic, or research settings and has been related in the main to the treatment of schizophrenics (12, 13, 26, 36, 51). As for joint interviews and couples' groups, published research reporting data drawn from sizable case samples and based on formal research procedures is still rare (19). However, many outstanding clinical articles are available on all the modalities (5, 11, 17, 32, 33, 34, 38, 52) and a steady expansion of conceptual thinking is evident in the voluminous literature (e.g., 6, 10, 31, 38, 41, 42, 43). In contrast, the more traditional group therapy approaches have attracted considerably more formal research attention.

Work based on sociologically oriented theory and research has concentrated in the main on large conceptual questions and studies of large population samples, on the one hand, and on highly delimited and measurable issues, on the other. To fill the research gap presented by this bifurcation, there is great need and opportunity for depth studies at the agency level. Here clinical material is richly available that could shed light on the dynamics of family processes and their treatment and on criteria for choice of treatment modality. Some of these possibilities have already begun to be explored. Illustrations include the studies and systematic clinical observation of marital treatment, family therapy, and multiple-

305

impact family therapy at the Family Service Association of Indianapolis (47, 48, 49, 50) and at the Jewish Family Service in New York (1, 2), as well as the methods study of the Community Service Society of New York, which includes multiple-client interviews as one of the experimental variables (44). A few agencies are also tooling up for detailed process research in these areas through the use of video-tape, one-way screens, and the like. Valuable contributions are also offered by some of the study groups undertaken as part of the present research project and cited throughout this monograph.

The National Experiment in Staff Development, which grew out of the present project, carried the study group approach further with the help of funds from the National Institute of Mental Health, which made possible regular field contacts and on-site consultation to the participating agencies. Through the study group process, local agencies on this project produced a variety of reports focused on multiple-client interviews as used in marital treatment. These concerned variously the values of joint and family interviews, the criteria for joint interviewing, and the findings from the follow-up of marital clients treated through joint interviews and couples' groups. Another group of papers probed such issues as separation, sexual adjustment, and ethnic and educational factors in marriage. The uses of social work concepts and other theoretical frames of reference in marital counseling were also examined, as was the applicability of selected concepts from small group theory to the development of preventive services (45).

There can be no doubt that clinical studies of the kind described can play an increasingly important role in the development of an over-all understanding of marriage and the family. At the same time, it must be recognized that to move from this critically necessary exploratory stage to the verification stage presents enormous problems. Specification of relevant dimensions and adequately defined and operationalized concepts would be required, as well as usable research instruments that tap the core variables involved. Rigorous and yet ethically acceptable designs and control procedures would also be needed.

Nevertheless, it is exciting indeed to realize that, given an adequate investment of effort and resources, the field may soon be in a position to contribute from its own unique vantage point not only to improved theory for clinical practice but also to family theory and research. In general, the enormously complex and varied

306

conceptual frameworks being evolved by related disciplines (4, 16, 22, 39) stand at this point in some isolation from the detailed studies and measurements ingeniously devised by sociologists and psychologists. If the pieces of the mosaic are ever to be put together, the linkage between the larger concepts and the clinically observable phenomena would need to be clarified further through theoretical study and research. Multiple-client interviews would seem to provide a fruitful arena for such research. To the extent that formal statistical data and clinical materials can be rendered increasingly relevant to each other, they can become mutually corrective. For example, as family interviews reveal the specific linkages between the marital adjustment of parents and the personality development of their children, it may become possible to untangle the seeming contradiction between clinical impressions suggesting a causal connection between the two and research findings indicating little association between them, at least at the gross level (29).

IMPLICATIONS FOR EDUCATION AND IN-SERVICE TRAINING

Expansion of the casework repertoire to include joint and family interviews and related multiple-client approaches calls for modified and expanded educational preparation for caseworkers. Whether and to what extent this should be provided at the university as contrasted with the agency level or whether both should have well-defined roles will not be debated here. Regardless of the setting where new information, theories, and kinds of interviewing are first taught, there will be a need for sharing new developments and for maintaining a liaison and supervisory structure suited to this purpose. For the time being, it must be acknowledged that many experienced workers and some novices have had little or no exposure to multiple-client interviewing or to marital and family theory during their professional education. Orienting them to these new approaches within the agency structure requires a substantial investment of administrative effort. In many agencies, the in-service training of workers for these new tasks is being given high priority.

What information is of special importance for developing skill in multiple-client interviewing? What special personal qualities and attitudes need to be fostered in relation to them?

307

First, the conceptual framework must expand to encompass not only the psychodynamic approach, but also learning theory and an understanding of the family viewed as a system within the framework of the larger social system. To be effective the worker needs to combine his concern for and understanding of individual psychodynamics with an attempt to assay his effect on the marital or family system, its impact on himself, and the way in which the needs and strengths of these systems and of the individuals within them may complement or war with each other. Information regarding typical family structures and attitudes for different socio-economic, nationality, cultural, religious, and ethnic subgroups within the wider culture should also be imparted as it becomes available, with due emphasis on the fluidity of such patterns within a largely mobile society and with stress on the maturational phases, maturational crises, and methods of crisis resolution often characteristic for individuals, marriages, and families within these groups. In the course of such teaching, the worker in training will also need to examine his own family background in these terms and probe his own values. He may then find these recalled, threatened, or otherwise confronted in actual interview situations. To deal with this confrontation in a fashion therapeutic for the clients will almost inevitably require not only careful training for self-awareness in the "live" situation but agency provision of opportunities for conferences or consultation with others in a position to help him maintain perspective and therapeutic functioning and to avoid being drawn into unconstructive or collusive alliances.

It is imperative that the worker undertaking multiple-client interviews be taught to see, recognize, and use individual and family strengths as carefully as he understands individual and family pathology. This should enhance his effectiveness and encourage him to develop a realistic therapeutic optimism, usually found more among highly experienced than beginning workers (15).

Since sex, money, and children are the areas in which couples applying with marital problems typically define most of their difficulties, factual, psychological, and sociological information on these topics should be considered essential teaching content, with special emphasis on the possible feelings of both clients and worker about discussion of these topics in a situation involving more than one client and one worker. The avoidance of normal adult sexuality—as distinct from infantile or pathological sexual functioning

—as a topic for casework teaching can hardly be justified in a curriculum designed to prepare students to help marital couples in conflict.

A further task of education and in-service training relates to the development of sensitivity to the special problems, opportunities, and methods for nurturing intrafamilial communication in multiple-client interviews. In particular, the worker accustomed to individual sessions will need to learn to help clients to communicate with *each other* rather than with himself. He must also become alert to the various layers and meanings of manifest and covert and congruent and incongruent communication in a multiple-client situation. Many will also need help in developing communication skills with children of various ages.

The conflict spiral concept also has some interesting implications for in-service training, since practitioners are likely to have a knack for dealing with families in a particular phase of conflict, but may need special training or consultation for coping with other phases. Those who have little difficulty in helping couples to bring out latent feelings, for instance, may find it hard to provide controls against the spread of conflict, and vice versa. The concept of conflict phases, by clarifying such strengths and weak points, should be of help in staff development, which is a crucial factor in the further growth and testing of the family treatment approach.

As the unique values of multiple-client interviewing become better understood, workers can more easily be trained to use them appropriately and to recognize the criteria that call for confrontation, ventilation, control, and so on. The difficulties of using these methods need not be underplayed, but those in the leadership role may well stress that joint and family interviews make most visible those worker pitfalls—such as forming unconstructive alliances with one client—that tend to exist invisibly in the individual interview and are therefore not usually dealt with.

Great flexibility is needed for multiple-client interviewing, which requires a caseworker who can be comfortable in the simultaneous presence of several clients—young and old, male and female—with possibly intense levels of conflict among them or with vastly differing maturity levels and capacities for verbal communication. While observation can be helpful as a teaching technique, more is needed. Perhaps such techniques as role-playing or psychodrama may also help the practitioner to become, at different times, active intervener, quiet listener, reticent enabler, blunt challenger, sponsor of greater freedom or greater control within the group, neutral interpreter, and temporary ally of the member who needs momentary support. No amount of training can ever be expected to produce the perfect caseworker. However, increased knowledge and awareness of the worker qualities required within given treatment systems is likely to help agencies to dovetail particular worker strengths and weaknesses with the needs of particular families through skillful case assignment.

Concluding Remarks

In comparison with the complexity of the issues in the treatment of marital problems and the difficulty of the tasks ahead, the contribution that any study can hope to make is indeed small. This monograph has tried to articulate and view in an organized way the concepts implicit in workers' views regarding multiple-client interviews, but has not ventured to test or validate these ideas. If it has been able to clarify a few relevant concepts, to place them in some order and perspective, and to stimulate their systematic study and appraisal, it will have achieved its aim. Some of the areas highlighted may be ready now for rigorous testing and evaluation; others need further clarification before they can be examined systematically.

The use of multiple-client interviews represents a major breakthrough in casework practice. These modalities offer new avenues for understanding and treating marital problems and for linking them conceptually to the problems of the family as a whole. They also promise some rapprochement between client expectations and agency services offered. There can be little doubt that experiments with these modalities have been at once the result of and stimulus for intensive self-criticism and practical and conceptual retooling among caseworkers. The continuing ferment about them reveals a profession come of age, willing to expose its doubts and failures —and even to question its apparent successes—in the interest of growth and increased competence. But eagerness for success in the daily struggle to aid suffering couples and families should not be allowed to obscure the fact that these modalities are likely to yield the richest benefits for service only if research and theory are widely used to probe, test, and evaluate them and their usefulness in conjunction with other approaches.

At times the advance of conceptual integration and research is bound to seem excessively slow or even wasteful in view of the urgent pressures of marital distress. Effort spent on service, however, even with the best intentions, is not invariably productive. It must sometimes be a groping in the dark on the basis of intuitive hunch and unverified theory. Multiple-client interviews offer a unique opportunity for establishing a more solid base of operations. Here theories about social interaction, social systems, and their treatment can be examined and revised in the light of directly observed interaction and system functioning. Practice can thus be adjusted and re-evaluated on the basis of clearer theoretical understanding. In the end, time spent on studies that can contribute to the mutual modification and enrichment of theory and practice should yield genuine benefit for client families. It should also enrich professional education and practice by delineating and illuminating more clearly the respective roles of intuitive art and scentific knowledge in casework practice.

The task ahead will not be easy. It is reminiscent of the anecdote about the plight of the driver who, setting out with new glasses, finds his accustomed road clogged with traffic and hazards he had not observed even the day before. It is not the traffic pattern that is new but the driver's direct experience of it. In a very real sense multiple-client interviews offer the caseworker new glasses with which he can see more clearly the intricacies and conflicting pressures with which his clients have been familiar all along. While these glasses are revealing to the caseworker greater complexity and new problems, they also should increase the chances that he and the family will arrive at their common destination and that they will do so with all the passengers intact.

BIBLIOGRAPHY

1. ACKERMAN, NATHAN W., BEATMAN, FRANCES L., and SHERMAN, SANFORD N. (eds.), *Expanding Theory and Practice in Family Therapy*, Family Service Association of America, New York, 1967.

2. ———, BEATMAN, FRANCES L., and SHERMAN, SANFORD N. (eds.), *Exploring the Base for Family Therapy*, Family Service Association of America, New York, 1961.

3. AIKIN, DOROTHY, "A Project on Family Diagnosis and Treatment," in *Social Work Practice, 1963*, Selected Papers of the National Conference on Social Welfare, Columbia University Press, New York, 1963, pp. 3–18.

4. ALDOUS, JOAN, and HILL, REUBEN, *International Bibliography of Research in Marriage and the Family, 1900–1964*, University of Minnesota Press, Minneapolis, 1967.

5. BEATMAN, FRANCES L., "Intergenerational Aspects of Family Therapy," in Nathan W. Ackerman, Frances L. Beatman, and Sanford N. Sherman (eds.), *Expanding Theory and Practice in Family Therapy*, Family Service Association of America, New York, 1967, pp. 29–38.

6. ————, SHERMAN, SANFORD N., and LEADER, ARTHUR L., "Current Issues in Family Treatment," *Social Casework*, Vol. XLVII, No. 2 (February 1966), pp. 75–81.

7. BECK, DOROTHY FAHS, "Marital Conflict: Its Course and Treatment as Seen by Caseworkers," *Social Casework*, Vol. XLVII, No. 4 (April 1966), pp. 211–221.

8. ————, "Potential Approaches to Research in the Family Service Field," *Social Casework*, Vol. XL, No. 7 (July 1959), pp. 385–393.

9. ———— (ed.), *The Treatment of Marital Problems*, Family Service Association of America, New York (in preparation).

10. BELL, JOHN ELDERKIN, "Contrasting Approaches in Marital Counseling," *Family Process*, Vol. VI, No. 1 (March 1967), pp. 16–26.

11. ————, *Family Group Therapy*, Public Health Monograph No. 64, U.S. Government Printing Office, Washington, D.C., 1961.

12. BOSZORMENYI-NAGY, IVAN, and FRAMO, JAMES L. (eds.), *Intensive Family Therapy: Theoretical and Practical Aspects*, Harper & Row, New York, 1965.

13. BOWEN, MURRAY, "Family Psychotherapy," in "The Family as the Unit of Study and Treatment," *American Journal of Orthopsychiatry*, Vol. XXXI, No. 1 (January 1961), pp. 42–60.

14. BRIAR, SCOTT, "The Family as an Organization: An Approach to Family Diagnosis and Treatment," *Social Service Review*, Vol. XXXVIII, No. 3 (September 1964), pp. 247–255.

15. CHANCE, ERIKA, *Families in Treatment*, Basic Books, New York, 1959.

16. CHRISTENSEN, HAROLD T. (ed.), *Handbook of Marriage and the Family*, Rand McNally & Co., Chicago, 1964.

17. COMMITTEE ON FAMILY DIAGNOSIS and TREATMENT OF THE MIDWESTERN REGIONAL COMMITTEE OF THE FAMILY SERVICE ASSOCIATION OF AMERICA, *Casebook on Family Diagnosis and Treatment*, Family Service Association of America, New York, 1965.

18. COYLE, GRACE LONGWELL, "Concepts Relevant to Helping the Family as a Group," *Social Casework*, Vol. XLIII, No. 7 (July 1962), pp. 347–354.

19. EHRENKRANZ, SHIRLEY M., "A Study of Joint Interviewing in the Treatment of Marital Problems," Parts I and II, *Social Casework*, Vol. XLVIII, Nos. 8 and 9 (October and November 1967), pp. 498–501 and 570–574.

Summary and Implications

20. FINESTONE, SAMUEL, "Some Requirements for Agency-Based Research," *Social Casework*, Vol. XLIV, No. 3 (March 1963), pp. 132–136.

21. FLINT, ARDEN A., JR., and MACLENNAN, BERYCE W., "Some Dynamic Factors in Marital Group Psychotherapy," *International Journal of Group Psychotherapy*, Vol. XII, No. 3 (July 1962), pp. 355–361.

22. FRAMO, JAMES L., "Systematic Research on Family Dynamics," in Ivan Boszormenyi-Nagy and James L. Framo (eds.), *Intensive Family Therapy: Theoretical and Practical Aspects*, Hoeber Medical Division, Harper & Row, New York, 1965, pp. 407–462.

23. GEHRKE, SHIRLEY, and KIRSCHENBAUM, MARTIN, "Survival Patterns in Family Conjoint Therapy," *Family Process*, Vol. VI, No. 1 (March 1967), pp. 67–80.

24. GIOVACCHINI, PETER L., "Treatment of Marital Disharmonies: The Classical Approach," in Bernard L. Greene (ed.), *The Psychotherapies of Marital Disharmony*, Free Press, New York, 1965, pp. 39–82.

25. GOOLISHIAN, HAROLD A., and RITCHIE, AGNES, "Multiple-Impact Therapy," in *Casework Papers, 1961*, from the National Conference on Social Welfare, Family Service Association of America, New York, 1961.

26. GREENBERG, IRWIN M., et al., "Family Therapy: Indications and Rationale," *Archives of General Psychiatry*, Vol. X, No. 1 (January 1964), pp. 7–25.

27. HANDEL, GERALD (ed.), *The Psychosocial Interior of the Family: A Sourcebook for the Study of Whole Families*, Aldine Publishing Co., Chicago, 1967.

28. HESS, ROBERT D., and HANDEL, GERALD, *Family Worlds: A Psychosocial Approach to Family Life*, University of Chicago Press, Chicago, 1959.

29. HILL, REUBEN, "Status of Research About Marriage and the Family," in James A. Peterson (ed.), *Marriage and Family Counseling: Perspective and Prospect*, Association Press, New York, 1968, pp. 19–43.

30. LEADER, ARTHUR L., "Current and Future Issues in Family Therapy," Paper Given at Biennial Conference of Family Service Association of America, Miami Beach, Florida, November 1967 (mimeographed).

31. LEADER, ARTHUR L., "The Role of Intervention in Family-Group Treatment," *Social Casework*, Vol. XLV, No. 6 (June 1964), pp. 327–332.

32. LEICHTER, ELSA, "Group Psychotherapy of Married Couples' Groups: Some Characteristic Treatment Dynamics," *International Journal of Group Psychotherapy*, Vol. XII, No. 2 (April 1962), pp. 154–163.

33. ———, and SCHULMAN, GERDA L., "Emerging Phenomena in Multi-Family Group Treatment," *International Journal of Group Psychotherapy*, Vol. XVIII, No. 1 (January 1968), pp. 59–69.

34. ———, and SCHULMAN, GERDA L., "The Family Interview as an Integrative Device in Group Therapy with Families," *International Journal of Group Psychotherapy*, Vol. XIII, No. 3 (July 1963), pp. 335–345.

35. LEIK, ROBERT K., and NORTHWOOD, LAWRENCE K., "Improving Family Guidance Through the Small Group Experimental Laboratory," *Social Work,* Vol. IX, No. 4 (October 1964), pp. 18–25.
36. LIDZ, THEODORE, et al., "Schism and Skew in the Families of Schizophrenics," in Norman W. Bell and Ezra F. Vogel (eds.), *A Modern Introduction to the Family,* Free Press, Glencoe, Ill., 1960, pp. 595–607.
37. MACGREGOR, ROBERT, et al., *Multiple Impact Therapy with Families,* McGraw-Hill Book Co., New York, 1964.
38. MITCHELL, CELIA B., "Integrative Therapy of the Family Unit," *Social Casework,* Vol. XLVI, No. 2 (February 1965), pp. 63–69.
39. NYE, F. IVAN, and BERARDO, FELIX M. (eds.), *Emerging Conceptual Frameworks in Family Analysis,* Macmillan Co., New York, 1966.
40. POLLAK, OTTO, "Disturbed Families and Conjoint Family Counseling," *Child Welfare,* Vol. XLVI, No. 3 (March 1967), pp. 143–149.
41. ——, "Entrance of the Caseworker into Family Interaction," *Social Casework,* Vol. XLV, No. 4 (April 1964), pp. 216–220.
42. SATIR, VIRGINIA M., "Conjoint Marital Therapy," in Bernard L. Greene (ed.), *The Psychotherapies of Marital Disharmony,* Free Press, New York, 1965, pp. 121–133.
43. SCHERZ, FRANCES H., "Family Treatment Concepts," *Social Casework,* Vol. XLVII, No. 4 (April 1966), pp. 234–240.
44. SHYNE, ANN W., "An Experimental Study of Casework Methods," *Social Casework,* Vol. XLVI, No. 9 (November 1965), pp. 535–541.
45. SMITH, NEILSON F. (ed.), "Family Phenomena, Problems, and Treatment: Some Family Agency Studies" (A Terminal Progress Report on the Project, "Casework on Marital Problems: A National Experiment in Staff Development"), Family Service Association of America, New York, 1968 (mimeographed).
46. TAVISTOCK INSTITUTE OF HUMAN RELATIONS, FAMILY DISCUSSION BUREAU, *The Marital Relationship as a Focus for Casework,* Codicote Press, Welwyn, Hertfordshire, England, 1962.
47. THORMAN, GEORGE, "Application of Multiple-Impact Therapy in a Family Service Agency: A Description of a Research Project," Family Service Association, Indianapolis, Ind., 1966 (mimeographed).
48. ——, "Casework Treatment of Marital Disorders—A Clinical Research Approach," Family Service Association, Indianapolis, Ind., 1964 (mimeographed).
49. ——, "Clinical Diagnosis of Marital Disorders" (diagnostic findings on Phase I of research project), Family Service Association, Indianapolis, Ind., 1964 (mimeographed).
50. ——, "Research in Family Therapy," Family Service Association, Indianapolis, Ind., 1966 (mimeographed).
51. WEAKLAND, JOHN H., "The 'Double-Bind' Hypothesis of Schizophrenia and Three-Party Interaction," in Don D. Jackson (ed.), *The Etiology of Schizophrenia,* Basic Books, New York, 1960, pp. 373–388.
52. WEISBERG, MIRIAM, "A Caseworker's Experience in Joint Interviewing with Marital Partners," in *Second Jackson Memorial Institute,* Family Service Association of Cleveland, Cleveland, Ohio, 1963, pp. 1–24 (mimeographed).

Appendix

Explanatory Note

The three tables reproduced here report the numerical results of the formal content analysis of the comments of project respondents on the key questions on which this monograph is based. The wording of two of the basic questions involved is given on page 7, footnote 2. All the analyses were prepared by the author. The details of the comments classified in each category in Tables 2 and 3 are discussed in the text of the monograph.

Several definitions are common to all the tabulations. The term *joint interviews* is used to refer to casework sessions in which only one married couple and one caseworker are present. The term *family interviews* denotes sessions that include the couple and one or more other members of the nuclear or extended family. The term *respondent* denotes either an individual practitioner who submitted a separate response or a group of practitioners who chose to pool their responses in a single written reply. To simplify table headings, all counts exclude the three respondents who indicated that they were fundamentally opposed to the use of multiple-client methods under any circumstances. Additional specifications applicable only to specific tables are as follows:

Table 1. This table reports ratings of the extent of experience in joint and family interviewing of respondents who answered the two basic source questions for the topics discussed in this monograph. Since the original questions did not include any direct queries on the extent of respondents' experience with these methods, ratings were based whenever feasible on a global assessment of experience clues found by reviewing the totality of each respondent's project comments as a whole. When such a review still left unclear the extent of a given caseworker's experience, a follow-up questionnaire was sent out, in 1965, requesting, on a retrospective basis, experience data applicable to the date of the original response. Where pooled group responses were submitted instead of individual responses, a composite rating was made that reflected as closely as possible the level of experience of the majority of the group's members.

Tables 2 and 3. Both these tables present the results of detailed content analyses of the responses. Table 2 concentrates on the values of joint and family interviews, and Table 3 on conditions favorable and unfavorable to their use. Owing to the paucity of comment on criteria for family interviews, Table 3 is limited to joint interviews.

Both tables cover the 146 separate responses to the question on use of joint and family interviews in diagnosis and the 59 responses to the question on the use of these modalities in treatment. In addition, Table 2 utilizes those 43 responses to a question on new approaches to diagnosis in which respondents chose to discuss multiple-client interviews.

Both Table 2 and Table 3 employ as their unit of count the "reference," which is defined to include the totality of comment from any given respondent regarding any particular value or condition classifiable in a single subcategory of the table in question. The needed consolidation of multiple references by the same respondent to a single theme required a process of unduplication through which multiple comments on the same theme from the same correspondent were assembled together and identified as a single "reference" unit regardless of the number of separate contexts or questions in which the points classifiable in the same category were made.

Finally, it should be noted that Tables 2 and 3 cannot be taken as reflections of the total volume of support among respondents for any stated position. Since the questions were open-ended and purposely included no reminders of specific themes to be covered, the counts reflect only the proportion of respondents who spontaneously offered comment on given topics, not the proportion who would have agreed with the total list if it had been presented as a checklist.

Table 1

EXTENT OF RESPONDENTS' EXPERIENCE WITH JOINT AND FAMILY INTERVIEWS

Extent of Experience[1]	Distribution of Respondents according to Extent of Experience with—							
	Joint Interviews				Family Group Interviews			
	Those Answering Question on Use in Diagnosis		Those Answering Question on Use in Treatment		Those Answering Question on Use in Diagnosis		Those Answering Question on Use in Treatment	
	Number	Percent	Number	Percent	Number	Percent	Number	Percent
EXTENSIVE— For both diagnosis and treatment	69	47	44	75	12	8	6	10
For diagnosis only (method used only occasionally or not at all for treatment)	68	47	12	20	14	9	7	12
OCCASIONAL ONLY (for either diagnosis or treatment)	9	6	3	5	68	47	40	68
NONE (or not enough information to classify)	—	—	—	—	52	36	6	10
Total	146	100	59	100	146	100	59	100

[1] The assistance of Lili Solomon in the coding of the experience of respondents and respondent groups is gratefully acknowledged.

Appendix

Table 2

SPECIAL VALUES CASEWORKERS SEE IN THE USE OF JOINT AND FAMILY INTERVIEWS FOR THE TREATMENT OF MARITAL PROBLEMS

Special Values (in Comparison with Individual Interviews Used as the Exclusive Method)	Number of Responses Citing Specific Value			Percent of Total References Citing Any Value [2]
	Total (Unduplicated) [1]	Number where Comment Applies to—		
		Joint Interviews	Family Interviews	
PART I: VALUES RELATED TO DIAGNOSIS				
A. INCREASED SPEED AND ACCURACY OF DIAGNOSTIC UNDERSTANDING (IN GENERAL)	38	28	18	12.2
B. IMPROVED UNDERSTANDING BOTH OF THE INDIVIDUAL FAMILY MEMBERS AND OF THE INTERACTIONAL PATTERNS AMONG THEM, WITH REFERENCE TO—				
1. Ways of relating, interacting, and adapting	94	80	48	30.2
2. Attitudes toward the marital difficulty	3	2	—	1.0
3. Patterns of leadership, control, and role allocation	19	17	4	6.1
4. Patterns of communication	18	18	2	5.8
5. Extent and nature of conflict				
a. Patterns and degree of mutual hostility, aggression, and destructiveness, and specific areas involved in the conflict	9	8	1	2.9
b. Extent and type of relationship of the children to the marital conflict	9	2	8	2.9
6. Operation and effectiveness of mutual defenses	15	13	2	4.8
7. Extent and nature of existing strengths	18	13	8	5.8
8. Sociocultural patterns and values	5	1	4	1.6
C. IMPROVED KNOWLEDGE OF THE REALITY SITUATION	50	22	31	16.1
D. FULLER REVELATION OF THE HISTORY OF THE COUPLE AS A COUPLE OR OF THE FAMILY AS A GROUP	3	2	2	1.0

[1] When a respondent cited the same value for both joint interviews and family interviews, the response is counted in the columns for both these modalities, but is counted only once in the total column; hence the total indicated is sometimes less than the horizontal total of the two components.

[2] Based on the unduplicated counts in the first column. Percentages are computed separately for Part I and Part II of the table.

Appendix

Table 2, PART I—Continued

Special Values (in Comparison with Individual Interviews Used as the Exclusive Method)	Number of Responses Citing Specific Value			Percent of Total References Citing Any Value [2]
	Total (Unduplicated) [1]	Number where Comment Applies to—		
		Joint Interviews	Family Interviews	
E. MORE DIRECT KNOWLEDGE OF THE REACTIONS OF THE COUPLE OR FAMILY TO THE CONDITIONS FOR TREATMENT				
1. Reactions to agency structure and policies and to the worker	6	3	3	1.9
2. Readiness for involvement in treatment	6	6	1	1.9
F. MORE ADEQUATE PERIODIC EVALUATION OF CHANGES DURING TREATMENT, SUCH AS—				
1. Change or impasse in the marital relationship	12	12	—	3.9
2. Impact of marital change on the children	1	—	1	.3
3. Success or failure (in split cases) in working in areas jointly delineated	1	1	—	.3
4. Areas needing further work	3	2	3	1.0
5. Progress after termination	1	1	—	.3
Total references to values for diagnosis	311	231	136	100.0

Table 2, PART II

Special Values (in Comparison with Individual Interviews Used as the Exclusive Method)	Number of Responses Citing Specific Value			Percent of Total References Citing Any Value [2]
	Total (Unduplicated) [1]	Number where Comment Applies to—		
		Joint Interviews	Family Interviews	

PART II: VALUES RELATED TO TREATMENT

A. INCREASED SPEED AND EFFICACY OF TREATMENT	17	15	3	4.4
B. BETTER MUTUAL CLARIFICATION OF AGENCY FUNCTIONS	17	17	1	4.4
C. INCREASED OPPORTUNITY FOR HANDLING MUTUALLY RESTRICTING OR DAMAGING ATTITUDES AND INTERACTION PATTERNS THAT ARE REVEALED THROUGH—				
1. Problems in interaction (in general)	34	31	15	8.8
2. Problems in communication	38	35	14	9.8
3. Problems in role perception and role functioning	7	3	3	1.8
4. Misrepresentations, distortions, denials, projections, and other rigid defenses, including unawareness of the link between problems ostensibly outside and those within the marital relationship	52	44	27	13.4
D. PROVISION OF AN ENVIRONMENT SUITABLE FOR THE CONFRONTATION OF MARITAL CONFLICT VIA CONTROLS ON—				
1. Acting out and excessive domination	8	8	4	2.1
2. Excessive expression of anger	8	8	2	2.1
E. PROVISION OF CONDITIONS FAVORABLE TO HEIGHTENING AWARENESS OF SELF AND OTHERS	21	18	13	5.4
F. INCREASED OPPORTUNITIES FOR PROMOTION OF CONSTRUCTIVE MUTUALITY THROUGH—				
1. Focus on common goals, values, and responsibilities	16	16	8	4.1
2. Provision of a structure to dramatize and activate involvement of both partners or all members	20	16	4	5.2
3. Fostering of joint acceptance of problems and joint problem-solving	15	13	3	3.9
4. Demonstration and reinforcement of positives	7	6	2	1.8

Appendix

Table 2, PART II—Continued

Special Values (in Comparison with Individual Interviews Used as the Exclusive Method)	Number of Responses Citing Specific Value			Percent of Total References Citing Any Value [2]
	Total (Unduplicated) [1]	Number where Comment Applies to—		
		Joint Interviews	Family Interviews	
G. PROMOTION OF DIRECT EXPERIMENTATION WITH NEW BEHAVIOR AND WITH PROBLEM-SOLVING, THROUGH PROVISION OF—				
1. Opportunities for observation of, and identification with, worker's way of relating in the interview	8	8	1	2.1
2. Simultaneous worker support to both partners, or all family members, for experimentation with new solutions and new ways of behaving	3	1	3	0.8
3. More immediate guidance in the facing and partializing of problems	2	2	2	0.5
H. GREATER EFFECTIVENESS WITH CERTAIN TYPES OF COUPLES OR FAMILIES OFTEN HARD TO REACH IN INDIVIDUAL INTERVIEWS, SUCH AS—				
1. Families where all or some of the members are very suspicious	11	10	2	2.8
2. Families characterized by excessive and overt mutual anger	3	3	—	0.8
3. Families where one or more members are suffering from an acting-out character disorder, or have been referred by coercive authorities	2	2	1	0.5
4. Families where at least one partner is excessively passive	5	5	—	1.3
5. Families who cannot tolerate the one-to-one approach	1	—	1	0.3
6. Young married couples	1	1	—	0.3

Table 2, PART II—Continued

Special Values (in Comparison with Individual Interviews Used as the Exclusive Method)	Number of Responses Citing Specific Value			Percent of Total References Citing Any Value [2]
	Total (Unduplicated) [1]	Number where Comment Applies to—		
		Joint Interviews	Family Interviews	
I. AVOIDANCE OR ATTENUATION OF DIFFICULTIES NOT UNCOMMON IN THE SEPARATE TREATMENT OF MARITAL PARTNERS, THROUGH—				
1. Increased opportunity to deal with stalemate or deterioration of family relationships that may have occurred during individual treatment of the partners	9	8	2	2.3
2. Increased opportunity to highlight, test, and support gains in the marital relationship that develop during treatment	12	12	2	3.1
3. More adequate coordination of treatment focus, pace, and goals of both partners	14	13	2	3.6
4. Provision of opportunities to seek or institute a change of treatment direction or focus, as needed	23	21	3	5.9
5. Better opportunity to help the couple or family, when necessary, to face up to and prepare for termination of treatment	13	13	1	3.4
J. AVOIDANCE OR ATTENUATION OF COMPLICATIONS ARISING FROM THE ONE-TO-ONE RELATIONSHIP WITH THE WORKER, SUCH AS—				
1. Arousal of false hopes and fears related to the one-to-one casework relationship	5	4	2	1.3
2. Development of strong secondary gratifications for the client	2	2	—	0.5
3. Distortion of the client's image of worker role and attitudes	11	7	4	2.8
4. Distortion of the worker's role or attitudes in relation to the couple or family	2	2	2	0.5
Total references related to values for treatment	387	344	127	100.0
Grand Total of References to Values	698	575	263	—

Table 3

Conditions Considered by Caseworkers To Be Favorable or Unfavorable to the Use of Joint Interviews for the Treatment of Marital Problems

Conditions Considered FAVORABLE or UNFAVORABLE to the Use of Joint Interviews	Number of Responses Citing Specific Condition			Percent of Total References Citing Any Conditions
		Number Indicating—		
	Total	Agreement[1]	Disagreement	

PART I: CONDITIONS RELATED TO THE PARTNERS AS INDIVIDUALS

	Total	Agreement[1]	Disagreement	Percent
A. Conditions considered FAVORABLE to the use of joint interviews:				
1. Both partners have some self-awareness	5	5	—	1.8
B. Conditions considered UNFAVORABLE to the use of joint interviews:				
1. One or both partners have very limited capacity to tolerate pain, pressure, and criticism	7	7	—	2.5
2. One or both partners show great rigidity of defenses	7	7	—	2.5
3. One or both are anxious or fearful about exposure to the partner or about the presence of the partner	10	10	—	3.7
4. One or both partners have very little capacity to control hostility and aggression	7	7	—	2.5
5. Severe pathology is present in one or both partners	6	6	—	2.2
Total references to individual characteristics as indicators	42	42	—	15.2

[1] "Agreeing" comments include those that concur only under special circumstances with the condition as phrased and disagree under others. These conditions are indicated in the text. Since totals are unduplicated, they do not always agree with sum of components.

Table 3, PART II

Conditions Considered FAVORABLE or UNFAVORABLE to the Use of Joint Interviews	Number of Responses Citing Specific Condition			Percent of Total References Citing Any Conditions
	Total	Number Indicating—		
		Agreement[1]	Disagreement	

PART II: CONDITIONS RELATED TO THE INTERACTION BETWEEN THE PARTNERS

	Total	Agreement[1]	Disagreement	Percent
A. Conditions considered FAVORABLE to the use of joint interviews:				
1. The couple want to come in together	41	41	—	14.9
2. The couple have problems in communicating with each other:				
a. The couple's ability to communicate verbally has broken down or ceased	16	10	6	5.8
b. The couple's ability to communicate has been impaired but not destroyed and can be improved	13	13	—	4.7
c. The couple's ability to communicate has reached a point of change, whether in the direction of increasing or decreasing communication	9	9	—	3.2
3. The couple show an increase in constructive mutuality	6	5	1	2.2
4. The couple's concerns are mainly interactional although intrapersonal problems may also be present	6	6	1	2.2
5. Progress in individual interviews is impeded by the fact that one or both partners constantly use individual interviews to attack the absent spouse	1	1	—	.4

Table 3, PART II—Continued

Conditions Considered FAVORABLE or UNFAVORABLE to the Use of Joint Interviews	Number of Responses Citing Specific Condition			Percent of Total References Citing Any Conditions
	Total	Number Indicating—		
		Agreement[1]	Disagreement	
B. Conditions considered UNFAVORABLE to the use of joint interviews:				
1. The partners are excessively locked in mutually hostile, destructive, or inequitable interaction:				
a. The partners are very hostile and destructive toward each other	24	20	4	8.8
b. The partners are caught up in deeply sado-masochistic or inequitable interaction patterns	4	4	—	1.5
2. Intrapersonal problems predominate:				
a. The couple's concerns are primarily intrapersonal	16	14	2	5.8
b. The couple's concerns are temporarily intrapersonal	3	3	—	1.1
c. One or both partners are immature or have an undeveloped sense of identity	4	4	—	1.5
3. The couple lack readiness to work together:				
a. The couple do no want to maintain the marriage	9	8	1	3.2
b. The couple have no sense of belonging together	7	7	—	2.5
c. The couple have no wish to share goals and to involve themselves in working on their marital problems[2]	6	5	1	2.2
4. One or both partners have feelings or information not acknowledged to the spouse	8	8	—	2.9
5. The couple have not used past joint interviews productively	3	3	—	1.1
Total references to interaction patterns as indicators	176	161	16	64.0

[2] While all other conditions cited in the table are phrased positively or negatively in accordance with the phrasing of the majority of those commenting, this comment is phrased negatively even though respondents mainly cited it in its positive form. The present phrasing was necessary to show the disagreement counts without seeming to say that any respondents thought a positively phrased favorable condition unfavorable.

Appendix

Table 3, PART III

Conditions Considered FAVORABLE or UNFAVORABLE to the Use of Joint Interviews	Number of Responses Citing Specific Condition			Percent of Total References Citing Any Conditions
	Total	Number Indicating—		
		Agreement[1]	Disagreement	

PART III: CONDITIONS RELATED TO THE RELATIONSHIP BETWEEN THE CLIENT OR COUPLE AND THE WORKER

	Total	Agreement[1]	Disagreement	Percent
A. Conditions considered FAVORABLE to the use of joint interviews: None tabulated in this form[3]				
B. Conditions considered UNFAVORABLE to the use of joint interviews:				
1. The couple cannot share the worker due to special needs of one or both partners	17	17	—	6.1
2. The couple are unable to share the worker due to rivalry and inability to understand worker's role	11	7	4	4.0
3. The client or couple are unable to trust the worker[3]	8	7	1	2.9
Total references to client-worker relationship factors as indicators	36	31	5	13.0

[3] References to the ability to trust the worker (B-3 in this table) were phrased positively in the main by respondents but have been reworded in negative form and tabulated in the unfavorable category for the reasons given in footnote 2 of this table.

Appendix

Table 3, PART IV

Conditions Considered FAVORABLE or UNFAVORABLE to the Use of Joint Interviews	Number of Responses Citing Specific Condition			Percent of Total References Citing Any Conditions
	Total	Number Indicating—		
		Agreement[1]	Disagreement	

PART IV: CONDITIONS RELATED TO WORKER SKILLS AND CHARACTERISTICS

	Total	Agreement[1]	Disagreement	Percent
A. Conditions considered FAVORABLE to the use of joint interviews:				
1. The worker possesses essential personal qualities	6	6	—	2.2
2. The worker possesses essential knowledge and skills:				
a. The worker has the capacity to handle complex transference and countertransference reactions	1	1	—	.4
b. The worker has a good sense of timing	1	1	—	.4
B. Conditions considered UNFAVORABLE to the use of joint interviews:				
1. The worker is unable to remain neutral between the partners	4	4	—	1.5
2. The worker has great difficulty in coping with two sets of demands, defenses, and hostilities	3	3	—	1.1
3. Workers to be present, if more than one, have not achieved comparable levels of skill	1	1	—	.4
Total references to worker characteristics and skills as indicators	16	16	—	6.0

Appendix

Table 3, PART V

Conditions Considered FAVORABLE or UNFAVORABLE to the Use of Joint Interviews	Number of Responses Citing Specific Condition			Percent of Total References Citing Any Conditions
	Total	Agreement[1]	Disagreement	
		Number Indicating—		

PART V: CONDITIONS RELATED TO REALITY FACTORS

A. Conditions considered FAVORABLE to the use of joint interviews:				
None mentioned.				
B. Conditions considered UNFAVORABLE to the use of joint interviews:				
1. Confidential material has to be discussed or interpreted to one partner alone	3	3	—	1.1
2. One of the partners is not available at the time feasible for interviews	2	2	—	.7
Total references to reality factors as indicators	5	5	—	1.8
Grand Total of References to Conditions	275	255	21	100.0